Southern Literary Studies
Louis D. Rubin, Jr., Editor

Brushes with the Literary

Brushes

with the Literary

LETTERS OF A WASHINGTON ARTIST

1943–1959

Marcella Comès Winslow

Louisiana State University Press

Baton Rouge and London

Copyright © 1993 by Louisiana State University Press
All rights reserved
Manufactured in the United States of America
First printing
02 01 00 99 98 97 96 95 94 93   5 4 3 2 1

Designer: Laura Roubique Gleason
Typeface: Garamond #3
Typesetter: G&S Typesetters, Inc.
Printer and binder: Thomson-Shore, Inc.

Library of Congress Cataloging-in-Publication Data

Winslow, Marcella Comès.
    Brushes with the literary : letters of a Washington artist,
  1943–1959 / Marcella Comès Winslow.
        p.   cm. — (Southern literary studies)
    Includes index.
    ISBN 0-8071-1761-7 (cloth)
    1. American literature—Washington (D.C.)—History and criticism.
  2. Authors, American—Washington (D.C.)—Friends and associates.
  3. American literature—Southern States—History and criticism.
  4. Authors, American—Southern States—Friends and associates.
  5. Washington (D.C.)—Intellectual life—20th century.   6. Portrait
  painters—United States—Correspondence.   7. Authors,
  American—20th century—Portraits.   8. Winslow, Marcella Comès—
  Correspondence.   9. Portrait painting—Washington (D.C.).
  I. Title.   II. Series.
  PS253.D6W56   1993
  810.9'9753—dc20   92-18920
                                                              CIP

Letters herein are quoted by permission of Isabel Bayley (Katherine Anne Porter's), Mary
Winslow Chapman (Anne Goodwin Winslow's), Giles de la Mare (Walter de la Mare's),
Marian Holland McAllister (Léonie Adams'), Elizabeth Shafer (Chauncey Stillman's),
Helen Tate (Allen Tate's), Dorothy G. Van Doren (Mark Van Doren's), Anne Weygandt
(Cornelius Weygandt's), and June Wilson (Cornelia Stratton Parker's). Ezra Pound Letters
copyright © 1991 by the Ezra Pound Literary Property Trust. Reprinted by permission of
New Directions Pub. Corp. The poem by John Peale Bishop is reprinted by permission of
Hippocrene Books, and Anne Goodwin Winslow's poetry by permission of Mary Winslow
Chapman.

The paper in this book meets the guidelines for permanence and durability of the
Committee on Production Guidelines for Book Longevity of the Council on Library
Resources. ∞

For my children
Mary and John

Such a sweet gift—a piece of handmade writing, in an envelope that is not a bill. You can't pick up a phone and call the future and tell them about our times. You have to pick up a piece of paper.

—Garrison Keillor

CONTENTS

ILLUSTRATIONS

FOREWORD

Art in America has always led a bifurcated existence, in that the country's political capital and its artistic marketplace are located in different cities. Unlike London, Paris, Rome, and Vienna, New York City, where books are published, paintings are displayed and sold, plays are produced, musical compositions are introduced, and so on, is more than two hundred miles distant from Washington, where laws are enacted and the nation is governed. The result has been philistinism in Washington, and irresponsibility in Manhattan.

Of the forty-one men who have served as president of the United States since George Washington was inaugurated, the number who can be thought of as having been conversant with what was or is most creative and exciting in one or more branches of the literature and fine arts of their times may be counted upon the fingers of one hand. Name Thomas Jefferson, John Quincy Adams, Theodore Roosevelt, John F. Kennedy, and Jimmy Carter, and the roster has been exhausted. And indeed, the artistic sensibilities of several of these are suspect; White House concerts and assemblages of poets and novelists at luncheons notwithstanding, it was said that when Mrs. President Kennedy was asked what her husband's favorite musical composition was, she replied without hesitation, "'Hail to the Chief.'"

Whether the political integrity of the nation is better or worse off because of this, or whether in fact it would make any difference either way, is by no means certain. What is undeniable is that traditionally the arts found it tough going in the national capital. For in a community where political power rather than personal wealth and illustrious ancestry conferred the greatest distinction, there was relatively little incentive

to seek social prestige through artistic patronage. Those politicos who
did go in for the arts did so mainly for reasons of personal predilection,
not upward mobility.

In recent years, however, the District's want of interest in the Finer
Things of Life, as belles lettres and the graphic arts used to be called,
has been changing for the better. A historian chronicling the pursuit of
high culture on the banks of the Potomac River would doubtless date
the change from the early 1930s, when the coming of the New Deal had
the result of attracting numerous intellectuals into the precincts of government. When not at work running the government, no inconsiderable
number of them read books, toured art galleries, and attended concerts
and plays. There was even an occasional congressman whose taste in
poetry ran deeper than Longfellow and Edgar A. Guest and for whom
Norman Rockwell did not constitute the outer limits of graphic mas-
tery. Moreover, the increasing importance of the United States in world
affairs after the First World War brought sizable deputations of diplomatic personnel and their families to Washington from western Europe
and Latin America, many of them with cultural leanings. All in all,
Washington, D.C., began to take on something of a cosmopolitan air.

In 1936, Archer Milton Huntington, son of the railroad baron
Collis P. Huntington and a man of widespread intellectual and artistic
interests, donated securities worth $874,000 to the Library of Congress,
one-half of which was to be used to maintain a chair of poetry. At Huntington's behest, the chief of the library, Herbert Putnam, appointed
Joseph Auslander as consultant in poetry the year following. Several
other substantial gifts were also received. Then in 1938 Putnam retired,
and during the next year the poet Archibald MacLeish was named
librarian of Congress by President Franklin D. Roosevelt. What this
meant was that a distinguished poet, respected by his peers and thoroughly involved in the melee of contemporary letters, headed the nation's most prestigious library. A program of public readings by leading
poets was inaugurated.

Four years later, in 1943, after several poets had been offered the
consultantship and declined, MacLeish was able to bring in Allen Tate,
who had previously turned down the job. Over the next two decades the
consultants were Robert Penn Warren, Louise Bogan, Karl Shapiro,
Robert Lowell, Léonie Adams, Elizabeth Bishop, Conrad Aiken, Ran-

dall Jarrell, Robert Frost, and Louis Untermeyer. At Tate's instigation the library established a set of Fellows of the Library of Congress in American Letters, with Katherine Anne Porter, Katherine Garrison Chapin, Mark Van Doren, Willard Thorp, Van Wyck Brooks, Paul Green, and Carl Sandburg receiving appointments. Tate also set up plans for a program whereby leading poets would record their poems. During the years that followed, most of the major poets, and no small number of distinguished novelists and critics, came to Washington for Library of Congress activities.

What all this signified was that the nation's capital was becoming a literary center of some intensity. The city's idea of what poetry should be no longer corresponded to that featured in the *Congressional Record*. In 1948, Robert Richman established the Institute of Contemporary Arts, importing more talent, and the Library of Congress mounted an ambitious musical operation. Painting paralleled the literary flowering, owing largely to the efforts of Duncan and Marjorie Phillips, who in 1921 had founded the first museum of modern art in the United States, now called the Phillips Collection. Not only did the museum bring artists inspiration through its holdings but during the forties and fifties it often invited local artists to participate in group exhibitions.

The considerable historical value of the letters that are included in the present volume lies in their spanning precisely the period when all that was getting under way. In 1943, Marcella Comès Winslow, wife of Colonel Randolph Winslow, of the United States Army Corps of Engineers, moved with her two small children to Washington, where the Winslows had lived before, with the idea of staying there for the duration of the war. Her husband, a graduate of the United States Military Academy, was in England, where preparations were under way for the cross-Channel invasion the following year. An accomplished painter, Marcella Comès hoped to supplement her rather restricted income by doing portraits, at a time when there were few commercial galleries to show or sell works of art in Washington.

Colonel Winslow's mother, Anne Goodwin Winslow, who lived on an estate near Memphis, Tennessee, was a published poet, and she had numerous literary friends, particularly among southern writers. In 1943, when she was sixty-eight years old, her prose memoir, *The Dwell-*

ing Place, was published by Alfred A. Knopf to much acclaim. She followed it up with five more books, among them several novels.

The letters that Marcella Winslow began writing to her mother-in-law from Washington, and continued writing for the next sixteen years, constitute a virtual blow-by-blow account of the District literary scene. For among her mother-in-law's friends, whom Marcella met in Memphis and whose portrait she had painted, was Allen Tate. When Tate arrived in Washington to be consultant in poetry at the Library of Congress, he and his wife, the novelist Caroline Gordon, were soon in touch with Marcella. It was not long before she decided to make a specialty of paintings portraits of authors.

The result is a gallery of likenesses of some of the more interesting and distinguished writers of the era, many but not all of them poets. Beginning with the Tates, those who sat for her were Katherine Anne Porter, Robert Penn Warren, Eudora Welty, Robert Frost, Ezra Pound, Elizabeth Bishop, Léonie Adams, Mark Van Doren, Karl Shapiro, Katherine Garrison Chapin, Robert Lowell, Richard Eberhart, Denis Devlin, Peter Taylor, Sally Fitzgerald, Juan Ramón Jiménez, Father Martin D'Arcy, Ira Glackens, Cornelius Weygandt, John Finley, Harry Levin, Walter Jackson Bate, and Anne Winslow herself. Marcella Winslow has also drawn Tate, Pound, and Walter de la Mare, and photographed the Tates, Katherine Anne Porter, Robert Lowell, and Peter Taylor.

From a literary standpoint, it is the letters that Marcella Winslow wrote to her mother-in-law that make this book so valuable a record of a time and a place. For she was gifted with pen as well as paintbrush, and she had an eye for the human, the idiosyncratic, the significant and revelatory. Her letters offer striking vignettes of the people she painted.

Happily, Anne Goodwin Winslow recognized the remarkable quality of her daughter-in-law's letters—and it should be noted, too, that as with all good correspondence, the person on the receiving end was of no small importance in the transaction. For Marcella Winslow knew that her mother-in-law in Memphis was fully capable of understanding and savoring the nuances, intricacies, and the often telling insights and observations being sent to her. All but forgotten today, Anne Goodwin Winslow was a remarkable woman, as these letters will show, and the reader who may be prompted by the letters to have a look at the books she wrote will understand why her daughter-in-law cherished her. Writing *for* Anne Winslow, she reported what Anne Winslow would be interested in reading.

The student of our national letters who consults this book will find many interesting things. The depictions of the Tates here recorded show those two talented and contentious writers in vintage form. Robert Lowell is present at a key juncture in his career, and the mental illness that caused him and his friends and several wives so much grief is tellingly on view. There are descriptions of visits to paint Ezra Pound during his longtime incarceration in St. Elizabeth's Hospital, a mental institution, following his pro-Axis broadcasts from Rome during World War II, and to Vermont to paint Robert Frost.

Perhaps the most colorful epistolary portraiture of all, however, is the sixteen-year view of Katherine Anne Porter that the letters offer. She lived with Marcella Winslow in the winter of 1944, occupied her house for a time, and was a frequent visitor and correspondent. The emotional extravagance, exaggeration, sensitivity, and kindness, and the alternating joy and misery, of that gifted and inconstant personality are marvelously captured over the span of years.

A large part of the usefulness of these letters is the picture they provide of the cultural life of the city of Washington, during war and peace, and in particular what they show of the peculiar mixture of artistic, political, governmental, and social life that goes on in a political capital. There are at least three constituencies here: art, whether authors or painters; politics and government, made up of persons who have moved to Washington for career purposes; and old Washington, the social set which has lived in the city for decades, many of whose members possess wealth. Cultural activity served to bring them into contact with each other, often with interesting results.

Marcella Winslow herself was thoroughly apolitical in outlook; one may read through this sixteen-year compendium of letters and not know whether she voted Democratic or Republican, or for that matter whether she voted at all. Almost the only political note sounded is one of sympathy for John Carter Vincent, the China specialist of the State Department who was pilloried by Senator Joseph McCarthy and fired by Secretary of State Dulles during the anti-Communist witch-hunting hysteria that pervaded the nation in the late years of the Truman administration and for several years thereafter. And even then, the sympathy comes because of the writer's personal ties with the Vincent family.

The political and military dignitaries who move through the pages of these letters, however, do so not in their official roles but as they figure in cultural activities. Yet they are important *in* the cultural milieu *because of* their lofty government status. A reception for a poet, the opening of an exhibition at a gallery are notable in terms of the legitimacy conferred upon them by the attention of politicos, generals, and the like. The distinguished guests have come for the art. Their attendance will in no way enhance their own renown in places where political power is valued, but it will add to their prestige in social-cultural circles.

The result is something like the situation embodied in Tennyson's "Northern Farmer, New Style": "Doänt thou marry for munny, but goä wheer munny is!"—with public renown rather than wealth the desirable ingredient. In these letters we encounter secretaries of state Dean Acheson and Christian Herter, General Lucius Clay, Supreme Court justices Felix Frankfurter and Hugo Black, Secretary of Air Harold Talbott, Attorney General Francis Biddle, Senator Lister Hill, and Congressman Hale Boggs, among others. Marcel Proust would have relished the spectacle. For different reasons, so would H. L. Mencken.

One of the most delightful episodes, fetchingly rendered by Marcella Winslow, describes her telephone conversation with a young lady calling from the credit bureau to check on the credentials and reliability of a man who had recently moved next door. The new neighbor was Allen Dulles, director of the CIA, who had subleased Christian Herter's house while Herter was away serving as governor of Massachusetts. The caller obviously had no idea who either Allen Dulles—she pronounced it "Dulls"—or his brother, Secretary of State John Foster Dulles, was, or what the Central Intelligence Agency was and did. In a collection of letters containing much that is humorous, this is the pièce de résistance.

Still another informative aspect to the letters is the picture they give of the commerce of art. As a young housewife with two children to raise and educate, Marcella Winslow very much depended upon the revenue she received from doing portraits of notables. A commission to paint a likeness of someone prominent in society, or of the individual's wife or children, attracted additional commissions. It was by no means always easy to reconcile the veracity of the artist's conception with the taste of the person commissioning the portrait or the self-image of the subject. There were times when the artist, no matter how much she needed the fee and how patiently she tried to please, could not adjust her own vision to produce what the patron required. The continuing account of a working painter's pursuit of a livelihood which these letters offer opens an interesting and sometimes wickedly humorous perspective upon the difficulties faced in painting portraits.

Yet from the standpoint of the reader, perhaps one of the most appealing aspects of the letters lies in the consistent view they provide of the gifted woman who wrote them. For they are no mere frivolous, lighthearted descriptions of literary and artistic doings. There is abundant humor, but there is also pathos, grief, even tragedy. This is a book about a love affair. As the letters open, the author and her husband are separated by three thousand miles of ocean and a world at war. The letters that he writes to his wife, some of which are included and others of which are paraphrased by the author in letters to her mother-in-law, were by a man of taste, generosity, and understanding, who as a career military man despised war and its inhumanity, and who was deeply in love with his wife.

We follow his progress from a construction area in England, across the Channel as the invasion takes place, and with the army as it fights its way across France, is counterattacked at the Bulge in the Ardennes, and prepares for the assault across the Rhine. Then there comes a telegram. Colonel Randolph Winslow is dead, of pneumonia, and his young widow is left in Washington, devastated, with two small children to care for and educate.

Their life will go on, as hers must, and through these letters we look on as she battles against loneliness and despair to look after her family, and throws herself into her art work as anodyne for helpless grief. Ultimately she recovers, and although what her husband meant for her will never be regained or replaced (she never remarries), through the practice of her art and the rearing of her children, wins her way to equanimity and even joy once more.

Her mother-in-law, Anne Goodwin Winslow, recognized the remarkable quality of the letters, carefully saved them, and left instructions that at her death they were to be turned back to her daughter-in-law. "I wonder if I have ever told you half enough of what you achieve in the matter of taking up your pen," she wrote to Marcella Winslow from Memphis in 1959, the year of her death. "At all events I have kept the letters—one of these days you will have a treat ahead of you . . ."

The letters that follow tell us much about what kind of a person their author was, but Marcella Winslow has relatively little to say about her personal accomplishments, either in the letters to Anne Winslow or in her prefatory remarks to the book. The reader, however, will not be satisfied with that, so I must say here what she does not.

The daughter of a distinguished ecclesiastical architect, John Theodore Comès, of Pittsburgh, Marcella Rodange Comès studied before her marriage at the Carnegie School of Fine Arts with Alexander Kostellow, and continued her artistic apprenticeship in London, Rome, and Florence. When, in early 1945, her husband, Colonel Winslow, died of pneumonia, having, despite two full years of overseas service, refused to accept a leave when his outfit was in the direct path of the final Nazi counteroffensive in the Ardennes, he was awarded the Bronze Star, the Croix de Guerre, the Legion of Honor, and the Distinguished Service Medal.

Marcella Comès, to use her professional name, is best known for her portraits of creative personalities, but she has had her large compositions shown at the Musée de la Marine, in Paris, and in Madrid and Warsaw through the Art in Embassies program. Some of her best-known subjects are displayed in libraries: Admiral Nimitz at the Nimitz Library, in Annapolis, and John Finley, Walter Jackson Bate, and Harry Levin at the library of Eliot House, at Harvard. In Washington, the Central Intelligence Agency commissioned her to paint their first director, Admiral Hillenkoetter, and the Stone Ridge School's overmantel wall painting is a requested version of Edward Savage's canvas of the George Washington family. Before her marriage, she did mural panels for the Children's Room of the Homewood Library, in Pittsburgh, as part of the Public Works of Art Project that was conducted during the depression. Seven of her portrait photographs are in the Brooklyn Museum's permanent collection, and her ongoing project is photographing residents of Center Sandwich, New Hampshire, for the historical society there. She has shown in exhibits at the Carnegie Museum, in Pittsburgh, in the Corcoran biennial, and in many one-man and group shows in museums around the country and abroad.

Both of her children live in Washington. Her daughter, Mary, Mrs. John Ward Poole, teaches English and is a college counselor at the Washington International School, and her son, John, also an artist, is a professor of art at the Catholic University of America, in Washington.

When I first saw this collection of letters, I was struck by the fact that in one way or another I knew or had known many of the people who figure in them. Not only did many of the writers later become friends or acquaintances of mine, but from 1948 through 1954, as a student and teacher at the Johns Hopkins University in Baltimore, and to some extent after that, I had made the acquaintance of a fair number of the residents of Washington who appear in the letters. The account of the literary and artistic doings that I found limned in the correspondence offered a remarkable picture of the cultural life of our nation's capital at a greatly interesting juncture in both its own history and that of twentieth-century American letters. Not only that, but the presence of Anne Goodwin Winslow and of such authors as the Tates, Katherine Anne Porter, Robert Penn Warren, Eudora Welty, Peter Taylor, John Crowe Ransom, and others in the correspondence made the letters of considerable interest to students of twentieth-century southern literature. So I encouraged Marcella Winslow to prepare the collection for publication in the Southern Literary Studies series of Louisiana State University Press.

My suggestion, which she followed, was to preface the letters with explanations of what was involved in them, to provide information through annotation about some of the persons mentioned, and to tell something about how she came to be in Washington and decided to paint portraits of writers. When I saw the results, my first impulse was to ask that the annotation be handled more systematically. But then I decided that to do so would be to imperil the overall nature of the presentation, which—letters, explanations, footnotes, prefatory remarks, and portraits—was very much a unit, and in no inconsiderable way a work of literary artistry in itself. There is, after all, nothing here of a specifically documentary and referential nature that could not be fully identified and verified through normal research sources by a scholar who wished to make use of such information. It seemed more appropriate to let what Marcella Comès Winslow had to say appear as she prepared it.

LOUIS D. RUBIN, JR.

PREFACE

In 1984, I was invited to show-and-talk about a group of portraits of southern poets and writers I had painted forty years earlier. Since the occasion was a symposium called "A Southern Point of View," held in a museum in the southern state of Mississippi, I felt I should draw material for my talk from letters I had written in the 1940s and 1950s to my southern mother-in-law, the poet and novelist Anne Goodwin Winslow. She had saved those letters without my knowledge and arranged to have them sent to me after her death in 1959.

I called my talk "Southern Exposure." It had been, after all, in mid-Tennessee that I first received my exposure to the southern litterateurs who frequented Anne Winslow's Memphis country house. Some of them became my good friends, too, and during the war years quite a few turned up in Washington, where I had gone with my children in 1943 to await my husband's return from overseas. Among those to sit for me there were Allen Tate and his wife, Caroline Gordon, as well as Katherine Anne Porter, Robert Penn Warren, Eudora Welty, and Anne Winslow herself.

Not all my subjects were southerners, however. I was painting the portraits of some Yankee authors as well, among them Robert Frost and Ezra Pound, Elizabeth Bishop, Léonie Adams, Mark Van Doren, and Karl Shapiro. Later, Richard Eberhart, Robert Lowell, Peter Taylor, and Sally Fitzgerald joined the company, although too late to be recorded in these letters.

The following pages describe—in letters not written for posterity —events, and collaborations between painter and subjects, that took place during what remains for me a vivid era. The letters were written for my mother-in-law alone, but the interest aroused by "Southern Exposure" led me to decide on trying to put them in order for a wider audience. Perhaps Anne Winslow's care in preserving the letters and getting them back to me means that she had that in mind all along.

ACKNOWLEDGMENTS

To all these go my heartfelt thanks:

To William McGuire, author of *Poetry's Catbird Seat,* a history of the consultantship in poetry at the Library of Congress, who was the first person to encourage me to put my letters together into a book, and who approved the result.

To Sally Fitzgerald, without whose encouragement I might not have persisted in this project. Her suggestions were invariably helpful, as were those of John Auchard, Jean Lawlor Cohen, Rosemary Gates, Joan Givner, John Howard, Dr. Francis V. O'Connor, and Huldah Sharp.

To my daughter, Mary Winslow Poole, an English teacher, who gave invaluable guidance on punctuation, the shifting of paragraphs, and doing away with "all those commas."

To Patricia Heard and Ruth Bowman, for their essential help in finding identifications for me when the ancient obituary clippings I had saved fell short of what was needed. All too seldom do the revealing and timely bits of information in obituaries find their way into proper dictionaries of biography.

To Mary Winslow Chapman, my sister-in-law, who never lost confidence that I could find time to "work" on the letters that had meant so much to her mother and that she was sure an audience was waiting to read.

To Theda Henle, who attempted with her computer to make sense of my poor typing—all the while being patient with my unearthing of "lost" letters, and as my daughter said about her grandmother, "laughing in all the right places."

Finally, and above all, to Louis D. Rubin, Jr., who, reading the work of a painter and not a budding author, gave me to believe that my efforts might be not only presentable but even interesting and suggested that I send the typescript to Louisiana State University Press for publication in its Southern Literary Studies series, of which he is the editor.

Brushes with the Literary

INTRODUCTION

Anne Goodwin Winslow, the recipient of most of the letters in this book, was the author of six successful works of fiction and a volume of poetry. I knew that Anne Winslow had a reputation as one of the "lyric southern poets" when I married her son, Randolph, in 1934. It was, nevertheless, a pleasant surprise to her when, at age sixty-eight, in 1943, her semiauto-biographical book *The Dwelling Place* was published by Knopf and got a rave review in the New York *Times*. Later, a reviewer in the Washington *Post* called Anne Winslow a "writer of wise and delicate books about gentle people like herself," adding that her work was widely praised by well-known critics in the United States and England and that, although she wrote of gracious southern life, she enjoyed the friendship of the more realistic school of southern writers.

Two friends of this school were the writers Allen Tate (1899–1979) and his wife, Caroline Gordon (1895–1981), whom I met on a visit to my mother-in-law at her country house in Memphis in 1936. Allen, one of the most distinguished figures in contemporary American literature, had been a founder of the periodical *The Fugitive* and had written biographies of Stonewall Jackson and Jefferson Davis. Caroline laid great store by her Kentucky and Virginia Meriwether ancestry. Devoted to literature and Allen with equal fervor, she was to write eight novels between her regular entertaining of other writers and her gestures of encouragement toward young authors, including Flannery O'Connor and Walker Percy. Allen was the first poet I ever painted, and he was to be instrumental in furthering my poet-painting career. He insisted only that my subjects be first-rate writers: "No Somerset Maugham." In 1936, he was teaching literature at Southwestern University, in Memphis, and Caroline was working on her novel, *None Shall Look Back*. Because Anne Winslow was interested in the book Allen had just completed, *Reactionary Essays in Poetry and Ideas,* I lost no time in asking him to sit for his portrait with that book in his hand. Allen was in his most Agrarian period, so I put in the background a view of his house in Clarksville, Tennessee: Benfolly, named for his brother Ben, whose "folly" it had been to buy it for them. I also included the "Dark-Fired tobacco" field. Allen's letters of the time describe his enthusiasm about the portrait. The first came to me in Washington after I returned:

September 17, 1936
Dear Marcella:

I think from the photograph the portrait must be perfect. If you wish to make it more perfect, go ahead. I like the dashing handkerchief: nihil obstat. The conception of my character that you seem to be putting into the portrait pleases me vastly. Of course I don't recognize it, but that doesn't mean it isn't true, and anyhow that's what I'd like it to be. I fear I am far from callous and indifferent, or take-me-or-leave-me. It is my greatest desire to please.

I will try to get you a pretty postcard of a field of Dark-Fired tobacco, but any kind of furrows will answer the purpose. The nice feature about the setting of Benfolly is the river winding around the bluff on which the house sits. I don't say it stands; it sits as Mrs. Winslow says I do. I am in suspense until the full-size photograph of the final version is here.

We shall not let you forget the promised party. I don't know whether I ought to take a cocktail in Georgetown where, in the old brick house, my great grandmother sewed her intoxicated consort into a sheet, applied the horse-whip and said years later, after his death, that "he never touched another drop."

The following month, I received another letter in Washington from Allen, impatient to see the completion of the painting:

October 29, 1936
Dear Marcella:

If your letter weren't so very nice, I should have to think that you wrote it to tantalize me before the photograph arrives. I always feel as you do when I think I have done something good: I feel like glowing. Your glowing description makes my mouth water. That is not a bad figure: so much of the background is edible vegetation that it is permissible. At least chewable. Now don't get to liking the portrait too well, because we want to get it away from you. I am convinced that Brother Ben will snap it up, so to speak. But there has been a little difference between Bro Ben and me recently over politics. He's for Landon; I'm not exactly for FDR but I'm more for him than I am for Landon—maybe Bro Ben won't want the visage of such an enemy of Liberty (of the Public Utilities) on his wall.

In November, after I sent the photographs, Allen wrote,

The portrait is fine beyond any quality that we could possibly have imagined. I suppose it is not out of order for me to thank you for thinking that I look like that! It is almost as if what one sees there were in the mind of the subject (meaning me), what he is thinking. Caroline says that the eyes have the cold, not quite open expression that is exactly right. If this is so—then I marvel that you got it so right in the three days that I could sit for you.

Anne Winslow wrote in a letter that Allen was perishing to behold the portrait in full color and had already had a photograph of the head enlarged to life size. Her comment on this was that Allen, whose chief physical characteristic was a bulging cranium, did not seem to know that there was anything wrong with his conformation. A reproduction of the portrait was used on the jacket of his first novel, *The Fathers,* in 1938, and accompanied a number of the reviews the book received.

When Archibald MacLeish appointed Tate to be consultant in poetry at the Library of Congress in 1943, he and Caroline moved to Washington. In the same year, my husband, Randolph, then a colonel commanding a regiment in the United States Army Corps of Engineers, was ordered overseas and I chose to wait out the war years in Washington's Georgetown, never dreaming that the seventy-five-year-old bay-windowed house on P Street would be my home to this day.

In 1943, Georgetown was recovering from its long doldrums and regaining its lost charm. Rents were frozen during the war, and houses were being snapped up at very low rents. Since my house was conveniently located, I was happy to provide a setting for gatherings where poets could meet—the Tates having kindly included me in their circle of friends. Being a painter and not a poet, I was forgiven if I got Hart Crane mixed up with Stephen Crane.

Of the nineteen writers that I have painted, all but two line my walls—a visual reminder of a time and a place that produced poets and writers as important as any in this century. I was not aware then of the place they would earn in history. My letters said that Robert Penn Warren was writing a book called *All the King's Men* when he was sitting for me; that I was glad the reviews were so good it might even be a smash; that I took Katherine Anne Porter out to meet Ezra Pound at St. Elizabeth's, where he was incarcerated, and that I made sketches of him surreptitiously; that I visited Vermont to paint Robert Frost, trying to keep my promise to paint him in two sittings ("I wouldn't want anyone to tell me I had to write a poem in some designated time," he said); that Juan Ramón Jiménez, the Nobel Prize–winning Spanish poet, had a strange reason for agreeing to sit to me. Painting Eudora Welty in 1946 was a surreal experience. It was accomplished between a garden party, given in her honor, and a chaotic exodus down my front steps, where weary renters waited anxiously to take possession of my P Street house for the summer. The letters often have more to do with living than painting.

My mother-in-law often visited me in the winter, when her Memphis country house became difficult to heat; she became involved in my life and, when she returned home, counted on my letters to keep her informed of writers she admired and the children's activities. The evident interest my letters had for her encouraged me to write often and, especially, not to leave out anything she might want to know. I stressed the events that had amused me and was always pleased by her enjoyment of them too.

She was especially eager to hear about Katherine Anne Porter, one of her favorite writers, and I was able to supply voluminous dramatic copy when Katherine Anne came to live with me in the winter of 1944. The only reason I was able to get Katherine Anne to pose for her portrait was that the room I used as a studio was next to her bedroom and I could capture her before she became too involved with her overflowing life.

Anne Goodwin Winslow was born in Memphis, Tennessee, in 1875, and reared in the cultural traditions of the Old South. She was educated at home under the tutelage of her father, a lawyer and a scholar of the classics. The kind of education she received was not unusual in southern families at that time. As she wrote in *The Dwelling Place,* "It consisted entirely of reading the things we wanted to read out of doors, with apples, for the most part." After she married Eveleth Winslow, of the Boston naval family, her life took her to many lands and places with her husband, an officer in the Corps of Engineers. When he retired, they returned to her old home, and there, after his death and the marriage of her two children, she remained and took up her writing again, this time in the form of the novel and short stories. Her knowledge of literature and languages was reflected in the cosmopolitan tone of her novels. At her death, the critic Jacques Barzun wrote, "Those who like Hardy's poetry and the shorter tales of Henry James will like Anne Winslow's fiction, though its view of life suggests neither. Rather it is Virgilian: epic grandeur lurks under Anne Wins-low's vision of Europe or the South of the nineties . . . while the tone is that of glory declined. Her disenchantment has not reached the point of disgust or self pity, but all her objects speak of the 'lacrimae rerum'" ("On the Death of an American Artist," *MidCentury,* No. 8 [January, 1960], 22–23). What the Agrarians felt they had lost was epitomized by Anne Winslow.

It pleased Mrs. Winslow to have Randolph bring an artist into the family, especially a painter. I was the first person to paint his portrait after her aunt, Lamira Goodwin, of Nashville, did one of him at age sixteen. It was while painting his portrait that I fell in love: he kept going out of focus. He did not need to propose; he just wondered how I would like army life. Like his father, he had followed the Winslow tradition of serving in the military; unlike his father, though, he did not graduate first in his class at West Point but thirteenth, which was good enough for me. He was a lieutenant of engineers, working with Rivers and Harbors in Pittsburgh, my hometown. We had met there when I returned after two years of art studies in Italy. (Florence had more appeal for me than Paris, where most American artists were heading in the thirties.) Since Randolph, known at West Point as Willy Winslow, was a blithe spirit, his brand of army life suited me fine—before Pearl Harbor changed everything. We spent five years in Washington, where our children, Mary and John, were born; one year in Fort Leavenworth, Kansas, he at the Command and Staff School; two years in Vicksburg, Mississippi, in the National Memorial Park while he worked with Rivers and Harbors; and short stints in Dothan, Alabama, and Alexandria, Louisiana, where Randolph trained Engineer troops for combat in World War II. He was in command of the 390th Engineer Regiment when he left for Europe.

As for my own career, the atmosphere in which I was raised left me no doubt that I wanted to be an artist. For two years I attended the Carnegie Institute of Technology's School of Fine Arts, endlessly drawing casts of Greek statues and anatomical overlays of skeletons—including structures of the facial parts of the unfortunate student in the next seat. That exercise so paralyzed me that I was never promoted to the life class, where I most longed to be. Fortunately I was able to spend the next two years in Italy working from live models, with the result that, when I returned to the United States, I won a prize in competition with my former teachers, who were still on their anatomical campaign.

My father, John Theodore Comès (1873–1922), an ecclesiastical architect who devoted his professional life to improving the architecture of the

Catholic church in the United States, lecturing and writing to that end, was a fellow of the American Institute of Architects and the founder of the Pittsburgh Architectural Club. The famous architect Ralph Adams Cram (1863–1942) wrote of him, "I cannot forbear paying tribute to John Comès, dead in the very prime of life, who, as a great architect, played perhaps the greatest part in restoring to the Catholic Church a noble art, where she stood for fifteen centuries. There must be no going back from the standard he established. His churches stand in many places, monuments of piety and real genius" (*Progress in Ecclesiastical Architecture* [New York, 1924], 17). My father encouraged my interest in figure painting, and the muralists he selected to embellish his churches no doubt influenced my decision to go in that direction, for it was "best figure" or "best portrait" prizes that I won when I started to exhibit. In the 1930s, when artists were asking one another, "Have you gone abstract yet?" I was still painting faces. I continued to do so as I met people willing to sit for me. As a student in Rome, I had found that a Swiss guard at the Vatican was amenable to posing in exchange for English lessons. His Michelangelo-designed uniform won the eye of a juror in a Pittsburgh Area Show after I returned to the States, and I received my first portrait prize. About the same time, a portrait of my sister Alice was accepted for the Corcoran Biennial National Exhibit in Washington. The Pittsburgh *Post Gazette* headline read, "Local Girl Looms to Fore." Looming was easier in the thirties.

Information and comments about Randolph's role in the war in Europe fill many of the letters from 1943 and 1944. Although his letters were censored, they were exciting—in striking contrast to how things were in Washington during those years. His mother and I were dismayed by his discomfort and exhaustion in the ankle-deep mud when he first got to England and was using his top-rated regiment for the vast construction work necessary for the coming invasion, but we rejoiced when the "landed gentry" discovered him. We knew he was in the wide-open countryside but only later learned more exactly his location, in Sudbury, Derbyshire. The hospitable British welcomed him to their "stately homes," where he enjoyed old brandy, real eggs, and occasional fox hunting. After he was moved up in the chain of command to staff engineer of the 8th Corps, under General Troy Middleton, he could tell us even less about his whereabouts, but we were still able to get letters after the events he described took place: the crossing to France (where he had come to know mentally, from maps, "every road and stream and town better than any in my own country"), the push through Normandy, the siege of Brest, and the Battle of the Bulge. In December, 1944, he was too busy keeping the roads to

Germany open, and in Bastogne, using his engineers as infantry, to write more than, "Rather a dreary Christmas, although busy. It has been a liberal education and terribly exciting. If all pans out, I wouldn't have missed it." It was his characteristic understatement. With no rest and with two years overseas, he could not, however, throw off the pneumonia he contracted in the bitter cold weather. Things did not "pan out" for him.

His mother was visiting me when the telegram came on March 6, 1945: "The Secretary of War asks that I assure you of his deep sympathy . . ." Mrs. Winslow could only say, "You have so much longer to live without him"—a tribute we both understood too well. Letters between Anne Winslow and me continued until she died, in 1959. That year she wrote that she wanted to thank me for writing to her "all these many years," adding, "I look forward to the book you are going to write—for me to read on high—when you are too old to wield your brush. I wonder if I have ever told you half enough of what you achieve in the matter of taking up your pen. At all events I have kept the letters—one of these days you will have a treat ahead of you; only take it in sections."

Thirty years later, I have delved into the box of letters. Although I can still "wield my brush," I have set it aside to work on "the book." I have selected letters that have made me laugh, or shed a few tears, and I put them together for Anne Winslow to read "on high," as she requested.

Randolph and I celebrated New Year's, 1937, with Allen and Caroline Tate at our P Street house in Washington. Georgetown was the locale Allen felt he needed for the novel he was writing, *The Fathers*. He wanted to find the owners of the house his family had occupied, not far from us. In 1936, he wrote me,

> In the book I'm trying to write now, Prospect Avenue and [George-town] University is a long section; and I want to observe more closely than I've ever done some of the physical details of the scene. If Mrs. Dulaney is walking down the street I've got to know what she sees every step of the way. That's the trouble about a writer with no imagination; he can't make it up.

Apparently my enthusiasm was sparked by Allen's words, for in a letter of 1939 he told Anne Winslow,

> Marcella went to *great* trouble to do me a charming watercolor of "the house where the action of your novel took place." Alas, she got the wrong house! She did the big gray house on the corner, where

indeed some of my people lived a hundred years ago; but the Poseys were in a house on the next block. I didn't have the heart to tell her—and don't you, *please.*

The only letter that survives from those I wrote my mother-in-law before she began keeping them in 1943 sets the stage for the correspondence that follows.

January 4, 1937
Dear Tat [a family nickname, pronounced "Tot"],

The Tates left yesterday. After the excitement of a busy holiday season, today seems unbelievably quiet and peaceful. The sun is streaming in the window and the weather continues in a peculiar warm spell, unbroken by wind or rain. It was nasty for most of the Tates' visit which didn't matter much except that Allen couldn't loiter about his old "haunts" as much as he would have liked. As it was, they left before he could meet the owner of his old home or look up deeds and wills.

Randolph and I thoroughly enjoyed having them. They grow on one. Villie, Caroline's dachshund, does NOT grow on one. Villie has left his mark on the French doors, scratching to get back in every time she put him out. He wouldn't even eat without her. I thought he would be fun for the baby, but he growled at her as much as he did the rest of us. Caroline was apologizing for him all the time. The little guest room was groaning with the honor bestowed upon it; Allen, Caroline and Villie all got in it at night and shut the door. As there was never a noise to be heard, we presumed they all slept there. They insisted on doing this, although we offered them the big bed and the davenport.

But I will go back to the beginning: last Wednesday, out of a clear sky, came a telegram from Caroline that they would arrive on New Year's Eve. Then came long-distance calls to Randolph summoning him to the flood area. I am so glad he did not have to leave immediately for I do not know what I would have done—before even taking lessons on how to work the coal furnace, which I am doing now. He has to give a talk at the War College on the 7th and plans to leave that evening. I am glad he can get a rest now as he didn't sleep a wink the night the Tates arrived, and, as they blew in with the new year, and we got to bed around two o'clock a.m., and had them the next two evenings with various comings and goings, it is only now he can relax somewhat.

Seward Collins, the editor of the *American Review,* and his wife, Doro-thea Brandt (who wrote WAKE UP AND LIVE) came over one evening. They had gone to Richmond to meet the Tates and were stopping at the Willard Hotel. After dining there and celebrating until midnight (when the Tates came to us), they returned to their rooms to discover they had been robbed of everything, including a new mink coat (which had plenty of minks in it as Mrs. C weighs about 200 lbs.), and $100 cash, and Mr. Collins' overcoat, hat etc. They spent the next night with us and had not recovered anything so I don't suppose they would. We had such a nice evening. Everyone downed highballs and plenty of waffles and sausage and we played paper games and Ghost. No manuscripts were spilled on. We all agreed that Mrs. Collins, who is brilliant and witty, had very much your type of mind. Allen and Caroline say they have never known anyone like you, Tat. That you are a never-ending source of interest, and a work of art in yourself and the way you live.

I think Allen is one of the most simpatico men I have ever met. The combination of his mind, manners, charm and simplicity is rare indeed and Caroline is simpatico too. I found that I was so keyed up with enthusiasm and pleasure in their understanding, that I hauled out all my available painting for them to see. I think they both have a genuine feeling for art—at least in my manifestations of it.

Your plum pudding was a blessing and received hosannas all around. We had it for New Year's dinner with champagne. Mary seemed to enjoy the company. She loves to get under a sheet or towel and say, "Mary's a Koo Kux Klan." Randolph and I both hope the new year will be a happy and peaceful one for you and Mary.

> Much love,
> Marcella

The war in Europe started in 1939, the year Randolph and I left Wash-ington, and when the Japanese bombed Pearl Harbor in December, 1941, and the United States got into the war, Randolph was assigned to train Engineer troops in the southern cities of Dothan, Alabama, and Alexan-dria, Louisiana. The children and I were staying with his mother in Mem-phis when he was ordered overseas in June, 1943, in command of a black Engineer regiment. Since he was not able to take leave because of a mutiny at the base camp, I flew to New York to see him on short trips he was able to make into the city before embarking. Not knowing when those trips could be worked into his schedule, I passed the time posing for an artist colleague, who gave me the painting.

In Memphis, Johnny, age five, came down with the measles, and when no help could be found for Mrs. Winslow, I caught the first train south I could get on, what with troop movements, and paused in Washington only long enough to see my mother and try to find a house to rent for the duration. Having just a day to look and being told that in wartime Washington there was no rental housing to be had, I called a friend in my old block in Georgetown and discovered that she was moving from her house on P street to join her husband. In record time, I took over her lease. The next day, I was back on the train for Memphis. I took possession of the old Victorian three-story in August, 1943, and in 1955 I was able to buy it. My letters to Anne Goodwin Winslow were for the most part written there, from August, 1943, until her death in November, 1959.

A HOUSE ON P STREET, 1943–1945

> I do not see how anyone can get along without at least one
> thing in his life that he can think of as being both intimate
> and permanent. Not a mountain, though a rock might do;
> a tree of course is better, and a house is by far the best.
> There he can really store his past and get at it again.
>
> —Anne Goodwin Winslow, *The Dwelling Place*

When Randolph was stationed in Vicksburg, Mississippi, in 1939–1941 with River and Harbors, we found a house in Vicksburg National Memorial Park. Few servants were willing to work out of town, so I decided to train a "yard boy" named Monroe who was living near us and could cook only turnip greens. We got him a white cap and jacket, and cooking became his great interest. The children loved their father's version of my efforts to instruct Monroe. On a visit, Randolph's mother, listening to me admonish Monroe to "break an egg, now clean up, now break another egg, now clean up," remarked, "The blind leading the blind." After the United States entered the war, I persuaded Monroe to move with me to Memphis, where I stayed with my mother-in-law while Randolph was in Louisiana training troops in the Corps of Engineers. Monroe remained with me until I left for Washington in August, 1943, after I saw Randolph off to the war in Europe.

P Street, N.W.
Washington, D.C.
August 30, 1943
Dear Tat,

I would give anything to have Monroe here to help me unpack and cook meals. Even if he doesn't read or write, he could wade in and clean up the mess and then, no doubt, go into the kitchen and come forth with those heavenly biscuits. When I think of all the steps he had to take in your kitchen, to say nothing of the pantry and the storeroom where he had to go every time he needed milk, and then the wood stove which had to stay going after it was once made to go, then I know I should have induced him to come, because all he would have had to do to produce meals here would be to lean forward and backward and pivot occasionally. He could repair the furniture and rub the "storage" off it, and, most important of all, teach me how to take care of the coal furnace when the time comes. I am appalled at all there is to do.

The children came through the two-day ride up amazingly well. They were so thrilled and excited. Mary played with Pamo most of the time; I must give him his due. He was funniest held out of the window, flying, with arms and legs blown back and eyes closed in joy. I, too, must close my eyes in joy at having found this place. It is going to be fine—a big cellar (the kitchen used to be down there; a dumbwaiter is still in the dining room), wood floors, old fireplace, lots of wall space.

I hated to leave you sweltering in 100-degree heat. We were so restless the first night (all we did was drink ice water) that we got up and left at 5:30 a.m. I figured to make time before the sun came up. I could hardly believe my good fortune when it did not come up. I drove 12 hours with only one casualty; Johnny has always had definite premonitions, so when he announced that he was going to throw up, he was right. He was sitting beside me so you can imagine that I was pleased to have a bath towel nearby, and not a thing under my summer dress!

I was so happy to see Wytheville, Virginia, at 7 p.m. Next morning this is what $1.00 got us for breakfast: oatmeal, bacon, eggs, grapes, green applesauce, orange juice, delicious biscuits, home-made jelly, coffee, milk and REAL cream. When I told the children I had stayed there once with their father, Mary said: "Don't make me worry about Daden. Be reasonable!"

Do you ever have any brown meat points that you don't use? I have only three books which have to do for purchasing butter, canned fish, and cheese and lard. Any kind of roast takes about forty or fifty, which is a week's supply. Would appreciate any J, K or L's which are good until December 5th. If you can spare.

Love,
Marcella

September 5, 1943
Dear Tat,

My house is surrounded by trees, front and back, so I don't get much sun except on the top level where my spare room is. It is quiet and bright and the sun pours in since it is on the south side. It overlooks the gardens of three other Georgetown houses which should encourage me to get mine in shape. I wish you could come up and visit me this winter before I get commercial and rent the room. It is really worth $32.50 a month which is what Cynthia got for it.

How lucky the one day I was in Washington, on the way back from New York seeing Randolph off, that I got in touch with Cynthia who, as it happened, was planning to leave in August. I could take over her lease—not bad at $82.50 for a house with three floors, two bedrooms on the second floor and three on the third.[1] One I will use for my studio. You don't mind the smell of turpentine, do you?

It will be two weeks since I started working on the house. In another week I should be able to sit down and look at it. I haven't uncrated the pictures, or even glanced at the studio room, which is high with the overflow, but that can wait. The agent promised to paint over the wallpaper in the halls with Kemtone, that highly successful, washable water paint. The dining room is so dark you can't see the wallpaper anyway. We grope for the toaster and feel our way to our mouths. I can't get over how nice Randolph's piano looks in the living room and regret forgetting Death Ray's peacock feathers to place thereon.[2]

A lot of food is scarce. Butter is very difficult to get, though Mr. Neam (at the corner grocery) lets us have a stick now and then. The milk is excellent. Chevy Chase Dairy has a homogenized milk that has the cream and milk mixed up: delivery every other day, the middle of the morning. Gorgeous fruit, but way out of sight in price.

I haven't lit the furnace yet. Randolph writes that I'd better lay in my coal early and told me to get Reading Anthracite even though it costs more. He is also concerned about the three floors and only one staircase in case of fire. We do have a balcony on the second floor from which we could jump over to the neighbors' roof if worst comes to worst. Can you see us practicing?

I had a birthday dinner for Mother last week.[3] Mr. Neam got me a large sea trout which I stuffed. Everett, the Bostonian, approved of it highly. I give all the credit to Mr. Neam. He wouldn't let me get a steak today, to eat *tomorrow*—because, he said, the red juice would come out of it. I argued, but it was no use. He wants me to *like* it. Naturally, he remembers Randolph's interest in food. He never forgot that we were his early and steady customers after the summer of 1938 when Randolph discovered him. R wanted to get a steak on a Sunday, and no other store was open so he had to take a chance on the corner grocery which looked suspicious with all those crates of food always sitting out on the sidewalk in front of his store, but he took a chance. We all agreed that we had never had such a delicious steak! That paid off, for now he takes care of me. His three sons are all in the war, but he carries on with his wife and mother. His place is called Neams Market.

Love,
Marcella

1. Out of my $300-a-month allotment, I felt that $82.50 a month in rent was quite enough for a seventy-five-year-old house with an antiquated kitchen and its four-legged sink, a soapstone laundry tub in the basement, and a coal furnace I had to learn to stoke. In the forties I thought $17,000 an incredible price to be asked for an identical house next to mine. It eventually sold for less.

2. I had not been married a year when a music store phoned to ask where to send the sheet music—the Brahms Lullaby—for my nine-year-old daughter. That is the way I learned of the music lessons Randolph was secretly taking, during his lunch hour, with a man who had guaranteed that he would be playing in music halls within a year. My husband had purposely avoided a reputable music teacher, who would have insisted on hours of scale practicing. He had gone to the store and asked for a simple version of the Brahms Lullaby for his little girl. Then suddenly we had a piano and he was playing the lullaby at home. When our baby girl, who was born a year later, came home, it was the first thing she heard.

3. My mother, Honora Webber (1877–1976), was of English pioneer stock. In her background were Indian-fighters and some of the founders of Morgantown, West Virginia, teachers and ancestors with names like Leander, Simeon, and Silas Lafayette. A grandfather, Marcus Aurelius Ellis, recalling that he was a remote relative of the Garfields, wrote to congratulate the president on his election but took pains to explain that he had been unable to vote for him because of the party difference.

In answer to my letter about getting started in the P Street house, Mrs. Winslow wrote: "This paper you gave me is lovely—my first letter was written on it today, to Mr. Robert Nathan who said that Knopf's had sent him my book [The Dwelling Place] and it had made him 'homesick for graciousness, kindness, gentleness and humor; all southern qualities, I think; we do not have them here [on Cape Cod].' I hear *you* saying ha-ha! but if you can remember this old dwelling place as quiet, I suppose we can let him imagine all those other things. We have laughed a lot over your letter (the picture you give of settling in) and I am again impressed with the difference between life and art."

October 2, 1943
Dear Tat,

Randolph's letters have finally come through. After a crowded passage over, on a ship where everyone wore life preservers all the time, with the only anti-submarine activity being an occasional sudden change of direction, he has landed in England. Although he has been working his head off, he has been aware of the beautiful countryside and is comfortable. His job is a very large construction one which he finds interesting, but the social situation is a real problem. . . . In July he had none other than Bob Hope and Frances Langford for dinner! They had put on a show. He said Hope was very friendly and easy and thriving on the tour but that Langford seemed worn-out with four shows a day. She perked up after he gave her half a pint of Scotch. He keeps the men working until 10 p.m. to take advantage of the daylight and the good earth-moving weather before the proverbial rains.

Love,
Marcella

Luxembourg and the United States opened diplomatic relations in 1940 under Franklin Roosevelt, and my sister Eleanor became secretary to the minister, Hugues Le Gallais, and worked for him and his successors for thirty-three years. She helped take care of the grand duchess Charlotte and her family when they escaped from Luxembourg, just ahead of Hitler's takeover.

Before returning to Europe, Charlotte visited New Orleans. Since my father had been born in Luxembourg, news of that tiny grand duchy always interested me. GRAND DUCHESS AMONG LAST TO ESCAPE FROM LUXEMBOURG was the headline in the New Orleans paper of February 2, 1943, that announced her visit to that city. The article related that Le Gallais had much to tell of the courage displayed by the people of Luxembourg in refusing to annex themselves voluntarily to the German Reich. The Nazis, he said, had been campaigning for over a year, sending professors and lecturers to even the smallest villages to expose the glories of Hitler's Greater Germany. A census had been ordered, requiring the inhabitants to declare their nationalities as Italian, German, or French—to the exclusion of Luxembourger as a nationality. When 97 percent of the people signed themselves as Luxembourgers, Germany decided to annex the country forcibly. Eight thousand residents were arrested, and many families were deported to Poland. Germans from Transylvania—in whom the Germans had more confidence—were sent to replace them.

October 5, 1943
Dear Tat,

Eleanor has been busy with the Luxembourg contingent ever since they came to the U.S. The Grand Duchess Charlotte's maid is going to Europe and has agreed to take Randolph some chocolate. She goes by boat with a great deal of luggage. The Grand Duchess left by clipper for England—after a good deal of waiting and canceling and so much trouble. I got 12 bars of chocolate, some penuche and two Pocket Book mysteries into a 10″ × 6″ carton. My practice in packing my car! Remember old Luther's remark "Nobody pack cars like Miss Marcella"? This will be Randolph's birthday gift in time for the 17th November. The Countess Lynar (lady-in-waiting) came to tea yesterday. I had plain bread with YOUR butter and coconut cookies which I had made. Coconut has gone off the market but I happened to find a box. Mary wondered how the Countess was going to like "cow's butter." She liked it, rest assured. She couldn't adjust her court posture to our low chairs, poor soul, and must have felt that her knees were touching her chin. But there was nothing for it. I have a low-slung house.

I tried to get some whiskey but the best I could do was a Mexican tequila which tastes awful. Wish I had a cellar saved up! Randolph has been able to get whiskey, beer and ale for his officers in England but it is seldom warm enough to want beer there. He was invited to cocktails at "the Hall" with an Earl and his wife—said she is a charming hostess. [1] He said the whiskey one gets in England now is about half water and rather green. Apparently he made an impression for he was invited back for dinner which, in his word, was a "gem." The hostess, Lady Vernon, has lived many years in France. The menu: Martini cocktail, vichyssoise, casserole of chicken with hock to drink, raspberries and cream, fruit (peaches, apricots and cherries), coffee, port, and brandy.

Love,
Marcella

1. Lord and Lady Vernon had a large estate in Sudbury, Derbyshire, and frequently entertained American officers stationed nearby. Sudbury Hall became an oasis for Randolph during the ten months he spent there.

October 7, 1943

Dear Tat,

Randolph keeps asking for your book. He sent me a check so I would like to order two of THE DWELLING PLACE for him from Knopf. Enclosing check for $5.00. As you see from his letter "gifts to hostesses" are not included in whatever stipend he is managing to get along on. I am so happy he is having such a variety of interesting experiences in the English countryside. Of course I am dying to read the book on THE HALL which he is sending to us. That should give us an idea where he is, but we may not receive it until 1944! I read recently that a Negro choir gave a concert in London and felt sure that must have been Randolph's outfit. I wasn't so keen on the Marquand book I bought to send R so exchanged it for WINTER'S TALES by Isak Dinesen.

Allen [Tate] took his portrait home Sunday after a diligent morning of sitting, correcting the final details.[1] His eye lights up every time he looks at it. The ear is now to his liking, the hair lighter and the eye a trifle bluer—with a cold glint. (This was Caroline's suggestion.) Nancy [Tate]'s first reaction was distinctly favorable. Allen would like me to paint Caroline. Nothing said about payment as yet, but I presume that will materialize some day. While waiting to hear from my allotment I go up to the attic and sit there brooding on being an artist in a garret. Fortunately I have credit at Neams Market. Mother had the Tates and me to a delicious lunch on ham and your pickles which are heavenly. Afterward they came here before going on to a cocktail and dinner party. Since I had to take the children to a birthday party, I left the three of them napping. They were obviously dying for one, after a late Saturday night outing, but how few could manage the doing of it so gracefully! Caroline's book will be called THE WOMEN ON THE PORCH, she says.

Love,

Marcella

1. The portrait of Allen Tate that I had almost finished in Memphis was completed in Washington, with corrections approved.

Mary started school at the Sacred Heart Convent. The Society of the Sacred Heart, a French order, had a school on Massachusetts Avenue near the Sulgrave Club. Later they bought the large Hamilton estate near the Maryland border and kept its name, Stone Ridge.

October 10, 1943
Dear Tat,

Mary adores her school. The Sacred Heart nuns are so sweet and jolly. Every day at 3, the class files out past Mother McDonald (who stands at the door, girls curtsying and boys bowing), shakes hands and says: "Goodbye, Mother." In the morning a colored maid stands there. . . .

A girl, half day, gets $12 a week and a full day from $15 on up (an 8-hour day). If you can get her.

I don't know how you can be eating mustard greens since I am sure I planted only turnips. If you are, I hope they are good.

Love,
Marcella

Anne Winslow and I first met Robert Lowell while visiting the Tates at Monteagle, Tennessee, in 1943. Mrs. Winslow was surprised to learn that Allen's invitation to us to come and meet our cousin was at the behest of Lowell, who with his wife, Jean Stafford, was sharing a house with them. Neither of us had ever heard of such a cousin. On our two-day visit, we were witness to various novels and poems coming to life: Caroline's novel *Women on the Porch*, Jean Stafford's first novel, *Boston Adventure*, and Robert Lowell's poems that he would revise and later include in his first book, *Lord Weary's Castle*, which won a Pulitzer Prize in 1946.

October 13, 1943
Dear Tat,

Have you read about "Caligula" [Robert] Lowell going to jail?[1] The headline on today's paper reads: LOWELL SCION ORDERED TO JAIL FOR FAILING TO OBEY DRAFT LAW. The piece always starts out with his cousinship to the president of Harvard and Amy Lowell, poet. It turns out that Cal had applied to both the Army and the Navy for a commission after Pearl Harbor but was turned down because of defective eyesight, but now he is a conscientious objector because he revolts at the bombing of whole cities and nations.

Caroline has finished her book and seems very elated. She has asked me for dinner tomorrow night so I will see the ménage in action. My portrait of Allen is over their mantel and they say they have no objections—unless, like the *New Yorker* joke, "someone shoot him down." So I hope they approve. They have taken a house with Lon and Fanny Cheney in Anacostia—of all places.[2]

Love,
Marcella

1. Robert Lowell (1917–1977) was born in Boston. He attended St. Mark's School and began undergraduate work at Harvard, from which he transferred to Kenyon College, where John Crowe Ransom was teaching. He was influenced by Allen Tate. In 1940, he converted to Catholicism, and in 1943 he was imprisoned for refusing to report for military service. His works include *Life Studies* (New York, 1959), *Confessional Verse* (New York, 1959), and *Day by Day* (New York, 1977). His *The Dolphins* (New York, 1973) won the Pulitzer Prize.

2. The Cheneys were old friends of the Tates' from Nashville. Brainard (Lon) was a secretary to Senator Tom Stewart, of Tennessee, and his wife, Fanny, a librarian, worked as a secretary to Tate at the Library of Congress in 1943–1944.

When Anne Winslow's book *The Dwelling Place* was published by Knopf in the fall of 1943, Orville Prescott, a staff book reviewer for the New York *Times,* devoted two columns to it, commenting that it was refreshing and encouraging to find books like it still being written and women like Mrs. Winslow still among us. "For Mrs. Winslow is that admirable rarity, a lady born and bred who has never had time or inclination to be just a lady. Instead she has been a wandering officer's wife, a poet, a celebrated hostess, a woman of gentle wit and rueful wisdom, a polished writer. With *The Dwelling Place* she takes her place in my private, imaginary filing system of American authors in the exclusive group limited to Southerners whose humorous and perceptive autobiographical books do honor to the South and to themselves" ("Books of the Times," New York *Times,* August 6, 1943).

Allen and Caroline Tate were disconcerted at the success of *The Dwelling Place.* They did not consider Mrs. Winslow a pro. To receive such good reviews, at age sixty-eight, for a semiautobiographical book! But to Mrs. Winslow, Caroline wrote,

> Your book came yesterday. I snatched it first and read it through at one sitting. It is an extremely readable book. Anybody who starts it will keep on reading, I think. It is also a beautiful, graceful and frivolous book. I hasten to add that I use "frivolous" in the Proustian

sense. . . . So, I think your choosing to write the kind of book you have written, is an assertion—or denial or something.

But the book itself is a delight. I admire the deftness and the economy with which the stories are presented and the skill with which they are woven into the narrative, for there is a narrative, though you don't realize it until you put down the book. . . .

With thanks for the beautiful book. . . . You'd probably never have even told us it was out, but having written it would have turned to gardening or something else. I enjoyed it—that is the proper word—and will dip into it often again. I don't really think that since you write so well you ought to write more and write more seriously—that is probably what Allen will tell you. I am just pleased that you write so extraordinarily well, and with such grace.

Caroline's flattering comments here were at odds with the derogatory ones she made to me. Allen remained silent. A letter dated September 20 from Anne Winslow concerning Allen's attitude states, "I hope you told Allen it was not only books I didn't like, but just about everything. Never shall I 'hash it out' with him or any 'sensitive artist'—except the very few I am trying to reform, but you might slip it to him, casually but often, that I think he has the most charming mind I have ever encountered; what he does with it is between him and God. As for Caroline, keep on telling her I like what she said about my book (not orally). I like her better for saying it now that I know what they think."

October 15, 1943
Dear Tat,

What about another book for Randolph? I think the other one got sent to his old APO number. I doubt if many ships are being sunk now.

I haven't seen the Tates lately. However, I made it clear that you considered them one of the most interesting and charming couples you know, and that you liked Caroline's letter better than any review you had had. I said you would have liked other reviews as discriminating. She seemed pleased and remarked that the way you had written the last chapter was superb. She also said she thought it was terrible of Allen not to write to you, but sparks were flying from Allen's eyes and I knew how those that he is "arrogant with" must feel. He said he would rather be in your company than most anyone he knew, and thought you completely charming but apparently this is not altering his formal mad.

They both hoped very much that you would come up and visit this winter. I hope so too.

> Love,
> Marcella

Food was an interest I learned to share with my mother-in-law. In "Food and Drugs," one of the chapters in *The Dwelling Place,* Anne Winslow wrote that experimenting with new dishes, making wine in the cellar, and having postmortems after meals were encouraged. Using raw materials—and no substitutes—was the norm: "If one makes a failure nowadays with everything pretested, pre-measured, and pre-mixed, there is no longer anything to blame for it" (p. 125).

October 17, 1943
Dear Tat,

There is a marvelous bread which comes from Pepperidge Farm, Connecticut. You may have read about it in the *New Yorker;* it costs twenty-seven cents a loaf but lasts about three days.

Every time I eat one of the fresh fish from Neams I think how you would approve of its divine lack of smell. (This means nothing to you coming from me.) Aside from their beautiful non-odor they fall to pieces after 15 minutes' baking and literally melt in your mouth. I have Boston lettuce every day too, and a choice of breads as difficult for me as choosing French pastry.

These last few days we have had long confabs about our luck in finding Vistula. As you can imagine Vistula is of the dark race and she is shared. She goes to Mother in the morning and to me in the afternoon, so she can make $20 a week, which she is worth. She is too good to be true and we hope that Vistula likes US. I am economizing as closely as possible.

> Love,
> Marcella

A family friend I had taken on, Betty Fisher, was devoted to Anne Winslow. Her mother had been a close friend of Mrs. Winslow's, and Betty had inherited "Miss Annie." Both Betty and her husband, Evan, had been brought up in the lap of luxury, but after marriage both lost their fortunes in the depression. Still, they continued to hang on to the threads of their past while trying unsuccessfully to cope with the present.

October 18, 1943
Dear Tat,

Betty Fisher wanted to come over last week, so I suggested dinner on the strength of Vistula, not knowing how long my luck will last. Betty looks more windblown as to hair, heavier and older, but has still the same light in the eye, and is being the brave little woman while Evan is away. She says she just manages to "scrape along" on $365 a month compared to my $299.50, which was one dollar short of my allotment last month! Here it is for your interest: Rent, $82.50 (I wonder what the landlady does with that 50 cents); Doctor, $5; School, $50; Maid, $32; Laundress, $16; Food, $60; Milk, $10; Utilities, $6; Frames, $14; Coal, $14. I hope to make some money if I can get started. I tried to get some of the smarter shops in Georgetown to display some of my paintings in their windows but the only reaction was: They are not antique enough, or, They are not modern enough. Antique shops make up most of Georgetown but the most popular store is Stohlmans, the homemade cake and ice-cream store, and the Tastee bake shop which you will love.

Love,
Marcella

October 20, 1943
Dear Tat,

I feel just as though my "salon" had started but the setting is not my house. I've just returned from a cocktail party around the corner where they had frightfully good tidbits to eat. The specialty of the house is anchovy in tiny pastry crescents. I took one every time they were passed (as I had passed up my own dinner for the gala occasion) but that was only three times so I came home with a ravenous appetite—after very good 15-year-old Scotches—and fried some mushrooms in your butter. Your can of butter came yesterday which means that my bought stuff can be released for cooking. Che gioia! You are wonderful to send it to me and I automatically reach for my brown points to give you 16! I do hope you are not sacrificing any you could use. Canary must be really performing now, and who is milking her?

Apparently Allen is saving up to pay me all at once for the portrait because he hasn't said anything. He had all last evening to breathe in my ear, when I was invited to dinner, but I fear, with the portrait on the wall so tangible, it will be easy to forget.[1]

We had a lovely dinner. Caroline has a real knack for living with people who can produce food as good as hers. Of course they have Jessie, but Mrs. Cheney, who shares the house, did a major portion of the cooking, I gather. When Caroline invited me she said the Huntington Cairnses were the only other ones coming, that she was wearing a long dress because she never felt much like a dinner if she didn't dress, adding that they might go walking in the woods first.[2] That was a clue that should have alerted me. It rained hard that day, though, so I figured the walk was off and I looked over my long dresses which have "sat" for so long. I picked out the least dressy one and, garnished with earrings and pearls, set out to drive to the other end of town. It might have been Baltimore or any strange town to me once I passed beyond the Capitol, but I carefully followed directions and finally arrived on a windswept hill without a name—new, cheerless, utterly devoid of personality. I was sure I must be all wrong when I saw in the lighted window the silhouette of the picture of Allen's family they had at Monteagle, and then from another window the brightly colored painting by Mrs. Ford Madox Ford [Janice Biála]. I prepared to make an entrance.

After all, Huntington Cairns was quoted in *Time* magazine as being the star performer on the radio program "Invitation to Learning," to say nothing of knowing fifteen languages. Caroline answered the door in a shirtwaist and skirt. What's more, the shirtwaist was hanging out the back. She had on moccasins and held autumn leaves in her hand. She had been wondering why they didn't look like the colored pictures in the Coca-Cola flower-arranging ads in the flat bowl she was using. I wasn't a bit disconcerted—the Tates being what they are—until I saw Mrs. Cairns. Then I wanted to surreptitiously remove my pearls and disarrange my hair. She had on what looked like hunting boots left over from World War I, which should have been in the Smithsonian. Her tweed suit might have been of the same period, judging from the back of the skirt which was sitting down when she was standing up, and must have required a good many years to get so perfect a bulge. Her shirt also escaped its moorings and her hair was, like the surroundings, windswept. By now, dear reader, you have guessed that they walked in the woods.

Mrs. Cheney completed the female trio appearing in slacks a trifle too tight, which she changed to a velvet dress when the slacks proved not slack enough after the Old Fashioneds and rich canapés.

A delightful evening and stimulating as always with the Tates. Allen read his poem translated, from the Latin ("Perivigilium Veneris"), "amavis, amat," etc. It sounded lovely, all about love. Caroline produced a good many pastels for criticism. She seems to have gotten the bug from a "post-Whistlerian nocturne" painter at Monteagle. She asked for a *real* criticism so I said one was good and one was poisonous. She acts toward the current dachshund as Mary does toward bedraggled Pamo, smothering him with amavis, amat. Huntington Cairns is a Pickwick-looking soul—very nice. Has something to do with the National Gallery and has just helped the Director write a book on same. Knows John Rothenstein and everyone else, it seems.[3] He had just read Albert Jay Nock's book from which he quoted Nock's idea that Pickwickian types commit suicide.[4] Everyone, at this point, decided that he or she had at some time contemplated suicide—except me (and I was in evening dress). Mrs. Cairns doesn't believe in democracy, which was so novel that the subject was dropped immediately. Outside of not believing in democracy, I couldn't find out anything else about her which would permit her to dress that way and call David Finley, David (Finley is a big shot in Washington).[5] The atmosphere was so exactly the same as it was in the Monteagle household, with the Cheneys substituting for the Lowells, that it was downright monotonous.

Will you engage the top room for the cold months? I think I will have to rent it.

Love,
Marcella

1. At some point I received a hundred dollars from Allen for the portrait.

2. Huntington Cairns, a Baltimorean, was an author, editor, and for two decades a secretary, treasurer, and general counsel of the National Gallery of Art. He also advised the Treasury Department whether books and works of art were pornographic or artistic. "Someone had to do it," he explained. "Most of the customs people don't know a Vatican mural from a French postcard. One customs man was suspicious of a Spanish version of the Bible." He graduated from law school when only twenty and once observed that Plato had dominated the first part of his life and Shakespeare the second. He was the author of *Legal Philosophy from Plato to*

Hegel, and editor of *The Limits of Art* and *The American Scene,* a collection of H. L. Mencken's writings.

3. John Rothenstein, a director of the Tate Gallery, in London, had as a young man given a course in art at the University of Pittsburgh, where our paths crossed. He asked me to paint his portrait when he became interested in my work, and I, being a student and very pleased with the result, offered to give it to him. He said, "No, it will do you more good. Keep it!"

4. Albert Jay Nock, a leading literary critic and author, was the editor of the *North American Review.* A great admirer of Anne Winslow, he published several of her essays in the 1920's, one being on Rainer Maria Rilke, whom she knew in Switzerland and helped to introduce to the United States.

5. David Finley was the first director of the National Gallery of Art in Washington.

[A week later]

Dear Tat,

I am getting prepared to paint Caroline when she gets THE WOMEN ON THE PORCH off her hands. We went to the Phillips Gallery the other day and she and Mrs. Cheney came to dinner. The men had gone somewhere over the weekend. She has bought an easel now so she is really into painting. I asked her point-blank about Mrs. Cairns. Sort of a Why-is-Mrs.-Cairns? question. And the answer is: "She reads!" Herodotus and stuff. You see, you were wrong when you wrote in your book that you can't say, "she reads." [1] She told me also that, at a dinner Mrs. Mark Van Doren asked them to in New York, Mrs. Cairns told Caroline not to dress, contrary to Mrs. Van D's instructions. So Caroline, who also reads, didn't dress and Mrs. Van D was furious and got out a black lace for her to wear. When Mrs. Cairns came, Caroline said—believe this or not—"she had on the same tweed suit she wore at my house." She described her in almost the same words I used in my letter to you—the braided hair having been done the day before, etc. However, she always dresses at her own dinners and expects you to. I believe I shall invite them to dinner and see what happens. Vistula is doing fine, but I doubt if she will stand the pace over any period of time. She shows up later and later.

Love,
Marcella

1. One of several explanations Anne Winslow proffered for a solitary way of life: "'Oh yes, she lives out there by herself,' my friends could say; 'she is writing a novel'; or 'she writes, you know.' How much better that sounds than saying she cooks, or she plays the piano, or even she reads, you know" (*The Dwelling Place*, 13, 14).

We met our Washington Winslow cousins in Georgetown in 1936 through a mistake in the mail. Harriet Winslow and her sister, Mary Winslow, maiden ladies, lived on Q Street, a block from our P Street house. Soon after our daughter, Mary, was born, Randolph received a phone call from Mary Winslow telling him that she had received a baby dress in the mail. Were we related? she asked. Randolph was not aware that he had relatives in Washington, but the ladies had known his father, so we welcomed their interest. Harriet was the acknowledged authority on the New England branch of the Winslows, and she took such a generous interest in her young male cousins, Robert Lowell and John Winslow, my son, that they each named a daughter for her. Robert Lowell's mother, Charlotte Winslow, was Harriet's first cousin, Harriet being the Winslow relative he felt closest to, "roguish and worldly enough [for Robert] to feel thoroughly at home with her—witty, generous and unshockable" (Ian Hamilton, *Robert Lowell: A Biography* [New York, 1982], 234).

November 1, 1943
Dear Tat,
Sunday I took the children to call on the Winslows. Miss Harriet received us and was very cordial.[1] Johnny, now five, who is usually mildness itself, after settling down in an antique chair in the beautifully furnished drawing room, suddenly, softly but audibly, announced, "I don't like this house." So much for the ritzy relatives! Harriet loved it.
Harriet had seen young Lowell [Robert] in New York a short time before. He is her first cousin once removed (which makes Randolph a fourth cousin to Lowell, doesn't it?). Jean [Stafford] had been here last week.[2] Harriet said she had cut her hair so that it hung straight down all around her shoulders and frightened them nearly to death when she peered in through the window before announcing her presence when she came out to tea.
I don't remember when I last wrote. I believe it was since the last butter—the large can—the nubbins of which I am still using. Caroline

said she intended to write and tell you what a treat it was for her to have real butter after the oleo they have all the time. She stayed with me several days this week to enable me to paint her uninterrupted. The fates had planned differently about the interruptions, though.

The day she came Vistula did not. It turned out she had left for good. Vistula told my laundress that I was going to take boarders and had not offered to pay her more! Poor Caroline never laid eyes on her so we painted, and cooked, washed dishes, and painted; tore downstairs to answer the phone and painted; went to pick up children at school and painted; tended the furnace, let the furnace go out, and then nursed it back again; and painted; and cooked. Bub is on her lap and I have included a colorful Meriwether scarf that Caroline insisted should be in the painting. It helps the composition, as well as the color scheme, and Caroline fell happily into a natural pose. The figure is life size, and characteristic with the dog—as she is never without one.

The evening Allen came to get her, [he had] with [him] Mark Van Doren (in town for a day), a bottle of Jack Daniel's whiskey and John Peale Bishop—in that order.[3] I put the JD before JPB because I liked it more. Mark Van Doren I am mad about on first sight. I put him in a class with Allen [Tate] and Walter de la Mare [the English poet I knew in London]. All three of the literary lights were interested in my paintings and approved of the start on Caroline and Bub. JPB kept saying: "Keep everything subservient to the dog—do the dog first and let the rest follow." My last portrait commission was brought out as a horrible example of American womanhood—my masterpiece! Allen and Caroline like to think of her as the mean rich girl with the hard mouth. B was merely dubbed "rodent." The composition of Randolph and me over the sofa was approved of highly. The portion particularly sought out for praise was the bit I had always intended to repaint but never got around to. Now, I don't know.

It is so difficult to get help. Employment agencies have girls who work by the day, but most want an 8-hour day so they can make 4 dollars. The men one gets are so unreliable and independent. They half-finish a job and promise to come back and one knows they never will.

Love,
Marcella

1. Harriet Patterson Winslow (1882–1964), active in musical circles in Washington (she studied singing for seven years with Nadia Boulanger in Paris) was responsible for the organization of European relief societies during both world wars. Harriet, whose Winslow branch had settled in Georgetown before Washington became the capital, was born in the family mansion, Brentwood, designed by Benjamin Latrobe, the architect of the White House. Her great-grandfather Daniel Patterson commanded the naval squadron defending New Orleans during the War of 1812. His flagship was the frigate Constitution, "Old Ironsides."

2. Jean Stafford (1915–1979) married Robert Lowell in April, 1940. Her first novel, *Boston Adventure,* was published in 1944, to immediate success. With the proceeds from the book she bought a house in Damariscotta, Maine. She and Lowell were divorced in April, 1948.

3. Mark Van Doren (1894–1972) was a poet, a critic, and the literary editor of the *Nation* from 1935 to 1939. He taught English at Columbia University until 1959. John Peale Bishop (1892–1944), a poet, editor, and essayist, had been managing editor of *Vanity Fair* in 1919 and served as the model for the radical poet in *This Side of Paradise,* F. Scott Fitzgerald's novel of Princeton life. Bishop collaborated with Tate in editing *American Harvest,* a collection of essays on American literature between the two great wars.

The American monsignor Francis Spellman was stationed at the Vatican in 1943 and later was to become the cardinal archbishop of New York. The first year I was in Europe, living in Italy with my mother and sisters, I was asked by him to paint a Bishop Murray from a photograph. Never having worked from a photograph—which I considered very commercial—I decided to get real props. The Duomo in Florence was happy to lend me a bishop's robe, never even asking my name; a lace store provided the lace (Americans were completely trusted), and a handsome Italian with fair complexion, Albizzo degli Albizzi, said he would sit for the proper skin tones. If only I had painted him instead of the bishop. Later, in Paris, the first magnificent painting I saw in the Louvre, on the wall as I entered, was by Ghirlandaio (1449–1494), *The Albizzo degli Albizzi Family.*

November 15, 1943
Dear Tat,

Guess whom I saw getting out of a taxi in front of the Mayflower? Archbishop Spellman! With his fantastic memory he recognized me immediately, although he jumped a mile when I tapped him on the shoulder. I guess no one does that to an Archbishop. He said he had just seen a painting of mine (the Swiss Guard that won the prize in the Pittsburgh

Area Show) and then asked why I had sent the portrait of the Bishop of Portland—the one I did in Rome—to Portland, Maine, instead of to Portland, Oregon. I never knew before that my very first portrait commission, which he got Mrs. Nicholas Brady to pay for ($300), had gone 3000 miles astray—via the American Express!

Still working on the house. The halls have been Kemtoned over the old wallpaper and I'm trying to hang most of my pictures. Washing hair all around, cooking and furnace-tending, I realize I must find another girl to take Vistula's place or I won't get any painting done. My top price, straining to meet, is $15 a week. The good ones won't take a job for less than $20 or so, because of government competition.

Love,

Marcella

Lieutenant General Lucius Dubignon Clay (1898–1978) was the son of a three-term United States senator from Marietta, Georgia. One of the military giants of World War II, with his rigorous standards and organizing genius, he helped not only win a global war but secure a lasting peace. His greatest achievement was the creation of a prosperous, stable, and democratic Germany. As military governor of Germany and commander of the American forces in Europe, he against all odds and advice ordered the airlift of food into Berlin when that city was threatened with a land blockade by the Soviets. His conviction was that the future of democracy required the West to stay there until forced out if it was to hold Europe against communism. Clay's successor, John J. McCloy, described Clay's military governorship as the "nearest thing to a Roman proconsulship the modern world afforded. You could turn to your secretary and say, 'Take a law.' The law was there and you could see its effect in two or three weeks . . . benevolent despotism" (Jean Edward Smith, *Lucius D. Clay* [New York, 1990], 201). What is less well known is the personal interest Clay took in preserving the art works the Americans captured, many of which the Nazis had stolen. After the works were sent to the United States for safekeeping and restoration, many congressmen and military personnel felt that they should remain there as reparations. Clay, however, had the authority to ensure that they were returned to the German museums from which they had been taken. Although Clay graduated from West Point at an earlier date than my husband, they were colleagues in the Army Corps of Engineers and were stationed in Pittsburgh and Washington about the same time. It was through Clay's wife, Marjorie, that I was initiated into army life when I came to Washington as a fledgling bride. She became interested in my art career and was disappointed that Lucius was too busy to sit for his portrait. She convinced me, though, that she could persuade Mamie Eisenhower to let me paint her before Ike returned from overseas.

November 20, 1943
Dear Tat,

I expect to learn a lot if, and when, I see Marjorie Clay (wife of Lucius Clay, an Engineer friend of Randolph's). General Clay has just come back from two months around the world with General Brehon Somervell.[1] I may get first-hand information on Randolph. No letter in a long time.

Love,
Marcella

1. Brehon Somervell (1892–1955) served as engineer, chief of army service forces, from 1942 to 1946. Lucius Clay never had a wartime command, for he could never be spared from the other assignments few others could do as well. When he returned from the trip with Somervell in December, 1943, he once more asked to go overseas and was willing to take a reduction in rank from major general to colonel if necessary. He wanted most to command a combat engineer regiment, saying that for a professional soldier to go through a war without seeing combat was about as humiliating as anything he could think of. Robert Lovett is quoted as saying, "Lucius Clay represents the fiery type of fellow that you see in old fashioned movies like *Gone with the Wind*. He's the kind of military leader the Confederate Army produced in good numbers. They were proud people. They weren't wild entirely, but they weren't afraid of anything" (Smith, *Lucius Clay,* i).

November 25, 1943
Dear Tat,

Randolph fulfills his quota of two letters a week. This must be a miserable time of year for them. If Lady Vernon can make up for the mud I am all for it. He has been discovered by another "Hall": people who have a huge estate, swans on the lake, boy at Eton etc. He says the only concession to the war in those houses is that maids have replaced butlers. A lot of the farm work is done by Italian prisoners who have complete freedom and a distinctive uniform. He says they make good farm hands and are popular with the local girls. His companies are scattered all over the place and when he travels he sees mostly Yanks. Few English on the roads.

I don't like to sound too confident after my bad luck with servants, but I think I have come to a turning point in my life. A girl named Lena Clifton has started to work for me. Her first job since she was married at 14. Practically no maid will touch $15 a week, but she is content with that as she wants only to keep busy and LOVES children and LOVES housework and doesn't care about a government job. Incredible?

Mary just called from the next room and asked: "If God is an Episcopalian, what would I be?" It is very difficult to explain about that! Just at present she feels God is a Catholic, but Daden isn't, which brings one or the other of them up or down, I don't know which.

Did I tell you that Allen has accepted the editorship of the *Sewanee Review* and that they will return to Monteagle in June? The Tates, as usual, are entertaining almost continuously.

John has written a letter to Santa Claus asking for a machine gun, a pistol in a holster and a soldier cap, which is where his interest lies now. Mary's letter to the same recipient is complete with drawings. I send you the original.

Dear Santa Clause,
Will you please bring me a dollar. And a jack-in-the-box. And a girls wallet. And a two-wheeler that I can ride and isn't to little or big and that I can learn to ride it in a jhife. with a case that faones on with everything I need in it even a hamer. And a tipe-writing mashein. and some staplers to put in my stapling mashein.

Love,
Marcella

When Anne Winslow's book, *The Dwelling Place*, received excellent reviews, Allen Tate acknowledged the fact after some hesitation. His device was to compose a letter in the style of Dr. Johnson, the irony of which was not lost on Mrs. Winslow. Written on Library of Congress stationery, it is dated December 1, 1943.

Dear Miss Annie:
I salute you thus, with a praenomen which I have hitherto neglected to use in our long and affectionate intercourse, because by this artifice I may hope to establish that 18th-century social distance

which will, I trust, give point to the elevated sentiments which I beg your permission to express upon the occasion of your recent book. I need not say to you, Madam, that with us Miss or Mister preceding the Christian name (usually in a diminutive form) is at once a symbol of social unity and a title so honorific as to be virtually an acknowledgment of nobility. I would not offer you less; nor, Madam, as a disciple of Mr. Jefferson's democracy, would my conscience permit me to offer you more.

Permit me to confess to a contemplation of the marvelous when I reflect that a widowed Lady could resume a career of authorship after a lapse of so many years had advanced her to a distinguished age.

In style, THE DWELLING PLACE is a shining model of perspicuity, and equally of liberality of view guided by the restraint of an elegant and fastidious mind. "My lord," said Horatio, "custom hath made it in him a property of easiness." The elegance and perspicuity of your language are qualities which you must allow us to distinguish, even though you, in your high station, unlike the grave-digger in his low, might discover a want of taste did you but acknowledge these superior qualities as present in yourself.

It hath been justly observed by the leading wits of our enlightened age that Elegance is an accomplishment which Art cannot create but can only improve; and it hath been doubted that Art itself is more than a particular refinement of the mind towards polite learning. My Lord Kames—a man of sense as well as a man of learning —abundantly proves that Poesy herself is a goddess of the best antecedents, who departs from polite usage at her peril, as we have egregious evidence in the poets of the barbarous age of Shakespeare, who was only Fancy's child.

I should distinguish, Madam, for my especial favor, if you will allow me the presumption, the equal mind with which you pass from the untutored wildness of the Yancui female to the savagery of the Blackamoor murderess. For this equipoise I have only the most abject admiration. And permit me to add that I can but approve in the highest terms of your failure, or may I say your refusal, to condescend to the nondescript race of scribblers who have imposed upon your generosity: they are unworthy of the glance of a Lady of Fashion. But, Madam, I would advert, if I may do so without offense, to a certain ingenuousness of observation as you direct your attention to bucolic scenes and even to Nature herself, although I must confess that, while there is just a suspicion that you have read Monsieur Rousseau, your pen has not strayed into the inelegant excess of that misguided Genius. There is everywhere order and proportion. I conclude these lucubrations upon your distinguished talent with the hope that you may take the first stage for Washington, where it will be our distress not to be able to offer you hospitality consistent with your Quality.

Until this happy consummation of our wishes, I beg, dear Madam, to remain

> Your most ob't friend and serv't
> Allen Tate

We pray that you will condescend to accept the accommodations which we, in a time of civil and military commotion, are able to provide.

When "Miss Annie" wrote Allen to say she enjoyed a letter from Dr. Johnson but would have preferred one from him, he answered:

December 13, 1943

Dr. Johnson retires; and we are again Mr. [Henry A.] Wallace's common man. I just wonder whether you see any hope of making him uncommon?

And now, I can say that it is a beautiful book, written with great skill and subtlety—a minor masterpiece, in fact, which I am sure you will not let your publisher persuade you to write again. They always want the same book, only slightly different. —What is next? There will surely be something.

Marcella being without a servant can't leave the house; so we go to see her. Yesterday we had a very pleasant visit and we all agreed that you must come up to see us all during the bad spell in February.

Caroline sends her love along with mine, for we love you very much and suffer the constant desolation of your absence.

> Ever yrs,
> Allen Tate

Anne Winslow and I were guests of the Tates at a poetic evening in their house in Washington some time in 1943. The guests were participants in an appropriate game. I kept the paper we used, with the handwriting of those present, though I can match the handwriting with names in only a few instances. At the party were John Crowe Ransom, Robert Penn Warren, Denis Devlin, Caroline and Allen Tate, Brainard and Fanny Cheney,

Anne Winslow, and I. One of the poets present wrote a column of rhyming words, and each person's part in the game was to compose a single line ending with a word assigned from the column. The paper was folded in a way that did not let one see what had come before; all one could see was the word one had been allotted. The resulting "poem":

I have gone all the way and ne'er have SEEN
The U-backed beasts at bay, now eye to EYE
Slithering, sliming over the moldering GREEN
She transforms boys to figs by ALCHEMY
From spook to gobbledegook, dour RIDE
Through elements reflecting horror's FACE
And boned 'neath folds and slabs of slimy HIDE
Gosh, it sure did look an awful DISGRACE
To see his pants and not his eyes thus SHINE
Expansive dewdrops sweated from his BROW
And awkward gestures spanned the thought not MINE
For what was then new, has come to be NOW
For further intonations she DISDAINETH
Whose lips the foul black curse word ever STAINETH

Here are some extracts from the letters my husband wrote to me from England in the fall of 1943:

SEPTEMBER 6, 1943

Rather quiet few days. Dinner last night at Vernons on some rather too high wild duck. These people like their game to be carrion before they cook it. Very fine brandy however.

Drove through the town of Chester on one of my trips. It is on the river Dee like the jolly miller. The most picturesque spot I have come across. Food terrible. The hotels can't charge more than 5 shillings which means you get soup, a paper-thin sliced piece of meat, cabbage and a piece of cheese. No napkins or butter. No wonder the British officers like to eat in my mess.

They talk about limiting the colossal tonnage of soldier mail but yesterday I got a Sears, Roebuck catalogue which followed me all the way from Fort Claiborne, La. A lot of good it will be!

We are having mosquitoes. Supposed to be unheard of here and no one has screens. Our mosquito bars were taken away before we left N.Y. I kept mine out of stubbornness. Comes in handy. I believe the only one in the United Kingdom.

SEPTEMBER 17, 1943

The invasion of Italy seems to have started, no details as to where and how well. Wish I were there but mountains of work ahead here. I would feel like a country squire except for my weekly trips to my farflung companies. Riding in a Jeep is rather breezy which will be an ordeal later on. My Jeep is fitted with Hartley black-out lights. I recently got caught in the black driving through Birmingham, the 2nd largest city, and thought I would never get out. Reading or even seeing road signs [is] out of the question. Finally made it by asking a dozen bobbies who are very helpful.

SEPTEMBER 20, 1943

My officers gave a dance Sat. night to break the monotony. It was in the local hospital—a Nissen hut, or rather 2 huts joined. Girls were half nurses and a variety of British girls, a surprising number missing all their upper teeth. Must be something in the diet.

SEPTEMBER 26, 1943

Went to London for the week-end. Stayed at the Savoy since it was impossible to get a room in a smaller hotel. A pound a night. The theatre starts at 6:15, which is daylight, and ends at 9, which is black. Your first step out of the theatre into the inky dark is rather startling. Only dim flashlights which people carry. A taxi is utterly impossible. I groped my way down Haymarket into the Strand and found my hotel. Next day had lunch at Simpsons. No beef at all. Had a piece of grouse you could put in your eye. Waitresses instead of men. Saw the most popular play in town, a revival of "Love for Love" with John Gielgud. Great. The signs of the Blitz are everywhere but you soon get used to them. My old hotel is a pile of rubble.

Will write you a V-Mail request for some boxes of candy that should be good presents for my hostesses. Any kind would taste great to them.

OCTOBER 5, 1943

Our 9th wedding anniversary has rolled around. Trust I'll be home before the next one. Spent an unproductive prewar British weekend this week. Quit work Friday at 2 p.m. and went to a place called Vernon's Oak which belongs to the local Master of the Fox Hunt and adjoins the Vernon property. We went partridge shooting, then had tea and, as dusk was falling, went to a little artificial lake and shot wild duck. Spent the night there and breakfasted sumptuously on broiled mushrooms, grilled tomatoes, scrambled eggs (a treat since our ration is all powdered and lousy) and English bacon. Then went fox hunting. I had a marvelous horse (I mean a real millionaire hunter) and had such a good time I don't unduly mind being stiff to the point of agony today. It was all done with great dash and true tradition. Pink coats and horns and much shouting of "tally-ho." They even had a man standing around with a terrier and spade in case the fox went to earth. We saw 5 foxes and had 2 very swell runs and didn't kill a single one. All of which suited me perfectly for, as you know, I don't enjoy seeing things killed. The partridge and duck shooting is rather necessary since they are hard up for meat. Not much sport though, as their partridge is so big, and flies so low it is like shooting fish. I don't see how I could be farther from the war. It rather embarrasses me.

There was a Sir Bertram Hardy at the shoot. So British it was painful. He had "his man" with him to carry his gun. I gave my share of the game to Lady Vernon and was invited to eat same at Sunday dinner.

OCTOBER 7, 1943

I'm sitting by my electric heater waiting for the 9 o'clock news. At first I missed the dramatics of Raymond Swing or H. V. Kaltenborn, but now I rather enjoy having someone give just the bare facts without embroidery. When there is nothing exciting in the news they just say so.

The nights are quite cold—4 blankets—and it gets dark at 7 o'clock in spite of daylight saving. I am comfortable enough but I get awfully restless when I am not busy. I think it is simply the feeling of impermanence that goes with everything we do.

My choir is getting quite a reputation. They have sung in at least a dozen churches around here and last Sunday they sang at Trinity in London. There is a rumor that they may broadcast back to the States.

OCTOBER 9, 1943

Am sitting by a coal grate in the castle which is occupied by one of my companies. This one belongs to the Hope family of diamond fame. We don't know where the diamond fits in and Captain (last war) Hope, who occupies what used to be the lodge house, is rather a pill, and we don't have much to do with him. The place is unnecessarily luxurious. Big enough for the entire company. They are in a dairy farming spot and get fresh milk and eggs to supplement the ration. A comedown when they have to move.

Thanks for the Engineer buttons. They came OK and look great on my new uniform—the best piece of tailoring I have ever had. Wish I could have some civilian suits made, but it is tabu and God knows how long before I could wear them. Opinions vary over here, ranging from those who guess a couple of years to those who think the bombing will finish it before the winter is up. Some, who went through the bad blitz in Birmingham and Liverpool, say that the country couldn't possibly have stood another 3 months if the Germans had only known it.

I have had a fireplace built by the regimental brick masons. It took a lot of improvising to fit it into the Nissen hut, but it works fine. There were a lot of stumps to be cleared on the job and I had the prisoners cut up the wood without upsetting the British "save fuel" program.

OCTOBER 27, 1943

Spring 1943 seems a long way off. My life continues placid. Have been hunting again. A great horse and I don't get stiff anymore. It rained this last time but no one was daunted. I had a raincoat and didn't get wet, but the Britishers just took it in their tweeds and went right on. Another dinner at the hall. We had jugged hare which I had disliked in various local hotels, but, if done correctly, is a casserole affair with a sauce of claret and beer and is simply swell. Shall get the recipe for Lady V's bread sauce which is an absolute MUST over here with game of all kinds.

Have received two requests from my officers to marry British girls. I have given them my blessing though I think it is foolish. I can't set myself up as a Dorothy Dix, however. They still have to get approval from the General which may take so long that they may change their minds.

NOVEMBER 5, 1943

No radical change. The fox hunting is still the great saving. Haven't missed a weekend since early October. There is a fascination which is genuine, at least to one who likes outdoors and horses as I do, and it grows on you. No one seems to get hurt and the horse I have is too good to be true. I get him from Major Newton, who is simply a walking, breathing fox hunt personified and who is also rolling in money (Bass ale). Last week we ended the hunt at an enormous house called Burton Hall. It is occupied by a formidable creature called the Baroness. We all held our horses out on her lawn while the butler passed cakes and ale (I mean really cakes and ale) all very very something. Am rereading Siegfried Sassoon just to get in the mood. I think the British feel a little self-conscious about keeping up hunting in war time, but not enough to stop it.

The rains have started and everything is mud. Being engineers, we have gotten a lot of what is called Blitz Brick from some of the bombed-out houses and managed to get walkways and roads in fair shape, but the rest of the camp just wears rubber boots and plods through.

Your description of P St. in the fall takes me back to our happy years there. Wish I could come back even for a day.

NOVEMBER 10, 1943

Today got your letter dated Oct. 12, as well as one of Oct. 22. Strange. To dinner with the Pearsons. Mrs. P is a very horsey lady who, as they say, goes well to hounds. Her husband is a storybook Englishman. Big farm. Much champagne. Won at poker—8 pounds in spite of trying to throw it back. The "pièce" was corn-on-the-cob swimming in melted butter. There are no grains on the cob. Not enough sunshine. My man, who was tried for rape, has been sentenced to be hanged, all of which isn't helping the morale of my regiment.

Churchill is out with a spiel about finishing the war in 1944, which should dampen some of the optimists who see it over this fall. Even the *Stars and Stripes* was full of the imminent collapse of Germany. I couldn't help feeling cheered by this although I felt it couldn't happen.

Have written the Luxembourg Legation giving my address and shall go into London and get your package when it arrives. I took two cakes of the chocolate you sent me to the Hunt yesterday. You should have seen the hunters go for it! I was lucky to get a little piece myself but at least felt very popular for a minute.

Have been invited to a special preview of the latest "new movie": *Random Harvest* with Ronald Colman and Greer Garson. My first movie since we saw Fred Astaire and Rita Hayworth back in Alexandria.

Enjoyed C's letter. Her friend, Averell Harriman, has been sent to Russia so I guess her trip is off.

NOVEMBER 21, 1943

Went to London for my birthday. Tried on my shoes being made by Maxwell. They better be special—6 guineas and 7 coupons. Found that the Grand Duchess and their Royal Highnesses had just arrived. The man at the Legation spoke no English, but I worked my French on him and it seemed to work. I got the chocolate. The best without doubt.

Took Major Newton and wife to the theatre and to Claridge's where I had a lot of near, but-not-quite, celebrities pointed out. It is supposed to be the hangout of the "Jeunesse Dorée" but this night they must have gone somewhere else. Car and chauffeur to get around the blackout. All coming to 7 pounds and 30 shillings, but definitely worth it considering the Thoroughbred he mounts me on every Saturday. Then went to be photographed for your Christmas present. An Austrian by the name of Fayer. Hot stuff. Charges plenty. Here is a coincidence. The first name on Fayer's registry book which I signed was a man named Frankenstein whom I had met the night before at Claridge's, then came the Grand Duchess Charlotte, her consort, Prince Felix, and the two princesses. The last name was a Miss Audrey Martin whom I met at tea with Lady Vernon the next afternoon. She is the prospective daughter-in-law. The trip left a pleasant taste as the dreary winter is closing in and it makes for depression and a bit of homesickness which need resisting.

Everybody is catching, or has caught, the flu. We are supposed to get turkey for Thanksgiving, but I fear it will be canned—the kind you put on toast, but better than nothing.

NOVEMBER 28, 1943

I finally caught the flu. No one is escaping. This is the first I have had since we were in Washington in the 30's. I was beginning to think I was immune. The doctor made me stay in bed for 4 days.

Thanksgiving better than I expected. Frozen whole turkeys, cranberries and pumpkin pie à la mode. (Ice cream made from canned milk.) I invited a few of the British officers in and they were quite flowery.

We've had freezing weather the last few days, which has been great as it stopped the rain and froze the mud, which had to be seen to be believed.

When you see Marjorie Clay, pump her well for news. She ought to be full of it unless Lucius has quit talking to her about business. Your life sounds well organized and makes me feel contented even at a distance.

DECEMBER 3, 1943

Much mud and much work until yesterday when we had a super inspection by the Chief of the European Theatre, General Devers. The entire camp went into a complete dither and did no work for a whole day previous, getting ready. I figured he wouldn't bother me since I was not a permanent part of the camp, but he announced on arrival that what he wanted to see was colored troops at work. So we all got inspected. The men were working hard so I assume he was impressed. Afterward I had supper with him on his private train, most de luxe thing ever. Three cars, a stateroom car, a lounge car with complete bar, and dining car. We had fresh oranges, sumptuous steaks etc. I realize generals have to live up to their name; nevertheless, the whole thing made me a little sick.

DECEMBER 16, 1943

There isn't much to put in a letter. On the military side I am not allowed to say anything except the most vague generalities. We are terribly busy building things. Just what it is all for, and how it fits into the scheme of things, I can only guess, and can't write what my guesses are. Socially, I have a rather unexciting routine, though pleasant. Manage to get out to dinner about 2 nights a week. Nice little parties, usually just talk after dinner. Back at midnight—suits me fine. Do you think you could send a few lemons? They are rare as fine jewels over here as they have nothing to mix their rum with except synthetic lime juice which is quite awful. HAPPY NEW YEAR!

DECEMBER 21, 1943

I am spending the evening at The Plough in a little town at the tip north end of Wales, on an inspection trip. Picturesque place with no bathroom I have discovered so far. The country is rugged with stone walls instead of the hedges of my part of England and all the towns are unpronounceable like Llyandudno or Rhyll. The people are named Lloyd or Llewellyn. *L*'s and *Y*'s take an awful beating.

Weather is brutal and my fire is as big as your hat. I feel very Wuthering Heights.

I have never felt better in spite of the weather, probably it is the horseback riding. I am so terribly busy that time seems to be escaping me. In spite of being here 6 months it is hard to get any feeling of accomplishment. We all seem like flies buzzing around a manure pile. Doubtless the war has to be won and doubtless we are all playing some small part in winning it. The feeling of utter futility persists however.

DECEMBER 27, 1943

My Christmas was quiet but awfully pleasant for one away from home. I was the only stranger at the Hall for a Xmas Eve party and dinner next day. Champagne at the first and Château Margaux 1929 at the other. They gave me a bottle of pre-war whiskey from the Vernon cellar and each child got a check for 100 pounds. For lunch the day after we had the plum pudding fried. The nursery rhyme about "The queen next morning fried" really meant it. On Boxing Day I gave all the servants a pound apiece.

The papers are full of Gen. Eisenhower's appointment to head the invasion. The English seem to feel it is a good choice. I believe I would have preferred Marshall, but we shall see . . . soon, I hope.

January 4, 1944
Dear Tat,

The children started back to school today after a nice long vacation. How I hate to get up in the pitch black again! The extra sleep in the mornings was so nice.

I rush downstairs and jiggle the furnace and put on the oatmeal and brush hair and get the car (wondering if it will start every time) and get Mary to school at 8:45—then I track back to Georgetown depositing Johnny at his kindergarten. Then comes marketing and a return to the dishes, beds, etc., walk up to get J at 12. Lunch. Rest period, so called. Pick up Mary at 3. Home. Dinner at 6. Lessons. Bed. DISHES.

One of Mary's schoolmates, whose father is at the Spanish Embassy, had a fancy party, complete with Mickey Mouse movies, in the Madison Suite at the Wardman Park Hotel. I took Johnny along with me to the hotel and, though he didn't want to stay at the party when invited, he very definitely insisted on going into the bar to have a drink. He said he was too thirsty to go another step and the place looked so dark and interesting to him. So, while Mary cavorted with the elite, J and his mother had a Manhattan and Pepsi-Cola respectively. Because J will soon be six I could practically hear the tsk-tsks as we walked out of the bar—"so young, my dear"! No good shutting my eyes and pretending he was Randolph. Speaking of whom, I think he is homesick. He seems bent on proving that he likes the Sudbury Hall cook. Certainly his Lordship is not the attraction. Lady Vernon is equated with the cooking which is dangerous. I hope she has buck teeth! He seems to have been gone such *years* already!

Nancy [Tate] married Percy Wood of Memphis and Sewanee yesterday. They will go to Monteagle for a while and then he goes into the Navy. He is a most attractive boy. Allen has taken it all nobly, if a bit dazed. Caroline is down in Florida with her father who is dying, but marriage can't wait these days.[1]

The Georgetown Library got your book, THE DWELLING PLACE, finally and it will be my barometer. I can gauge its popularity.

Love,
Marcella

1. Caroline's father, James Maury Morris Gordon, was the inspiration for her most successful novel, *Aleck Maury, Sportsman* (New York, 1939), for which Maxwell Perkins was the editor.

January 21, 1944
Dear Tat,

Your box arrived in perfect shape—just a TEENY bit of the Ginger Pears sweetening the pickle jar. The Ball glasstops seem not too perfect a lid for traveling jams. Everything looks delicious and will be consumed with relish—not the traveling kind.

Do you know who will be here for dinner next Saturday and whom you will meet if you come? None other than the great Katherine Anne Porter. She is supposed to be just out of what the Tates call "the nesting period," and all ready for something or someone new. She is taking John Peale Bishop's place at the Library of Congress, as JPB almost died of heart disease and has been away since before Christmas. Do come.

Caroline and I took in an exhibit at the Corcoran yesterday, then she and Allen came in to discuss my dinner party for them that has been brewing for so long. There will be about nine or ten people all hand-picked by the Maestro himself. Included will be a war correspondent; the secretary of the Irish Legation, Denis Devlin; my sister Eleanor; and the Cheneys—along with KAP and me.

Until I get out of the Secretary class and into the Minister class I can't be said to have a real salon. However, I am working up by degrees. I almost hooked a real celebrity but unfortunately, he won't be in town for the party—the painter George Biddle. He is the artist I met in the little hill town north of Rome, Anticoli Corrado, where I spent my last summer in Europe in 1931. Biddle and I used to take long walks over the Abruzzi mountains and then paint them. He is visiting his brother Francis just a block up 31st Street.[1] When I asked him to dinner to meet the Tates, he said he couldn't come, but that Katherine, his brother's wife, would love to. Allen says he is on a jury to judge some poetry with her, which includes some of hers. He says her poetry is not as good as yours.

Now the Attorney General and family, I fear, would be way beyond my capacity in the liquor line—not that the Tates aren't, heaven knows, but I can at least tell them about it! Allen has offered to supply the liquor, thank goodness. It pays to know a few Senators.

Love,
Marcella

1. Francis Biddle was attorney general under Franklin Roosevelt, and his wife, Katherine Garrison Chapin, was a poet and a consultant in poetry to the Library of Congress, judging poetry awards. She resisted giving the Bollingen Prize to Ezra Pound. Her obituary declared her to be "like her husband, Francis, a thinker and a writer."

February 12, 1944
Dear Tat,

I have met Katherine Anne [Porter].[1] She is more attractive and interesting than I expected—which was a lot. She strikes me first of all as being a very sincere artist, and then a very attractive woman. Rare combination.

I have already gone out to the Tates' to make sketches for the portrait I am going to do of her. They all came over here last Sunday. A most memorable evening. She is pleased with the idea of a portrait and will probably make a good model though, perhaps, a bit difficult to catch for sittings.

KAP has pure white hair, short, curly. She is short, about your height [5 feet, 2 inches], thin, and has lovely gray-blue eyes, a youthful unlined face, high forehead, pointed chin. She is animated in a very lady-like way and fascinating to talk with. No airs or mannerisms, a good sense of humor and the ability to say devastating things in a charming way, like Allen. I will find out more about her while I paint her.

Thanks for the uniforms which seem to fit Lena well enough. I am not here to reason why I was so fortunate to be the one—the only one—whose ad she answered. She is really SWEET. She never worked out before and doesn't need money. Her husband makes over $300 a month. She has two fur coats, diamond rings etc. Her friends are amazed. They probably think she is slumming. Both of her sons are in the service. One gets leave in a few weeks so, of course, I will give her a vacation then, or she will give me one, or something. I get a bit mixed up in our relationships since she holds all the dough—and now mine too. Somehow she can say she prefers nylon hose and it sounds all right.

Come see my wonder woman who, like Cinderella, will vanish the moment her boys return to her—after the war—if not before. I pray they won't get hurt and worry every time she says one doesn't feel well.

Mary made her first communion on a cold snowy day with only one other girl in the Convent chapel. With white veils, white prie-dieu and 3-foot white candles tied with long white ribbons the whole effect was terribly chaste and also terribly cold. Why do pure things have to seem so icy?

Love,
Marcella

1. Katherine Anne Porter (1890–1980) was born in Indian Creek, Texas. Her books have become classics and have been translated widely. During her lifetime, she received the highest literary honors, and she is today considered one of the most distinguished masters of her craft, particularly the short story. Her master-piece is *Pale Horse, Pale Rider* (New York, 1939), her best seller *Ship of Fools* (New York, 1962).

February 19, 1944
Dear Tat,

The Scarlet Fever sign is on the house but the worst is over. Johnny is getting along nicely now but I have had a nurse for three days—lucky to get her, after many phone calls. She is fat, jolly and utterly devoted to John. She has never taken a child's case before. In all his suffering the little darling said, upon first seeing her, "I never knew nurses weren't tall and thin and young!" You know how appealing he is—more so when sick.

The health authorities permit a maid to come in, but of course we are quarantined and Mary is home from school. We are allowed to go for walks and do errands. Everything has to be soaked in Lysol and we smell like a hospital. Lena's boys are leaving tomorrow so she will return steadily Monday. She is so fond of Johnny that she isn't going to tell her family that she is in a scarlet fever house for fear they won't let her come. I don't know how I would manage without help. She is true blue just as I thought she would be.

> Love,
> Marcella

A new experiment in radio in the early 1940s called "Invitation to Learning" was an unrehearsed program, instigated and moderated by Huntington Cairns for CBS, that presented panel discussions on the classics from Plato and Aristotle to Henry James and Proust. The panel included Allen Tate and Mark Van Doren and frequently brought in guests such as Katherine Anne Porter. Random House published transcripts of twenty-seven of the conversations in 1941; the one on Defoe's *Moll Flanders* had Katherine Anne as the guest.

February 22, 1944
Dear Tat,

The very night J got sick, Katherine Anne came down with Pneumonitis. She is recovering rapidly, I hear. That morning I had gone to the Library of Congress to make some sketches of her, taking her a valentine box of [the] cookies which I had made for the children. I enclose a copy of a letter I sent to her. Did you hear KAP on "Invitation to Learning" last Sunday? This was her 13th time on the program, the only woman so consistently invited.

> Love,
> Marcella

Dear Miss Porter

In this same mail is being sent to you a bit of fungus. Did you ever think that fungus, even masquerading as a lapel flower, could enhance your delicate beauty? I believe its color to be the key to my portrait of you, whether you wear it or not. I am willing to stake my reputation as a painter of literary celebrities that if we follow this general color scheme we will have the knockout picture you deserve. Caroline and Allen know that I get things out of the astral. When I sketched you, one portion of me was functioning, the rest was quietly getting in touch with my astral medium. The result: one gray suit, one gray-blue blouse.

I hope you are recovering rapidly and that we will both feel like a mighty burst of work, come spring, when we are out of our respective incarcerations.

Marcella Winslow

On February 13, 1944, Randolph wrote me a letter containing his impressions of some English attitudes about class, politics, and the influence of Americans.

Dear Marce,

The fruitcake came and is awfully good in spite of its long voyage. It seems to travel better than chocolate.

Friday I went to a political rally for the local Conservative candidate for Parliament who is running in what is called a by-election. The candidate is Lord Hartington, a Marquis and son of the Duke of Devonshire. He is very tall, very good looking and a very very young man, and certainly no public speaker. When he finished his speech and began answering questions he displayed an abysmal ignorance on a number of points the farmers seemed to find important. No one seemed to feel any doubt about his being elected as his district has always been represented by a member of the Cavendish family and he is *it*. It is all very simple but not overly democratic. On the other hand we have our Bankheads etc. so I shouldn't criticize. The best part of the evening was a remark by Lord Vernon after the rally. The conversation turned on the British educational system and the fact that one can at once tell a well-educated Englishman by his accent. I mentioned one of the other speakers at the rally, a young MP who I thought was a man who obviously went to the right schools. His Lordship said, "No. Not quite right. I should think that most likely *he* went to the right schools but that his father didn't." I thought that was swell. The funny thing is that the old boy is quite democratic and utterly unsnobbish about everything else.

The papers over here are discussing seriously whether the chewing gum the Yanks are introducing will spoil the shape of the faces of British women. A learned group of doctors says No.

Rumors are being spread, aided by the newspapers, that the American troops are bringing venereal disease over here and that public health is menaced. Of course this is utterly wrong since if there ever was a group of men free from VD it is our soldiers when we put them on the boat. If one of our boys catches same we lock him up till he is cured. On the other hand, when names of ladies are reported the police do nothing about it. International amity is a tenuous thing which is based on strangeness and fewness and will never survive familiarity and the crowds of Americans who must come over, waiting for the second front to get going.

Love,
Randolph

February 24, 1944

Dear Tat,

Johnny has just passed the half-way mark with his scarlet fever. Mary seems to have escaped. People are amazing about that disease—or the getting of; on the street today I met a friend who drew me aside, so I wouldn't give scarlet fever to her, who was next to a woman who has children, who would get scarlet fever from her, after meeting me! I feel that all I need is a scarlet letter.

Caroline is taking a course in art at the Phillips Gallery so she is tied up for a while, but I intend to get her portrait finished and then go on to other literary personages—perhaps getting a whole group, so that being asked to sit will seem to confer an honor. All being chosen by the chosen, so to speak!

Love,
Marcella

March 2, 1944

Dear Tat,

Eleanor has a lead on a nice cottage at Rehoboth Beach. We decided to take it for 3 months as it will be so good for the children. E will try to get a month's vacation and I will beg, borrow or steal a maid—even if I have to import the Tates' Jessie, who wants to return to D.C. If mother is with the children, I may be able to make my fortune in the big world.

I am returning Lady Vernon's letter. Something always seems to happen to the letters we treasure. She sounds charming. Not just because of things we want to hear about Randolph but she is so frankly friendly. Letters of "reserved" English people always surprise me because of the lack of said reserve.

Randolph's letters are interesting about the Labourite winning the election over the Conservative, Lord Hartington.[1] Lady Vernon seems to feel "they" are on the way out—at least out of their large estates. The election could not have changed that impression. I hope you get over for a visit before it all folds up like the Arabs' tents.

If I go to New York, I will try to get Mark Van Doren to let me sketch him for my "series." Allen is writing him. This is all a pipe dream but MAY work out. I have had nibbles on my house for the summer.

Won't you come up this month? I realize the main attraction is missing and there is only the side show but, with the Tates, Katherine Anne etc., you will find everyone turning out to show you a good time. You could sleep in either twin bed, moving out of whichever one has the pea under the mattress. You can wear the new dress and I will throw a party as, goodness knows, I am ready for one now. Prospects of gold, no matter how faint, make me a trifle light in the head. (A West Point portrait seems pretty definite.) Get C—— to fly you up. That would be elegantissima and quite worthy of the RISING novelist.

I have a wonderful start on a portrait of Mary—which may be the only good thing to come out of the quarantine.[2] She is in her element inventing games and stories for Johnny to keep him happy, so she doesn't miss school at all.

Love,
Marcella

1. February, 1944, saw a by-election in West Derbyshire in which Lord Hartington, son of the duke of Devonshire, was opposed and defeated by a Labour candidate. On losing the election, Hartington returned to the army. In May, 1944, he married Kathleen Kennedy, sister of John Fitzgerald Kennedy. He was killed in action in France on September 19, 1944.

2. This painting won a portrait prize in a Corcoran area show in 1946.

Late March, 1944

Dear Tat,

I have no idea of the date. Sorry I didn't get a letter to you before I started working on Caroline again, for then I never find time. She went home this evening with Nancy and Bub, the dachshund, and Allen and a whole trunk of wood in the back of the car. Also, a bottle of sour cream and several painting boards. I have an excess of wood from all the packing crates, as you might surmise, and I am rather afraid rats will get into the pile. This last cold spell has taken most of my coal so maybe the crates will be needed if I can't get another order. It was a beautiful snow and the worst ice of the winter. Everyone fell on it—including myself—down the front steps! No harm done.

I finally got Caroline in a state of rest. She has been utterly exhausted all winter—ever since I started her—but she agreed to give me two days. She says writing isn't easy like painting.

I bought a $5 canvas and started in gaily from the colored sketch I had made last November, only to find that I loathed the canvas, though it was the best in the market these days, so, after losing one futile day of my two promised ones, I started over on a board today and, voilà! She is there. Upstairs. Just a little something about the mouth as usual, which I must fix.

Allen is crazy about it. No doubt he isn't so hard to please but Nancy was convinced of the likeness. I had my usual struggle and worked all day since Caroline posed madly and magnificently. Bub is in the picture as well, lying on her lap, making both of them happy. I am happy too to have this be my exhibition portrait for a while. I expect to finish it in one more sitting.

When I finish I will consider that I have done my duty by the Tates' posterity, as I painted a head of Nancy last week. It is the best head I have ever done, and came like a flash, without a struggle, in just two sittings. It is a wedding present, long promised. The posterity is on its way too as Nancy expects a baby next October. Her husband, Percy Wood, is in the Navy and Caroline is resigning herself to raising the child. Just as she got Nancy raised!

When I finish Caroline next week, I plan to go to West Point April 4th to try to clinch the portrait of "Brother" Wilby. [1]

Then Katherine Anne. So why can't you come after that? I made a good goulash today out of some left-over sirloin tips—which Caroline almost gave Bub with an "Is this any good?"—and a bit of left-over ham, cut up and fried with spring onions, peppers and celery in olive oil and then baked in a casserole with a lot of tomatoes.

I know your garden must be lovely. I get the urge to dig now but, if I were digging, I wouldn't be painting—and painting is important to my state of mind—and being.

Love,
Marcella

1. Major General Francis Bowditch Wilby graduated second in the class of 1905 at West Point. He was superintendent there from 1942 to 1945. The $500 commission to paint him came through his son in the Corps of Engineers, who had been on Randolph's staff in Alabama when they trained troops.

April 1, 1944
Dear Tat,

Harriet Winslow asked me to go to the symphony tonight to hear Hoffman, but I knew I would be tired and it is such an effort to prepare to go out. Caroline offered to stay with the children. She is such a dear. Isn't she one of the really nicest people on earth?

By the way, Allen thinks your conversation is far more scintillating than Katherine Anne's. She talks a bit much, and apparently tries them some with her vanity. She is the Prima Donna—but fascinating. Vamps all the young men who come to see Nancy. They just fall for her and ask, "Why isn't she married?" KAP may rent my house this summer with two other women.

Please keep it under your hat, but Mother and I have sleuthed out Randolph's whereabouts. The clue was on the back of a recipe from Lady Vernon that I had asked for. On the back of the paper was a scratched-out letter to her from the Sudbury Parish Council thanking her for some work she had done for the American hospital people. In Baedeker, mother found that Lord Vernon has a model dairy farm near Sudbury at Ashbourne, Derbyshire, not far from Derby as well as the famed Haddon Hall, the Dukeries, and 40 miles from one of the most famous fox hunts. Her Baedeker is vintage 1906. So, we can visualize him in the Midlands.

What do you think of L'Affaire Patton?[1] An unsavory mess, but no good in airing it for the edification of the enemy, I should think.

Something big seems to be brewing abroad. The bombing of Berlin is so devastating I don't see how it could fail to bring results. Can you imagine what it would be like to hear that New York was being evacuated?

Allen asked me to dinner the other night (Caroline being away and no Jessie) but I couldn't get anyone to stay with the children, so invited him here, though I had been entertaining some of Mary's friends and was not prepared. He arrived just as the last guests were departing (a mama and daddy who were interested in their child's portrait) so I said: "Read some poems, Allen," and dashed about frying chicken and got up a pretty good dinner (he said) in about half an hour.

Surprisingly enough, Allen took my suggestion literally and read poems—the surprising part being they were not *his,* but yours. He said he had never seen your book of poetry before. He thinks you very gifted, of course. This has been a remarkably bad winter for them, ending with Nancy's marriage, which wasn't sudden, but she is so young.

Love,
Marcella

1. A slap was heard around the world when General Patton took out his frustration on a hospitalized American soldier in Sicily. The media played it up.

No one reckoned with the jealousies that could flare between two southern women writers struggling for recognition in the literary world. A fight erupted between Katherine Anne Porter and Caroline Gordon Tate over some spilled perfume, which I gather was the reason Allen phoned me to ask if Katherine Anne could rent my third-floor room. I was not only glad to have the extra sixty dollars a month she paid for room and board but flattered that someone whom my mother-in-law had always said she would rather write like than anyone else was willing to share my old bathroom with the clawfoot tub on the second-floor landing—and share my life as well.

The Superintendent's Quarters
West Point, N.Y.
April 5, 1944
Dear Tat,

I finally made it to West Point! The last few days have been full ones. The excitement of having a letter from Randolph telling of his new job as staff engineer of the 8th Corps was almost too much—unless, of course, it was Mary breaking out with the mumps the day after I left.

Aside from these two excitements, Katherine Anne Porter moved in to take my spare room and had a fever of 101! Nothing to worry about. She seems to get fevers even moving across the street, she says. She is rather frail and given to bronchial trouble, having once had tuberculosis. It is nice to have her and especially the $60 a month for room and board. I have the first check!

Mark Van Doren has written that he would sit to me but I have to put that off for now—maybe after a few more contagious diseases. The only one left is whooping cough.

I have a good idea of how I will paint Superintendent Wilby. I hope they won't be expecting one of those dark brown portraits that one sees all over the place. Gen. Wilby met me at the station and has been showing me around. Not as much fun as being with a cadet but simpler and easier. At a party, four or five ladies were gushing about your book [*The Dwelling Place*]. Not only the hostess—who is actually going to buy one—but a Mrs. McCandless who stayed up late to finish it. Caroline calls this the bedroom test. I tried to get some interesting opinions but nothing to pass on; just the "I loved the part about"—and then they would tell it to me, unfortunately in their words and not yours. We agreed that I can return in the fall to paint the portrait.

I went to a posh chamber musical and tea at the Harriet Winslows'. The place was ribbed with important dowagers, crusty Senators, and Justice Frankfurter etc. Not a soul was doing the honors when I walked in, or so much as looked at me—all busy talking in small groups. I recognized the Attorney General, Francis Biddle, from his pictures, and introduced myself since I HAD to do something. He graciously asked me to sit beside him for the musical in the biggest chair, front row center. I felt like apologizing to the cousins, saying: "Taint my fault I have the best chair—he asked me to sit here!" The "cave dwellers" did a bit of wondering. Later we had cocktails and all breathed easier. The Quartet was delightful.

Love,
Marcella

P Street, N.W.
Washington, D.C.
April 13, 1944
Dear Tat,

I seem to be getting more letters from Randolph, which pleases me not a little—the V-Mail combined with air mail assures me of news at more frequent intervals. Of course, every name and place is neatly cut out by the censor. He writes that he is getting quite a reputation as a fox hunter which amuses him a lot. You remember that I heard he was the only engineer at West Point who played polo? One of the English officers whom he had to dinner presented him with a first edition of Surtees, which he says is a hunting classic and a must for all experts. He loved the Rosemarie candy. On one of the last days for hunting, the colonel in charge of venereal inspection in Randolph's district who was always in R's hair about his regiment, was at the hunt. Being a cavalry man he had been dying to go and had been quite jealous of Randolph being invited. To R's delight, after only 1/2 hour he got "neatly thrown." R was glad he was not hurt but wrote: "It made my day."

I have had a houseful of convalescents. Katherine Anne is no trouble —in fact, a great help—since she is an artist of a cook, but I had the 3 meals to think of, as well as keeping her and the children apart since she had never had the mumps.

I forgot to tell you that while I was away tracking down General Wilby for his portrait, KAP dosed herself so effectively with the medicine the doctor had given her that she passed out cold for a day. No one could rouse her and she has no recollection of about 48 hours! She had a touch of her usual bronchial trouble so when the doctor came to see Mary she asked him for some sleeping pills and said later they made her feel so good that she kept on taking them every time she woke up.

When I left for West Point, I asked Mother to just "look in" on things in the house. Lena was here during the day but I felt sure there would be little for Mother to do. However, Mary immediately came down with the mumps and mother moved in to nurse her. So, besides the unusual situation of KAP dead to the world, Mary had raving, yelling nightmares that even aroused the neighbors. Naturally, Mother got no sleep but when she took an afternoon to go back to her house for some much-needed rest, and lay down exhausted in her empty house, her doorbell started to ring and ring. Thinking it must be a telegram from me, she dragged herself downstairs and answered the door. It was a man selling lots in a cemetery! This, of course, appealed to her at that moment but she told him, regretfully, that she already had one.

Lena returns today and I suggested she bring a friend to help her as all I have had time to do is to blow the dust off tables.

Love,
Marcella

April 15, 1944
Dear Tat,

The doctor told us the only thing wrong with KAP is exhaustion. It seems the Tate household was too much for her. She simply caved in. Allen is sick with a cold now after returning from John Peale Bishop's funeral in Maine. If they don't give up the hectic life they have led this winter, they will all cave in!

KAP has a tremendous appreciation for Allen's writing. Feels he will be considered the greatest poet of his day after T. S. Eliot. She told me how sorry she was that I didn't ask Harriet Winslow's permission to take her to their last musical, as early chamber music is her all-time favorite. Had I done so, SHE would have been the one in the biggest chair, front row center!

An Epitaph written for Allen Tate by his friend John Peale Bishop:

The verses should never
exactly scan
If the poet is a gentleman;
This poet was; he could
have either
Made his family a livelihood
Or written odes to praise
his blood:
He couldn't do both; so he
did neither
He died like a hound in a
wayside ditch,

Calling the world a son-of-
  a-bitch.
There he lay, refined and
  thin
With his small Scottish
  nose and his large Irish
  chin.

Randolph wrote to me about his new job, which he could not describe except that it was still in England.

Love,
Marcella

April 18, 1944
Dear Tat,

No doubt you have Randolph's new APO address and news about his
giving up the regiment. As he says, not without mixed feelings, being
Chief Engineer of the 8th Corps is considered a big step up but he DID
like being his own boss before. He wrote me that, in spite of some
problems, he had a feeling of accomplishment as he was doing a job with
the blacks that he felt he could handle. Although he got weary of keeping the racial peace, he enjoyed having his contemporaries congratula-
tory instead of commiserating. He feels the change will be good for him
even with his "loss of liberty" as he was becoming too independent.
No doubt having sixty officers all working to do what he wanted them
to do, and handling the largest unit that one man can command, and
seeing concrete results would, in some ways, be more satisfactory than
working with twenty other Colonels who take orders from the big boss.

On the other hand, he has about four times as big a command as the
regiment but, instead of taking the whole load of responsibility, is content to share administration, discipline and morale. After the load he
has carried it should be a great relief.

Mrs. [Ethel] Jasspon [a Memphis neighbor] had me to one of the
more sumptuous dinners at the Mayflower, with interesting company.
One was Roy Hendrickson, Director of Food Distribution. He has the
girth of one who knows how to distribute the food in the places he wants
it to go. I took the opportunity of telling him of cornmeal shortage and

bad cow feed (that is, for you) and he said the situation had been remedied. However, I haven't seen cornmeal or grits for ages. Maybe it's all down your way. Along with roast beef we had an endive salad which impressed me because Eleanor says the Minister of Luxembourg, Hugues Le Gallais, sends for $25 worth to a country place nearby, from time to time. Onions are completely passé, but there are plenty of leeks.

Allen sat for his portrait to a New York artist named Littlefield. Caroline says L's method is to keep one portrait and give the subject another. Can you imagine? C considers it pretty bad, which I would assume it must be. As though Allen doesn't have portraits enough by now! I think my portrait of Caroline turned out to be the best one I have painted recently.

Love,
Marcella

April 23, 1944
Dear Tat,

So much to tell you—now that I have a fascinating "Femme Fatale" in the house. I don't have as much time for letter writing as formerly. I don't, however, find Katherine Anne a Prima Donna—at least, as yet. She wears remarkably well, so far, and is most considerate. She is too popular for her rather frail person, though, as the slightest extra exertion knocks her out. She runs fevers for nothing at all and, literally, seems to be a too high-tension person. One has a feeling the fuse will blow. How she has managed to keep her feet so firmly on the ground with all the attention, adulation and emotional strain of her tempestuous life I can't imagine, except that she has a tremendous interest in *everything*. I have hardly hit upon a subject that she does not know something about (usually a great deal) from old colonial silver to astrology. She could run for political office as easily as she could get a chef's job at the Ritz. [1]

She tells an amusing story about going to a French cooking school where the Maître Albert asked her loftily if she (naturally) desired to learn to make pastries. She answered, "No, I desire to cook a wild boar." Which she proceeded to do, and if you want the recipe I can supply it.

Today, being Sunday, I am taking my cooking lesson. By the time Randolph returns I will have mastered a few tricks. We are having a chicken in garlic and Worcestershire sauce which we will eat with noodles and sour cream. Next, I shall learn to make an onion pie. She stuffed a capon for our Easter dinner. Superb!

So far, she has given me $52 for board this month. We arrange that she pays me $1.00 for a dinner she eats here, as she goes out often. That helps quite a bit, especially as I haven't realized a cent from those pictures that I supposedly sold. My trip to West Point cost $50. I always get to rock bottom every month. Even Mary's dentist hasn't mentioned paying for the *Magnolias* he has in his office. Which brings me to, how much do you think I can charge C—— for his portrait if he likes it? Betty [Fisher] and KAP think he couldn't possibly like it for under $500. That price may go in New York but I am not sure it would go here. When he said something about shipping the portrait south (getting ahead of me like that always makes me nervous), I merely said: "I'm not sure I will let you have it!" Which is true if it doesn't suit me.

Johnny's case of the mumps was very slight. Mary had it bad enough for everybody. She is getting to be quite a personality. KAP is, fortunately, interested in children, and thinks Mary a tremendously forceful character. She talks about Mary's violent eyes! Last night, we had some red wine with spaghetti for dinner and Mary, who has a huge capacity for anything of a consuming nature, got us in stitches. She announced she felt funny and then began . . . lasso[ing] KAP and "muscling" us, as she called it, saying over and over: "I've never before been able to try my muscles on real people." She is so strong for an 8-year-old! We couldn't cope with her, but I walked her around the block and she quieted down some, though she told me I had better take her home before she "tore up the town"!

Mary takes KA's authorship very much for granted and has said she will write a book herself as soon as she gets a typewriter. She refers to publishing as "Knopfing" the pages. She has decided it will be about death and hell. I think she gets carried away with Katherine Anne's interest in her.

Everyone here is impressed with Randolph's new job. I hear that it calls for a Brigadier General's rank eventually, depending on the Commanding Officer. It is a great step up and, since the army is Randolph's profession, I am all for it.

Love,
Marcella

1. This line was adopted without modification by a television documentary on Katherine Anne Porter in the 1980s.

April 26, 1944
Dear Tat,

Florence Cairns is what's called a "headhunter." She is on KAP's trail now and phones to ask to speak to her. Although she knows who I am, she pretends not to, and this week she invited KA to come for dinner to meet Blanche Knopf [the wife and partner of the publisher Alfred Knopf]. I was sorry KA couldn't go as I wanted to hear all about it. Florence's famous dinners I have heard about and would like to partake of myself.

Maids are impossible to find now. Everyone is offering fabulous sums but getting none. I am glad Lena is not that interested in money.

I had a real fright the other night. When I went out for dinner I had left a high-school sitter, as KAP was off somewhere. When I returned I rang and rang but got no response. I finally had to go next door and, fortunately, found my neighbor home, so I climbed over the fence (in my long evening dress) and was able to get into my back door. No sign of the sitter. Expecting a murder or suicide, I discovered Katherine Anne had returned early, let the girl go, gone upstairs to bed and never heard the bell.

I have been fixing up my back yard. It has been an eyesore all winter with old lumber, leaves and general debris. I now have two peonies, some lilies, wisteria and exactly six lilies-of-the-valley, whose fragrance reminds me of the thousands I picked in your garden last year for the flower stores. Mrs. Frank Simonds, my neighbor, asked if I was a professional gardener—no doubt in sarcasm—but I do feel like one after my contacts in the south! [1]

Betty [Fisher] is not at all impressed with Katherine Anne, so you will get a different version of her from that source. However I will know her better after I paint her.

Have you talked to C—— lately? I never thought I would be relieved to have missed a chance at making so much money (or would it be?) but I am. He told me when we started that what he expected, in having his portrait done, was a detailed likeness with a flattering expression. As he put it—"the way Lord Nelson looked when he steamed back to Lady

Hamilton after the battle." When I made the mistake of letting him look at the start, his comment would be: "Do I look that haggard?" or, "Doesn't look like anyone I know," ending up with, "I don't know how you feel about it, but I wouldn't have it on my walls." So I painted it out. Now he wants to have another try but I have no desire to go through what would probably be the same procedure. Ordinarily, I would be in despair, after such a failure, but I am relieved. Not to have to worry whether he would like the painting enough to buy it, not to worry how he would carry or not carry or have shipped the final result is a great relief. I had to go through all that and his love life as well. I have learned a lot and will be stronger next time. No looking at starts.

Mrs. Ford Madox Ford is in town with her husband—a new one, Alain, the cartoonist. KAP and I were invited to a picnic with them but couldn't make it.

Love,
Marcella

1. Mrs. Frank Simonds, widow of the syndicated journalist and war correspondent (who wrote *History of World War I*), told me she had bought her beautiful Federal house without her husband's knowledge since the house was run-down and Georgetown had an unsavory reputation at the time. He told her he would never live there but came to love the place after her remodeling. The Christian Herters bought it from her son in the forties.

April 30, 1944
Dear Tat,

These summer days which have come on the heels of winter are so lovely. I call them summer, not spring, because we are sweltering already.

No doubt you are eating greens, and more greens. We had our first tender ones yesterday with some ham. I am so glad the points have been taken off because I am going to contribute a ham to Katherine Anne's birthday party on May 15th.

It is going to be a select little group of her choosing—mostly from Mexican days—the painter Federico Castellone, who is at Fort Belvoir; another, a young Alabama painter named Shannon, who has shown in New York and been stationed in the Pacific; several influential South American diplomats; Lincoln Kirstein; and Monroe Wheeler if he can make it from New York. The Tates aren't even being invited—hush-

hush—that is another story; anyway, they don't know many of this group. I am being invited because I live here. KAP always makes a lot of her birthday. She is already talking about having chicken liver pâté, which is one of her specialties, and beaten biscuits, and a very special vegetable salad. We will probably overflow into the garden.

I started painting her portrait today. If I can keep the quality I started with, it should be one of my best. I also made a sketch of Allen for his new book of poems.

KAP's mumps passed so quickly that it is a great question in my mind whether she had them at all. She is very open to suggestion. She had a stiff neck and fever and swollen glands so, maybe it was a sort of mumps, though she never got puffed out at all the way Mary did.

Today, Lena was off. I was tired after painting so we went out for dinner. John got dressed up in his new white suit, walked in shining after his bath, hair curly and brown eyes huge in his little face, and said, in a tone exactly like Randolph's, "Fantastic!" And he was.

Love,
Marcella

May 1, 1944
Dear Tat,

Last night, KA and I went to the opening of an exhibit at a new little gallery, saw a few friends (one of whom, she informed me today, she was madly in love with once and, literally, almost murdered—a South American), among whom was the young Bart Barber who is getting KA to talk on his radio program. On meeting me, he asked if I was related to Anne G. Winslow and then turned out to have been 12 years old when he last saw "the gracious lady." Do you remember him? He is a smart boy with a delightful sense of humor. He enjoyed THE DWELLING PLACE very much, his favorite story being about the miniature. He worked in Brentano's awhile and said your book had done very well. I found out this meant selling several hundred copies! He also said most of the buyers were the wrong ones, from his point of view, and he was distressed because he thought they would miss the irony which was so delightful. I gathered they were mostly the Helen Hokinson [New Yorker cartoonist] type who got a Gardener's Guide at the same time.

Can you believe it is almost a year since Randolph left? Just too long to have him away. This invasion is giving me the jitters.

I'll send Bill [Lee]'s picture down when I SEE the check for $100. I don't trust these authors!

Katherine Anne is having a book of short stories out in a few months. She has been taking it easy since her "mumps." Comes downstairs and lies on the sofa to save the tray running, which is a great help. Caroline's book, THE WOMEN ON THE PORCH, is out now, but I have not seen it. She says she is not sending [it] to anyone. Broke as usual!

KAP is in "your" bedroom on the third floor next to the studio. That is the only reason I can capture her for sittings. She adores the idea of a portrait, but is hard to catch. Her social life is demanding and her health is frail. She seems always in a state of exhaustion. That doesn't stop her from wanting to experiment with gourmet dishes. Nor does it stop her from entertaining anyone willing to sit at her feet and listen to her stories about her colorful past; her loves, won or lost; her tales, true or false; her writing success ("I could publish my laundry list") and her inability to find time for her writing. I am willingly one of the feet-sitters. I drink in every word and believe every one of them.

Love,
Marcella

May 4, 1944
Dear Tat,

Katherine Anne has been here a month and has settled in as though we had known each other for ages. I spend most of my time just listening to the stories of her life, as she tells them so dramatically. She delved into my guest book and wrote the following:

> May 1, 1944, and first month at P St. Georgetown D.C. Melancholy little ditty, one of four published in youth from among perhaps four hundred—all gone but this one, and it might have been a good thing to let this one go too. But here it is!

> *Little Requiem*
> She should have had the state
> Of a king's daughter

Or a hut of willow branch
Near running water

Or a scaled silver armour
For a breast cover
Or a sweet lie on her mouth
For a lying lover

Since she had none of these
But a song instead
She has well hidden herself
With the indifferent dead

Since for lack of these things
She knew herself lost
She has well chosen silence
With her hands crossed.

Katherine Anne's new book will be called THE LEANING TOWER. She was interviewed on the radio last week about the stories in it. Mary and John sat fascinated, wondering why you aren't also on the radio, since you wrote books too. Recently she has been offered $250 for the use of her story called "The Cracked Looking Glass" for a radio program. She says she has made $2000 on that story alone. The title of the story she is now working on is "Season of Fear."

Love,

Marcella

May 13, 1944
Dear Tat,

My life, as Randolph puts it, is in a whirl. I have two or three pictures to finish before I pull up stakes for the summer. I have a beautiful color scheme for Katherine Anne's portrait, but I don't have her head yet—at least the expression I want to get. Her eyes say it all and are her finest feature. Sometimes they look blue or blue-gray, or almost a violet, and are deep set, so I try everything, getting very frustrated when they elude me. I love painting her noble brow and the ringlets in her white hair. She is wearing a gray dress that we chose which has long full sleeves, one of which drapes nicely over a deep blue chair, featuring her hands in a striking characteristic pose which she takes often, as she likes to be dramatic. I am very excited about it and will use a soft rose background to express her femininity which will complement the cool colors.

KA was hoping that I could get her spinet in the painting. She owns this small musical instrument of the Elizabethan Age called a Virginal which I never heard her play, and doubt that she ever did, but which she loves and keeps with her in her wanderings. Of course, it did not fit in the composition, and isn't needed anyway. She doesn't require props.

I didn't think there would be time for a Tennessee ham to get here . . . for KA's birthday party on the 15th, so I bought a Smithfield. She is spending about $50 on the party. Besides a capon she is ordering a cake at Avignone Frères, pistachio ice cream, candles, nuts, and liquor (brandy!). We expect a big evening. She has hired a man to do it all— thank goodness.

Love,
Marcella

May 20, 1944
Dear Tat,

You are right, the party is over, but I have put my brushes aside. The house needs attention again. It has a way of collapsing. It will be almost like moving to get it ready for three tenants this summer but, at $150 a month, is definitely worth it. I will be making enough to pay the cottage rent and still clear about $80 a month. Katherine Anne so far has been very reliable about money. She keeps up to date on payments and remembers meals she has had here and pays me promptly. Her friends will be two old maids (almost), sisters who both have jobs and seem very reliable women. Nice too. One of them, Mary Doherty, is her heroine in FLOWERING JUDAS and has lived in Mexico for 20 some years. She is quite out of step with American ways and anxious to get back to Mexico and her life there. The three are even going to hire a maid and live like civilized people!

KAP's party was a delicious treat—I particularly liked the salad (after the ham of course) which was a combination of French-style beans, asparagus, celery, with sour cream and mayonnaise. Lincoln Kirstein, one of the directors of the Museum of Modern Art, who is a private at Fort Belvoir (and worth $40 million, I hear), was the best known of the guests, but so rude that his goose is cooked with me. He walked out after dinner and never returned. Not a word was said to either of us and his friends merely remarked: "Lincoln isn't feeling himself; he is worried about what they are going to do to him." He published FLOWERING JUDAS and is a very old friend of KAP but nothing could excuse him in my eyes. KAP says she has seen him at a friend's house lie down on a sofa after dinner and go to sleep in front of everyone. Federico Castellone and Charles Shannon, young artists at Belvoir, were very pleasant. I was especially taken with a young, very handsome German poet named Schaumann, who is now in our army having forsaken the Nazis, like the Manns. He was the most intelligent on my paintings, like your friend Alex Böker at Harvard. S could place the periods and tell which were my most recent things. He thought Nancy's head the best. Shannon seemed to think all I have to do to get a show in New York is to ask for one.

Love,
Marcella

May 23, 1944

Dear Tat,

A letter from Randolph which I know you will love. One of the light spots in the war. He took the first holiday he had had in a long time, spending the day at his old station visiting Major Newton, the friend who lent him the Thoroughbred horse he used to ride. On the way back by train (he said on a 30-mile trip he couldn't use official transportation) he found the first-class car was locked up tight. He said he didn't think much of that since the ways of the LMS [London-Midland-Scotland] railroad are always devious and strange, so he climbed into the baggage van and walked from there into the car, which turned out to be loaded with Italian officers. He took a vacant seat and made himself at home and finally broke out his Italian, which he said was lousy but got a very eager reception.

They were just beginning a "beautiful friendship" when a British Major came in and told him the men were all prisoners on their way to some new camp and that he was violating every law in the book by even being in the car, much less talking to them! So he went back in the van and talked to the conductor who finally unlocked a whole vacant car on the end of the train and there he rode in solemn de luxe state all the way home. He said he never did find out where the Italians were going. He has been overseas a year and feels no sense of accomplishment. Still no second front which he has been expecting ever since he got there. It's a will-o'-the-wisp. General [Omar] Bradley made a speech in which he *s⁺J. Perse*

pooh-poohed the idea of blood and said it would not be nearly as bad as people think, which no doubt Randolph thinks is preparing the troops for invasion. He tries to think of news he can write but knows it would be censored so he just says his job is indoors now and can't say more.

He wrote that the news of Katherine Anne's birthday party sounded exciting, especially the food, but he doubted that he could have stood the array of temperament she had for guests.

Love,
Marcella

In May, 1944, I met the exiled French poet Alexis Saint Léger Léger (1887– 1975), who wrote under the pen name Saint-John Perse. A brilliant diplomat, he became one of the most influential figures in Europe between the two wars, and as a poet, he won the acclaim of Proust, Gide, Eliot, and Claudel for his early work. After his escape in 1940 from the invading Germans, who ransacked his apartment in Paris and destroyed his manuscripts, Archibald MacLeish offered him a job at the Library of Congress as a literary consultant. Léger and Allen Tate became close friends in 1943, after Tate's appointment as consultant in poetry, so I was privileged to see this famous man on many occasions. Léger had a small apartment in Georgetown on R Street. In 1960, he won the Nobel Prize for literature. A book-length poem, *Anabasis,* was translated by T. S. Eliot in 1930, and *Exile and Other Poems* was translated by Denis Devlin while he and Léger lived in Washington in the early 1940s.

Although kind and agreeable, Léger was not willing to pose for his portrait. I had given up asking him and was surprised when one evening, as he happened to sit adjacent to me in a box at a concert, he leaned over and, in a conspiratorial tone, announced that he would let me paint him. "I want to send it to my mother in France." So, alas! I was not painting for a mother in France.

May 27, 1944
Dear Tat,

The Tates gave a great party last night for some of the Fellows who are here in conference: Van Doren, Willard Thorp (Professor of American Literature at Princeton), the Cairnses (Cairns is not a Fellow at the Library of Congress though) and, most important of all, the French poet and diplomat Alexis Léger. He is a power in France, they say, except that now it would have to be "they SAID" Alas! Allen thinks him one of the best living poets so you must know him, I'm sure. Léger was most enjoyable and recounted stories of the dictators (as seen and heard by him). He seems to loosen up with the poets, as perhaps he does not do with the diplomats. You may be seeing the Tates before I see you so get Allen to tell you Léger's story on Stalin and the vodka. Katherine Anne and Katherine Garrison Chapin (Mrs. Biddle) are the only women Fellows. The Tates were in top form and the food was excellent, as usual. There were even flowers—and nicely arranged too. Mrs. Biddle had a luncheon for them today so Van Doren couldn't get here sooner or longer for the promised portrait sitting.

Today Mark Van Doren came to the studio at 3:15 and left at 5:15 to get a 6 o'clock train to New York.[1] In that time I tried to do a small painting—an utter impossibility in so short a time, but I may get another day to finish it. Obviously no time for a guest book to record the names I should be catching these days. I never seem to remember, or have the time, to get my camera out either.

There has hardly even been time to give you news of the children. Johnny is almost over his chicken pox and so far Mary is OK, but Mum is floored! Poor little J is still accepting his fate stoically. I am itching to get him to the beach and sunshine and away from the possibility of getting the only disease he hasn't had—whooping cough. We will probably be leaving about June 15th. I am trying to find a maid to go with us which is very unlikely.

Love,

Marcella

1. Mark Van Doren wrote me on June 7, 1944, "Dear Marcella: Please let me call you that. I'm glad the picture turned out as well as it did. The circumstances were all against you—a painter, I realize, is cruelly dependent upon circumstances. As for your social manners, I thought them quite right—exactly suited to the occasion, which would have made any others wrong. I liked the way you got down to business after I had come an hour late. Such concentration always fascinates me, and especially so when ability is present. . . . Sincerely, Mark Van Doren."

Sunday June 11, 1944

Dear Tat,

No letters from Randolph and I have been so busy. All the mail was held up, General [Lucius] Clay told me, awaiting the invasion.

The invasion has kept me jumping from radio to easel. On D Day I painted all day trying to finish Katherine Anne's portrait before I go away but, owing to the excitement perhaps, or getting up at 6 a.m. (not early for you) I succeeded only in undoing what I had done before. I finished her once but was dissatisfied with the eyes, despite the likeness, so have put it aside for a short time and painted a head of Allen.[1] It is excellent if I do say so and I feel better about art and life in general.

I have been too keyed up to rest well lately. It is so much like the other spring when France fell—almost too exciting to live. It is better to be too busy to think about it.

Too bad your garden is not going well. That seems a long way from me now though I would like nothing better than a good dig in the earth. Painting has taken the place of gardening for me. I realize how absurd it is for me to spend my time on nonessentials. Essentials are irksome nowadays too since no one delivers anything anymore, which means trips to the market, bakeries and all the rest.

In spite of distractions, however, and a succession of the children's diseases (scarlet fever, mumps and chicken pox), I have managed to complete six portraits since the end of February. I painted heads of Nancy and Allen Tate, Tommy Fisher and Mark Van Doren, and did large portraits of Caroline Gordon with her dog, Katherine Anne and the one of Mary which I did when we were quarantined. Just as I get going well something happens. Like a move. We will be leaving for the beach next week.

The Tates are leaving July 1st and I will miss them. KAP and I had a mint julep party for them. We got bourbon through one of the Senators and Allen made the juleps Kentucky style. He drank seven and got quite lit. He is on the wagon now. Posed for me yesterday and today, slightly subdued. Do you think I can qualify for a salon yet? Present at the party were Attorney and Mrs. Francis Biddle; Mr. and Mrs. Archibald MacLeish; Senator Lister Hill; Procope, Minister to Finland; Alexis Léger; Denis Devlin; Major General and Mrs. Lucius Clay; General Miles Reber and his ma (he became a General that very day); the Misses Harriet and Mary Winslow and Miss Guest, Asst. Director of the Freer Gallery, as well as the home team.[2]

Love,

Marcella

1. It took some years for me to complete the painting of Katherine Anne Porter, since I took the eyes out and kept waiting for Katherine Anne to return to Washington so I could put them back in. It was not until 1953 that she wrote

from New York after a visit, "I do like to think of that portrait finished and hanging in there, the eyes really looking somewhere now, after all these years." Before plans fell through she hoped it would be in the Texas library named for her, sold at a "good Texas price."

2. Archibald MacLeish (1892–1982), a poet and verse dramatist, was a three-time Pulitzer Prize winner and the librarian of Congress from 1939 to 1944. A graduate of Yale University and Harvard Law School, he first practiced law in Boston but lived in Paris between 1923 and 1928 to concentrate on writing poetry. He became absorbed in Yeats, Eliot, Pound, and the French symbolists and was active in founding UNESCO. From 1949 to 1962, he was Boylston Professor at Harvard. He continued teaching at Amherst until 1967. Lister Hill (1894–1984), a United States congressman and senator from Alabama, served as Democratic majority whip from 1941 to 1947 and was coauthor of the Hill-Burton Act (1946) authorizing federal funds for hospital construction. Denis Devlin (1908–1959) was an Irish poet and diplomat. He was first secretary of the Irish legation in Washington, then counselor of legation in London. He was appointed Irish ambassador to the Vatican a few years before his early death. General Miles Reber was a friend and classmate of Randolph's at West Point.

June 15, 1944
Dear Tat,

Katherine Anne was very pleased that you liked THE LEANING TOWER. Allen thinks her novel is very good (the one she has been working on for so long [*Ship of Fools*]) as far as it goes. He feels it might even be a best seller; but the publisher has already advanced her so much it is hard to see how she will make anything on it when, and if, she finishes it. Her job at the Library goes until September 1st. And then she does not know what she will do. She can't write holding down a job, or being unsettled, yet she has to have one to live. It is a vicious circle.

How did you like Caroline's novel, THE WOMEN ON THE PORCH? I haven't had time to read it. I know Allen thinks it her best and KAP thinks it well written. Edmund Wilson wrote C and said he could not give it a favorable review so was turning it over to someone else for the "also rans" column. Wasn't that unnecessary?

Mary and Johnny call Katherine Anne "Miss Pota" with a southern accent. They used to chant: "Miss Pota has the grippe. Miss Pota has the grippe," which changed to: "Miss Pota has the mumps. Miss Pota has the mumps." On her birthday, May 15th, they drew a large paper cat for her, under which they printed in large letters: "To Miss Pota.

We aire glad you aint got no more grippe and no more mumps. Mary and Johnny."

Love,
Marcella

On Wednesday, June 7, 1944, Randolph wrote his version of D Day in England:

Dear Marce,

The show is on at last as you have no doubt heard probably ad nauseam ever since yesterday morning.

Having been working with the plans for so long and having spent so much time mentally in the country on the maps and scale models, I seem to know every road and town and stream better than anyplace even in my own country. Like any land, however, that has been visited only on paper, it all seems a little unreal and it now appears almost fantastic that it is all working out exactly the way it was planned. Of course, the real test will not come until Friday or Saturday when the Germans can get off their coordinated counterattack. If we can stick it after that it should be more or less in the bag.

I decided to stay up Tuesday night to see what I could of the start but got so sleepy I went to bed. I was awakened at midnight by a mighty roar of airplanes, that distinctive pulsating hum that comes from nowhere in particular but fills the whole atmosphere. I looked out but couldn't see anything because of the clouds. I went back to bed but was called after a few minutes by the excited voice of the sentry outside my window. I got up again and here they came. On both sides as far as one could see to the east and west the sky was filled with red and green and yellow lights like some enormous Christmas tree. A gorgeous spectacle which kept on for two solid hours—plane after plane—thousands of them.

In the morning we rushed to the radio but it didn't say a thing. Even our own radio messages, which are so tightly coded that it takes forever to decipher them, gave only snatches of information. I finally gave up and went up to the hilltop where the gunfire could be plainly heard like distant thunder. It wasn't until night that the picture came into focus. So far it is all going about as expected, although some of it has been pretty tough.

Am fine
Love,
Randolph

Rehoboth Beach, Del.
June 18, 1944
Dear Tat,

These snapshots were taken the Sunday I was painting Allen, the weekend after the mint julep party KAP and I gave for the Tates' farewell. We four went up to Montrose Park next to Dumbarton Oaks to do them. I think they are better of Caroline and Allen than KAP. She puts on poses for pictures and does her mouth the way you do, so there is no use, unless you get her unaware of the camera. I left for the beach directly after that weekend so I hardly got to study Allen's portrait but Katherine Anne is crazy about it. Allen told me "Brother Ben" (his wealthy brother who lives in Cincinnati) should want to buy it and I should ask $500 for it. Nothing like that has ever happened to me though!

I know you are chortling about the captured liquor, as I have been, over Randolph's description of the spoils of war. It must be too thrilling for those men to have it all happening, not on paper, or on maneuvers, but the real thing though that is a heartless way to look at it. Do you think he is helping to direct the repairs to the Cherbourg harbor? Will we ever be able to catch up on all he has done so far away? Do you realize these are the first letters that are purely optimistic? No doubt he feels that he is accomplishing something at last, and can really see it happening.

My life is as quiet as a stagnant pool here, but I like it. After Washington it is almost too big a change, but no doubt I am benefiting. The children certainly are. You should see Johnny jumping the waves! Today he announced that sometimes the big waves take his "walking feet" from under him.

Love,
Marcella

I discovered that Katherine Anne had told me what she wished were true: that she had had a privileged childhood. Eventually she may have come to believe the stories. My letters describe her as I saw her at the time. Her fiftieth birthday party was actually for her fifty-fourth year.

Research by Joan Givner for *Katherine Anne Porter: A Life* (New York, 1982) uncovered the facts of the painful early life that Katherine Anne seemed determined to put behind her.

June 22, 1944

Dear Tat,

Since you liked Katherine Anne's letter so much, I am sending you another. You can tell how nice she is. And that is not just her letters. She IS a really sweet person. However, she is restless and dissatisfied and put off by so many worthless things—as well as people. She likes people but they distract her. She lets them distract her and then she worries because she can't write. Allen says she does everything she can to prevent herself from writing—it is almost as though she is afraid to tackle it. Usually she writes in a blaze of inspiration from numerous notes. Practically never has to write anything over. Just gets stuck and then waits for the proper mood—but tires herself out with distractions, so the mood gets waylaid. She never could write at Yaddo, or places where she is expected to write.

She is a genius. Unpredictable and undisciplined about her life and work—not her manners. Strangely enough, she cannot bear to be late for an appointment, and is usually prompt somehow, some way, for interviews and parties—yet, if I had not picked her up, bag and baggage, and dumped her in my car, she never would have made the train to New York for a radio program recently.

She is a LADY, and one never forgets it for an instant. She was educated by the nuns in New Orleans, and still bears the imprint of their training—little feet crossed under her when she sits down, modest in her dress and ways. She told me she wanted to be a nun, but her father squelched that idea, giving her anti-Catholic literature to read. Now she is hoping to return to the church. She sent away for a huge silver Mexican rosary which she has hung over her bedpost, perhaps expecting that to do the trick. She adores beautiful things. Likes just to hold a piece of old silver in her hands to feel its beauty. The most sensitive person I have ever met—so much so that one wants to do things for her and remove some of the worry—but she can't bear to be under obligation. That is torture to her. Considering how she can't find her way about on buses and streetcars, one wonders how she has found her way through these 50 years of her life doing absolutely everything and experiencing extreme poverty as well.

Katherine Anne's life is unbelievable. I'll tell you about it some day.

In the meantime, if you have it on hand read "Old Mortality" which is an exact true story of herself and her family. She is Miranda in the story, herself when a child.

On June 27, 1944, the day before the Tates left Washington for Sewanee, Allen wrote to me at Rehoboth Beach:

> Dear Marcella:
>
> It was very sweet of you to write me. Everybody is crazy about my portrait. Archie [MacLeish] came to the office the other day and of course admired it. When you get back you must call him. He will be expecting to hear from you. —I write this headlong note in between last minute rushes of all kinds. We leave tomorrow morning. Late this afternoon we go to your house for a drink with Katherine Anne, who by the way returned from N.Y. much exhausted.
>
> Our address is simply: Sewanee, Tenn.
>
> > Love,
> > Allen

Rehoboth Beach, Del.
June 29, 1944
Dear Tat,

Imagine you not telling me that you have another book on the way! I could be right hurt if I were the type, but I have learned that artists seem to do things in their own way, and the ways are many and devious. Am I allowed to know the title? If you write a book every year you will soon catch up to Caroline and then she cannot say you are not a serious artist. A second edition of THE DWELLING PLACE is good news indeed.

Of course we would be delighted to have another distinguished author-boarder next winter. How can I be sure you will really do it? It is a logical solution to your winter problem and would be nice for the children and me to have you. I can produce a few interesting people, if they are still around, such as Alexis Léger, whom you can charm into sitting to me, and Denis Devlin, who will charm you into sitting by him. Allen likes Denis better than anyone else he met last winter. KAP likes him a lot too, as do I. I could take you to the Library of Congress musicals, to the National Gallery and to the Phillips Gallery exhibits and so many other places you would love as much as your favorite Dumbarton Oaks Gardens. Do let me count on you.

I have read a book lately that you might like: Anne Lindbergh's THE STEEP ASCENT. Who strives to get books that you are willing to read from the library the way I used to do in Memphis? At least the way I used to TRY. Do you remember when I thought it would be safer to phone you from the library, before you rejected the armfuls I hopefully brought for your edification, and I asked if you would like to read Rumer Godden's BLACK NARCISSUS—and you told me with conviction that you would read no book with "black" in the title?

It is lovely here at Rehoboth. Very nice people—quiet and refined as the "ads" might say. You would fit in nicely.

Love,
Marcella

Rehoboth Beach, Del.
August 7, 1944
Dear Tat,

Thank you for all the red points. We promptly bought two lbs. of butter. It doesn't go far with this gang. I got a letter from Randolph and Monroe in the same mail. R is in Normandy and Monroe is somewhere in the Pacific. Monroe got someone to write the letter but he enclosed his photograph. He looks handsome and extra black in his white navy uniform. I hope he returns from the war to the cooking he has learned to love so much.

I took Mary in to Washington to see the dentist. The city was like an oven. I spent an afternoon in the National Gallery—air cooled. When I came out at 4, I tried to breathe but felt so stifled that I returned until the doors closed—just sitting, cooling in front of masterpieces!

I dropped into P Street to see Katherine Anne and found her in a state of dishabille and bad shape. She was so distraught over the departure of her most recent love (Charles Shannon, years younger, the painter who is doing his military here), and the discovery that he was married as well, that she completely forgot she had invited the Edgar Ansel Mowrers to dinner. I was sitting by the window and exclaimed: "Katherine Anne, there are two people in evening dress coming up the steps!" She didn't even have makeup on and became panicky. She exclaimed: "My God, this is the second time I have done this to them!" But they had to be admitted and the conversation was strained to say the least. E. A. Mowrer is a distinguished journalist and his wife, who is English, also writes. She knew them in her Paris days. I don't know how KA lives these things down but maybe they happen so often she takes them in her stride. Her typewriter had to be repaired but she can't remember where it went and how she will get it back. I doubt she had occasion to use it much this summer with Shannon in the house.

In a recent letter she wrote that she didn't think I needed her offices in getting MacLeish to sit to me as Allen had that arranged, but she might be able to round up Alexis Léger, adding: "Heaven knows he is a slippery article when he wants to be; I think he has been rounded up by experts in his crowded past. He comes when I call, but he never calls me, and of course that cannot last. But get MacLeish first; he is all prepared in his mind and will make a fine interesting subject." I hope I will have the courage to ask him.

Love,
Marcella

> Joan of Arc at point of lance
> Drove the English out of France
> Madame Poulard better yet
> Brought them back with omelet.
> —Anonymous

Madam Poulard's Restaurant was in Mont-Saint-Michel.

Rehoboth Beach, Del.
August 17, 1944
Dear Tat,

If Randolph can eat a Madame Poulard omelet during an invasion things must be going well for us.

He writes that he took a longish trip through sniper country in an armored car and drove like the wind. "It was worth it—little fresh radishes and a sumptuous omelet about 4 inches high, also good Pouilly to drink. This country still eats just about like always." As he gets further into France, he says the people get friendlier and better looking than the Normans. However, what they are waving is mostly gasoline cans, hoping for the free *essence,* and what at first was taken for a V-for-victory sign they soon learned was a smoking sign asking for free ciga-

rettes. In sum, the Free French are well named. Also, he says that during this period of comparative calm, my "friend" Homer Saint-Gaudens
(director of the Carnegie Institute in Pittsburgh) dropped in as a cam-
ouflage consultant and was being given a junket to show him a good
time but, since his ideas are definitely First World War, everybody gives
him a big hand but few pay attention to him. He loved the trip Randolph arranged for him going over the front in an observation plane.

A note from Katherine Anne with the last month's rent, saying she
is rushing to New York to see about the imminent release of THE LEAN-
ING TOWER. You should be glad you are far away from publishers.

Glenway Wescott's new book is a novel, but not the one you are in.[1]
Do you still keep in touch since that memorable meeting on board ship?
He was one of the early ones to sit at your feet, I recall.

Mary made a "book" for my coming birthday which she illustrated
and calls THE MINANITE POPELE. She was fascinated with a group that
we saw here one day bathing in their long-sleeved bathing suits with
their bushy-haired and bearded men.

"Popele" are here in droves, and all swimming. Johnny learned and
goes along just like a little dog. He says "real people" go much slower
than he does.

Love,

Marcella

1. Glenway Wescott (1901–1987), a prizewinning novelist, is best known for
stories of Wisconsin settlers, especially *The Grandmother* (New York, 1927).

September 1, 1944
Dear Tat,

Your birthday gift arrived being what I hoped it would be. You will
know how much I love ginger pears when I tell you I am eating them,
glass and all. I had to pick out the brandied peaches one by one, but
the blackberry and peach preserves are OK. Many thanks. We seem to
be able to get most everything in the food line now except good beef,
ham and butter. The butter is spasmodic and then only 1/4 lb. to a
customer. I must confess I miss the southern dishes I learned to love,
like greens and cornmeal muffins. Maybe Monroe someday will be able
to make me those muffins after his journey in the world.

I have heard from General Wilby, who is back from Europe and ready to sit for his portrait. I will go to West Point as soon as I get the children settled and in school. Lena has promised to stay with them. I hope the polio has calmed down by then. Washington has been one of the hardest-hit cities.

Katherine Anne plans to return to Yaddo after she goes to New York for a party to be given by her publishers. She will try to finish her novel which even she, herself, says is good. Allen thinks it is remarkable as far as it goes. KA writes that "it seems as if things were only beginning and that, here it is, the end of something and the beginning of something else." It is the end of something interesting for me—living with her—genius, beauty, prima donna, femme fatale, fascinating person. I have enjoyed all of it.

You must keep all the gadgets that I left with you. Every gadget I own has had to be repaired—lamps, clocks, fans, radio, vacuum. I could use the clock for your room. KAP never knew the time except when she borrowed the Tates' radio. When they took it away she was lost.

Love,
Marcella

Rehoboth Beach, Del.
September 6, 1944
Dear Tat,

It is 8 a.m. and, according to the *New Yorker,* we are to get up early and see if Nostradamus' prophecy comes true. Mother and I felt last night that something was in the wind, with all the predictions of sensational reports from the Third Army, but I am waiting for the 8:55 radio. As I remember, the war is to end on Sept. 16th, according to old N. It begins to look as though it will too. Hard to believe that Germany can hold out. I gloat over the news, except for reports on the damage to Florence. How could any civilized nation vandalize such a city? I am glad to have made my little painting of the Ponte Trinita when I did.

Randolph writes that they are now authorized to tell what they have been doing, provided the news is two weeks old. His outfit, the 8th Corps, started with the battle of Carentan and then held the line from Carentan through St. Sauveur Le Vicomte while Cherbourg was being taken. Then they pushed south which was slowgoing with terrible casualties till they broke through at Periers and Lessay. His outfit was the one that made the grand rush down through Coutances Avranches to Lorient and Brest. He couldn't say anything about his last two weeks but apparently they are having a breathing spell. Although it was hectic, he said he thought it should not take more than a couple of weeks to clean up all of France. However, breaking through the Siegfried Line would be something else again. He says Lyon was taken and if he got a chance he would try to get down there and get news of Maurice Terry and his family.

He wonders if rubber overshoes are still being sold. Also, hot-water bottles, both of which he would be happy to have. Weather is a problem always. The *New York Times* has a piece about the overworked word FANATIC, as in the fanatic resistance by the enemy's fanatic Elite and fanatic SS troops. Randolph's word is HECTIC, as in the HECTIC days they experience. Now they are just quietly freezing to death.

Love,
Marcella

P Street, N.W.
Washington, D.C.
September 17, 1944
Dear Tat,

Back home. How good it is to feel the solid protection of brick after that hurricane in a frame cottage! A rather terrifying experience but no harm done except to the nervous system and scratches on the car where a tree fell across it. The tree was a large pine. It cracked first and swayed dizzily against the roof, ripping a bit of it each time a new gust came— which was too often. Then it fell, landing on my car which the branches enveloped. Had the car been crushed I would be really out of luck since one of the first pieces of mail I saw when I returned was an unforwarded notice that my auto insurance had expired!

If I hadn't been able to get out from under we would probably still be there as everything was disrupted and the damage was awe-inspiring: roofs blown off, trees uprooted, a large freighter broken in two and boats stranded on the beach. Ocean City feared a tidal wave and evacuated the citizens. The worst aspect for me was that we were packing to leave and when the electricity went off we had to sit in a chaos of trunks and boxes unable to see a thing. The food had been packed and the towels were sopping wet and the candle butts were used up! Well, I have no more curiosity about what a hurricane is like. Not a good end to a perfect summer but interesting in retrospect.

Katherine Anne is pictured on the front page of the *New York Times Book Review*. The enclosed article is a little gem of a review from Glenway Wescott. Mutual admiration there. The drawing by Paul Cadmus—done about a year ago. He is very talented and has caught her at her best. My portrait of her concentrates on her unusual brow, but I have also got her rather weak mouth. Allen says: "Noble brow, weak mouth." His last letter says: "Poor KAP is now at Yaddo, as you probably know. I imagine she is in pretty low spirits but, as you know, nobody can help her."

Love,
Marcella

September 20, 1944
Dear Tat,

The 8th Corps captures Brest! I have discovered that the 8th Corps is Ninth Army and is composed of three Infantry divisions commanded by General Troy Middleton. I get most of my information from the *New York Times,* but you should get it in the *Commercial Appeal* too. I have had no letter from Randolph since September 1st. Of course he hasn't had time if he has been capturing Brest! It was a 48-day siege and 36,000 Germans taken prisoner. The Nazi leader escaped. It was the second largest prisoner bag of the war. Brest was a pile of rubble. Can't you see Randolph enjoying the irony of turning over "liberated" Brest to the city authorities complete with beards and bad breath in a ceremony of which no one seemed to appreciate the irony but he? He says his wit is lost on the army.

Katherine Anne seems to have gotten her typewriter back as she typed the news of her leaving Washington with this charming paragraph: "My dear, you know how pleasant it has been to know you, and how you really saved my life last spring by taking me in here; and we must keep in mind what a very small world it has become, and how we shall be seeing each other at all sorts of odd times from now on."

She prepared me for finding the house a "little dusty as there was bound to be some wear and tear" but she thought it really looked pretty much the same. The garden, though so pleasant, was getting raggedy and she planned to send Mary and Johnny some inscribed books and was so bone-tired that she never expected to get rested again and there was still New York to go through and everything that should be a pleasure had simply become an ordeal but maybe she would get some rest at Yaddo.

Jean Stafford seems to have a best seller with BOSTON ADVENTURE. A really auspicious sendoff for a first novel, isn't it? I read parts of it when the proofs were sent to Katherine Anne. KA thinks she has great talent, but that this book was too borrowed and piecemeal and not completely her own, and that she should scrap it and wait, but who would do that nowadays except KAP herself? Especially with reviews like she is getting. Caroline will love the Proustian angle every reviewer has mentioned.

You can see why KA has a hard time getting to the novel. The letter sounds exactly as she talks. She always finishes with love to her "darling Mary and Johnny" whom she "thinks of a great deal." She also hopes that we can get my portrait finished—the eyes which I took out at some point. She is happy to have Whyte's Gallery show the portrait at the same time she could autograph her book. She doesn't consider that plan commercial, just "normal."

> Love,
> Marcella

Katherine Anne Porter wrote a letter to me on October 4, 1944, after the party given for her in New York for the publication of *The Leaning Tower:*

The book is selling, a great change for the better in my life. Gone into a second printing already, which means more than ten thousand in the first week or ten days. Simply not bad, all considered. The day I went to sign them there were none left in the office. I could only get 16 when I needed about thirty copies. My party took place the day of the hurricane, beginning on the very same hour. Everybody came though and slogged through the wet, and it was a serenely gay pleasant affair. Everybody was so friendly and sweet and the reviewers really did me proud. By now you have seen the *New York Times* and the *New Yorker?* I liked those best because those two men, Wescott and Wilson, are the best critics. But Red Warren, the best of them all, did one for a Chicago paper, and I am waiting anxiously to see that. Well, after the party, there were no taxis, and I walked with Charles through the flood and wind for five blocks to my hotel; it was wonderful, but I paid for it with a week mostly in bed, coughing my head off. I still have the cold, but not so noisy. Just the same I got in cocktail parties, a lunch for Henry Wallace, dinner parties, theaters, it was altogether gay and pleasant and I loved it . . . now I am in a little cabin in the woods at Yaddo, wanting to work on the novel and still trying to catch up with letters.

After Anne Winslow had read *The Leaning Tower,* she wrote me,

I agree with you about Katherine Anne's gift for analysis. That one little story of hers ["The Leaning Tower"] has done more to explain the war than anything I know. I am always telling people to read it and shut up.

October 6, 1944
Dear Tat,

The date to paint General Wilby is set for October 12th. And I am set to go.

The Secrecy has been lifted on the siege of Brest so Randolph can write about the tough fight they had and how depressing it is. The town was in such appalling chaos. Not one single house left standing, what with the shelling and bombing and the German demolition and over it all the dank smelling white dust from shattered masonry and the sticky stench of dead rats, horses and men. He has been getting the engineers started on taking out the mines and clearing rubble from the streets. Mother and I were sure we detected Randolph in a remark—was it in *Time?*—quoting an engineer on Brest: "We better scrap this and start from scratch." He says the French don't feel so friendly towards them around there.

The children need everything new this fall so, since I have an aversion to shopping in wartime Washington, I have discovered the Sears catalogue. A very convenient telephone service that brings things right to your door and calls for them if they have to go back. I just sit down with a list and buy brooms, hairpins, silver polish, galoshes, toilet articles, writing paper, etc. and then have a field day when they show up. I had to go to town however to look for some curtains, and finally found what I wanted (the last three pairs) only to forget them when my arms were full of packages—one being the long-sought prism light needed for so long, which was lugged everywhere, only to fall and break, still in the wrappings, the minute I got home as I reached for your letter on the hall table. Then Mary tipped over a bottle of perfume as she eagerly examined the purchases and there was little left in my hands but three ersatz curtain rods. So who needs to go shopping?

When I asked you to send Johnny's climbing rope I didn't realize you would have to go into every trunk, box, basket and cracker tin. Sorry. It is probably in Monroe's room in the box where the blocks are. Never mind.

Love,
Marcella

Anne Winslow and Allen Tate collaborated on a play based on Henry James's story "The Turn of the Screw." There seemed a possibility at one time that it might be sold to Hollywood. While they were waiting to find a producer, though, another play on the same theme, called *The Children*, had a successful run in New York, so the work was abandoned. Later Tate had it put on at the University of Minnesota with help from Isabella Gardner, his second wife.

October 14, 1944
Dear Tat,

I am like Allen. I can't think of the Hitchcock Hollywood venture for more than two minutes at a time. Even if they don't follow through, it is most exciting. Will it be called *The Governess?* I have always been fascinated by "The Turn of the Screw" and hope you and Allen have shed some light on the mystery. Did SHE do it?

The children are very disappointed that the General has a cold and had to postpone posing for a week. They had all been planning a great time in my absence. John is so utterly delighted over rediscovering his rope that it was all I could do to keep him from going to bed with it tonight. He wanted to tie it to the pipe in the bedroom, but I persuaded him to wait until he could connect with a tree. I know he is climbing in his sleep.

The 8th Corps is having a rest after the fall of Brest and Randolph managed to get to Concarneau and Quimper. No china but good lobsters. Do you know of a town called Roscaf, north of Brest? He said he

Saturday Dec 9, '36

Dear Marcella –

I had
a nice trip home
and found the Tates
here to greet me. –
Everything looked
very festive, thanks
to Mary's efforts, with
big fires burning
and an elaborate
tea set forth. Mr.
Meeman was also
among us and he &

From Anne Goodwin Winslow to me

Thursday

Dear Tat — I should love to read the Emily Dickinson book. I got so interested in everything about her last year ——

Just for a commission to paint the Episcopal bishop of Harrisburg, Pa in all his robes. He is staying here for the summer. It will be large with hands. At least $500 — depends on size!!

Working steadily and really terribly busy. How I wish I could see Colonel Reeves. You didn't tell me anything he said — Can you remember to?

Must run now —

love,
Marcella

Nice letter from Betty. She wrote me a long one about Guatemala.

To Anne Goodwin Winslow from me

In 1931

One of my two mural panels in the Children's Room of the Homewood Library,
in Pittsburgh, painted in 1933.

Courtesy the Homewood Library, Pittsburgh

My first portrait of Randolph, 1933

With Randolph and Mary, 1937

Goodwinslow, in Raleigh, Shelby County, Tennessee, built by Anne Winslow's father.

Looking down P Street, 1947

Allen Tate, painted at Goodwinslow, 1937
Courtesy Nancy Wood

Anne Winslow arranging magnolias for my painting *Southern Sunday*

Southern Sunday, 1943

The Goosepickers, 1943

At Monteagle, 1943, left to right, Caroline Gordon, Anne Goodwin Winslow, Andrew Lytle, Mrs. Lytle, Nancy Tate, Allen Tate, Robert Lowell, Jean Stafford.

David Fentress with his portrait, on the steps of Goodwinslow, 1943

With Allen Tate and Robert Lowell, 1943

Lena Brushing Mary's Hair, 1945

Caroline Gordon, with Bub, painted in 1944

Nancy Tate, painted in 1944
Courtesy Nancy Wood

Katherine Anne Porter and Allen Tate in Montrose Park, Georgetown, 1944

With Katherine Anne Porter in Montrose Park, 1944

Katherine Anne Porter, painted in 1944

Mark Van Doren, painted in 1944

Robert Penn Warren, painted in 1945

Accepting Randolph's Distinguished Service Medal from General Robbins, 1945

Back Fences, 1935

would like to see this charming place under pleasanter circumstances. He says it is so cold and asked for a heavy wool sweater as he expects the war to last through the winter. The Germans they are up against are stubborn and good soldiers and he can't see their morale fading at all. Not hopeful when you consider that it took 48 days to capture Brest. He is getting fed up with the war and must need a rest after more than a year of unremitting responsibility.

I am trying to put the garden to rest. It was a wilderness after I returned last month. Daniel Boone's descendant, Katherine Anne, liked that effect but I don't.[1]

Robert Penn Warren has taken the place Allen had last year. He is red haired and from Kentucky. Very nice. His wife, Cinina, is a sort of invalid, I believe.[2]

Whyte's Bookshop has sold over 100 copies of KAP's book. I never saw Edmund Wilson's review. The *New Yorker*s are always sold out the day they appear on the newsstands. I renewed R's subscription.

Love,
Marcella

1. An invented lineage.

2. Robert Penn Warren (1905–1989) was born in Guthrie, Kentucky. He entered Vanderbilt at 16 and afterward went to Oxford as a Rhodes scholar. He was cofounder with Cleanth Brooks of the *Southern Review* at Louisiana State University in 1934. In 1942, he became professor of English at the University of Minnesota, and he moved to Yale in the 1950s. He was consultant in poetry at the Library of Congress from 1944 to 1945 and the first poet laureate just before his death. His novel *All the King's Men* (New York, 1946) won a Pulitzer Prize. In the 1920s, Warren married the daughter of the conductor of the San Francisco Symphony. Caroline Gordon felt "Cinina tried to live up to her descent from the Borgias" (Anne Waldron, *Close Connections* [New York, 1987], 59).

October 18, 1944

Dear Tat,

It looks like this time General [Wilby] and I are really connecting. I leave tomorrow so I have lots to do. In fact, there is a lot I have *just* done. Your room is ready for you. Ernest calls himself "helping me." You must remember the guy I took in who, when he washed the windows, would wipe out first the words "Buy War Bonds and Stamps" or "Mary and Johnny Is Nice Children." I have the telephone numbers and addresses of lots of decrepit, inexperienced, or very young help who are willing to come and let me give them lessons in housework, and Ernest is one. I swore I would never have him back because I had to spend hours cleaning up after him. However, I was desperate and when he wrote me a card saying he was available, I took a chance, or rather a leap, and permitted him to do some work in the garden. Ernest IS earnest, and clumsy too, but willing, and never cares what I pay him—or even cares what he is doing. He did so well in the garden that I thought he could finish the Kemtone job I had bogged down on in your bedroom. As he "finished" the walls, I was on the floor scrubbing the paint as it splattered in all directions. Please don't look too closely at edges, especially where the ceiling begins, or wonder why the window sash was left the same color as the mantel.

Love,

Marcella

My father's maternal relatives, the Rodanges, never forgave his artist father for acting on the supposition that there might be more opportunities for artistic achievement in the United States. Although my father was only eight years old when he left Luxembourg, he never forgot the language. When he sat with my mother in the piazza in Luxembourg City on their honeymoon, he enjoyed overhearing the Luxembourgers discuss them at great length.

October 20, 1944

Dear Tat,

Imagine Randolph in the Grand Duchy of Luxembourg! Eleanor is so delighted and is sending him the Prime Minister's address as well as Major Konsbruck's, aide to the Grande Duchess, so he can meet up with royalty. The Minister at the Legation here returned a short time ago driving from Paris to the ship in a Jeep. I have met Konsbruck; he is on Eisenhower's staff and as high as they go in the Luxembourg army.

Mother tells me that there are three ancient cousins of my father—children of the national poet, Michel Rodange—still living in the family house in Luxembourg. It seems two surviving spinsters take care of their unmarried brother, the Chief Engineer of that Graustarkian country, who is the Albert that a bridge he designed is named for, unofficially probably . . . the Albert Bridge. None of us can read the poet's work in the language, which they call a dialect, but it is still taught in the schools. Monsieur Bech, the Minister of Foreign Affairs, told Eleanor he keeps the Rodange political fables as bedside reading, which appeals to me.

Love,
Marcella

West Point, N.Y.
November 6, 1944
Dear Tat,

It will be almost three weeks since I came to West Point. I never would have believed it, but you should see the spit and polish I am having to put on "Brother" [General Wilby]. Every little detail has to be gone over, and a perfectly good hand has to be repainted because it looks "dead" compared to the other one. I have had an unbelievably difficult time and was so discouraged at one point that I went into N.Y. to see Alexander Kostellow (my old teacher) who suggested that I go from oil into tempera, since I didn't want to keep working over the oil and lose the freshness which is so important for vibrant color. (Not that color is the important thing here. Likeness is all.)

In order to use tempera I had to make an emulsion which requires an egg. I asked the waiter at the Hotel Thayer where I am staying if I could have an egg for the General's portrait. He looked surprised and was gone for some time. When he returned he handed me the largest egg I have ever seen. He asked if it was large enough. Anything for the General has to be the biggest and the best, even in eggs. I carried it as carefully as possible to the studio and it served me well. Somehow the word had got around; everyone knew an egg had to be used for the General's portrait and the curiosity was intense. At a cocktail party that afternoon everyone was talking about the egg. When a particularly insistent young man got me in a corner and demanded why I should need an egg for the painting, I supplied what seemed to me the logical answer: I had arrived at the point where I threw it at the portrait.

This was my first experience doing an "official" portrait and I was not aware that, after many hours painting the colorful ribbons (denoting rank and honors), other hours would be necessary to make sure they looked like moiré ribbon. The four stars had to glisten with the highlights in the right place; the wrinkles on suit, as well as face, did not need to be highlighted—or even noticed. The overall effect just had to be of a distinguished military officer, who was distinguished enough to be the Superintendent of the U.S. Military Academy at West Point. I trust I succeeded.

Love,
Marcella

Randolph wrote an account about a boar hunt in the Ardennes to his mother:

November 1, 1944
Dear Tat,

This is pretty country to be out in. The pine forests are all interspersed with a lot of deciduous trees, ordinary ones, and the color combinations are gorgeous. Even the woods and fields have a manicured look. The weather sure is nasty however. It is not too bad on us in the higher headquarters as we have stoves, but the men out in the line are pretty uncomfortable. Our uniform, in spite of all the millions that are squandered on it, is inferior to either the British or Russian when it comes to keeping out the cold.

I have heard that nostalgia is mostly smell. I have been getting an intangible but strong feeling of Swiss in the towns around here. It wasn't until yesterday however that I found it is the smell of burning briquettes. I never smelled them anywhere else.

Sunday I decided to overcome my dislike of killing things and went on a boar hunt. Our ration has been rather on the lean side since we used up the last of the eggs and captured German stuff we got at Brest, and the thought of roast pork was too much. We began at the hunting chalet of the host, M. Myrisch de St. Hubert, who owns most of the land around here, with a large glass of straight holland gin. I found out that this custom is a bit of liquid courage because the wild boar of the Ardennes is deemed very fierce. We went to the hunt two dozen strong—eight guns, twelve beaters and a host of gun bearers plus a pack of large shaggy gray dogs that I was told were boar hounds, all in charge of the game keeper with green tabs on his collar, feather in hat and Kaiser Wilhelm mustache. I felt (under the influence of the gin) like singing a few bars of "So ja, so ja, gar lustig ist die jaegerie" etc. but refrained as they all carefully avoided any German. They spoke Walloon to the servants and French to each other. The only other American was my Jeep driver whom they treated as though he were a General. The hunt was tame but afterwards we returned to the Chalet for wild duck and beer. When you think this all happened in a country which is allegedly suffering from malnutrition, and only 15 miles from the front line it sounds fantastic, but a lot about this war seems more and more phony to me every day. Am fine

Your loving Randolph

Thanksgiving
November 23, 1944
Dear Tat,

We missed having you at our festive board today, but will have you for Christmas, which will be nice. Mr. Neam got me a turkey from a farmer we saw bring it in and it was the kind that Mother says has personality. She can always tell, she says. I spiced it according to THE JOY OF COOKING, which is now my food bible.

Randolph's Nov. 3rd letter expresses a hope to get on with the war since he writes that the British seem in a fair way to clean up Antwerp. Also, that it wouldn't mean much to be awarded a 48-hour leave to Paris since it didn't look like the old Paris he knew when he went through it. Le Gallais [minister of Luxembourg] was so excited about R being in the Mayrisch de St. Hubert Château, as he says he almost grew up there. The old Countess was a sort of foster-mother. Eleanor has to write and ask Randolph a lot of questions. He is about 30 miles from the center of Luxembourg. I hope he doesn't go into Germany but continues to fight the wild boar instead of the wild Boche. The Grand Duchess' lady-in-waiting, Countess Lynar, says the old Countess M. de St. H. is a freethinker and would not be likely to turn her place over to the nuns. I would have loved to see that boar hunt in a Jeep.

I have settled down after my busy week of parties. After my cocktail party for the Fellows [of the Library of Congress] I went with them to the Biddles' dinner. Marquis Childs [the journalist], Alexis Léger and Francis Biddle were the only non-Fellows, besides myself, to be invited. Katherine Biddle is lovely. You two must meet. Allen thinks more of you (if one can compare woman poets). As much as he likes her he thinks her a little too well disposed toward everyone—which is certainly not the case with either you or me! Allen likes a little bitter with the sweet—as who doesn't really who is any fun to know?

Theodore Spencer, one of the new Fellows, who teaches at Harvard, is terrific—huge, amusing, smart, attractive and much savoir faire.[1] Ever hear of him? Louise Bogan was a nice enigma.[2] Sat in one place drinking one Martini after another without changing her facial expression. I decided at last it must be a manner she puts on for parties, as one could hardly be so inert.

I missed Katherine Anne, who had sent a wire that she was in the Saratoga hospital and couldn't make it. Archibald MacLeish is nice but not informal like Allen (at least with me) so I don't know how far I would get in bidding for sittings with Allen gone.

I went to a party at the Cheneys' one night and met Hodding Carter who is a Major in the army here now.[3] No doubt you would not want to read his book, which is supposed to be "nasty"—but very good. He is very attractive and has a beautiful wife. He has it in mind to come to the dwelling place to meet you. He knew William Alexander Percy very well, of course, and said he might have met Randolph—how could he not have remembered?[4] I told him of our visit to Percy and how much we liked him and his LANTERNS ON THE LEVEE which you felt paved the way for Knopf's interest in publishing THE DWELLING PLACE. Allen is supposed to come back once more this winter so he is looking forward to seeing you.

You ask if Randolph is still in the 9th Army. I presume so, although it doesn't necessarily follow. The corps change around. I think he was with the 1st Army when he went to France, according to General Wilby. I am saving Wilby's diary for you to read, which he lent me. He saw "everyone" last summer in Europe and he left nothing out, not even the pills he took for the "trots."

Love,

Marcella

1. Theodore Spencer (1902–1949), with degrees from Princeton, Cambridge, and Harvard, was Boylston Professor at Harvard, specializing in Elizabethan literature but also an authority on contemporary fiction, poetry, and drama. Fond of stylish clothes, bright bow ties, and the piano, he was a popular teacher of Shakespeare.

2. Louise Bogan had the chair of poetry at the Library of Congress from 1945 to 1946. The New Yorker was willing to hold the job of poetry reviewer open for her while she was in Washington. Although critical of poets in politics and a number of poets in particular, she declared, once her year in the capital was over,

that she had begun to feel warmly about Washington, Georgetown, and the Library of Congress.

3. Hodding Carter moved to Greenville, Mississippi, to take over the *Delta Democrat Times* at William Alexander Percy's instigation.

4. William Alexander Percy, author of *Lanterns on the Levee* (New York, 1941), was a poet, teacher, lawyer, and planter, and the son of a senator. He was a southern aristocrat "born and raised within the shelter of the old traditions," as I recall the New York *Times* put it. His famous book about the South was reissued in 1981 by Louisiana State University Press with an introduction by his adopted cousin Walker Percy.

On November 25, 1944, Anne O'Hare McCormick wrote from Luxembourg, in her customary column on the editorial page of the New York *Times,* about the Thanksgiving service in the cathedral given in honor of the Americans who had helped liberate that "tiny fairy-tale grand duchy" after four and a half years of annexation by the Reich. She quoted an old man: "We owe you everything for our deliverance. All we can do in return is to sing a Te Deum and invite your soldiers to have Thanksgiving dinner in our homes." She described the state as being comically small, with its tiny schlosses, its romantic dynasty, and its miniature towns, and she explained how, although Luxembourg boasted the highest standard of living in Europe, its Thanksgiving was held in fear and heartbreak, because no state is too small or too harmless to its neighbors to be safe from aggression.

Randolph wrote in a letter to his mother dated December 1 that he was glad to get the clipping about Luxembourg since he had not yet started to get his New York *Times.* "It is a nice tight little country and much better under control than either France or Belgium. Prosperous too. There is considerable undernourishment in Belgium and actual suffering in Holland." He went on to describe the picture painted by the newspapers about the accelerated pace of the war, which he felt was a distortion caused by the battle between press agents: "Our generals have become so publicity-conscious that they actually have press agents working on their staffs and the competition for headlines is something to see . . . all of which could be probably classed as innocent fun except for the fact that the truth gets buried in the process."

Katherine Anne Porter had expected to come to the Fellows' meeting in mid-November but had to cancel because of illness. Working at Yaddo, in Saratoga Springs, on a grant, campaigning strenuously for Roosevelt, and attending parties in New York for her book had depleted her small store of energy.

The previous summer had started out with such promise. She was renting my house with two sisters, old friends from Mexico days, all happy to be together sharing a maid named Edna, who was "slow but of the best will and humor," but it turned out to be a sort of disaster in more ways than one. Katherine Anne could not remember where she had sent her typewriter to be repaired. Edna was soon to be declared a "born saboteuse" who had added her "not inconsiderable heft to the war between the races" and had to be let go. Each tenant let her one-third of Edna go. Katherine Anne had to see doctors all summer for bronchial troubles, an infected lung, and "other little ailments," and at the same time get to her job at the Library of Congress.

Somewhere along the line one of Katherine Anne's admirers was housed on the third floor, to the dismay and disapproval of the sister tenants, one of whom "sabotaged the whole summer, simply sitting with her arms crossed staring, saying 'I don't want this or that to eat,' 'I don't feel like doing this or that,' 'I'm not used to this or that,' etc. winding herself around the neck of her sister like an albatross," according to Katherine Anne, who expected nothing less than a home for psychopaths to be the end of it. "All in deepest confidence, my dear," she added to me.

In spite of all these setbacks, Katherine Anne managed a good amount of social life, "Denis and Léger and Shannon all over the place" (Shannon was on the third floor), and "lunch now and then with rather high-ups in the State Department." Her July letter added that she really preferred the society of artists as they seemed somehow to be the "realest people I have found and I know my own when I see it." She was able to say in October that the time on P Street had not been all wasted, that she had "tender recollections" of it as did "someone" else too. The "someone," Shannon, was the last great love of her life, described in detail in Joan Givner's biography—a sad ending for Katherine Anne since she had never been told there was a wife.

The day before the Tates left Washington, a party was hastily put together with Katherine Anne's "little crowd"—Léger, Denis Devlin, Eleanor Clark, and the sisters and the Tates. "Allen brought your portrait of him from the office, showed it, and then, up to their ears in strong drink, he left it," she wrote. "I know he will want it . . . it is a triumph."

William McGuire, in *Poetry's Catbird Seat,* published by the Library of Congress in 1988, states that Allen Tate emerged as the most influential figure in the early years of the consultantship, that he gave the office credibility with his peers, made recommendations of lasting significance in regard to appointments, and drew other poets to the library's cause by the force of his reputation and stature. And it was Tate to whom the Fellows turned as a leader and a spokesman.

November 29, 1944
Dear Tat,

Randolph seems to be more bothered by the cold weather than the war. When he was in that large château, the one in the middle of a pine forest, which was so dreary and dark, there was a heavy frost as early as October 4th. He wrote in the huge oak-paneled salon where there were stags' heads all over the place and said he was as cold as hell. Now he is in cold Luxembourg which, though very beautiful, is rugged and gets two meters of snow which he is not looking forward to if he has to spend the winter there. His main occupation is riding in a Jeep which can be an ordeal. He is living in another château which has been a monastery. A countess turned it over to the nuns after the Boches ran them out of their real home. Crucifixes all over the place but also boars' heads which evidently go back to some not so religious Count. On the way to Luxembourg in a car, he enjoyed a stop at Chartres, but was disappointed not to see the stained glass which had been buried since 1940. He also stopped in Paris. It is declared "off limits" to troops but he pulled his rank on the M.P. only to find that food is literally unobtainable. Wine was plentiful, however, so he sat outside a buvette opposite Notre Dame, ordered a bottle of Château d'Yquem and ate his K ration!

He says he is finding nothing inspiring about the war now and plenty that is depressing and phony, but says he wouldn't have missed it and it surely can't go on very much longer, although he sees nothing too encouraging in the news from where he is.

I will be at the station to meet you when you come so you won't have to take a taxi. They are crowded and sometimes you wait to get a Georgetown one. No one ever seems to live in Georgetown at such times, though, from the papers, one gets the idea that everyone lives here. There are those with chauffeurs of which I am not one. I wish you could have seen the Christmas calendar Mary made for her father. A whole day's work showing him boar hunting in the deep snow with a Christmas package in one hand and a rifle held high in the other.

Johnny has stopped being an angel and become a boy, like Pinocchio.

Love,
Marcella

December 2, 1944
Dear Tat,

The invitation to the possum hunt is inviting. How Mary and John would adore to come! Johnny wanted to get right on a train and come down. He is going through a tough stage now. When you come I am wondering how long it will be before he tells you he will "beat your teeth in"—this all came with the first grade and going with the boys he always stood in awe of before. For Christmas he wants a rifle, Dick gun, cowboy suit and airplanes.

I am going to serve at the Luxembourg booth for United Nations relief next Wednesday. Randolph writes that the Luxembourgers seem much more prosperous and unhurt than either the Belgians or the French. This is probably because they were incorporated into the Reich proper rather than treated as conquered people. He sent a copy of MEIN KAMPF which was captured at Brest where there was a whole warehouse full of them. Johnny was so fascinated with this touch of Hitler that he sat mesmerized with it for an hour. One would think he could read German the way he was turning the pages with great concentration.

Someone at a ritzy luncheon I went to yesterday said to me: "It must be wonderful to have such a *hobby* as painting" (how I hate the word "hobby" used for "profession"). I was pleased to retort that I had been occupied for a week looking for a dead rat in my basement.

The hostess told me that an architect friend, the one who designed the Apostolic Delegation, said my father was one of the really great ecclesiastical architects, and, if he hadn't died so young, would be very famous by now. Since he has been dead for 20 years it is seldom I hear such things, so I was pleased.

A nice card from Theodore Spencer who wrote: "Your cocktail party was great fun and I enjoyed your pictures greatly. I should of course be most pleased to sit to you—if ever there is time."

Love,
Marcella

I realize how unfortunate it is that there never was time for Spencer to sit, especially since I later painted his colleagues John Finley, Walter Jackson Bate, and Harry Levin, who were teaching English literature at Harvard and were all at Eliot House, where the portraits now hang.

On December 30, I wrote Katherine Anne,

Dear Katherine Anne,

When one says, "Writing Long Letter," on a Xmas card, of course no one is expected to believe it but I, being the soul of honor, am writing "long letter" before I even get my thank-you notes out. Since "Miss Annie" is with us now, hardly a day goes by that we don't talk about you. She is so fascinated with my stories about you. I wish you two could meet. Only today I told her she was taking to brandy the way you did when you came to stay with me. What is it about Georgetown that creates such a strong urge for brandy? I gave her a bottle of Pedro Domecq for Christmas and Mary told her grandmother yesterday that every time she looked at her she was drinking something. It's true. The Fundador is about gone. However, she has not yet taken it to bed! Sherry is more her thing as she won't touch hard liquor. For a while, the war news was so distressing, with our beloved Randolph in the very path of the advancing Germans, that we both imbibed heartily to drown our worry. With things going better, we are drinking out of pure joy. Of course it will be some time before we hear just what happened where he is. His last letter sounded tranquil, which I am sure he does to allay our fears. His V-Mail letter written on the 22nd says that they are finally able to get mail out for the first time in a week, and, although he was short on sleep, he thought they finally had got the situation under control.

Mrs. Winslow's new book of short stories comes out March 15th [1945]. The publishers seem quite enthusiastic from a few letters she let me read. Wilson Follett, on the editorial staff at Knopf, writes delightful letters to her, although she has never met him. She calls the book A WINTER IN GENEVA. That story draws on her experience living in Switzerland with Mary, her daughter, when Gen. Winslow was working on the Panama Canal. There is still fan mail from her last book, which gives her great satisfaction. She will be returning to Memphis as soon as spring beckons to get her garden going. Have I told you that Caresse Crosby is interested in my work? I know you aren't that interested in her after her behavior in Paris when you lived there, but she does have a flair, or is it courage masquerading as foolhardiness, or the other way around? At any rate, she has opened an art gallery near Connecticut Ave. and, judging by the first two shows she has put on, I am not sure I would care about a one-man show there myself. There is something so obviously arty about it—mainly the audience, or should we say, "clientele"? Yesterday, at an opening of one Sam Rosenberg, a sort of Doodlebug who draws eyes stuck onto fingers and wires, a *Life* photographer covered the scene. All the people (including myself) who wanted to be pictured in *Life* magazine crowded the rooms. I escaped to a back room and met up with a handsome naval officer who was having his first showing of naval action pastels, slick and pretty, and, while [I allowed] him to rave about them to me, someone brought Sam Rosenberg up to be introduced and we were snapped by the *Life* photographer! Not a chance I'll get in, but, if it does make the magazine, I'm the one with the drooping black feathers in my mouth, and the coat is my Saks 5th Ave. $135 number, bought with the West Point General. I want so bad to send it to Randolph to prove I am now going to the right places, even if they are the wrong people.

Our Christmas holiday has been a cozy if not an entirely happy one, on account of the war. The children have been wide-eyed and excited beyond belief, first for Christmas and now for snow. Mary got a transformed Pamo "lamb." She is fully convinced that Pamo's soul is inside a beautiful new blue bear's body. She doesn't know it is a bear, just thinks the ears got shorter and the body fatter. All she could say for days was: "We are such a happy pair!" Schwartz Fifth Ave. doesn't have the lamb anymore—the white lamb she has loved so much for four years. Mother is blooming as ever. All the rest of us pale into insignificance beside her. She had us all to a magnificent Christmas dinner. Mary and Johnny send their love, which they reserve in their best Anne Hutchinson-Winslow manner, for VERY special people, to their dear "Miss Pota," and I send my plain variety, which is none the less potent.

As ever,
Marcella

Bostonian Caresse Crosby's autobiography, written in 1953, was rightly named *The Passionate Years*. As coeditor, with her husband, Harry, of the 1920s' notorious Black Sun Press in Paris, she helped publish Joyce, Hemingway, Hart Crane, Gertrude Stein, Pound, Dali, and Picasso. In the 1940s, she opened an art gallery in Washington, became a patron of Mexican artists, and published *Portfolio,* a review. Caresse and her husband were members of the "lost generation" of Parisian fame—He less lost, since he was the nephew of J. P. Morgan. Malcolm Cowley made this rich amateur an emblem of the exiles of the 1920s after he became notorious for arranging a double suicide with a girlfriend. He was thirty-one at his death. Caresse died at the age of seventy-eight in a castle she had purchased near Rome in 1970.

Katherine Anne was intrigued by the relationship of Anne Hutchinson to the Winslows. She admired this religious liberal from England who had been banished from the Massachusetts Bay Colony for preaching salvation without church laws. Anne and all but one in her family were massacred by Indians. The son who escaped was an ancestor of the Winslows, one of these marrying John Copley, the painter. Katherine Anne expressed a desire to write a biography of Hutchinson after she finished her biography of Cotton Mather. Neither was ever done.

Mrs. Winslow came for Christmas of 1944 and stayed through March. Her letter to her daughter, Mary Chapman, says it was cold and icy, and that she had seldom been so glad to be where she was. Compared with the vast fireplaces in her house—a method of heating that needed strong men to lift huge logs—my coal furnace was a welcome relief, even if my efforts to keep it going sometimes failed. She wrote how much she enjoyed the parties given by the Robert Penn Warrens and how sorry she was not to have known them better when they were in Memphis. On a Sunday in January she wrote to Mary Chapman, "Marcella and children have gone to church, rain and all. She was up with the furnace at both ends of the night, and I found a note tacked to the bathroom door saying she was also up with a bat. It said: 'There is an animal concealed somewhere in this room.' She says if I tell her she didn't see one, she will not be able to bear it." This recalled the famous note I left for Monroe when he was working for me in Tennessee. Knowing how petrified he was of snakes and how important he was to us in the absence of Mrs. Winslow's servants, who were holding war jobs, I feared that the little snake I found one evening in the kitchen would send him back to Vicksburg on the next train. I carefully placed a pan over the small reptile with a note. The very large letters cautioned, "Monroe, do not lift the lid. There is an animal under here." That he could not read gave me pause, but I had to take the chance. It worked perfectly. Monroe knew a note had to mean something.

Anne Winslow and her daughter, Mary, wrote daily to each other, with news from both ends, always the weather and country matters (gardening and fence building) from Memphis, parties and the weather (icy winds but warm house) from Washington. Occasionally Mrs. Winslow included comments on visitors such as John Crowe Ransom, the poet and critic. About Ransom, she wrote, "We have been festive in his honor—a cocktail party. Nobody has tea anymore, it seems, but this time, a little less whiskey and a more sustained brand of conversation."

Ransom taught first at Vanderbilt University, in Nashville, and later at Kenyon College, in Ohio. At Vanderbilt his voice joined those of the Fugitive group, which included Allen Tate, Donald Davidson, and Robert

Penn Warren. At Kenyon he founded and edited the *Kenyon Review*. Among his pupils were Cleanth Brooks, Randall Jarrell, Robert Lowell, and Peter Taylor. His *Collected Poems* (New York, 1945) came out three months after his visit, so he obliged me by writing the last two stanzas of one of the recent poems it contained, "Painted Head," in my guest book. The title seemed appropriate in a painter's house.

> For Marcella Winslow . . .
> Beauty is of body:—
> The flesh contouring shallowly on a head
> Is a rock-garden, needing body's love
> And best bodiness to colorify
> The big blue birds sitting, and sea-shell flats
> And caves, and on the iron acropolis
> To spread the hyacinthine hair, and rear
> The olive garden for the nightingales.
> —John Crowe Ransom

Randolph's letters written after the Battle of the Bulge began to come in. He had not been able to write until December 27, and all mail going to him had been lost, since it was his outfit, the 8th Corps, that had taken the brunt of Hitler's counteroffensive in the Ardennes. His V-Mail letter said, "As you have undoubtedly heard, things have been rather exciting up here. This is the first time in a week that we have been able to get mail out, but all is well and I am fine though a bit short on sleep. I think we have finally got the situation under control." He said Christmas had been a bit dreary and that he was not as optimistic as the high command seemed to be. By New Year's Day things were quieter although it was bitterly cold, and he wrote that the boys up front were really suffering.

January 5, 1945
Dear Marce:
The slippers finally arrived yesterday and just in time as we have had a two day heavy snow about a foot and a half deep and it is very cold. I wear them inside my galoshes with two pairs of socks and they work fine. As you can probably imagine we have been moving about a good deal lately (and not all voluntarily either).

I am now in the biggest château yet—at least 50 rooms and decorated with very rococo furniture and the most amazing collection of boars' heads and stags' heads and horns and stuffed foxes you ever imagined. The owner, a Count, has moved into one wing and seems friendly although I am sure he must have collaborated to have prevented the Germans looting the place as they have done pretty universally.

Wish I could write the news which is nothing if not interesting but of course I can't.

Astonishingly, the Christmas package sent by my sister Eleanor got through to Randolph. Since the food supply had been erratic, the fruitcake tasted especially good.

Only the extreme northern part of the duchy of Luxembourg had been hit; most of the combat had been in Belgium. Fighting the weather proved to be more difficult than fighting the Germans, and finding shelter became as difficult as both together. In January, Randolph was living in a former sanitarium. The windows had been blown out, and the water and steam pipes were frozen. Most buildings had been shelled out of recognition. General Somervell, chief of the supply services, announced that winter clothing was on the way. Randolph felt that the general's reassurance would have been funny if it had not been so tragic. Injuries from frozen feet were running way ahead of gunshot wounds.

In early February, Randolph's disgust with the politics that had erupted increased. He wrote, "While we jockey with the British the Russians will probably win the war which will be fine, though disgraceful." His last letter was written on the twelfth of February saying he thought I should make my plans for the summer inasmuch as it would take months to ship all the troops out. A touch of sunshine had helped because they were about to bog down completely in the mud.

We were so happy at the thought of his return, after we received this letter, that we were not prepared for the telegram that came on March 6 announcing his death from pneumonia on February 24. Although the news was delayed, I remembered that I had been mysteriously ill on the very days he had been dying. With no discernible ailment, I had been unable to leave my bed, with a heart so heavy it had been painful. Mrs. Winslow said that I was overtired, but I had never before felt this way. I had not even been worried about Randolph, convinced that the worst was over. My last V-Mail letter to him was dated March 3. When it came back marked "Deceased," I found my words hard to believe. I had written, "After a spell of depression (unusual for me) I seem to be feeling that all is well once more, that you will be coming back to me one of these days—but the days and months go by and we are missing them—two years is too long to be without you." It was just as well that I had not been informed of Randolph's orders to return to the States on December 18: he had refused to leave his besieged outfit when the surprise blow overwhelmed them on December 16. I was proud of him for that, and for all the awards and commendations, but grieved most for our children, who would never know the richness their lives had lost. The letter that meant the most to me was from Randolph's adjutant, Captain Gordon Watts. He wrote that the relationship between a commanding officer and his adjutant at such a period is unique and that, going through the good and the rough times, he could judge well from the very first the deep loyalty, honest love, and respect from the regimental staff—that they would have gone through hellfire for Uncle Willy, as they called him. He judged Randolph singularly well balanced and tolerant, brilliant, with a vast store of knowledge, but as understanding of the simple men as of the army's "brassiest." Watts ended his six-page letter by telling of the "esprit de corps" engendered in the "Fightin'" 390th by Colonel Winslow, whose personal qualities built a family feeling among the officers which remained as a memorial to him.

As for Randolph's feeling about his place in the war, he wrote a letter to an old friend, who sent it to me after his death. It was written on October 10, 1944.

War is a messy business. I have been fighting the thing, man and boy now, from the beachhead on down through Normandy, St. Malo and out to Brest and thence up to Luxembourg, which is where I am now. Being a professional soldier with an introspective mind, I may not share the common outlook, but I am sorry to report that it is, for my money, no fun. The utter terror, however well controlled (and I flatter myself that mine has been moderately well concealed), which accompanies all the front line activity completely robs it of all pleasure. One is conscious only of the sickening fright which leaves you no room for thought, except for the craving to get it over with. Of course, after it is over there is a certain exhilaration and, no doubt, after the passage of time the whole thing will take on the glamour and excitement which will engender the garrulousness common to most veterans. The actual experience, however, is anything but pleasant.

After the first beachhead days we had a long nasty stalemate, particularly nasty because, while we were stymied, the casualties were awful. The so-called "bocage" was ideal for delaying tactics and the Germans were skillful as hell. Then we had the breakthrough and made the big run down the west coast of Normandy—exciting—but an engineer's nightmare. Even I was amazed at how fast the boys built the bridges. Then we split off from the rest of the war and took St. Malo and, finally, Brest. A tough show, even though it missed the headlines. The place was garrisoned by some 40,000 fanatical troops, and old Vauban fort with modern machine guns and 88's shooting was as formidable as in 1710. When we finally got in, the place was devastation. We got the port along with 38,000 prisoners. I suppose it was worth the price, but I am not sure. Now we have rejoined the war.

Mrs. Winslow stayed with me until April—very dismal days for us both as we tried to adjust to the insurmountable loss of son and husband. One of the letters she wrote in March to her daughter, Mary Chapman, describes a visit from Allen Tate that she tried to make cheerful.

Allen is now with us. Up here to talk over cultural relations with "Archie" [MacLeish] who wants him to represent same in France. "Declining," says Allen. "Why?" says I—for form's sake, since of course I knew already it was because he wouldn't have a free hand to teach the French his brand exclusively—he would much rather edit the *Sewanee Review,* with 1500 subscribers—a 100 more than when he took over (or is it 500?). "Where are most of them?" I asked in an underhanded manner—"South? —West Coast?" "East, almost entirely," he answered with poorly concealed pride. He, himself, is as delightful as ever, completely unspoiled, unchanged. Everybody seems to feel a little funny about Katherine Anne making two thousand a week doing something nebulous out in Hollywood. "Maybe she will advise him to take our play," I suggested. "I thought of that right off," he said frankly.

April 20, 1945
Dear Tat,

Your letter was very welcome. I hope, because food was available here, you will not find it unavailable where you are. As you say, the world is so beautiful and so sad. I find each day so much harder to get through without giving way to almost despair at some time. The full realization of losing Randolph seems to mount to unbearable proportions. I do everything mechanically and there is no letup at all of this heavy weight.

The latest on the literati. Sewanee—the Tates: all Caroline's Meriwether clan has descended to see Aunt Lu, and Caroline has gone so completely Meriwether that Allen and Nancy have to get out and leave them talking clan. In spite of all the company, Caroline has written a short story which will be published in *Harper's*. Allen is due here some time in May. Katherine Anne has bought a car to save the $7-a-day taxi fare and leads a quiet life, but is not well. I wish I could get up more joy over the close of the war in Europe. Such terribly momentous events, as the death of Hitler, Mussolini and Roosevelt seem to come as great anti-climaxes. And Randolph had to miss the fruits of victory after all his efforts! I am torn to pieces. I do hope you are eating and taking care of yourself.

Harriet Winslow is amazed that we didn't get invitations to the launching of the *Kearsarge* and intends to see "some Admiral" about it. She knows that the first *Kearsarge* launched was christened by Mary [Chapman] and apparently thinks the second one should be christened by Randolph's daughter, but I think Mary is too young, although I know she would be plenty strong enough to break the bottle!

I have been telling the children about the famous battle of the *Kearsarge* and the *Alabama* and Johnny is glad that his "big ancestor" won, although he is not sure he wanted the South to lose—they hardly understand what the Civil War was all about. They knew that the battle took place off the coast of Cherbourg because we have a copy of the painting Manet made at the time, which is now in the Philadelphia museum.

Love,
Marcella

Letters of condolence poured in after news of Randolph's death. So many of my old friends, fellow artists and teachers wrote to me—among them my former art teacher Alexander Kostellow, who taught me at the Carnegie School of Fine Arts, in Pittsburgh, and often visited us in Washington.

Randolph used to listen attentively to Kostellow's theories on plastic recession and, using only that knowledge and my best paints, made a composition of a lush nude holding a bowl of melons and entitled it *Multiplicity of Melons*. The work's title derived from an abstract painting we had seen at the Phillips Gallery. It had elicited from him the classic comment "I could do as well myself," and he had set out to prove he could, incorporating the artistic ideas he had picked up from me and my teacher. He told me he had worked over the composition so that certain lines drew your eye into the picture; he added that by drawing certain other lines, he had ensured that the eye could never get out again.

I learned of the painting only when I found it hanging over the mantel in my most expensive frame the day I returned from the hospital after the birth of John. I almost dropped the baby. Randolph did not stay to see me see it. He later related how he had moved my easel into the living room during the stifling days in July, 1938, where he painted stark-naked and unobserved. He resisted taking the picture down, holding that everyone would think Matisse had done it.

April 23, 1945
Dear Tat,

A lovely letter from Alexander Kostellow, who feels a distinct personal loss. He was so fond of Randolph—felt him to be more understanding of his theories than were my artist friends. Mournful, Nikolaki "gives me" one evening a week so I can go out.[1] He took the children for a walk last Sunday—very mournfully. Maybe he cheers up in the park.

I am glad your winter here was so comfortable, and also that Randolph knew you were enjoying being here. Your room will certainly be saved for you next winter, unless I hear to the contrary this fall. I took a nap there yesterday and realize how soothing and quiet the room is. The leaves now shade one of the windows, which is pleasant for warm weather.

I must go now and wrestle with the meat problem. A few pieces of bologna was all I could find recently. The children need sustenance for their playacting. For Mother's Day they put on for me an Indian Chief performance, complete with conversation—"ugh" and "how."

Love,
Marcella

1. Nikolaki—Nicholas Mimopoulos—was a Greek poet and scholar who had once given Greek lessons to Anne Winslow. He offered to sit with the children when I was invited out in the evening. I loved telling friends that my new sitter was a Greek philosopher, poet, and scientist who invented on my nights out.

The second book by Anne Goodwin Winslow, published by Knopf in the spring of 1945, was *A Winter in Geneva,* a collection of eight short stories presented as reminiscences. The title story was singled out in a number of reviews as Jamesian in its setting and theme. Mrs. Winslow's depiction of the American woman in Europe could easily have been drawn from her own experience, but she never explained her sources to anyone. Having the book come out at a gloomy time was a welcome distraction for us.

Many of my friends were convinced that they needed their portraits painted, or knew someone who did. That helped pass the days—days that had to be lived with no outward change. They are only a blur now. One of the sitters was Robert Penn Warren. I remember the sittings well, but have little recollection of the conversation. I wrote in a letter to Mrs. Winslow that I wished she were still in Washington to talk to Red while he sat for me—perhaps about the book he was then writing, *All the King's Men*. When the portrait was finished, I wrote that it was one of the few bright spots in my life, since it had turned out so well: "Only 9 × 12, but quite a nice head, all in browns and reds with a bright green background." I also mentioned that Warren had liked the reviews of her second book and planned to read the stories in the summer. My portrait of him was shown in Brentano's window in downtown Washington when *All the King's Men* came out to excellent reviews.

Mrs. Lucius Clay had me paint her pretty daughter-in-law, who considered having a portrait painted a glorious adventure. She didn't mind the tedium of finding the right pose. The decision was for three-quarter length, at $250, to be paid in installments. I invited Marjorie to come for one of the sittings and later wrote to Anne Winslow that she had been filling up at the font and "doing" the National Gallery and was chuck full of Art and Posterity and what not. After I had made a charcoal sketch of the pose, she suggested that it be put into the back of the frame. I visualized posterity thinking so little of Grandma they would rip her open.

April 25, 1945
Dear Tat,

Some dreary drizzly days and me at rock bottom. To think that I have merrily paddled around on the surface for so long!

Mrs. Biddle's talk on Poetry was canceled because of President Roosevelt's death. Rumors have it that there will be a new Attorney General so they may be leaving Washington. The President's death was a shock, coming so suddenly and at such a bad time. I feel sorry for the Trumans but he may be better than Dewey anyway.

I took the children to Lafayette Square to see the funeral procession and a few other people thought of the same thing, including young Douglas Fairbanks, just beside us. I felt it was something the children would always remember. Sad and solemn.

I am too full of the smell of turpentine. Not a canvas this time, but the bathroom. I am painting it blue like my clawfoot bathtub—up to the top of the doors and gray from there on. I may put a posy on the door panels. Since the bath has to be so familiar to us all, I am putting my soul into it.

Randolph's footlockers have arrived, some with the locks broken. I am giving most of the contents to the Luxembourg relief, but Lena is selling some. Strangely enough the only two things I broke down on were a golf score and a barrette of Mary's in his raincoat pocket.

The children are fine. Johnny is full of beans. He told me he wanted to be a boy scout but didn't want to start at the bottom!

Love,

Marcella

At one of the Winslow musicals I met Miss Grace Guest, assistant director of the Freer Gallery of Art, the museum on the Mall that specializes in Far Eastern collections and the work of James McNeill Whistler, including the famous Peacock Room he had decorated in London. Miss Guest had known Mr. Freer, having worked for him in Detroit, had supervised the installation of the collection when she came to Washington in 1920, and had aided its growth since that time. After her retirement, in 1946, the gallery published her book *Shiraz Paintings in the Sixteenth Century*.

Miss Guest lived a few houses from me on P Street and became my mentor, introducing me to the Dumbarton Oaks concerts (arranged by Mrs. Robert Woods Bliss), and the chamber-music Budapest String Quartets at the Library of Congress. Anne Winslow admired her more than anyone else she met in Washington, and we enjoyed the friends we met through her. Mrs. Winslow wrote to me, "Glad to hear of our beloved Miss Guest—our 'favorite person.' She is as wonderful as ever. Always shining. I so often think of the way she looked to me the first time I saw her—standing by your dining room table and telling something to make me laugh. She was so different from anybody I had ever seen—or have seen since."

May 2, 1945
Dear Tat,

Dear Miss Guest took me to hear the Budapest String Quartet at the Library of Congress. These concerts are a great treat since chamber music is my preference. She knows everybody. She introduced me to Millicent Todd Bingham, whose family knew Emily Dickinson. (Her mother is credited with helping to get Emily's poems published.) We always see her friend, Mrs. Eugene Meyer, who bought the first painting I sold in 1935—the year after I came to Washington.[1] Miss Guest tells me she owns a Cézanne, so I am in excellent company! I doubt that Mrs. Meyer would remember me or my painting, but I distinctly remember asking

$60 for the scene I did from our apartment window at 2222 Q St. of women hanging clothes in their yard, and was so pleased to sell it.[2]

I saw your good reviews in the *New York Times* and *Tribune* last Sunday. More "lady" stuff. Fanny Cheney likes best your story called "Memorandum." My favorite is "Allen Percy's Son." A number seem autobiographical, especially the title story, "A Winter in Geneva."

Love,

Marcella

1. Agnes Meyer was an accomplished writer, art connoisseur, lecturer, lobbyist, and philanthropist. She married Eugene Meyer, president of the Washington *Post,* and published a number of articles in that newspaper. In January, 1970, her three-page article on Charles Freer told of their common interest in oriental art and of his gallery, to which she had bequeathed some rare pieces from her collection. She was also responsible in 1935 for arranging an exhibit of the paintings of Washington artists to help them sell their work during the depression.

2. I learned in 1970 that Mrs. Meyer did remember buying my painting *Back Fences,* painted in 1935. She told me it had been hanging over the mantel in her office ever since. When I asked if she would permit me to come and photograph it, since I had no record of it, she wrote, "You may come and do anything you like with it since it is, after all, your painting." When I phoned to request a date, she said, "When you come, get them to show you the Cézanne." I learned after she died that she had willed *Back Fences* to her secretary of many years, Frances Landry, who had lived with it for so long—the only painting in her office.

575 Park Avenue
New York
May 7, 1945
Dear Tat,

This may seem incredible to you, but Mary and John and I came to New York to see the launching of the *Kearsarge.* The trip was all arranged through Mrs. Fitch, the Sponsor and wife of the Navy Commander, who apparently felt guilty about having taken the place of the descendants of Admiral John Ancrum Winslow who commanded the *Kearsarge* when it sank the *Alabama* in the Civil War. She blamed the oversight on the "new navy."

Harriet got us the train tickets and arranged for us to stay in her brother Pearson's apartment. It is very elegant, in the Beekman Hotel, so we can get service and breakfast sent up. Harriet was very emphatic about finding the key to the liquor cupboard! I gave a drink to the young aide who came to get us and drove us out to the Brooklyn Yard.

It started to pour just as the launching took place and we had to run. There was a huge crowd. The children were angelic. A real pleasure to show them off. A very nice man took an interest in them—the only children there—and spent a lot of time with us. When he heard we were from Washington, he asked if I knew his nephews, "the Rockefeller boys." He turned out to be Mr. Winthrop Aldrich, president of the Chase Manhattan Bank! He was amused when I said I thought he looked important. A darling, looks like "Life with Father." Just as we were warming up to what we should do on Sunday, and he had taken my address and said a Mrs. Richard Whitney would phone and advise the children (as they had never been to New York), a voice was heard over the crowd: W-I-N-T-H-R-O-P! So that was the end of that.

Mrs. Fitch was just lovely to us and said she wanted to have her picture taken with the present John Winslow, 7 years old. She was delighted with the idea of my giving an autographed photograph of the Admiral to the SS *Kearsarge* when it would be commissioned. That ship was the hugest thing I ever saw.

The children were made much of and took it quite in stride. In our special car (one of the Admiral's) we took back to New York some young decadent New Yorkers named Livermore. Mrs. L was so drunk she couldn't get her words out and had to be helped out of the car. Mary asked, "What made that lady talk so funny?" So I gave her a lesson on ladies and liquor. Very timely too.

Sunday John's godmother took us to lunch at Longchamps—wonderful steak at $2.20 and ice cream at .60—then we went up to Radio City Skyscraper and saw the city and took in a bit of the Metropolitan Museum and had tea, after which we took a bus along Riverside Drive. Mary said, "We are really doing things." Indeed we were.

Love,
Marcella

On May 11, 1945, Anne Goodwin Winslow wrote to me her thoughts on death.

Marcella,

You mustn't feel that you have to write, if you are too busy, or too sad. I will understand a spot of silence now and then. You say you "don't see how I stand it"; and I wish I could tell you. I would love to hand on to you some beautiful clear belief. But I am not good at that. There are so many things I cannot believe—more and more of them all the time. Hardly anything really is what it seems to be. All this death, for instance. I feel that we are in a darkened room where we see everything dimly, or not at all. If we could raise the blind, it would all look different. We would see all sorts of things we did not know were there. We might even see Randolph.

I am glad Allen [Tate] is coming. He will help you more than anybody. His thoughts can be trusted.

If you will accept a thought from Ernest Hemingway: "It was so much better to be gay, and it was a sign of something—it was like having immortality while you were still alive."

P Street, N.W.
Washington, D.C.
May 11, 1945
Dear Tat,

The first sunny day in weeks and Lena still home with pneumonia. I have been afraid of writing because of gloom which I do not want to impart since I know you have enough of your own. I am hoping these months are going to be as low as I can go so there won't be anywhere to go but UP. I simply cannot believe that I will never see Randolph again, but I awake with a sudden start with the horrible reality. How you can stand it with your 40 years of memories as stacked up against my ten I do not know.

For some weeks I have been receiving my letters to Randolph returned from overseas. I dread seeing the envelopes in my handwriting stamped "Deceased" and dread even more reading the contents, which so often contain enclosures from the children. One of the most appealing is from Johnny, which I know Randolph would not have been able to resist . . . the painfully written note will enchant you too: "Dear Daden . . . Please send tin dollars too me because I want Boxing Gloves very Badly But if you dont have that much Money You dont have to Send it But they will be real Boxing Gloves. Love Johnny."

Lena was here fortunately to get dinner the day Allen came to town. He was able to put away hamburgers (coaxed from Neams Market), asparagus, salad, fruit cup and cake which he loved. By the next day, after committee meetings and a dinner at the Huntington Cairnses (other guest, Mrs. Nicholas Longworth), he was developing dyspepsia and, by yesterday, he was definitely on the ragged edge. He said it was from anger at the stuffy members of the Rockefeller Foundation and the lack of lunch. However, when he and Betty [Fisher] came over for a spaghetti dinner, he was able to eat little dinner and looked rather green.

He left early but, from a telephone report this morning, he is now OK and all primed for a week in New York! In his usual gracious manner he sent the most gorgeous box of yellow tulips, pink gladioli, lavender sweet peas, and baby's breath, as well as red wine which we had for dinner last night.

Latest news from the literary front: Léger is in San Francisco and DOES read the translations Denis made of his work and found two very minute mistakes.

Caroline's short story in the June *Harper's* is not as good as the one she just finished and her book is postponed because of shortages. She still paints and the mean, dying aunt won't eat the food she cooks. She is cured of doing her noble duty. Nancy's husband, Percy Wood, is stationed on Admiral Halsey's flagship. Allen says because he is so good looking. Allen loves his work as editor of the *Sewanee Review* but is a little bored with Sewanee in general and considers buying a violin.

Your friend B—— came by and is much improved. Has a human coloring and is almost manly. He is the only one of your "pale young men" who is much in evidence these days.

Love,
Marcella

May 21, 1945
Dear Tat,

A delightful person named Helen Coxe has made a pleasant dent in my life. She appeared at my door telling me that Miss La Mont had told her I was going to Eaglesmere this summer, and she wanted to let me know that she would be there. Because she worries about her husband, who is in the army, she wanted to console me about Randolph. Although she didn't know I was a painter, when she saw my work she immediately asked me to paint her and even offered me the use of her sister's studio in Eaglesmere. She is from Philadelphia and was a student of Miss La Mont at a school in Connecticut, and came away with a copy of THE DWELLING PLACE from her. My Eaglesmere prospects for portraits may be rosy because of this fortuitous connection.

Randolph's decorations from the French Government came Saturday and are very handsome and imposing. They are for his help in the liberation of France. The copy was dated January, so R must have known about them but, of course, he never told us about any of the honors he received.

Katherine Biddle's talk on poetry has taken place. She was so natural—referred frequently to Robert Hillyer's article on poets in the *Saturday Review of Literature,* and spoke well of a young poet's first book, and read a lovely war poem of his. Francis sat near me and beamed with pride. Mrs. Arthur Paul, who knew her in earlier days in Philadelphia, said K had blossomed out amazingly here, as she used to be so shy and still never knows what to order for dinner.

We took in an Infantry show in Potomac Park for the 7th War Loan Drive. Hot sun but coolish breeze. After the infantry did its stuff with bazookas and flamethrowers, we sat on the banks of the Potomac and drank in the breeze. Johnny wants to do every little thing the way his Daden would do and keeps asking me what that would be. I had to dissuade him from wearing the medals, but I let him try them on.

Allen looked fine when he stopped by. He is on the wagon. Saw everyone in N.Y. of the "correct" literary group. Jean Stafford is enjoying her money and sitting back basking in glory after BOSTON ADVENTURE was published.

> Love,
> Marcella

May 23, 1945
Dear Tat,

I will order one of Randolph's photographs sent to you from Fayer in London. How fortunate he had those made by such a good photographer! They are all good but, since he had no vanity, he selected the least flattering one for me. Too bad Lady Vernon had to complicate matters by taking the best one! She writes me reams about him—the way he loved the days at Sudbury Hall when he could enjoy duck shooting on the pond and reading in the "long hall." He kept his rifle there by a window and once made an unbelievable shot, hitting a duck 200 yards away on the pond. She said he could often be found in the unused music room playing the piano. No doubt that kept him going, as he worried a lot about his black regiment and their problems.

Mother and I went to the Luxembourg Legation to meet Prime Minister (he is also Foreign Minister) Joseph Bech, who had just returned from the San Francisco conference. He is a great favorite with everybody and I can see why. We were entranced with his stories and his charm. He told us a lot about my father's great uncle, Michel Rodange, the Poet Laureate, who wrote a political fable called "Raynard." Apparently it made Rodange a lot of political enemies in his day, but Bech says he is adored by the younger generation. I hope some day the fable will be translated so we can read it. He told us that the Germans were within 12 miles of Luxembourg city but he wasn't worried because General Bradley was there.

He took all the information about R's grave at Foy and will attend to sending me the Luxembourg decoration for his work there.

Did I tell you Mrs. Biddle invited me to be her guest at her poetry reading? Harriet Winslow told her I wanted to paint her and Francis spoke up and asked, "Why doesn't she want to paint me?" Katherine then declared, "Certainly not. No one ever wanted to paint me before!" So it is in the bag.

Love,
Marcella

May 28, 1945
Dear Tat,

Marjorie Clay finds a small defect on Betty's mouth in her portrait that I considered finished. It will be removed today. I should have had on view the suggestions of a photographer, printed in 1887 in a New England newspaper, which applies to female sitters:

> When a lady sitting for a picture would compose her mouth to a serene and bland character, she should, just before entering the room, say "bosom." If, on the other hand, she wishes to assume a distinguished and noble bearing, not suggestive of sweetness, she should say "brush." If she wishes to make her mouth look small, she should say "flip," but if the mouth be already too small she must say "cabbage." Ladies may observe these rules with some advantage to their appearance.
>
> —*Quincy Patriot,* December 3, 1887

I think just before Betty entered my studio she must have said both "bosom" and "brush." But "brush" didn't work as well as "bosom," as she does look sweet.

Love,
Marcella

Roman Spring, the memoirs of Mrs. Winthrop Chanler, had been published by Little, Brown in 1934. That was just after my return from two years of art studies in Italy, so I was fascinated by her stories of growing up in Rome with her artist father, Luther Terry, who, in spite of his unreconstructed Calvinist views, lived out his life there. They were well-to-do, well known, and well connected, and there were few interesting people they did not meet. She wrote chapters about her prolific, very successful half brother, the writer F. Marion Crawford; her uncle Sam Ward, the famous and brilliant bon vivant New Yorker; old Roman families like the Orsini and the Borghese; and, especially interesting, her close friendship with the writers Henry James and Henry Adams. She described Adams as curiously shy, self-conscious, and inaccessible to foreigners, but very fond of children. He knew how to charm them and stimulate their half-awakened minds.

Her youngest daughter, when sixteen years old, went to stay with him in Washington, and Mrs. Chanler wrote in *Roman Spring* of a strange evening the young girl spent alone with him. "Adams began to talk, he spoke of all that lay on his mind, the mysteries of time and eternity, man and destiny, his aspiration and helplessness. At last he paused and said: 'Do you know why I have told you all this?' Of course she had no answer. 'It is because you would not understand a word of it and you will never quote me.'"

June 2, 1945
Dear Tat,

I went to tea at Mother's yesterday to meet a Miss Chanler and she said she had four irons and would sell me one. That is because my iron had just melted. My new laundress thought she had left the iron on "low" when she went out to hang some clothes, but, when she picked it up, the bottom fell off. There it was, when I saw it, molten lava, looking like one of Dali's watches, sort of wretchedly hanging over the laundry tub. I am glad to have the iron of Mrs. Winthrop Chanler's daughter who was the one "talked to" by Henry Adams.

I have always wanted to meet the mother since I read her book called ROMAN SPRING, but the daughter will do. She is a refreshing and charming person, very amusing. Here is the story of Clover Adams' suicide as

told by her mother: Mrs. Adams came of a family inclined to melancho-
lia. One evening she sat on Henry's lap, threw her arms around his neck,
and said, "Darling, I love you very much and I just took potassium
cyanide." Like Himmler, she died, but clothed in more than her socks,
I hope. She said Adams was rather precious and smug, but interesting,
of course. A bit abnormal, especially in his aloofness. Did you get traces
of that in reading THE EDUCATION OF HENRY ADAMS?

Love,
Marcella

June 4, 1945
Dear Tat,

Evan Fisher may be putting out more flags, but Betty is mad at him.
Seems he left for Guatemala without taking his per diem which he needs
to draw his pay, and had blithely overdrawn his account so that she has
not only had no money but has spent a small fortune in taxis and tele-
grams. Yesterday, in a hailstorm, I had a party for Betty's farewell. I had
asked her special friends and had not demurred when she asked if she
could bring Evan's English cousin, Lottie, even though this meant an
extra girl. However, I had not expected Lottie's mother, too, who came
without a by-your-leave. I had met the mother before and we had soon
exhausted our repertoires on each other. Lottie was very condescending
about looking at my paintings (she paints too) and the mother got in all
the bits about Lottie's portraits. After many mint juleps were partaken,
I was asked to lend my canvas stretcher to Lottie. Johnny and Peter were
playing wild-eyed commandos in the back yard all this time (no grass,
just gravel and nicely fixed up for prospective summer tenants), where
they had built barricades and the pebbles were flying like machine-gun
bullets.

Betty got out of her house finally and is staying in her Aunt Muffie's
apartment until some money turns up somewhere. I lent her two blankets and she was as thrilled as a refugee, Muffie being the kind of housekeeper who has blankets sent away for the summer. WILL the careless
husband find a house in Guatemala to bring his impoverished family to?

I am still wrestling with the meat problem. Be sure to send me any
red points you don't use. You people in the country are lucky about
meat and food in general.

Love,
Marcella

June 13, 1945
Dear Tat,

Nikolaki came in Thursday . . . an evening when he was sitting only for me. I stayed home. He brought a dozen eggs carrying them like jewels—got them from a Greek friend who deprived his restaurant clientele because of Mary and Johnny—who won't eat them—which I did not have the heart to tell him.

I had a few people for cocktails with the Robert Penn Warrens, all but one of them having been painted by me. We ended up having a showing for Mrs. Warren who couldn't make the stairs. First, Bill brought his own portrait down lovingly, and then Red offered to get Katherine Anne's portrait, and his, until they were all trekking up and down with everything. Red's had been framed so he took it to be photographed. It is nice that they never ask if the portraits are for sale. Perhaps that never occurs to them.

Mrs. Staunton, wife of one of Randolph's best friends, Colonel Staunton, came out with General Troy Middleton (R's commanding officer) to see me. She was the one who told me she had had such a vivid dream about her husband (so upset, so far away in thought and looking toward the battlefield) that she wrote him about it and found out it was the day Randolph had died. More of those currents.

The General is a sweet Southern gentleman. Regular army but retired now. He was a financial advisor at Louisiana State Un. in Baton Rouge. Has every medal going. He said Randolph was one of the finest officers he had ever known and had received the most superior ratings he had ever given anyone. Apparently Randolph would have emerged as a Brigadier General from all I have heard. Middleton had also gone against regulations and ordered a coffin made which was not being done then. He said they were in Bastogne at the breakthrough. Randolph was in great danger as the fighting was all around and he had to be on roads directing etc. The Corps was spread out 88 miles and Germans and Americans were all mixed up.

Every time the General would mention Randolph he would seem to be acknowledging his presence by nodding to his portrait (the one with me over the sofa which was hanging across from him), completely unaware, I'm sure, of this gesture of recognition.

Love,
Marcella

Although Randolph had expected the war to be over without a doubt by summer, he had not expected to be home by then, so I had made plans with my mother to take a cottage in Eaglesmere, Pennsylvania. We arrived there on June 22.

Seven Knots Cottage
Eaglesmere, Pa.
June 23, 1945
Dear Tat,

Left Washington at 10 o'clock. Arrived Eaglesmere about six. A perfect day for a ride through the most beautiful country. We went through Gettysburg, Harrisburg and Frederick (Maryland) and there isn't anything lovelier, or cleaner, or more luxurious than those rolling hills, farms and beautiful barns. On the drive Johnny asked if there was such a thing as a one-way mountain.

I told you there was to be a presentation of the Distinguished Service Medal just before I left D.C. at the War Department for me to accept in Randolph's name. General Robbins read the Citation which I am sending to you. Pictures were taken and were supposedly to be sent to the home papers. R and General Middleton were the only ones to receive the DSM from the 8th Corps. Apparently it is reserved for very special accomplishment, so the presentation is special too. A car was sent for us and we met all the brass hats. General Reybold, the chief of engineers, was supposed to present the medal, but he was called away just before we came. Robbins remembered you and General Winslow, and said Randolph, as a child, used to play with his boots at the War College.

The day before I left I had a last sitting on Diane Poel's portrait. I hadn't time to even look at it since I had repainted the head as I had to dash to Miles Reber's wedding, and was barbecuing a steak when Mrs. Poel came to pick it up. I was sure she wouldn't like it, and hadn't decided whether to tell her she couldn't have it or what I would do. Then she raved! Quite a surprise. The steak caught on fire and the mashed potatoes were soggy, but I had another $150. Mr. Poel is concerned about getting an "expert" to clean the picture every so often! They act like they had paid $1000 for it! They seem quite enraptured—or are you tired of being told that by me about my pictures?

Love,
Marcella

Mrs. Winslow had responded immediately to Johnny's request for "REAL boxing gloves." I thought they were awfully expensive, but Sears had two pairs for $7.75 and they arrived in time for his birthday on July 5. I had already told her that the only thing John wanted more than boxing gloves were sneakers (rubber soles, size C1), but they could not be found. He needed sneakers more than boxing gloves because he climbed on everything and boxing gloves require someone to box with and not climb on.

Eaglesmere provided enough combatants to suit even Johnny, so I took pictures of the bouts and sent Mrs. Winslow the shots with no bloody noses in evidence. In response to John's thanks to his grandmother, she answered, "I was crazy about your letter—all written in REAL WRITING."

In the library of the Lakeside Hotel in Eaglesmere, I found *An American Idyll,* a book written in 1920 by a writer unknown to me, Cornelia Stratton Parker, about the death of her husband, who had been an exceptional man. The analogies in our loss seemed exceptional: both husbands died of pneumonia after an idyllic ten-year marriage, at about the same age, and both were brilliant, promising men who could do everything and charm your socks off. I felt an impulse to write to her to find out how she survived her loss twenty-five years before, since I did not see how I could face my future. Taking a long chance, I wrote to her at the publisher's address and was surprised to receive a reply—an understanding, encouraging six-page letter, closely spaced in a large, bold handwriting. In part, she wrote,

Swiss Meadows.
Williamstown, Mass.
July 17, 1945
Dear Mrs. Winslow,

I wanted to answer your letter as soon as I finished reading it. If only we could sit down in front of my farmhouse fireplace and talk instead of this slow putting down of words on paper—Yes, I have been able to "pick up the pieces of a shattered life and find happiness and peace," as you put it. Time is very kind, it heals as nothing else can.

I thought back to how I felt five months after my husband died— my August 1918 was your July 6 1945. Nobody then could have made me believe that I would ever again know happiness or peace. I wrote the "Idyll" about then, because in my desperation it seemed it would help. Nothing helped nights nor Sunday. The relief of Monday!

I said time was—is—such a wonderful healer. I combined it with work. For one thing I had to earn money, for another it kept me thinking about something besides my own situation which then seemed all but impossible. I couldn't pull myself up out of the black when the next turn of a street brought me to some remembered experience with Carl.

I have found such peace and happiness in my 5 acre farm house— as I wanted our roots to go down someplace . . . along with the worst financial worries and never ending hard work I ever knew. I'm a toughened old woman of almost sixty, feeling like forty—or twenty . . . as far as my eagerness for each new day and all the labor it means. Children carry one along from problem to problem and keep one thinking or planning and, before you know it, you are having fun again with them. At first I almost resented the children and their insistent and unconscious intrusion into my desire to live in the past. Perhaps the formula for ever again feeling whole is time, children, work.

But right now, five months after your husband died—it's hard to believe there is any formula. Every day and night is a fight to keep from giving in to complete anguish. Many find comfort through God and prayer. I couldn't that way. I should have mentioned friends, new and old. I've gotten much out of the children's friends.

All I can tell you is that I KNOW you will feel very different a year from now. Time does that, with no help. But the children will help. And just life helps . . . all that is going on around you. I've seen women who don't seem to get hold of themselves. Invariably they are innately selfish and egoists.

Certainly life is never again lived on the same plane we once knew. But lower than such happiness is much indeed to make one glad to be alive.

My warm greeting to you,
Cornelia Parker

After that, I learned that Cornelia Stratton Parker (1885–1973) was an American writer and lecturer on labor problems. Anne Winslow remembered when *An American Idyll* (Boston, 1919) came out. She wrote, "Cornelia's father was a professor at the University of California, and she was a bit untamed, even for California—her children were left to 'express themselves' to the terror of all peaceful citizens etc., but I thought she did a bang-up job on the *Idyll*. She went on writing for the magazines, socialistic stuff—all well done. Lived in New York, disguised herself as a 'working girl' in steam laundries and whatnot to get her material." By September, 1941, *An American Idyll* had gone through thirteen impressions.

Seven Knots Cottage
Eaglesmere, Pa.
July 12, 1945
Dear Tat,

The enclosed thank-you from Johnny consumed about one hour—or as long as it took me to bake his birthday cake for his 7th. Mary wrote out the letters which he laboriously followed. Just before the "Love, John" he came to the kitchen and said he was worn out. You will just have to guess what the unwritten portions of the longer letter he *might* have written would be.

Needless to say, they are his proudest possession and such BEAUTIFUL boxing gloves I have never seen—REAL Boxing Gloves!

That evening John asked to wear them taking a walk. And he DID right into the fashionable Lakeside Hotel while we looked for books in the library. Of course he took them to bed too. Only one pair fortunately. Mary says they should take the place of Pamo with him. You have made a very happy boy. He should have them for years.

Love,
Marcella

Seven Knots Cottage
Eaglesmere, Pa.
July 15, 1945
Dear Tat,

Helen Coxe, who is lending me her sister's studio, has been so kind, introducing me to the Eaglesmere cave dwellers, most of whom she has known for ages. Her family has been coming here for many summers, since her father bought a lot of land when it was starting as a resort. I am painting Helen's two children and an Episcopal bishop!

You will never guess whom I met at a cocktail party, none other than Rosemary Paris, who had a story in the last *Sewanee Review!* Her husband is Arthur Mizener. He will have an article in the October issue on F. Scott Fitzgerald. They are a most attractive couple. He teaches English at Wells College and, of course, they are good friends of Katherine Anne and the Tates. I happened to mention Louise Bogan and some girl from New York said: "Oh, she was one of the four wives my uncle married!" So other people do it besides KAP. Writers HAVE been heard of here even if they haven't been read.

I am working on the portrait of another lady named Cox, spelled without the "e." The children call her "Hi-Hairdo Cox" to distinguish her from the other Coxe. She has been painted by the great English portraitist Augustus John—but I am not competing with him. She was cherry red for him. I am making more of her "line."

Johnny was so pleased when a little girl asked to see how far he could swim without a preserver. When he gets up in the morning he puts on his sailor hat before his pajamas are off, and then he asks for his hair to be brushed straight and not curly. He is Mary's shadow. Thinks everything she does is perfect—except she doesn't box so the gloves are now more make-believe than REAL.

Love,
Marcella

Seven Knots Cottage
Eaglesmere, Pa.
August 15, 1945
Dear Tat,

I have just returned from 7 o'clock mass, which was a double celebration for peace. Little Eaglesmere did the best it could in a wild spree of joy last evening when the news finally came through about Japan's surrender. Church bells rang, horns honked, sirens blew and the fire engine took all the children on rides around the lake! For a minute this morning I thought of all the tons of paper which must have been thrown in New York when I saw a few struggling lines of toilet paper on the main street! Having nothing personally to celebrate was hard in all the joy.

Love,
Marcella

Seven Knots Cottage
Eaglesmere, Pa.
September 16, 1945
Dear Tat,

Mary and her cousin Sara have gone back to Washington by themselves on the train as their grade school starts today. Johnny is utterly lost without them. He woke up in the middle of the night and asked:

"If two little girls got on a train and forgot their quarters to tip the porter what would happen?" He has been philosophical about his earache. I would hear him muttering through it all, "Life is Life," or, "I wish the end of the world would come." Etc.

You ask about the Augustus John woman. No, I didn't "torture" her face as you suggested. I don't want to spoil it. I was pleased that her sister-in-law liked mine BETTER than A. John's and asked me to paint one of her!

Allen writes that he had told Louise Bogan that she could ask me for KAP's room. She is taking Red Warren's place at the Library, but I am saving the room for you. He was to read a paper at Wells College in Aurora, N.Y. Says they have been well but weary—too many summer visitors and parties for, and by, people whose names he couldn't remember.

Enjoyed ANCESTORS' BROCADES by Millicent Todd Bingham but got a bit tired of Mr. Higginson. Would have preferred more gossip on family and Emily Dickinson, and less of vindicating her mother.

This has been a profitable summer for me. I have made $1430 which seems like a fortune. Every painting to Philadelphia—perhaps I should go there too.

Love,
Marcella

P Street, N.W.
Washington, D.C.
September 23, 1945
Dear Tat,

Back on P Street. Your understanding letter came yesterday at a point when I thought I would have to run back to Eaglesmere, run anywhere, and try to get away from everything—this house and my intolerable sorrow which, as you seem to know, bears down so terrifically at a homecoming. Randolph rushed back to me in everything I looked at, every thought I had. . . . To go on living like this is such utter misery that I hardly see how I can do it. I seem to get more and more hopelessly involved with this blank wall. My house particularly depresses me. I don't intend to stay on here if I can possibly help it after this year's lease is up. There are so many things that have to be done, as usual, that it tires me even to think of them. All this, in spite of the fact that I found the house as immaculate as a pin—everything as I had left it—and even a few improvements such as freshly laundered curtains in my bedroom!

The one bright spot in my life now—the only one—since temporarily I have gone sour on painting—is the children. They are so gay and attractive. Nothing bothers them at all and just hearing them chatter about nothing, in their joy at being together again cheers me up.

Helen Coxe, who has meant a lot to me, has gone back to Philadelphia. She is so vital and amusing. I helped her pull out of their rented furnished house down a block on P Street, and she needed SOME pulling. Things were found in drawers at the last minute. Everything too big to pack was just given away. I got a folding bar, a Dripolator, a beautiful black hat (I had given her my small hat embellished with your peacock feathers, which she had been smitten with), and the negligee she had worn that morning. The dozen champagne glasses I can't see myself using until Mary gets married!

Love,
Marcella

October 7, 1945
Dear Tat,

I am consumed with curiosity about KAP and "cette galère" since you forgot to enclose the clipping. I can't imagine whether it is very high or very low company she is keeping this time.

Mary Doherty had invited us all to gallery seats for the Nimitz parade from her office on Constitution Ave., and I wanted to take her the latest news about Katherine Anne.[1] However, it didn't matter as the parade went down Pennsylvania Ave. Instead we were left without anything except a good view of the 1928 airplanes which flew in formation overhead. Quite spectacular in itself. Johnny said: "I hate parades—I never see anything!" He no doubt will be marching in one himself some day, so I think he is entitled to a good seat.

I wish I could get in the mood to finish Carleton's book on the Roosevelts. I should do that instead of rereading THE DWELLING PLACE. What moods, what nostalgia, those familiar scenes and words evoke! I like it more every time I read it. I laugh again over Uncle Robert howling; or the servants' comments on your guests at teatime; or my one entrance when I ask where the flies go. I still want to know. I think that was a logical question after your remark that we would have tea outside "after the flies go."

Did you read that Lucius Clay is mentioned as a candidate to succeed Eisenhower as Supreme Commander of the United States forces in the European theater? I hope he gets the job because I would be a little closer to the top drawer in military circles.

More of Randolph's footlockers have come as well as a big carton with his bedding and all sizes and shapes of boots and rubbers. I had a man in to Kemtone the studio and wash windows. He not only charged me $8 a day, but stole two of R's coats. I asked him to return the next day and then called the police. I got only one coat back, by telling him he had taken it by mistake, but he spotted the police car and disappeared. I fear Randolph's watch and West Point ring were stolen when his things were packed.

Love,
Marcella

1. Mary Doherty was a supportive friend of Katherine Anne Porter and is said to be the model for the character Laura in *Flowering Judas*. A genuine Mexicophile, she embraced communism in order to help oppressed Mexicans.

October 28, 1945
Dear Tat,

There was a very good review of Caroline's book in the *New York Times*. Mary Doherty had a long letter from KAP which she brought over. It seems KAP is "settled" in a small apartment in Santa Monica spending her time sending sardines and coffee to the French—and just ABOUT to write something. KA says the film celebrities are dull as a group. She isn't affiliated with Hollywood now, but apparently is living on the proceeds of her recent work. She is in good health and has a maid! It is nice to know she is settled.

Yesterday I started a portrait of the young Sturgis girl. Because of Lena's illness, and ditto laundress, I have not had time to do much housecleaning, so I just asked her to step over the debris. The studio is uncluttered, however, nothing but the model stand and a table. Since the guy who stole R's coats left so precipitously, I have no one to move the heavy stuff—like Randolph's trunks.

Joe Battley, who is a General now, is the biggest help to me.[1] Anything I have wanted he has done immediately—getting me the name of the doctor in charge of R at the hospital, also checking on the theft of the watch and West Point ring. Everything else came back: the Surtees book given to him in England, your autographed books of THE DWELLING PLACE and the snapshots of the children. These were in the last trunk, along with his 6-guinea riding boots which he wore such a short time. But how good to know he had them—the wonderful fairy-tale fling in England!

Glad you are having a nice autumn. Knowing how much the outdoors means to you (the way you literally RAN to Dumbarton Oaks this spring where you found some respite) I can imagine the beauty you are taking in . . . but I couldn't bear to be there. I take the children to Dumbarton Oaks to see the chrysanthemums. They are a mass of golds and reds now—the trees the same, as far in the distance as one can see, a fiery forest.

Love,
Marcella

1. General Joseph Battley was a West Point friend of Randolph's. They shared an apartment while they were stationed in Honolulu after graduation.

November 5, 1945
Dear Tat,

Lena and I have been doing a man's work on this house. If it weren't for her I would not be heaving things around the way I am doing. Ever since Fred stole the coats Lena has been off men. She says: "Let's do it ourselves and then we won't have to depend on no mens."

When you come up bring along any nice old felt hats you have discarded, because I have found a wonderful hat-fixer-over. It is possible, sitting quietly, to have a new hat blossom on your head before you know it, with a punch here and a ribbon or feather there. For $11 I have two new hats made from one old one.

Can you tell me when you plan to come up? Nikolaki has never asked me what your plans are so I haven't told him you won't listen to reason. I would like you to be here when I have a party for the Fellows when they meet about December 8th. Mark Van Doren has resigned but there will be someone to take his place.

You and I are invited to a theatre party to see Ethel Barrymore and our mutual friend Craig Kelly, the good-looking actor I painted this summer.

State of the Union has even the N.Y. critics ecstatic. Such reviews I have never seen. No hope of getting a seat. I will get tickets for the Lunts in January.

Ken Fields is back from Europe and working on the Atomic Bomb under General Groves.[1] He was closely involved in the Remagen Bridge affair and has an outstanding record, almost equal to his being No. 1 at West Point and All-American Football.

I was delighted to get your note that Mr. Wilson Follett at Knopf wants your new book.[2] Something to look forward to—there are things to be thankful for.

The other day I told Johnny that his Daden knew the answer to everything. He quickly asked: "Did he know where flies go?"

Love,

Marcella

1. Brigadier General Kenneth Fields graduated from West Point in 1933 with more awards than anyone else except Douglas MacArthur. For four years he directed military atomic energy programs for the United States Atomic Energy Commission; for the next three years he was general manager of the commission itself. I have heard from his family of an interview in which he said, "It's there. Unfortunately the bomb was let loose on the world. . . . Whatever is physically possible man will discover. Some will want it for good and some for bad, but we have to live with it."

2. Wilson Follett (1887–1963), author of *Defender of the English Language,* and an editor at Knopf.

November 13, 1945

Dear Tat,

The news seems to be out now so I might as well tell you that Caroline and Allen are getting a divorce. I don't know if this will come as a surprise to you after our conversations of last winter, but apparently it has been brewing for a year. Allen has fallen in love with Elizabeth Hardwick (watch for her story in the next *Sewanee Review*) and of that, and all of it, lies many a story. Last winter was given over to Katherine Anne Porter, but this winter can be devoted entirely to the Tates when you come up!

One of the most amazing things is that Allen says KAP always has to take sides and in this she is on Caroline's side. All is now well between the two ladies, Caroline having deeply regretted the incident in Washington 1944 vs. Katherine Anne. There is something inevitable about it all. Allen and Caroline are still in love—he says the two loves have nothing to do with each other—but they can't live together. Those terrible scenes—can you believe all this, having seen them so many years together, inseparable? They have gone mad along with the rest of the world.

Johnny has gone back to your German Fairy Tales and can't wait for you to come and read some more to him. Today he took the book to school for a "read a book" review of the REAL story of Red Riding Hood. He says yours is his next favorite after MEIN KAMPF. As you wrote in it "Johnny's Kampf." He loves school and says it is "funner" to have a desk than to sit at a table.

Love,
Marcella

P.S. This divorce news explains a cryptic letter I had from Allen on October 23rd, in which he writes that he couldn't call me when he was in Washington for a day because he wouldn't have been able to suppress things that he wasn't ready to talk about at the time—that the most he could say was that Caroline had gone and might not come back. He ends with: "The other matter, which shook me so deeply when I saw you, will probably not come to anything. So there I am—wherever there is, which is simply nowhere." Now I can't remember what the "other matter" was!

November 23, 1945
Dear Tat,

I am so glad my house-settling episodes have amused you. When you say I am powerful, I am beginning to think you are right. To the amazement of a carpenter (so-called) who was pondering how to remove some large coat hooks, I pulled them out by the roots, so to speak, which also amazed me. I am at the place where I stop at nothing!

This man came from the hardware store which had sold me some paint which had not dried. I had followed the instructions carefully the night before, when I painted the linoleum on the vestibule floor, and I was confronted with the possibility of my important tea guests getting stuck in the entryway like the rabbit and the tar baby. The tea party was to show off my portrait of the Sturgis girl (daughter of Gen. Sam Sturgis) to friends and family, all of whom were unknown to me and whom I naturally wanted to impress. I did not want them to be put off by the shabby linoleum as they entered.

The paint can label made a promise of drying "immediately." Then why was my morning paper caught and fastened like a fly to flypaper on the floor? I was frantic. The hardware store which sold me the paint rose up to a man with suggestions and cluckings, but the only practical thing to me (in view of the imminent party) was a new piece of linoleum, since the paint would make a perfect cement for it. This I got done 10 minutes before the first guest arrived, little realizing what had been GOING ON, in the real sense of the word. In Johnny's way of expressing it—it was "REAL" linoleum!

The party was a big success. I got two commissions—to paint the son and daughter of General and Mrs. Philip Fleming.[1]

Today we had our second transit strike in two weeks. No streetcars or buses. I had to drive to get Lena and take her home as she stayed with the children when mother and I went to see *The Late George Apley*. That play should have remained a book—there isn't enough action.

A letter from KAP. She says she hasn't felt as well since she was 20! Still in California.

Love,
Marcella

1. Major General Philip B. Fleming (1887–1955), a graduate of West Point and in the Engineers, was administrator of the Federal Works Agency from 1941 to 1949.

November 28, 1945
Dear Tat,

A letter from Mark Van Doren wanting to know more about the Tate divorce. They were so shocked saying that the Tates were positively the last pair they expected would ever separate, much less divorce. He wrote that Caroline had called them from Princeton and told them there was "trouble," but they wondered if I knew the reason so they would know what to write them, not as gossip but because they really cared. Mark resigned from the Fellows. He says he isn't a librarian. He doesn't know when he will return to finish the portrait sittings, but he likes to think of himself in gold leaf even if parts of him are missing. He also wants to see the painting of Red Warren. I answered immediately telling him the little I knew but his thank-you note merely said: "and Allen was such a monogamist! . . . I think I won't go nuts."

Lena has been bringing me HER poetry. The most recent is titled "Why" and I will give it to you as she wrote it. (I want to keep the original.) Have I told you that Lena became a Catholic and I am her godmother?

> Why cant they treat these African
> like they are human bein, All
> they are doing now is treating
> them terrible mean
> Why is it that Man want to
> destroy another Man soul We
> Know it is Wrong in the bible
> We have been told.
> Why dont they remember they
> are going to die and go,
> I hope they don't forget they
> got to reap just what they sow.

I think we will soon have enough for a little booklet. I will send you the best ones.

Love,
Marcella

November 30, 1945
Dear Tat,

I am very pleased to have a painting accepted in the Phillips Gallery December show. It is the one of Mary having her hair brushed by Lena at the window. Do you remember how shocked you were when the painting slipped and Mary's face was wiped out? You said you had been holding your breath for fear I would lose the likeness and away it went! I'm not sure the second attempt was as good as the first, as I was tired by then—painting in one day, standing up, in that room and not using an easel—but I will never know as I never had time to judge the first face.

I had my family for Thanksgiving dinner and asked Nikolaki too. He always gets sad, instead of happy, on joyous occasions, and by the time dessert came on, his face was a mile long. He is better [at] less gay gatherings. Of course he was thinking of Randolph missing it and our missing him.

We haven't had too much time to "miss" Allen. I was amused last time he was here when, after much talk about his sleepless nights, he mentioned that he was still carrying in his pocket a long letter from Betty [Fisher] written in longhand so you can well understand why he hadn't read it. (I always brace myself for one of her letters.) He said he just couldn't get around to reading it. A constructive suggestion was then made by me. I offered to exchange the recent typewritten letter from Betty to you, which you sent to me, for his handwritten one, since I doubt he will EVER read it. He may be sorry that he didn't take me up on it.

Yesterday, Mary and Sara made a moving picture—a box with a curtain, carefully wallpapered inside. The movie, called *Human Murder,* was a strip of drawings like the Disney cartoons pulled across the opening. This was so successful that they made another one called *Human Love.* The next in the series will, naturally, be *Human Nature.*

Love,
Marcella

December 11, 1945
Dear Tat,

I am so glad about the interview for your new book, CLOUDY TROPHIES. What pictures it brings up!—you "playing" with the peacocks etc. I am glad the book is a novel, and especially because the scene is Washington. Let's hope for a best seller.

I will meet your train on the 15th. My house is cozy and warm. Plenty of coal in the bin. Get good and cold so you will be happier to be here. Better get your reservation before they crack down on civilian travel. Can you bring up some butter? The food situation is as bad as it ever was. I enclose a clipping about the butter famine—worse than during the war. Why would there be a national milk shortage? The local restaurant frequenters will have to do without. Apparently there is none in storage because it all went to the military.

The awards keep coming in, among them Chevalier of the Legion of Honor and Croix de Guerre with Palm from France, Croix de Guerre of Luxembourg, Officership in the Order of Leopold II and the Belgian Croix de Guerre with Palm as well as the Bronze Star which was held up before. I think I treasure most the letter signed by President Roosevelt since he died so soon after Randolph did. They are all put away in a drawer, these fancy documents and medals. I wonder who will ever look at them! Certainly R never would have although I'm sure he was thrilled to get them.

Helen Coxe is settled at her country place—at Penlyn, near Philadelphia—and hopes I can bring the children for a weekend. A friend told me it is a huge place (requires four house servants). When her 4-year-old son saw the house, after traveling around in the army all his life, he asked: "What's this hitched onto?"

Love,

Marcella

In December, 1945, Alfred Knopf paid us a visit. After telling us that he would let us know in advance (Mrs. Winslow said that Alfred did not proceed by indirection), he arrived on a busy afternoon while I was finishing a portrait of the young actor Craig Kelly, who was in a play with Ethel Barrymore and had a free afternoon. An account of this visit is in Mrs. Winslow's letter to her daughter:

In the afternoon came the great Alfred A. worse (and better) than anything you can imagine—huge green shirt—green handkerchief etc. Colorful! "How long can you stay? I want you to see my daughter-in-law's portraits," sez I. "An hour," sez he, looking at his watch. After which he settles himself in the big chair and has a lovely time for goodness knows how long—climbs to the studio room and recognizes the literati. Climbs down again and has fruitcake and sherry (hooray!) and from all I could gather, has no immediate idea of canceling my contract. Allen Tate came by and is so sunk in his woes that he is quite a wreck. You know he had nothing to lose in looks but he has lost it. He and Mr. Knopf both believe the end has come (atomically) but Alfred A. is too busy to notice the crack of doom and Allen rather likes the idea I believe.

When Knopf went to the studio he recognized Allen Tate, Mark Van Doren, Katherine Anne Porter, and Caroline Gordon, though he had not met any of them. Knopf wrote a nice letter to Mrs. Winslow about how she had come up to expectations and sent her the cover sketch for *Cloudy Trophies*.

LIFE MUST BE LIVED, 1946–1949

I stand face to face with
lost Love—my breath is life, the
rough, the smooth, the bright, the
drear.

—Robert Lowell, "No Hearing"

Katherine Anne Porter became very fond of my mother after the sleeping-pill episode and wrote to her frequently after she left Washington. In this letter, I am mentioned. Katherine Anne also tells of her arrival in Washington two years before.

843 6 Street
Santa Monica, Calif.
Dearest Honora,

The 21st of January, almost here, will be two years since I landed in the station at Washington, in what appeared to be a real madhouse, and spent the most awful night there—until four in the morning, trying to locate the Tates, who had invited me to stop with them. They had not got my telegram, had gone on a late Saturday night party. A little tired girl who had come from Alabama to meet her soldier husband and who was going overseas shortly, attached herself to me, and I must say her difficulties made mine seem nothing at all. I was getting the flu—that was my year for the flu, I had it three times—and when finally I got the Tates by telephone, they were drunk. I took a taxi and went out and slept on a canvas cot in the basement, and my Washington career was launched.

Golly, it seems a thousand years ago, further away than some things that happened when I was twenty. But that may be because more things have been crowded into the world's life than ever before in so short a time. And my little personal life has been as crowded and changing; and almost everybody I know has had such violent displacements and upheavals, a whole lifetime has gone into these little twenty-four months.

Santa Monica is still the nice little town I found it at first, but now I really have my affairs in order. After not knowing just where I was going to be—I have moved from hotel to hotel house to house four times, staying here or there wherever I could arrange. After my nice four months with my niece on 25th street, I landed—believe this—in a little birdcage of an apartment just six blocks from the sea, a semi-furnished affair, but complete with four little rooms (rent 65 dollars a month), and can stay here as long as I like. . . . If you had any lingering fears that I was going to join the goldplated-swimming-pool crowd, I hope this will disperse them. The place is full of sun and air (it doesn't smell like a house at all), is clean and quiet and the yard is full of oranges and lemons and almonds and a big peach tree . . . I have a new contract, at Paramount this time, working on a play about Madame Sans Gené. I work at home in a bright bay window, and just show at the studio now and then for a talk with my producer; nothing could be better, and I am still at that point where I hope I may even help make a good picture . . . we'll see about that. Of course it can't last, even shouldn't, perhaps, because this is not what I do, it must be temporary, but it is a great help. My health is perfect, I have not even sneezed once this year. I found a fabulous doctor who knew exactly what to do about me, and did it, and it is like a miracle. So when my work at Paramount is done, I shall just stay on and finish the novel and some other work. It would seem rather silly to change for the sake of changing just now—a thing I never held with anyway.

Sweet Marcella it seems to me has a very heavy load to carry. But what I always loved about her is just that vitality and faith in life. You may know, naturally, that I hope she may love and marry again, but it is just true that I never knew any one so purely in love as she was—simply wholehearted and wholeminded, a beautiful rare thing and maybe it can happen only once in a lifetime. Indeed, it doesn't happen at all to most persons.

I wish you would come to California for a little while. Just take a plane. It's so simple and there really is space to be got now. My niece flew back to New York—bless her, she was so full of sunshine and vitamins I thought she would take off ahead of the pilot—and last October I had a mad moment of thinking I would run up to New York and down to Washington for fifteen days, and had no trouble at all getting reservations. That is the one way to travel, anyhow . . . If I had my way, I'd never go anywhere that I couldn't reach either on foot or by plane . . . I am fed up on motor cars. An average of three people every day are killed outright in this vicinity, and who knows how many wounded in traffic accidents. I sold my car and depend on taxis. They are expensive, so I have a very good reason to back my natural love of just staying at home . . . I saw Elizabeth Bergner in *The Two Mrs. Carrolls,* a really pernicious piece of trash, and it was discouraging to see a great talent so egocentric and dishonest it would waste itself in such a play because it had an opportunity to show off in a few scenes . . .

I still hope I'll get back to Washington so Marcella can finish my portrait, which I loved. It flattered me, of course, and so my judgment might be too personal. But really, I do believe I can be impersonal enough to see that her painting, just the brush and color on canvas, was good . . . but I don't know anything about painting, I shouldn't talk about it . . . Well do come here if you can, I'd love to see you. Greetings to all and to you.

Katherine Anne

On Tuesday, January 1, 1946, Orville Prescott, a staff book reviewer for the New York *Times,* summed up the literary output in 1945. He wrote: "During the final climactic year of the second World War, while civilization was either saved by victory, or destroyed by the debut of the atomic bomb, the unprecedented book boom in the United States never flagged. Books sold as they never had before, to the public in fabulous quantities and to the movies for fabulous sums." He cited authors such as Steinbeck, Sinclair Lewis, Glenway Wescott, and William Maxwell, among many others, ending with, "Three of the year's best works of fiction were not novels at all . . . one of these being Anne Goodwin Winslow's one novelette and seven short stories, *A Winter in Geneva.*"

Mrs. Winslow was with us over Christmas. She enjoyed the play *The Magnificent Yankee,* with Louis Calhern playing Chief Justice Holmes and Dorothy Gish as Mrs. Holmes. Calhern was entertained by former Attorney General and Mrs. Francis Biddle at a reception for him after one of the performances, at which Chief Justice Fred Vinson and other Supreme Court justices were present. Material from Biddle's biography was used in the play, but he had not been to it during the previous year because he was serving as a judge at the Nuremberg trials.

As Mrs. Winslow said, the period of the play was the same as that of her new novel, *Cloudy Trophies,* and it gave a feeling of nostalgia for the "good old days." Discussing the play at an eggnog party at Harriet Winslow's house, Felix Frankfurter said that most people who knew Holmes thought he was portrayed very well by Calhern, but that Gish was not so much like Mrs. Holmes.

A letter from Mrs. Winslow to her daughter, Mary, in Memphis says,

"Allen Tate came to see us yesterday. He apologized (to Marcella) for Jack Daniel, and asked her if I minded very much. 'She doesn't like you drunk,' was her answer. All the same I am sure he thinks it winning and modern. He is leaving *Sewanee*, he says. Under a cloud, we gather. Caroline has an apartment in New York and is writing a mystery story. So she may be able to pay him alimony!" In fact Tate resigned as editor of the *Sewanee Review* in January, 1946, because of a scandal caused by his attentions to Elizabeth Hardwick and Alida Mayo, which brought about the divorce with Caroline.

In February, 1946, I started a portrait of Anne Winslow sitting by the front window in the living room with her hand on a book. In it she is wearing a deep blue sweater and is seated in profile in front of glass curtains, in her usual meditative pose. I had chosen a difficult setting that made me look into the light as I painted, and I was nearly blind from the snow outside but I managed to get a striking likeness. Her pose was so familiar to me—looking out on P Street, as I had seen her so often, her hand under her chin, determined that no hint of age must show. She was of an era when ladies she knew were described as beauties in their youth. Although she was pleased enough with my rendering, she really preferred portraits of other people. She never permitted photographs of herself unless the camera was at the long distance she herself decreed. The only time the portrait was reproduced was with her obituary. It amused her to think I might use a "mother-in-law for publicity."

A young Engineer officer, Tom Carruth, contributed to the distractions Anne Winslow and I were always looking for in early 1946. We first learned about him from the issue of the Washington *Post* of December 20, 1945, in which an article told of a number of German flags to be exhibited in the National Archives. The flags had been captured by a Major Carruth and presented to General Troy Middleton "in memory of the popular Staff Engineer of the 8th Corps, Colonel William Randolph Winslow," who had died after the Battle of the Bulge. When we finally succeeded in tracking down the elusive Major Carruth, we found him charming and informative and altogether amusing. He was an officer in the Corps of Engineers who had served under Colonel Winslow, and he soon became a steady visitor. Before he left Washington, he posed for me with all the military accoutrements he said had to be in the painting—a large war map, a revolver in a leather holster, and binoculars on a table. In the painting, he is wearing a trench coat with his uniform and seems to be remembering the astonishing things the Engineers accomplished in the war.

Mrs. Winslow left for Memphis at the first signs of spring to get her garden started.

It was in 1946 that Harriet Winslow introduced me to her friend Anne

Archbold, a colorful character who was a Standard Oil heiress, her father having been a partner of John D. Rockefeller. She lived in the house with the highest tax assessment in Washington. An Italianate mansion named Hillandale, her forty-four-room villa had a music room with two Steinway grand pianos and a pipe organ. The walls were hung with thirteenth-century tapestries and Sienese banners, and the house displayed many trophies of Mrs. Archbold's safaris. One was likely to run into a stuffed giraffe's neck in the sun porch (she shot it on her honeymoon; the feet were in the basement), along with an elephant's ivory tusks and an African drum. In 1939, she had a Chinese junk built—with an engine—so she could sail to the South Seas. This house with its thirty-eight acres is in the upper part of Georgetown; forty acres of the original tract had been donated to form Glover-Archbold Park soon after the house was built in 1922.

Harriet told me that when Ann Archbold discovered that her Irish husband was unfaithful, she ordered one of her father's oil tankers to come alongside his estate in Ireland to bring her and her four children back to the States, declaring that she would disinherit any who tried to see their father again. Then she resumed her maiden name.

Gretchen Green heard about me through Mrs. Archbold. She wanted an artist to design a mural for a room she was furnishing for returned service men in the United Nations Club, and approached me out of the blue by telephone in such a commanding way that there was no way I could not accede. Gretchen was a good friend of the sculptress Malvina Hoffman (1887–1966), for whom she had worked as an advance agent on an expedition looking for types that could be modeled for the Field Museum in Chicago. She took an early interest in serving humanity. Daughter of an itinerant preacher and granddaughter of a bishop, she was at one time a big sister to the poor, and operated a clinic at Tagore University, in India. She wrote a biography, *The Whole World and Company* (New York, 1936).

P Street, N.W.
Washington, D.C.
March 28, 1946
Dear Tat,

I have started my overmantel design for Gretchen Green at the United Nations Club. Her idea is to express PEACE which she visualizes as a world with a white dove pulling a transparent gray veil across it. I will paint it directly on the wall.

Today I am asked to the Archbolds to meet Malvina Hoffman, the sculptress whose work Mrs. Archbold prefers to all others.

Mary and her cousin Sara had a special privilege last week. Mother was given a box to an Artur Rubinstein concert to which we all went to hear the great man play Rachmaninoff. The girls were so excited and puffed up with importance. August Borglum (Mary's piano teacher) was also there in tux, as the guest of Mrs. Gertrude Whittall who, as it turns out, used to be a pupil of his in Omaha.[1]

Marjorie Clay is leaving for Germany to join Lucius. She came by yesterday and raved about your portrait. She said it has so much inward light.

Love,
Marcella

1. August Borglum told us that a concert-pianist pupil of his had met Rubinstein and said he could play absolutely anything from memory—selections from opera, symphonies, concertos. On hearing that, Johnny asked me, with that serious, big-eyed look, if Rubinstein could play "Swans on the Lake." Gertrude Whittall bequeathed a number of Stradivarius violins to the Library of Congress, as well as money for poetry readings, concerts, and literary events. She lived into her nineties and seldom missed the Budapest String Quartet, which played regularly in the Coolidge Auditorium.

April 2, 1946
Dear Tat,

I am going to retire to a nunnery as soon as I get the children launched in their respective careers. The more I see of people the more I'd like a quiet nunnery. This is brought on by my experience with the United Nations Club. Miss Gretchen Green is one of those rare wonderful souls who TRULY is not interested in anything for herself. I believe she is the first person I have ever met like that. She is furnishing a room in the club for a library, is giving it and doing all the work, and their attitude is WHY? My mural over the mantel is the theme she wanted, with the motto Wisdom Is the Principal Thing (her idea, all of it). Molly Thayer, in her column in the *Post* today says Gretchen Green is the only woman who lives permanently on Ellis Island—sleeping in a bed with 4 posts made from giraffe necks (perhaps Mrs. Archbold's contribution). She spent several years in India as a disciple and follower of the poet Rabindranath Tagore and is a founder of the school for Seeing Eye dogs.

Gretchen asked me to bring the children to tea at the Archbolds'.

She likes children, no doubt, unlike Mrs. Archbold who has disinherited some of hers, I understand. They were expected to play outdoors, of course. There is everything there—three large stone peacocks (easier to take care of than your unruly birds), and a swing from a big tree. Later they came into the tremendous drawing room and each took a piano. Luckily we were on the porch and couldn't hear them.

Sam L. M. C. Smith liked the portrait I just finished of his mother.[1] I had to paint it in their house since she turned her ankle coming down the turn on my stairs when he brought her over to see my work. In spite of the accident, Sam told me I was the first painter she was willing to sit to. I enjoyed being with her and the painting went quickly. Don't tell me I should push all my prospective sitters downstairs!

Sam has just bought a whole tract of land in Freeport, Maine, on the coast, 250 acres—a huge old house and small cottages. They hope to get artists and professional people to come in summer but want to keep the "resort" idea out of it.

Love,
Marcella

1. Sam and Eleanor Houston Smith were active in the arts, reared six children, and helped many causes.

April 6, 1946
Dear Tat,

The portrait of you, which I will refer to as Madame X, has been much admired. Even though you think it makes you look older than you want your admirers to know you are, it is right for future generations and so exactly YOU. I am sorry you won't use it for your publicity. I think the photograph Knopf took of you is so NON-you.

Johnny has a sore throat, and home from school, wanted me to give him something to do. I called from upstairs: "What do you want me to bring you?" He answered, "Never mind. I am reading a grown-up book now and don't want you to bother me." Fifteen minutes later I saw him deep in a very small brown book and the title was SONNETS FROM THE PORTUGUESE! He said it was like all grown-up books, all about love and God.

I started a painting of Dumbarton Oaks. I got permission from Mr. Thatcher (who is in charge of the place) when I met him at the Archbolds.

He is an attractive bachelor and I should have liked him to have asked me, à la Carruth, to a hunt in Virginia, or a prizefight, or an ice-skating contest—or even to walk through Dumbarton Oaks. But, alas! he didn't. (There is no lineup at the door, not even three, much less thirty, as you seemed to expect.) He told me the magnolia was shedding fast, so I tore up there the following day. It will be a view of the whole mansion, a group of trees, and a long view of that grassy green lawn leading up to it.

Mrs. Archbold and Gretchen Green asked me to a party which GG says they, and the fruit trees, are giving for 100 people. There will be a guitarist playing, Generals and Air Marshals etc. Gretchen runs to Air Marshals. I went to Fredrica's house today. She is still decorating—both doorways are to be draped. Freddy's slogan should be "Be draped or be damned."

Tea at Pauline [Dodd]'s. Her husband looks older. In fact, he looks like Louis Calhern as Justice Holmes in the last act [of *The Magnificent Yankee*].

I have been grateful for my new boarder since paying my numerous bills. He is a very neat and erudite former professor of English. We leave each other little notes, and his room is a model of a model English teacher. Slippers carefully put away heel to heel in his cupboard, and not a single thing in view in the room except the large copy of his Ph.D. thesis on Whittier's Early Boyhood. He, so far, has treated me as a somewhat errant pupil, giving me to understand how fortunate I am to have him for just the length of time I want to rent the room.

Incidentally, he got me down to $10 a week, even though he was told $12 beforehand. The last little note left on the maple table (the "mepple table" is where all little notes are left) told me he would be back Sunday before midnight. He is going to be smelling turpentine—I haven't warned him—because the hall is being painted. Not bad: $10 for a pale cream in the kitchen, $15 for all the hall, which includes nine doors altogether, and $22 for the children's room. Can you believe it—with those high ceilings?

Lena is the usual great help, but I think she is getting ready to collapse. Since that day when I had to admonish her for coming so late, which I had never done before, and she almost left me, we have been so nice to each other. She brings me a stick of butter, if she ever finds it, and I give her chocolate. She allows me more minutes' grace before dinner, and I insist on her taking sick leave. Perhaps this is the way it is meant to be. Don't miss Evelyn Waugh's letter in *Life* magazine.

Love,
Marcella

April 12, 1946
Dear Tat,

Allen stopped in here Sunday, driving to Princeton for his wedding. He was as excited as a new groom and bubbling over. It seems he has been "courtin Caaline" since his last visit here. Maybe we did some good talking to him—though the remarriage was inevitable. He will be editing prestige books for Henry Holt publishers in New York. The wedding was on the 8th. No doubt you got the printed announcement? THIS IS TO ANNOUNCE THE MARRIAGE OF MISS CAROLINE GORDON TO ALLEN TATE ESQUIRE April 8, 1946, IN PRINCETON, NEW JERSEY. THE CEREMONY WAS PERFORMED BY THE MINISTER WHO OFFICIATED AT THE WEDDING OF THE COUPLE'S DAUGHTER. Second wedding after one divorce. Same people.

George Hamilton, the nice man who takes people on tour at the Phillips Gallery every week, was brought over one evening by Miss Guest, who knows all the art people in town, and he liked your portrait. His taste is neither conservative nor modern, and he is an excellent critic. He thought the portrait of Caroline had the best composition with the dog, and would be the kind of modern portrait that could get in the exhibits of today.

I had luncheon with Mrs. Denis who has taken a country place which belonged to the Mrs. Minnegerode Andrews (a Washington cave dweller) who wrote the book you read about Washington. A nice old house, but all the old paintings, which may have passed for good once, hang around like ghosts—family portraits and dados painted with cherubs and vines and Auld Lang Syne poems. Depressing to me, but reminiscent of very old Washington and the way it must have been not too many years ago.

The illegible note enclosed is from one of your fans. Have you ever seen more aggravating handwriting? She liked THE DWELLING PLACE but is sorry you didn't include the Spice Round recipe. I am telling you this in case you never read the note.

Since you like to think of me in bed I will tell you straight off that is where I am writing so-o relaxed after a successful day of painting. Successful art-wise, not the way you may imagine. Today I started an oil of Gretchen Green who agreed to let me paint her seated in a window-seat in the upper hall of Anne Archbold's house. She is wearing an exotic robe (the kind one picks up on foreign travel) and is holding a sprig of flowers and gazes out the window where wisteria is visible. She is shown three-quarter view and there is quite a bit of architecture—the window and long hall, at the end of which is a flight of steps. I decided to take Mary over and show her coming down them at a distance. It is a good touch; with Gretchen, humanity is ever present.

Yesterday the mansion Dumbarton Oaks "sat" again for me. Not as much trouble as painting people, I find, and far more amenable.

Love,
Marcella

Marceil and Russell ——— had two grand pianos in their living room and played them together on musical evenings to delight their guests. Marceil gave music lessons. She was very efficient and a great arranger, particularly of me, letting me know that if I did not get Mary into Miss Shippen's dancing class she might never meet the "right" boys. Mary (taller than any of the boys) stood it for a while, but when she left, a full scholarship was offered to Johnny—the only stipulation being that he would be expected to attend every class, unless, I inferred, he was in the last stages of pneumonia.

Russell decided to have me paint his portrait as a surprise birthday gift to Marceil, but when it was completed, she was definitely nonplussed.

April 14, 1946
Dear Tat,

Marceil has finally gotten used to the idea of the "surprise" portrait. It was a dash to Russell's ego, after she worked to get herself pleased over it, to have her say he looked too young—even though he laughed heartily over the remark. She hasn't been well. She says her throat is her Achilles' heel.

Mary is in another painting too. I took my easel into the living room to paint her having her piano lesson with August Borglum. What a nice man he is! Mrs. Whittall must have enjoyed her lessons with him. (Brother of Gutzun—famous sculptor of presidents' faces on rocks at Mt. Rushmore, South Dakota.) I'm sure you know.

Love,
Marcella

In 1943 Malvina Hoffman's popular autobiography, *Heads and Tales,* was published, dedicated to Paderewski. It told of her very successful career as a sculptress studying with Gutzun Borglum and then Auguste Rodin, and attaining the greatest fame with her interpretations of the famous ballerina Pavlova, a good friend. Her most courageous project was a lifework in itself, begun in 1930 for the hall of the Field Museum in Chicago—a hundred bronzes of racial types drawn from all over the world.

April 16, 1946

Dear Tat,

I have bought Malvina Hoffman's book HEADS AND TALES, in which she mentions Gretchen Green often. I want you to read it. G brought Malvina, who was visiting Anne Archbold, over to see me, and I showed her the life mask of Randolph that you all made for fun one time, and wrote about in the THE DWELLING PLACE, and I asked her if she knew of some student who could make a head from the mask. Since his forehead was one of his best features I have always been sorry it was not more in evidence. To my great surprise, she said she would oversee having it done and asked for a photograph and one of his hats. I gave her his overseas cap. I may be paying for it for years, but I don't think she cares. Her price for a death mask alone is in the thousands so we mustn't mention it. I would go to New York to pass on it before it is finished. I could trust her to do the best possible, and would mortgage anything to have a fine head of Randolph.

Dinner with some interesting young things—would-be poets. Around the fire they spouted poetry all evening in a most spontaneous manner. From Vachel Lindsay to E. E. Cummings, but NOT to Allen Tate. One of them, a Tom Riggs, knows the whole Tate family and mentioned the last scandal—as having been the cause of the divorce. No one understands anything about it, but they will all give their respective versions—which is not too good for the Tates. Or is it? They seemed to feel that Allen's poetry was too cold and intellectual, which means, no doubt, they probably have a healthy respect for it, but no love.

Went to a cocktail party which Alex Böker gave at the house of Penelope Saltonstall Pattee, niece of Senator Saltonstall.[1]

In fact, this odd knowledge is all I carried away with me from a huge crush of people, all of whom looked like most people one sees at cocktail parties. No. There were some nice-looking girls and some nice old professors. One, a German from Marburg and a research historian, told me that my friend the very distinguished Max Dessoir [a famous professor in Germany], whom I had met on a boat going to Europe, had died a natural death. I was worried about him since he was Jewish. He had written me a most enigmatic Christmas card: "Sometimes on one leg, sometimes on two. Something to think of, something to do." Perhaps avoiding the Nazis?

Love,

Marcella

1. When Alex Böker had finished his studies in Oxford in 1937, he came to this country to avoid Nazi Germany and, while in Memphis, made a living teaching at Southwestern University. He spent most of the war years in the United States, mostly at Harvard, and became a diplomat after he returned to Germany in 1949. In Memphis, he became devoted to Anne Winslow, appearing at Goodwinslow on all occasions, accompanied by friends who enjoyed the literary atmosphere. His was not the group we always referred to as her "pale young men," who were most often to be found clutching their manuscripts while enjoying the same atmosphere.

April 24, 1946
Dear Tat,

Today was HOT and I had promised to take the children to the country in spite of the pain I had from sitting in poison ivy. Having sat in it to begin with, I am now unable to sit at all! After a long wait at the doctor's office, I came home to see the children sitting patiently—or just the opposite—so I didn't have the heart to tell them that the doctor said I shouldn't go near a plant of ANY kind.

Friday, Johnny is having some of his friends over. I can't tell you how the prospect of entertaining 8-year-old boys frightens me! The last time J had a friend over he called and asked me to tell the boy to get off the balcony rail as, Johnny said: "We don't want to pay for him if he falls off."

Sam and Frances Sturgis (he is now a General) came to see me.[1] Sam had such a long siege in the Pacific. He is another, like Carruth, who can tell us the true facts about the war. Said he had heard that Middleton's and Collins' Corps were the best in Europe. That same evening dear Dr. Fairbank (Mary's teeth straightener) came in with two $50 bills and 5 twenties! He hasn't even seen the portrait he asked me to do of his daughter and baby. The money does come in at low tide. It always has for me, so I seldom worry.

My very UNdear top-floor boarder left me a note I wanted to stuff down his throat. He suggested that he have a change of linen. The week previous he had been here only two nights on pristine sheets. He is insisting on his money's worth—$10 a week! Every week he brings one book and leaves it neatly on his bureau. He is now reading THE LIFE OF JACKSON. Last week it was Thomas Mann. I would suspect him of being a Nazi spy, as he looks so Germanic, but he could probably prove that his family came over on the Mayflower. It is so nice to dislike him heartily.

The children went horseback riding today so tomorrow none of us will be able to sit.

Love,
Marcella

1. General Samuel Sturgis was an officer of the Engineers whom Randolph worked with in Vicksburg, Mississippi, in 1941–1942. He became chief of engineers.

One of the most beautiful, authentic Federal houses in Georgetown, at N and 34th streets, was bought by the Noel Macys, of New York, in late 1945. Mr. Macy organized, and was the first president of, the Foundation of Historic Georgetown. Mrs. Macy, who still lives in the house, opens it for yearly tours of Georgetown houses and continues to welcome my use of the fabulous studio on the top floor. I feel that in painting there for over forty years, I have been not exactly an artist in residence but more like an artist in the attic. I can, and do, say I am the living proof of their generosity.

May 4, 1946

Dear Tat,

Excellent news which verges on the fantastic. I have been offered a beautiful studio in a private house complete with revolving model stand and velvet backgrounds! Don't gasp. It happened because a Mrs. Albrecht (whom I "picked up" on the day coach coming from New York after my West Point job painting General Wilby) had me to lunch to meet an old friend from New York, Mrs. Noel Macy, who has just been married and whose husband has bought a house in Georgetown near my mother's at N and 34th Street.[1] The house is in the row of identical red brick ones with garlands on the front. Try to remember that I pointed out to you the big window on the rear that I said must be a studio the day we walked down 34th St., and asked if you could imagine anyone lucky enough to work in such a studio. There is a side gate and a back entrance, but Mrs. Macy is going to give me a key to the front door. It seems she has wished someone would use the studio.

The studio window had been put in the old Federal house by the former owner, John De Blois Wack, whose wife painted. They were here for the war years from California. Attractive, charming Mrs. Macy is a bride of eight months. I told her I would like to paint her or the house or the husband or the pets or anything she liked for the use of the studio. With such a light, I could become a sensation!

My party for Johnny's friends was a WHOOPING, HOWLING success. Yesterday I took Mary and John through Dumbarton Oaks Park (not garden) which is like walking into paradise. The paths took us as far as the Naval Observatory. A sign said we were leaving the cultivated part and going into the bird sanctuary. Mary was fascinated, as she is with all signs, and on coming into a clearing, exclaimed: "Oh, look! there is civilization having a picnic!" The Misses Winslow are having one of those frightening musicals on May 12, to which I am invited.

Love, Marcella

1. During World War II, J. Noel Macy worked in the United States Information Agency in the State Department. A Quaker, with roots in Nantucket, he grew up in New York in a prominent family. His grandfather was associated with John D. Rockefeller, in oil. The grandson owned newspapers in Westchester County, known informally as the "Macy chain."

Harriet Winslow's sister, Mary, arranged for my mother-in-law and me to have tea with Mrs. Jouett Shouse, who wanted to meet Mary's cousin, Anne Winslow, whose books she was enjoying. We found Katherine Filene Shouse to be a delightful person, very interested in the arts, particularly music. We were not surprised to hear, later, of her plan to give a hundred acres of her Virginia property, Wolf Trap Farm, to the United States government as a cultural park for the performance of concerts and operas and other artistic events. After the war, Kay Shouse founded the General Lucius Clay Fund to educate young German musicians. She had been the first woman to be awarded an M.A. from Harvard's Graduate School of Education. Her husband had been President Wilson's assistant secretary of the treasury, as well as Democratic chairman from 1929 to 1932.

May 6, 1946
Dear Tat,

The Jouett Shouses have moved from Georgetown to F Street, across from the F Street Club downtown. Mrs. Shouse is putting on a "Have Fun Carnival" at her country place in Virginia, which she calls Wolf Trap Farm. She has asked me to help out. The Hon. Mr. Shouse has told me he would like me to paint Kay, if I can catch her, and I can consider it a commission. Catching her will be the problem. She is not keen on the idea.

I completed Gretchen Green's portrait in two sittings and Jocelyn Fleming's has been hung in their house. Both gathering compliments. Miss Grace Guest told me I could paint her—at the Freer Gallery, in her office. She plans to retire soon.

Love,
Marcella

May 20, 1946
Dear Tat,

In preparation for making a painting of Miss Guest in her office at the Freer Gallery, I was making a sketch for the pose, when David Fentress was announced. Knowing David over the years, you may not be surprised to know that he had come with a small bronze, for which he had paid 25 cents, and which, he had been told by someone who knows Chinese, . . . was Ming or some other dynasty. He wanted the Freer Gallery to tell him that he had stumbled on a rare treasure. Miss

Guest told him it was a nice copy and we went home to lunch. David looks so dried up and old. Since it has been so long since I have seen him, I was not prepared either for his size, which seemed inadequate, or for his conversation, which was mellow and charitable. David has finally snatched his mother right out of his father's hands and packed his father off to Memphis! Somehow, I was reminded of your peacock Old Eye relegating Fine Chick to the backyard.

Malvina Hoffman has the head of Randolph ready to be seen, so I will go to New York when I arrange things here. She kindly wrote to Portraits Inc. to tell them I do portraits, so I will take some paintings when I go. She thinks it would be wise to have Randolph's head cast in bronze now. She said she would give her note at the foundry and I can pay her when I have some good luck with portraits—that there is no hurry. What an amazing woman!

I am asked to Wolf Trap on June 4 to talk over plans for the Carnival on the 8th. Mrs. Shouse is very deep in it but I hope she will find time to pose for me to please her husband.

Miss Guest took me to a beautiful concert where I saw Harriet Winslow and Mrs. Eugene Meyer. The latter was telling us about the special articles she is writing for the *Washington Post*. I do not know if you would care about reading more of her articles on the South, since you wondered why she wanted to do one on Boss Crump. Miss Guest said her pieces on the Kentucky coal mines are magnificent. They had been planned long before John L. Lewis got obstreperous. Mrs. Meyer says she wants to see my portrait of Miss Guest when it is finished. She already owns one of my paintings.

Love,
Marcella

David Fentress had been one of the perennial visitors and standbys at Good-winslow, completely attuned to its ways and its occupants. Sometimes in the Winslows' absence he would take over and run the whole place, so he felt almost one of the family, which was the way the Winslows felt about him. In their creative endeavors he was the first to take part.

Cloudy Trophies, Anne Winslow's first novel but third book published by Knopf, came out in May, 1946. On June 21, Orville Prescott again devoted his entire column to the review of a book by Mrs. Winslow. He felt that "this beautiful but baffling little novel" was more a display of Mrs.

Winslow's allusiveness than a creative work of fiction, that in spite of her cultivated mind and her alluring prose style, the central situation was smothered by subtleties of expression and an evasion of issues. "The characters think interesting thoughts, well expressed but are shadows without flesh and blood." He wrote that those who prefer writers like Edith Wharton, Henry James, and Katherine Anne Porter should admire Mrs. Winslow, although she was not really like them. He also wrote that the beauty and the wisdom and the wit of this novel would have been more effective as a short story or elaborated into an essay.

The action takes place in the quasi-southern town of Washington and in Mississippi at the turn of the century. Most of the reviews were complimentary about the author's craftsmanship and understanding and commented on her philosophical musings about the mysteries of time, life, memory, loss, and death and on her literary allusions.

May 31, 1946
Dear Tat,

This IS going to be difficult, knowing where to begin. I should have dashed off a note as soon as I got back from New York but I sat down and read CLOUDY TROPHIES 3/4 through. I wanted to give you my impressions fresh but had to write Malvina Hoffman which has taken a lot of starch out of me, so I will finish the book later. This is just for straight news: I drove with Mrs. Albrecht to New York last Friday in spite of the Railroad strike, or because of it, since I refuse to let labor unions interfere with my plans—and arrived about 4:30 (adding an hour for daylight saving). I got to MH's studio in time for tea. The light was waning but there was Randolph, or almost Randolph. With a half hour of suggestions, she made it right. She seemed to sense my corrections of the head. After dinner with Gretchen Green in a small restaurant nearby, we returned to the studio and, in the dim light, the resemblance was startling, even in that dull Plasticine. We spent the evening in her quiet third-floor living room and it was perfect.

Malvina amused us by telling us stories about her last sitter, the great tycoon Thomas Watson, President of International Business Machines, then showed us through her large place. She has the whole building, with three or four studios in which there are replicas of most of her famous statues, as well as a few things of Mestrovic (the Yugoslavian sculptor she studied with) that he had given her. She gets $2500 for just a bust.

She has Randolph's head slightly tilted—with the whole neck showing. No shoulders. The question now is whether I can afford to have it cast in bronze. That procedure alone costs $250. A colored plaster made to look like bronze wouldn't be permanent of course. I told her I would let her know. You could have a plaster if you wanted one. She said it would be easier to have the two done at once, but of course you would want to see a photograph first. So far I have given her two checks for $50. She said I could pay any time I felt I could manage it. The only price she ever mentioned was $250, so I am presuming—or hoping—that is IT.

I must get her book HEADS AND TALES for you to read.

I stayed over with Frances Eldridge and did some shopping. Saks Fifth Avenue is showing only two styles of black shoes now so I bought three pairs for $42. Sounds silly, but you can't find shoes yet and I wear theirs forever. Then I took two portraits to Portraits Inc., 460 Park Avenue. Fortified with a letter from Malvina Hoffman, I was able to see the top lady. But not before I went through a line of snooty subordinates, one of whom—a well-dressed very elegant dame who looked like she needed a greyhound struggling at the leash—looked straight past me, as I talked to her, nodding her head mechanically and saying, "Uh-uh" in a sing-song voice. After the top lady accepted my pictures, the greyhound suddenly came to life, patted me on the shoulder and said how lovely my paintings were. "Portraits" takes 1/3 commission and my price list cannot vary until I get so many commissions that I can charge more. At present I can ask $350 for a 16 × 20 size; $500 for a 20 × 24, and $650 for a 25 × 30.

Gretchen Green had given me some books to bring back to her UN library here, and I couldn't get rid of them. Post Offices wouldn't take anything over one pound (and these must have weighed ten), and I didn't want to make a trip back to the apartment so they went along to Saks and Macy's with me complicating a hot crowded afternoon. I just kept thinking how kind she had been to me and how she made the head possible and grit my teeth. It is impossible to buy *anything* for children. No bedroom slippers—no underwear—no pajamas—so I gave up and had lunch at Schrafft's where I sat with a business woman who owned a machine shop. She was *burned up* over the labor situation and these "foreigners." It developed that her father was Italian and her mother Irish, straight from the old country!

Next day I returned to Miss Hoffman's studio to see what she had done to the head that morning and approved the changes. She was entertaining Miss Anne Morgan—very deaf—so we shouted. Then I said farewell.

Malvina Hoffman had told me not to miss seeing the French Fashion Mannequins in the old Whitelaw Reid house on Madison Ave. I think they are worth a visit to New York if for no other reason than to wonder if France has gone mad. A French Relief Benefit which must have required a million dollars to line that huge place with yellow velvet—walls and ceilings—with elaborate and beautifully staged settings for some 250 wire dolls about 1 1/2 ft. high dressed in the most exquisite way, complete with REAL jewelry made by the Parisian jewelers. There were shoes, hats, gloves, and elaborate feathers to complete the costumes. Hard to visualize without actually seeing it.

I had been able to get the last ticket McBride's had for *The Glass Menagerie* so I spent a moving evening with Laurette Taylor as Amanda Wingfield. She is wonderful. I still cannot get her voice out of my mind. Eddie Dowling is every bit as good. It couldn't be a play without those two, especially as I saw it all in 4th row center! I cried all the way home in a taxi. Broadway affects me that way, anyway, as I have never been there without Randolph, and it isn't right that he should not be there, since the theater was one of his passions. Your book CLOUDY TROPHIES, coming on top of the play—exactly seven hours later (as I was in Washington at 6:30 a.m.)—seemed somehow to sharpen my sensations and, although I had no intention of reading it at the time, I opened it and fell into it and didn't come out until 12 o'clock. I kept thinking what a wonderful play it would make.

I sent THE DWELLING PLACE to Malvina, as she knew Will Percy. She made the memorial statue to his father. I had everyone in Brentano's looking for the book.

Love,
Marcella

June 13, 1946
Dear Tat,

Such a nice letter from Malvina thanking me for your book. She says the plaster is finished and she thinks it would be wise to have Randolph's

head cast in bronze now. She said she would give her note at the foundry
and I can pay her when I have some luck with portraits—that there is
no hurry. She seems to feel I will have some lucky commissions this
summer.

I am painting Miss Guest in her office. Life size, seated at her desk
with books. Lavenders and whites. Her hair is a lovely off-white. The
Freer will surely miss her when she retires, as will I.

So glad to get your letter and the one you enclose from Tom Carruth.
It isn't at all like him, but then he probably evaporates when he pulls
himself together to write. I think being eligible is hard on him. I don't
know what I would do without your letters just knowing you are there
to savor every little thing and, what is more, get the point. Sometimes
my life seems too difficult to bear without Randolph, and since there
seem to be fewer and fewer people to love, I want to hold on desperately
to the ones I do. Of course, John and Mary are my one and only joy.
Painting is a close second, but joyous only now and then. Betty Wharton is sitting for me now. She is wearing a pink dress and a yellow straw
hat with a big bow and it should be fun to do—especially as the Macy
studio is the most perfect place to work that I have ever known. We
never hear a sound in the house, being on the fourth floor, and there is
a lovely breeze up so high and the surroundings are so luxurious. Perhaps I am not geared to the "lusso."

Mrs. Shouse's Carnival was held Saturday and my job was to take two
artists and two dancers out in my car. For this, I found that I was listed
in the program as the manager of the artist group, along with some very
grand names indeed. My artist sketchers were impressed to be served a
drink by the Secretary of Agriculture! An Englishwoman, a Mrs. Glassford, having heard what I planned to do, asked me to take her to Wolf
Trap last Sunday. I took the children too and, on the way home, she
insisted on buying us all iron pills. She volunteered the information that
the zodiac signs were all in my favor this month. I have been counting
on this a good deal, but, since the 7th and 8th were supposed to be
particularly good days and were, instead, the worst in a long time, I am
a little worried about the whole rest of June. To say nothing of what the
iron pills might do, judging from Mrs. Glassford's own face which was
a white mask with blobs of black where the eyes were. The tight purple
turban perhaps had something to do with the effect or maybe it was the

dirty rain coat which she wore on one of the nicest days we have had so far. Anyway, the Wolf Trap ham with hot biscuits was delicious. To continue my "good fortune" yesterday, just as I was going over my canceled checks (because the grocer's bill said I hadn't paid in April) I heard a terrible crash. The bar table had broken its straps and four prized glasses smashed and a full bottle of rum spilled all over the floor!

Lately Mary has been giving her skit on *The Mighty Iron Pills of Mrs. Glassford.* Her monologue consists of pinning medals on all her ancestors who have contributed to her artistic makeup: "This medal goes to the renowned Anne G. Winslow, who gave me book writing. Thank you. Next, Mum. Step up and get your medal for painting pictures, a talent I greatly appreciate. Wait, I must take a mighty iron pill from Mrs. Glassford's kitchenette etc."

Sam and Eleanor Smith told me that they would have a farmhouse on their new place in Maine fixed up by the middle of August if I cared to rent it for a nominal sum and bring the children up after they go to camp. I thought that some cool weather at that point would be what they could use and told them I would love it. I would like to look over their place for possible future summers, since the idea of bringing a picked group of artists (preferably) to rent cottages to make the thing profitable appeals to me.

Mr. Whyte, of the Whyte Gallery and Bookshop, told me he was going to stock up on your book. I wonder what he calls "stocking up."

Love,
Marcella

June 20, 1946
Dear Tat,

This is a warning which I hope arrives before the fact, that a Mrs. Regler may call you or, more important, drop in on you with her bedding roll. She is on her way to Mexico and I suggested this since I think you will like her. She has had an amazing life and I found her very interesting. Brought up in a wealthy scholarly household in Philadelphia, she married young, but in spite of three lovely children the marriage didn't work, and she went to live in Mexico. There she fell in love and married a German refugee poet and archaeologist named Gustave Regler. He wrote a book on the Spanish Civil War called THE GREAT

CRUSADE. (Denis Devlin says it is very good.) Although he worked in the Underground in Germany against Hitler, the Communists are blackballing him, so he has been unable to get into this country where he wants to continue his writing. Last night I had Alex Böker over so he could advise her about various congressmen who might help her. Of course he mentioned Senator Eastland of Mississippi. Denis Devlin came also with the new Irish Secretary at the Embassy. He is a delightful unspoiled young man from Tipperary, with a beautiful brogue. Looking at the ice cubes from the Frigidaire he showed surprise saying: "Oh, they make themselves, do they?"

Love,

Marcella

Frank Lyell, a friend of Eudora Welty's, told me that Eudora was planning to come to Washington and he wanted to give a party for her but didn't know where to have it. I immediately suggested that she could stay with me and the party could be in my garden. I had heard so much about her from Katherine Anne, who wrote the foreword for Eudora's first book, and I wanted to meet her.

Late June, 1946

Dear Tat,

If Eudora Welty *does* come next Tuesday and Wednesday, how in h—— am I going to get DELTA WEDDING read before then? Perhaps it is better to just say I haven't. Miss Guest has been talking about it for weeks. How she has time to read now that she is packing and leaving that house where she has lived for 26 years I can't imagine. She has no one to help her either. On top of her days at the Freer and posing for the portrait in her office there, she has managed to read CLOUDY TRO-PHIES—with a magnifying glass—and can quote all the good lines. She found the book enchanting, cultivated, and witty. She felt Sabrina was the only one who comes through clearly but I believe she didn't worry about the book's meaning, which is what everyone seems to be doing.

My "good luck" for June, promised by Mrs. Glassford's zodiac, has finally come through with a bang, and the unexpected money, also pre-dicted, has materialized. The Navy people who thought they wanted my house for the summer decided they didn't want to be in the city and didn't like Georgetown anyway. So I phoned my other prospects who came right out and wrote me a check for $450 for 2 1/2 months, just like that. They were a nice mining engineer and his wife from Connecticut who spent the war years at Santo Tomás Concentration Camp in the Philippines. He was a Lieut. Colonel of Engineers at Corregidor. After that, it is no wonder everything looks wonderful to them. He is doing research and they are not the type who entertain.

My really fabulous luck was being asked by Mrs. [Philip] Fleming if I cared to "try out" a completely furnished house in New Hampshire which she has just bought near her summer place at the foot of the White Mountains. A place called Center Sandwich. I have never been to New England and would love it. To have a place for August, rent-free with a fireplace [and] furnace, and near a lake for swimming, seems too good to be true and I owe apologies to Mrs. Glassford for not believing her prediction. Mrs. Fleming is so delightful. I had always gazed from afar at her as the wife of an Engineering General in my early years as an Army wife and she is certainly tops in my estimation now. A person with breeding, background, culture and a great sense of humor—a trait that I value more and more as time goes on. The portraits of her children Jocelyn and Carson turned out well and she likes them a lot. She told me that when Randolph was just out of West Point, stationed at Belvoir, she was flattered when he singled her out for a dance as the handsome bachelor looking over the field. Safe, because already married, he must have thought, shaking off his pursuers!

Love,
Marcella

O St., N.W.
Washington 7, D.C.
July 2, 1946
Dear Tat,

Eudora DID come! [1]

Please notice the above address which I will be using for the next two weeks. I arrived here at Mother's house a few days ago and have been moving out of MY house ever since. Never has there been such an exodus—but perhaps we had better draw a veil over it. All is well now as I have rested and am all in one piece. You see I felt sorry for the nice tenants who have taken my house for the summer, because they were having to move from hotel to hotel (3-day stay) waiting until I moved out. I had told them they could come the day after Eudora's visit. I knew it would push me but I wanted to oblige them and they had said I could take my time, and since I was going to stay two weeks with Mother I could store my things on the third floor, which they would not be using, and pack at my leisure. I hadn't reckoned on painting Eudora's portrait, of course, nor, when I planned a party with Frank Lyell for Eudora, had I known about the tenants descending so soon. However, I don't regret any of it, except not having more hours in the day. The portrait is a smash hit and is being photographed and framed and dressed up like a movie actress for a trip to New York where I expect to take it next week.

Eudora will still be there. I will go on to Connecticut from there to paint the young Eldridge before I hop off for Les Cheneaux on July 14. There I expect to stay put until Aug. 4th, and perhaps paint someone before I return here to pick up the children and drive to New Hampshire. There is where I will really relax, as Mrs. Fleming says it is just country, near a lake, and not at all fashionable.

Mrs. Maynard, my tenant, is a wonderful housekeeper. Everything neat as a pin when I go over to my third-floor packing. When I left last Friday I had Lena, Charles and Myrtle cleaning the house while I nonchalantly painted Eudora from 10 to 1:30, and then things began to buzz! At 4 o'clock both "colored ladies" said it looked as though there wasn't anything more to do and they had to leave on their own business, so I paid them and then Charles brought up a bushel basket from the cellar and in it [were] dumped all the things the ladies forgot: medicines, jewelry, contents of my desk, perfume, gloves etc. All was piled on the third floor—and I mean in heaps! (I have spent two solid days there, since then, just sorting things out.) The Maynards were at the door when Eudora and I left, with our respective suitcases, on the way to tea at Katherine Biddle's house up on 31st Street. The packed car was full to bursting but Eudora managed to straddle the paraphernalia with her long legs as I carefully placed the wet portrait in her hands. As we pulled out, Mrs. Maynard appeared at the door and shouted: "What about the things in the icebox?" I just groaned and told her she was welcome to all of it. If Eudora wrote it up, no one would believe it, but it amused her no end, my life, which I said was insane.

We carried her picture—only 14″ × 10″—in triumph into the tea party as the one clear, distilled drop that had been squeezed out of the crush of her two-day visit. I was so exhilarated that I asked the ladies present, none of whom I knew, if they didn't agree it was wonderful! I hadn't time to even wonder how I did it. I still wonder.

Eudora loves the painting. She says she has never had a decent picture of herself. She is not a beauty but one of the nicest persons I have ever known. She has a quiet soft manner that would seem to still any noise that might disturb the impressions that are getting to her. She has invisible feelers and imparts a power that one is not conscious of until she leaves and then there is the realization that other people are awfully busy and talk too much. I am reading her book DELTA WEDDING now with her portrait propped up in front of me. So far I like it—the book—very much. I don't see how she can give the whole picture of people and places in so few words.

The party for her was a great success. Her attitude was one of regret that the party was not for a "glamour girl," and trepidation at meeting such people as Alexis Léger and the State Department (as represented by the Macys, Coxes and John Vincents). She was so obviously a creative person who would never be spoiled by success that she stood out for what she is—the real thing. Miss Guest agreed, as did so many others. They all loved her.

I had rum punch in the garden and it was a lovely day. Everyone feeling very informal and happy. Mrs. Landon, who wrote ANNA AND THE KING OF SIAM, was there, though not sharing honors.[2] She was attractive—looking like a suburban housewife. I was glad Mrs. Vernon Kellogg could come.[3] She is one of my favorites and the sort who would most appreciate a writer like Eudora, since she has done a lot of writing herself. Betty Vincent asked where in the world I got so many attractive men. They outnumbered the ladies 3 to 1! About 30 people.

Mary is adjusted to camp after writing a few homesick letters asking for Pamo. Johnny has taken to eating everything in sight just as prices for food are rising, and there has been no meat for days except frozen corned beef hash and chicken.

Jocelyn Fleming, who works at the Francis Scott Key Bookshop, said your book CLOUDY TROPHIES is selling well. Bart Barber, who was at the party, said eight copies sold was not enough. His generation should have more appreciation. I thought the *Herald Tribune* review was the most sympathetic of all.

Love,

Marcella

P.S. Eudora's portrait has a Delta background. The sky color blends in well with her green-blue dress. I spent about four hours on it. Miss Guest calls it a minor masterpiece. When I realized how much I liked Eudora, at some point, I asked: "Don't you think I should paint your portrait?" She replied, "Yes, I do!"

1. Eudora Welty, born in Jackson, Mississippi, in 1909, is among the most honored of American writers. She is known chiefly for her stories of the South, where she has lived all her life—in the house in which she grew up. In five decades she has produced an impressive body of work: four collections of short stories and six longer works. Her numerous literary prizes and honorary degrees reflect the lofty position she holds in American letters with succeeding generations of writers and readers.

2. Margaret D. Landon (1903–) went with her husband, a Presbyterian missionary, to Siam (now Thailand), where they remained until 1937. As principal of a girls' school there, she heard much of the strong-minded Welsh woman Anna Leonowen, secretary to the king, who tried to introduce Western ideals of freedom. Mrs. Landon based her story, *Anna and the King of Siam,* on Anna's two books of memoirs. Her best seller of 1944 was turned into the musical *The King and I.* Mrs. Landon also wrote a novel, *Never Dies the Dream,* in 1949. The Landons lived in Washington with their four children.

3. Mrs. Vernon Kellogg, a poet, was the wife of a professor who had been in charge of relief work in Belgium, Poland, and Russia in the years from 1915 to 1921.

Eudora wrote on June 30, thanking me for her visit, "every bit of which was a pleasure." She felt it was a feat to do the painting under the circumstances and wondered if I had started painting someone else, such as Denis or "no telling who." The following year she sent me a copy of *Delta Wedding* published by the Bodley Head, in England. They had used a reproduction of my portrait of her on the book jacket, stating, "The photograph on the wrapper is from a painting by Gomez." Eudora wrote on the flyleaf, "To

Marcella with love to Comès and apologies for Gomez." The book was recommended by the Book Society.

Southport, Conn.
July 11, 1946
Dear Tat,

Tomorrow I leave Connecticut for Washington—have you got my itinerary memorized? There will be a party and showing of the portrait tomorrow and then I go to New York on the 6:30 train to meet Eudora for dinner. I saw her on my way here for half a day and let her buy her portrait. We agreed that if I let her have it she would have a box made and would send it to me anytime I wanted to show it. She wants it so much that I don't have the heart to refuse as I like her tremendously. We had lunch with Caroline at 108 Perry Street. Caroline looks thin but about the same. It seems strange to see her in a small place with no people around—if one can except the mother cat and her 4 kittens she has given shelter to. Allen had gone to Utah. He seems to be working hard. She whipped up a delicious lunch (with the ubiquitous sour cream) in short order. It was nice to see her. She was as sweet as could be. Apparently all is well in that quarter.

This house Mrs. Eldridge has bought has a great deal of charm though there are some amazing aspects about it, such as a separate little house of one room WITH a cellar and three locks on the door—situated in the garden. The whole place was expensively fenced in by the recluse who lived here who never asked anyone to come in. Southport often has Theatre Guild tryouts. We saw *The Young Woodley* with Roddy McDowell—he being the young movie star who has played in all the Flicka movies. Excellently done, but naturally rather dated in lines and situations. You probably saw it at one time. I wondered afterwards if that was the play that made Randolph wary of women! The discussion of sex in the play, which took place in an English boy's school, was no doubt quite shocking twenty years ago.

The two ladies who went with us were old residents here. The majority of people live in New York in the winter, one of them being Mrs. James Truslow Adams. She asked us to come in afterwards to meet JTA.[1] What a garrulous and fascinating old man! He was so thrilled to show off the family portraits to someone who showed an interest and have the opportunity to talk about Great-Aunt Jane "on my father's side who gave me that highboy" that I thought we would never get away. Of course he tells you right off that he is Virginia and NOT New England before anyone has a chance to ask him about Henry and John Quincy. He was completely in character—tweed suit and vest (this was a VERY hot day), cane, red face, portly, reading a Life of Jackson and [with] the living room completely lined with busts of Socrates, Plato etc. in their respective niches. Many old pieces "from Great-Aunt Hattie on mother's side" and incongruously—and probably the thing he REALLY loved—a small nude drawing tucked away in a corner. Of course the Metropolitan has been begging for the portrait of his Spanish grandfather, because it was painted on copper (here there was produced a flashlight to see if I could guess what the medium was), but he had no intention of giving it to them. (I would never look at it if it were there.) His father was painted by Eugene Speicher (the famous portraitist) in 1911, and it encouraged me to realize that ES had to do potboilers at one time. It had no distinction. Adams' own portrait even he didn't like! Somehow that discouraged me about asking him to pose for my literary group, as I feared the Adams influence at this point.

> Love,
> Marcella

1. James Truslow Adams (1878–1949) was a scholar and writer who won a Pulitzer Prize in history in 1922.

P Street, N.W.
Washington, D.C.
July 22, 1946
Dear Tat,

Glad to get your letter, especially to know that James Truslow is quite satisfactory as a writer, even if he does go on and on. One would think he would be used to being an Adams by now. Caroline and Eudora both approved of adding him to the literary group to be painted, so if I get the opportunity I will ask him.

> Love,
> Marcella

Anne Winslow had just written to me:

Marcella:

James Truslow Adams!!! It hasn't been long since I was ransacking in the tower room for an essay of his in the *Atlantic* that I remembered and wanted to read again. I found it, too, and found it just as good. I can hardly believe such charm, wit, style, and above all, such depth, can belong to an old windbag in tweeds! Your description is perfect—but it grieves me. It just shows the truth about genius. It is not the person. It is just a light that breaks through. But what is he doing up there in New England if he is not a REAL Adams?

During July, she also wrote,

Marcella:

The photographs go back to you today, with thanks and admiration. I thought as I was wrapping them up they really represent about as important a piece of work as anybody anywhere has accomplished this year. And I am not excepting what has been done in the White House or the Kremlin, or points between.

More and more am I convinced that life is only the raw material of art. Mary was quite overpowered. She likes Eudora better than anything, and next, Tom Carruth! But that is a romantic judgment— Eudora is just a miracle—and so, in my opinion am I! What did you do to me? I am quite satisfied with that rendition. In fact I am already seeing myself on the front page of *The New York Times!*

Center Sandwich, N.H.
July 30, 1946
Dear Tat,

New Hampshire is calming my nerves! It is so peaceful here after all I have gone through this month. I wrote you last from Connecticut and returning to D.C. stopped over in New York. I had dinner with Eudora and Caroline Gordon and the inevitable hangers-on around Caroline— this time a Meriwether cousin—and took a sleeper to Washington. I couldn't find my ticket to Detroit on my return and telephoned Mrs. Eldridge to inquire. They found it in my waste basket and it had to be sent special delivery!

I have just returned from a devastating visit of two weeks in Michigan where painting portraits of the wealthy, which is what I had been led to expect, did not materialize.[1] It was embarrassing to have my hostess, Peg, show off photographs of my portraits at every party we went to—and that was mainly what there was to do (on this island butlers presented invitations to cocktail parties at one's door), but that was not as bad as having Peg stand over me while I attempted to paint her husband.[2] Having no success selling my artistic abilities, she definitely knew how her husband should be portrayed. She liked smooth dashing paintings and didn't appreciate what I unfortunately labeled a "Renoir touch" after the first sitting. She was always saying, behind my ear: "Now, the way I see it, Marcie, is shiny black—no highlights— and lots of contrasts—and I can't tell anything until you cover the whole canvas."

In the meantime my host was holding me personally responsible for everything President Franklin Roosevelt had done in Washington. Remember the great cartoon of the rich New Yorkers meeting at the Ritz to "hiss Roosevelt"? On the first day of my visit, he had asked me if I approved of Roosevelt and when I said I did, that subject was brought up at every meal for the purpose of making me feel guilty. I hated to toss aside $500 when I need it so much, but there was no way I could paint in that atmosphere. I destroyed the painting half completed. I can't tell you how it comforts me not to be rich.

It was such a relief to pick up the children after their month in camps and they are so happy here in this little village of Center Sandwich. The house which Mrs. Fleming has lent me is a dream. I invited a young couple, willing to share the driving and two blown-out tire changings in my old Ford, to come and help me with the detailed instructions—finding the unmarked dirt roads—that led us through a forest of trees to this red clapboard charming house with a view of the White Mountains in the background. When we arrived there was no one in the house, but the door was open, the kerosene stove was going and fresh flowers were on the table. It seemed to be waiting for us and it WAS. We fit in as though our destiny says we belong here—and I think we do.

Love,
Marcella

1. Anne Winslow: "Rich people are either the worst or the best. I think the lily when gilded properly is a fine flower."

2. In my days as an art student in Italy in the early thirties, I met Peg ———, a wealthy lady from Indianapolis who traveled yearly to Europe. She wanted to be an influence in my life, and especially my career. I was at the age and

time when I listened to her advice—since I considered her cosmopolitan. "Marcie, you must never wear red—it doesn't become you—too overpowering," she would admonish me. On her annual trips to Washington she always expected me to drop everything and entertain her—and for some reason, I always did.

Center Sandwich, N.H.
August 22, 1946
Dear Tat,

Nothing could have pleased me more than your and Mary's reaction to the photograph of Eudora's portrait. It is really the best I have ever done. Although I did not want to part with it, I am glad she wanted it and was able to get me to part with it, particularly since she will have the box made for shows when I want to exhibit it. I may ask her to send it up for the next Phillips Gallery Christmas show they always put on for local artists. I had a letter from Homer Saint-Gaudens [son of Augustus], Director of the Carnegie Institute, simply repeating what his secretary had written me (that Saint-G already has his artists selected for the International), and calling Eudora an "interesting" portrait, and [saying] that it had been a long' time since we had seen each other and nothing more. Not a word about seeing Randolph in the war zone when R helped him get around to see things! No hope held for the future at all. But then I am not famous. Although LOCAL GIRL LOOMED TO FORE, I am still LOCAL.

I am glad you enclosed the *New York Times* review of Robert Penn Warren's ALL THE KING'S MEN. Do you think it possible he has a smash hit? I was disappointed that the *New York Times Book Review* did not use the reproduction of my portrait of him which they requested after Eudora told them I had one. It seems I gave them the wrong address up here. I know it is better than the photo they used. Today's *Times* quotes nine eminent critics who rave about his book. I am so glad for him. Maybe Caroline will be the next with a smash. It is all in the timely idea, no? Politics. Crump. Huey Long etc.

I received the following letter from Ellen Lewis Buell, Editor of the *New York Times Book Review,* which she wrote on August 1, 1946:

> Eudora Welty told me the other day that you had painted a series of portraits of Southern writers and that you might possibly allow us to reproduce them in The Book Review from time to time as books by these authors appear. She said she thought you had the

photographs of the paintings and we would appreciate it greatly if you would let us have a set of prints of these to keep on file. We should, of course, be glad to pay for the extra prints and if you haven't photographs perhaps you would allow us to send a photographer from the Washington bureau of The Times. She mentioned a portrait of Robert Penn Warren and I am especially interested in that at this time because he has a new novel coming, as you doubtless know, and if it were possible to secure a photograph of his portrait by next Tuesday we would appreciate it very much.

Love,
Marcella

Center Sandwich, N.H.
August 28, 1946
Dear Tat,

We went up the Maine coast to Freeport to visit Sam and Eleanor Smith to see their new place, where I might have gone if it had not been for Mrs. Fleming lending me this adorable place. They have bought, along with a point of land, a fantastic house. Huge, ungainly, way off in the woods away from everything except the ocean and a view. They have bought cottages around it, to accommodate their six children.

Can you imagine a pseudo-colonial pillared gray stone house with a tremendous chandelier and a tiled mantel, along with the Smiths' very modern paintings? The piano is painted green and the draperies are orange. The Smiths enjoy all this and don't want to change anything, it is such a period piece. Sam's mother was there and has failed greatly. She seems lost in another world of the past, and has no more that bright look that I was able to get in her portrait. How fortunate I painted her when I did! All her stories of her past! She said she was still a good friend of Katherine Hepburn, divorced from her son, Ludlow. I know you treasure the visit we had with her—when you said it was the first time you had ever made a visit just for being invited.

The children are now loving everything about New England. They argue violently about whether they are Southern or Yankee, and can't decide which they prefer. I believe Southern has won out. I am reading them Kate Greenaway's THE SECRET DOOR—struggles of an artist. In Johnny's words: What's-so-hot-about-you sort of thing. A good lesson in going one's own way artistically. When I expressed a wish to paint an evening light effect later on, but was too busy to do so, preparing dinner, Mary dashed off to get my paint box and Johnny set up my easel on the spot. Art won out.

Love,
Marcella

Center Sandwich, N.H.
August 31, 1946
Dear Tat,

Unexpected company. One of my "friends" who likes to get me organized (of which there are many) succeeded in short order. After she appeared just before dinner, and got settled in the children's room (they had to sleep on the couch in the living room), where she stayed for two nights, she made picnic lunches for the following day by boiling the chicken "FAST," so that we had only one pot to wash and no skillet and mess; screwed on the toilet paper holder and put the electric grill where I will never use it (looks better) and decided to get me some new shelf paper; and boy, wasn't it fun to live the country life? Next day she wanted to find out how much a nearby house would cost (over my dead body) so I found out from Mrs. Fleming that the house was not a good buy but she did know of a good buy and we went to see it. I am amazed at the low price and though my unexpected company was only curious I am more than that. I have never owned a house in my life and am beginning to think I should. Should I?

The last imperative from my departing guest was suggesting that Mary and Johnny cut the grass around the walk as their daily task, to please the owner, Dorothy Fleming. She was really on the way to getting my life all neat and orderly when she had to go.

Center Sandwich, N.H.
September 13, 1946
Dear Tat,

I returned from Connecticut, my mission accomplished (painting the Eldridge son). Sometimes I feel like eloping with a millionaire to get out of doing portrait commissions. As much as I like to paint people, commissions are different. None of the literati were commissioned which is why they are good. No one standing over me saying how they wanted me to see them, the way they always wanted to have themselves be seen. In this case, a full face was ordered. The most difficult to do. The portrait I made of his mother earlier apparently is "too delicate" in tone, they say, and I saw her as delicate. Looks as though I will have to change my style to be successful. I am a little sick about the whole business—in fact I AM sick as a result of the strain of the trip and working under such difficult conditions, knowing, as it was in Michigan, that my best work wouldn't necessarily be what would please them. There is a terrible wooden portrait by that good artist Wayman Adams [1883–1959], done of Mrs. E's father which she said was ruined because the family asked for so many changes. I was glad to get back to the clean White Mountains with the nice human understanding Flemings. Mrs. F wants me to stay as long as I can. I am delighted because it means more days of sunshine and fewer to spend in that dark, depressing house in D.C. before the leaves come off the trees.

The children were well taken care of while I was gone by nice Elspeth. Mary had set up a WINSLOW ART GALLERY in the garage and hoped to make some money for me while I was away. Her sign, fastened to a tree, read: MODEARN FRAMES. ANY REASONABLE OFFER ACCEPTED. PLEASE SIGN REGISTER. NO SMOKING. There was even a jar for the money beside a note which said: "Mrs. Winslow, Gone to Connecticut. Come Again." No sales. The frames were too "modearn." But also, few ever travel down that rural road. General Fleming thinks there will be a depression in 1947. Cheerio! Did you see the *New Yorker* copy about the Hiroshima bomb? I sat up until 1 p.m. reading it, unable to stop.

Love,
Marcella

Hardly knowing how it had happened, I found I had made a commitment to buy a neglected Cape Cod–style house with an attached barn—I had plans for a studio—by the time I returned to Washington. When I showed all my friends photographs of the little house with its green shutters, surrounded by open fields and woods (40 acres, "more or less"), and said it could be had for $2750—the entire parcel—they declared, one and all, that they would buy it if I didn't. The picturesque village of Center Sandwich at the foot of the White Mountains by Squam Lake was some miles from the nearest railroad and, during the war, with gas rationing, a number of houses had been left to rot in the fields. The "summer people" had not been able to get there and many villagers were desperate to sell. I thought about escaping the torrid Washington summers and what it would mean to the children, and to me, and threw caution to the winds. Soon after I had made the down payment of $750 and arranged a $15-a-month mortgage, Anne Winslow had one of her novels condensed for the *Ladies' Home Journal*, for which she received $3000. She decided to buy the place outright for us. Alfred Knopf had phoned to ask if she would feel it demeaning to let the book be condensed for just money. He was no doubt startled at her quick acceptance. Few realized how difficult it was for her to keep up the big house after she had lost so much in the depression.

Making plans for my new house and garden and painting in the grand studio of the Noel Macys' in Washington provided the stimulation I needed to regain my interest in life. I used the new studio to paint a portrait of Denis Devlin and made plans to paint a portrait of Mrs. Jouett Shouse, which her husband wanted and she did not.

During the war years, when male help was hard to get, I often hired whomever I could find. That resulted in a robbery, which won the sympathy of some gracious neighbors who decided to "lend" me their beloved Charles to help out. Our pleasant association lasted until his death, and I was happy that after a few years with me he agreed to let me paint him.

P Street, N.W.
Washington, D.C.
October 8, 1946
Dear Tat,

My return to the city offers better prospects than last year. Etta has taken Lena's place and seems perfect for my needs. Plans meals, comes at 9 a.m. and is willing to stay late. Please send Bessie's uniforms which should fit. Also, I have been "permitted" to have Charles (who has worked for Mrs. Hyde for sixteen years) to take the ashes out and mend, paint or fix anything. He is a darling. Old-timer. Has his own car which is an ancient flivver, highly polished. Mrs. Hyde was worried about me taking so-called helpers like Fred (who stole Randolph's coats) off the street, and decided to share Charles with me—if three hours a week can be called sharing. He gets 65 cents an hour and has his own tools. He started to work for a white family in Virginia when he was a boy and stayed with them until they all died. They left him the Ford.

I have enjoyed the sittings with Denis Devlin. He gave me his new book of poems with the inscription "A word and a metre for a color and a form." Charming!

I also won the portrait prize in the Washington Society of Artists' show at the Smithsonian Museum: the one I made of Gretchen Green in Mrs. Anne Archbold's house. The prize is $100 which is mentally spent already. It is all going into changing the back yard into a garden. The men have just brought in (down all those front steps and up all those back steps) 20 bushels of topsoil, ditto gravel. They are yanking out the snowball bush and bricking over the stagnant pool, planting four ever-greens and a forsythia. I am protected with a two-year lease and would rather spend my prize money that way than any other way I know.

I took Johnny and Mary to see *Henry V* with Laurence Olivier and, though the words were over John's head, he enjoyed the battles and the costumes. A perfect performance with breathtaking settings that look like primitive paintings. I have never forgotten how impressed we (you, Randolph and I) were with young Olivier's performance in *The Green Bay Tree*—his first appearance in New York. Was it 1936? Mary was inspired to make costumes for the paper doll she has drawn of Olivier. She has made an array of medieval costumes for quick changes while Olivier waits patiently in shorts and a helmet for a suit of armor—which seems beyond her capabilities at the moment.

She has been examined for anemia. The mighty iron pills are being brought into action.

Malvina Hoffman writes that she told Gretchen the good news about her portrait winning a prize and that she had so much pleasure reading THE DWELLING PLACE that she has lent it to friends who were full of enthusiasm for your "wonderful originality and charming style."

Love,
Marcella

In October Eudora let me know that she was back home and my portrait was on her wall "looking too elegant to be me," and that an artist friend would come "just to see IT." Eudora had enjoyed meeting the Tates in New York, she said, liking Caroline especially. She had become so involved in her writing that she sometimes went out to her car to work to get away from the phone. I was glad to hear that Italy had bought *Delta Wedding* and that the New York *Times* was "in high delight" over my photos of the writers. According to her, the editors were "just waiting for your subjects to turn out the first peep of a new book to splash them on a page."

The first painting I made for the Macys out of appreciation for the use of the studio depicted their house on a fall day. A letter I wrote to Anne Winslow mentions that I was talking up the idea of painting people's houses with her friends and contemporaries but felt that they had all stopped liking pictures painted after 1898. The group came to see my portrait of Gretchen Green, whom they all knew, walked up to within an inch of it, and never said a word. If they were confounded, I was more so.

Once, earlier in my career, I had decided to find out what it is that creates this confusion. Soon after I came to live in Washington, I entered a painting considered one of my best (at least it had won prizes in other shows) in the competition for the Phillips Gallery Christmas show. When I found out that C. Law Watkins, who had selected the show, was running a life class at the Phillips, I signed up for it. At some point I asked if he would come to my house. When I produced the painting he had turned down, along with others, he got excited and asked, "Why don't you submit these paintings to the Phillips shows? This is just the sort of thing Duncan [Phillips] would like." That boosted my morale but left me confused.

This sort of experience most often happens in connection with portraits. The subject's first viewing of the finished work is usually a shock. Time is needed to become accustomed to seeing oneself as the artist did. Most people have their own image of what they look like, or how they think they look, or especially, how they would like others to see them as they think they look.

November 4, 1946
Dear Tat,

Having people fall down my steps seems a good way to get portraits! Yesterday at 5:15 Mrs. Vernon Kellogg tripped on those circular treacherous three steps where Sam Smith's mother was laid low, and at 5:30 asked me to paint her.

Friday at 10 a.m. Mrs. Kellogg will pose for her portrait. I have a secret guilt though I assure you I was on the top landing and can prove it by Millicent Todd Bingham. MTB was brought over by Mrs. K as a future victim and will, apparently, also submit to sitting for her portrait although she got down the stairs safely. We had a delightful time at tea. I can't wait for you to meet Mrs. Bingham who has had a full life and other interests besides Emily Dickinson. I am distressed to know Mrs. Kellogg will be leaving Washington for California. She is enthusiastic about my work and is helping no end. Because her daughter is an artist, she takes a special interest and is rounding up more writers for me to paint so I can exhibit them in my show next spring. Her friends seem to think so much of her that they all want to do what she suggests. Both Mrs. Biddle and Mrs. Eugene Meyer have agreed to let me "do" them. She herself has published a volume of poetry so can qualify.

I love the way the mountain is continually going to Mohammed in your case. I can't wait to hear more about Mr. Strauss at Knopf. To rhyme with him I have Mrs. Shouse coming to me. Next Monday we start the sitting with hopes of having the painting for a Christmas present. So far the size has not been decided so I don't know the price. Kay Shouse was in Europe this summer and was telling Betty Vincent and me over a cup of tea about the gaiety of Paris and the dreariness of London.

Thanks for the clipping on Randolph. I think I have a very complete record in print for the children now. How proud they will always be of their father, but how little does it take the place of having him to grow up with!

Hurrah for authoress with Hollywood options and London editions!

Love,
Marcella

Soon after Thanksgiving, 1946, I began to make plans for Anne Winslow's visit. She stayed over Christmas and left in April, when her house in Memphis had lost its chill and she could start her garden. During the winter there were letters from her to Mary Chapman, her daughter, mentioning the plans I had to paint Ezra Weston Loomis Pound (1885–1972), the American poet. Born in Idaho of Quaker parents, Pound had studied at Hamilton College and at the University of Pennsylvania under Cornelius Weygandt, who told me he didn't think much of Pound as a student. He was known for helping other writers—Joyce and Eliot among them—but he was a controversial figure. His Pisan Cantos, written after his arrest in 1945 for making anti-American broadcasts while he was in the United States Stockade in Pisa, won the Bollingen Prize in 1948. Tried for treason, he was imprisoned in St. Elizabeth's Hospital, from which he was released in 1958. My mother-in-law wrote, "Funny things do happen. One of the funniest is that Marcella wants to do a portrait of Ezra Pound for her Series. The fact that he is at present an inmate at St. Elizabeth's Hospital impressed her, when she heard it, as simplifying the problem—'For after all if I can get into his cell there won't be very much he can do about it.' The idea that the thing might work the other way didn't occur to her. I laugh over that one after I go to bed at night."

My paintings were a never-ending source of interest to Anne Winslow.

Anne Goodwin Winslow, painted in 1946

Major Tom Moore Carruth, painted in 1946

Gretchen Green in Anne Archbold's house, painted in 1946 (Smithsonian Portrait Prize, 1946).

Grace Dunham Guest, painted in 1946 in her office at the Freer Gallery

Eudora Welty, painted in 1946

Courtesy Eudora Welty

Denis Devlin, painted in 1946

Mrs. Francis Biddle, painted in 1947

Courtesy Randolph Biddle

Mrs. John Carter Vincent, painted in 1947

Karl Shapiro, painted in 1947

Charles, painted in 1947

Courtesy Greater Latrobe School District, Latrobe, Pennsylvania

Self-portrait, 1947
Courtesy James Street

Drawing by Léon Masson in my guestbook, 1948: "All most beautiful, oldest, profitable Georgetown houses surrounded Mr. Masson, the famous French artist, in order to have their portrait done by him."

Mrs. Harold Talbott, painted in the 1950s

Rose Standish Nichols, painted in 1948

Juan Ramón Jiménez at his house in Maryland, May, 1948

Juan Ramón Jiménez, painted in 1948

Ezra Pound, sketched in 1948

Léonie Adams, painted in 1949

She had her favorites, however (front yard in preference to back). When I got four pictures accepted in the Corcoran Gallery area show in 1947, she was as pleased as I was. We often found things to be pleased about.

In January we were pleased to get letters from Walter de la Mare, in England, and Allen Tate, in New York. De la Mare (1873–1956) was a leading contemporary poet in England. My sister, Alice, and I were often invited by his son, Colin, to their house in Taplow, Buckinghamshire, the winter we lived in London. De la Mare enjoyed our Americanisms. After a year in Italy, we sailed back to the States from Southampton in 1931, staying with the de la Mares for a few days before Colin drove us to the ship. In 1946, I wrote to ask him if he would mind my showing the sketch I had made of him when I was living in London. He responded, "I was delighted to have your message at Christmas with that lovely drawing. It is very good news to hear that you are busy painting and that you won the Portrait Prize last year. I know the names of some of the authors you mention but by no means all. If you actually want a 'head of Sir Walter' he assures me he will be proud to be one of your gallant assembly. Alas, there is no chance of my ever coming to America again; but there is every good reason why you should give England another chance. We are all, I am thankful to say, well, and in spite of certain little disadvantages, such as bread units, clothes coupons, strikes, nationalizations and so forth, are happy enough."

Allen Tate was liking New York less and less. He wrote that it was more difficult living in that machine city than it was living in Kentucky in 1780. He liked my report of Denis Devlin's wedding, which he could not get to, owing to Caroline's flu: the report helped to "fill the void." As to my thinking he might help in arranging for me to paint Ezra Pound at St. Elizabeth's, he said, "I suppose you don't know how intensely Ezra dislikes me. But when the Fellows appear for the Spring meeting I will ask Ted Spencer to arrange everything. Will April be too late?" Allen also wrote that he was glad I planned to paint Huntington Cairns and I should ask him a good price since "Florence has the cash." He added that he might be able to run down to Washington in February and, if he did, he would count on taking "Miss Annie" and me to dinner, at that "pub of the writers, the Cosmos Club." It was not until the following year, though, that Robert Lowell offered to take me to meet Ezra.

Neither Mrs. Winslow nor I was pleased at the outcome of Huntington Cairns's portrait. It didn't work out and had to be abandoned, to his chagrin. Had Anne Winslow been able to come to the Macys' studio and engage him in conversation while he was sitting, that probably would have distracted his interest from my efforts to make the "little gem" he was so obviously expecting. I couldn't live up to the National Gallery expectations and his face continued to look Pickwickian. The only thing that resulted from the portrait sitting was an invitation to one of the famous Cairns dinners, special and rare. I had often been told that Florence Cairns's dinners were always beautifully served by a maid or butler but that no guest was ever informed that Florence prepared the meals herself. She especially made memorable desserts. I looked forward to experiencing her culinary skills and was not disappointed. Sitting near her when an elaborate concoction was first offered her at dessert time, I was amazed at the surprise in her voice when she said, approvingly, "Oh, goody, Tipsy!"

Rhymed couplets were passed around after dinner, with instructions from Huntington that we—mostly poets—were to say which of the couplets had been written by Alexander Pope. I was terrified! Everyone would see how ignorant I was about this English poet, whose work I had never read. By the use of what my children call my astral, however, I selected the rhyme that turned out to be the correct one—and it also turned out that I was the only one to get the right answer. It made my day. It also "made" my evening—the one and only dinner I ever had in the Cairnses' book-lined apartment.

I wrote a letter to Mrs. Winslow telling her of Denis Devlin's marriage and of my comment, on presenting him with a large photograph of the portrait, that it was a shame he had to leave "himself" behind on his next posting to London.

On March 9, 1947, in an article called "Town Talk" in the Washington *Star,* Eva Hinton wrote that before Denis Devlin left Washington to take up his new post in London he brought his bride to see the portrait.

> The poet, who has a rather prominent nose, told his wife, "One day while Marcella was painting me at an intense rate, I asked her, 'Must you make my nose so red?' Her unanswerable retort was, 'Yes, I must!'"

The article went on to say,

> Also on her display easel is a portrait of Mrs. Jouett Shouse with her prize-winning Boxer. Forthright, Mrs. Shouse arrived to pose carrying a beautiful black velvet gown which she had acquired in Paris last summer. Suddenly she threw the dress on a chair and said, "I just can't see myself being painted in a Paris gown!" So she and Mrs. Winslow jumped in a car and motored to Wolf Trap in Virginia where they chose a huge locust tree for a background and allowed the friendly Boxer to wag his way into the picture.

Malvina Hoffman had finished work on the head of my husband, after asking me for any suggestions I might have, and had it cast in bronze. She secured my permission to show the head at an exhibit, and she was pleased by a poem it inspired. She undoubtedly felt this sculpture was her contribution to the war effort, since she asked me to pay only for the plaster cast and the casting in bronze.

It was in early 1947 that Anne Winslow and I met Rose Nichols at a Georgetown dinner party. Beforehand we were told, "Only ladies, but wear evening dress." Miss Nichols impressed us from the start—not because she had received a half-page in *The Proper Bostonians* but because of her appearance. She was tall and bony and wore cascades of pearls, an embroidered pouch at her waist, and an old-fashioned long lace dress. I thought for years that her dresses came from a trunk in her Beacon Hill attic but discovered that she had Worth make copies of them in Paris. At the Georgetown dinner party, she monopolized the conversation: "Do you believe there is such a thing as a holy war?" Sipping her after-dinner coffee in the living room, she suddenly turned to me and asked, "Mrs. Winslow, do you know of a writer named Anne Goodwin Winslow?" I pointed out my mother-in-law, who, amused by this Boston Brahmin, had been quiet, and said, "She is sitting next to you, Miss Nichols." There was delight all around when the conversation turned to books and Miss Nichols could express her enthusiasm for the novels this quiet and unobtrusive southerner had produced.

We learned later that Miss Nichols was a well-known landscape architect who had designed many famous gardens and written books—now collectors' items—on English, Italian, Spanish, and Portuguese pleasure gardens. It has been said that her acquaintance with a wide variety of people enabled her on one occasion to give a Europe-bound friend letters of introduction not only to Bernard Berenson but also to the daughter of the queen of Romania and to the head of the French Communist party. Burke Wilkinson's biography of Augustus Saint-Gaudens describes Rose Nichols as the sculptor's favorite niece and says that she was very possessive of her "Uncle Gus," who admired her boldness and high spirits. Wilkinson wrote, "Tall, with a Diana-like figure, Rose had certain marked predilections: she liked the limelight, celebrities, travel, and having her own way" (*Uncommon Clay: The Life and Works of Augustus Saint-Gaudens* [New York, 1985], 271).

When Mrs. Winslow returned to Memphis in April, I wrote in my first letter that I had the "Lost Lady" feeling—one of the most poignant—when there is a leave-taking. Although two years had passed since Randolph's death, I could still write, "To hear Mary at the piano sounds so cheerful and, if I could only learn to be happy with the children instead of unhappy without Randolph, all might be well. When all seems too bad I think of

New Hampshire and your new book and hope you dash off many more."
Time was too slow in healing, but I never had enough of it.

I painted a large portrait of Mrs. Fleming in her house in exchange for
another summer in her cottage while my house in Center Sandwich was
being made habitable and I acquired furnishings for the move into it in the
summer of 1948.

April 21, 1947
Dear Tat,

Helen (Philadelphia) Coxe asked Mary and me to drive to Middle-
burg, Virginia, with her to look at Foxcroft, the school where she is
entering Betsy next year. We got a grand tour by "Miss Charlotte"
herself. Miss Charlotte is so perfect in the role of headmistress at the
swankiest school in the country (at least the most expensive) that she
seemed like a stage version of herself. Completely dressed in riding
clothes (for sidesaddle), skirt and boots—white hair, patrician nose,
tiny feet and signet ring. She was far more interesting than the school,
which is lovely. It aims to give the "Suthen" atmosphere to the east—or
what they think is southern. I asked what percentage of Yankees there
were in the school. Ninety-nine, she said.

A New York mother, an alumna, drove us around and, passing a
nice-looking Negro girl, called out: "Hello Mazekia!" or some such
name, and told us she had been "given" to Miss Charlotte when Miss C
was a child. I must say the girls looked nice and were pleasant and
natural. The trees, avenues of pink blossoms and the garden were very
beautiful—the country all around bursting with spring. I continue to
find Helen delightful.

I am starting a portrait of Katherine Biddle tomorrow. Francis wants
me to paint her in profile. Almost an order but it is not a commission.
I will see.

I had an appointment with Reverend Mother Barry, head of the Sacred Heart School, Stone Ridge, where Mary is going. A charming
person—sister of the playwright Philip Barry who wrote a play about
her which featured Ethel Barrymore, you may remember—and she got
right to the point. We discussed art. She wants me to give the senior
group some idea what modern art is all about (oh boy, what a field!),
composition, color etc. She is planning something so she can keep Mary.
The tuition has been raised to $500 so it would be a great help to me.

Betty [Fisher] is wistfully longing but will not be able to afford to rent her mother's former house on Leroy Place for $400 a month. She saw it today and said it looked bigger than her memory of growing up there. A case of log cabin birthplace in reverse.

Love,
Marcella

April 30, 1947
Dear Tat,

Katherine Biddle has sat twice for her portrait. She is wearing a purple and rose gown and, yes, it is a profile. She is seated at a table with a book but the picture is only 9 × 12, smaller than the one I did of Eudora. It is the first time she has ever posed. Surprising, since the artist George Biddle is her brother-in-law and her sister, Cornelia Van A. Chapin [Princess Caetani, head of the Italian magazine *Bottega Oscura*], is a sculptress. Tomorrow the Hattie Carnegie hat gets taken to the studio for Betty [Mrs. John Carter] Vincent's pose. Kay Shouse was supposed to come for a sitting last Monday but is too busy. She has become self-conscious about her looks, perhaps I should say her girth, but her face is pretty; and she is attractive.

Love,
Marcella

Georgetown's Dumbarton Oaks is a great attraction. The gardens and the mansion, and the concerts, were made famous by Mr. and Mrs. Robert Woods Bliss. At the northern tip of Georgetown, Dumbarton Oaks is an enduring legacy to the city of Washington. Combined with the Byzantine collection, housed in a dream pavilion designed by Philip Johnson, and the incomparable library, which provides scholarships for scholars, this is a treasure known all over the world.

May 3, 1947
Dear Tat,

I went to a private showing (in a very grand house off Massachusetts Avenue) of frescoes and paintings done by a Prince Merchersky. Mrs. Hewitt (Higginson, Boston) apparently has taken up this Russian painter and given him a beautiful place to show for several days. Mrs. Robert Woods Bliss helped her prepare the list—printed invitations. Being a Prince is no end of help. Eleanor Smith brought Mrs. Hewitt to tea yesterday and Mrs. H wanted to see everything, upstairs and down. She is horsy too. Her horse, Phalanx, is the favorite at the Kentucky Derby. I wouldn't mind being her favorite for a few days but who would prepare *my* list?

I have drawn a self-portrait for an exhibit titled "Meet the Artist." Johnny's remark "I might know you would make yourself thin" may be to the point. I have pictured myself holding a mask and will title it "How do you do?" The show will be at the Dupont Theater and most of the better-known artists will be in it. Alice [Mrs. Dean] Acheson has sold seven paintings, so far, in her exhibit at the United Nations Club which the Whyte and Bader Gallery arranged.[1] They were so pleased because six Ambassadors came to her opening.

You have now become a museum piece! I was offered $800 by J. Lionberger Davis (the collector from St. Louis) for the portrait I did of you.[2] He wants it for his museum in St. Louis. He fell in love with your face. You should have heard him! "Cultivated, spiritual, fascinating!" I didn't sell it and won't unless I can paint another just as good! He buys what he likes and doesn't give a rap for anything else. He then considered my portrait of Fredrica, and I hope he will buy her instead. He also offered me $300 to paint a copy of my head in the painting of Randolph and me that hangs over the sofa.

Since Malvina Hoffman got me into Portraits Inc. in New York, I have had two inquiries, so I have a number of prospects which I may have to put off until the fall as I want to paint the poet Karl Shapiro and get on with Kay Shouse.[3] She can give me only a morning a week.

Love,
Marcella

1. Alice Acheson, well-known artist in Washington, had shown in an exhibit of paintings with her artist mother and her grandfather John Mix Stanley at the Smithsonian, and had also had a solo show at the Corcoran Gallery. She was a member of the local art societies.

2. Lionberger Davis (1878–1973), a lawyer and banker and patron of the arts, was founder and chairman of the J. Lionberger Davis Art Trust in his hometown of St. Louis.

3. Karl Shapiro, who was born in Baltimore in 1913, received the Pulitzer Prize in 1945 for *V-Letter and Other Poems* and, soon after, a Guggenheim Fellowship. He was the consultant in poetry at the Library of Congress in 1946–1947 and was an editor of *Poetry* magazine. He is now professor emeritus of English at the University of California in Davis, where he lives. His most recent book is *Reports of My Death* (Chapel Hill, N.C., 1990).

May 12, 1947
Dear Tat,

The cat, who is now to be known as Bunchy, since she will soon produce kittens, I'm sorry to say, is lying beside me obviously indicating what Johnny told the 3rd and 4th grades in Jackson school was a "big bump" in her side. That started a discussion on cats in their news-giving period at which I learned from two children that the kittens always come at night, so I am prepared with a box. When I asked Johnny if he ever gave any news of me in class (cats and medals for his father having been well received), he replied: "No. What's so hot about you?" Perhaps you will make the news period when you get those movie rights. Mary has named several of the bumps already. She is solicitous and I hear her often say: "Poor Kitty, I'm sorry about your figure and your fleas." Kittens at this moment are one little complication I could do without. I found this priceless document in John's dungarees: WE ARE IN JUNIOR PARTNERSHIP WE CAN ONLY BREAK UP AFTER A MONTH OF WANTING TO AND WE BOTH WANT TO. David Auld AND John Winslow.

I send you my favorite poem by Lena just as she wrote it—I encourage her to bring the poems for a little booklet:

Let My Peoples Go

> The southern Men dont want to pass the bill of Civil right
> If a war start the Colored will have to fight
> God made us all he was very please
> he made us in his image Not
> Walking on Bending Knees
> What we want while on this earth
> Is all to be treated the same
> Not to be insulted and hang our head in shame
> God love us all this I know
> That why he told Pharaop to let my peoples go.

Love,
Marcella

May 17, 1947
Dear Tat,

When I finished the portrait of Katherine Biddle I invited her to bring Francis to see it. Since I was pleased, and had posed her in profile as he had suggested, I fully expected some enthusiasm. Instead, they seemed to be outraged. They stayed only fifteen minutes and, most of the time, they looked longingly at your portrait which they liked very much (and you won't use in your publicity), and the rest of the time he stared at my small rendition of her—even making a face at it! She said she looked like a sunburned Semite just returned from Atlantic City, and a parrot with a sharp beak. She does, too, you know. Then they walked out leaving me crushed. I wanted NEVER to do another portrait. I wanted to die. I couldn't sleep that night. I thought of what awful things they would say about it and I would be ruined! Also, I couldn't understand their criticisms. By chance, next day, Alexis Léger, K's good friend, called and I asked him to come in. He told me not to change a thing—that I had caught, not only a likeness, but K's spirit—the psychological essence—that reserve she has. Then he gave me excellent criticism on my other paintings proving he knew quite a lot more about painting than I ever had an idea he did, so I felt better. Emily Amram, who is an old and good friend of Kay, felt the way Léger did, only more so—said the portrait had a feeling of repose and grace, whereas the Biddles felt it to be stiff and hard.

Do you blame me, or any other painter, for dreading painting portraits because of the agony one goes through trying to express what one sees with one's eyes? I have a chance to get even—which I will pass up. June 1st the Biddles have invited me to the unveiling of the portrait of Francis done by his brother George—the official one. Léger says it is awful—that he has made Francis evil looking. But I shall see . . . That is the weekend just before the Ann Bullitt–Tony Biddle wedding, so I should see many faces heretofore only viewed in the newspapers.

I have made a sketch of Karl Shapiro in his office at the Library. He was a good subject—sitting by an open window with his tie blowing in the wind, which I put in the painting. I will try to remember to include his glass poem, which I know I like.

Love,
Marcella

May 20, 1947

Dear Tat,

Fish House Punch will be partaken by the poets in my garden before the Biddle dinner tomorrow, to which I am also invited. The Philip Rahvs (he is the editor of the *Partisan Review*) have come from New York and I had them for dinner and, unexpectedly, overnight as well, since their plans had fallen through. [1] Allen Tate felt, as they were his guests, he could suggest my third-floor bedroom, which was hardly equipped for the likes of them. However, I will always make room for the literati.

I had James Whyte (who owns the Whyte Gallery and Bookshop) to my garden party and he wrote me how pleased he was to have met Robert Penn Warren and have him inscribe a copy of ALL THE KING'S MEN. He says Warren is having a collection of his poems coming out shortly. He also wrote that Franz Bader and he were keeping the month of March open for an exhibition of my paintings next year.

Harriet Winslow had another posh musical on Sunday the 25th with the usual cave dwellers and other recognizable people. One being Felix Frankfurter [1882–1965; Supreme Court justice, 1929–1962]. I had a long amusing chat with him about painting. I sensed that he enjoyed a little repartee so when he asked me if I were as good a painter as Alice Acheson, I said: "Certainly!" And everyone he named, I would say: "Much better." Finally, he told me Sidney Dickinson was going to paint him and would I be able to do as well as he. I answered: "Well, I'd make you the way you are." He guffawed and called his wife over to repeat my remark. Harriet's music room was added on to her house for just these occasions and I am glad she invites me.

Painting Mrs. Shouse. I have an excellent likeness but she doesn't like the expression. Apparently she has been dreading her "ordeal"—the portrait that her husband wanted and she did not. If she still doesn't like the expression after another sitting there will be no $600.

Love,

Marcella

1. Philip Rahv was a leading American literary critic—an expert on Kafka, Dostoevski, and Tolstoy. He founded the influential *Partisan Review* in 1934 but left it in 1969 to start a new quarterly that condemned both the old and new Left in America. He taught at Brandeis University.

June 28, 1947
Dear Tat,

My last days in D.C. were quite hectic trying to get portraits finished and I was so tired of portrait painting, and everything connected with doing them. When Marceil called, before I left, to suggest that if I visited her in Nantucket I might make some "profitable contacts" for portraits, I said, "Marceil, I'm tired of profitable people. They never pay up and I never want to meet another. They can start looking me up and I mean it." My situation with the Shouse portrait was typical. Betty Vincent came to one of the sittings with Kay Shouse who was restive and self-conscious and didn't want the painting to really look like her, and yet did want it the way she used to look some years ago. Betty told me later she didn't see how I could do it, but was quite struck with the pose. I ended changing the dog from a Boxer to a miniature Doberman pinscher and hav[ing] it sitting on her lap. I discarded the riding habit for a dress and have put a garden hat in her hand. I have her seated on a circular bench that surrounds a tree (a famous one with a plaque on it for something or other), and behind the tree is a vista of a landscaped field. I have been out to Wolf Trap 3 times to get the setting and background landscape. Kay apparently had asked Betty to come and help her go through her "ordeal." I think Betty bolstered her sagging ego as she enthused enough to help things along. I like Kay. She is so outgoing and natural. How she has managed to escape the Washington mildew is a mystery.

Johnny has been taking music lessons. When his music teacher got a group together to play, an engaging new friend of J's, when introduced to the teacher, rose to the occasion to say, "I am musical too. I don't play any musical instruments, but I like to whistle and sing." I loved him immediately.

Love,
Marcella

June 30, 1947
Dear Tat,

We went to Kay's place in Virginia, Wolf Trap, so I could paint the tree and get her placed correctly on the seat. I put the painting on the mantel to study it while we had lunch, and Kay invited her two servants to look at the painting asking for their opinion on the likeness. (I won't let this happen again.) They both in so many words said: "Dey's jus somethin 'bout de eye, de mouth and de expression." I proceeded to paint the background and never touched the face. When the canvas went back on the mantel for study, the same women exclaimed that I sure had improved it and the face now favored their mistress exactly. Nearing the final sitting later in my studio, Kay's husband, Jouett, came along with an old friend and the two flatly contradicted each other . . . "The hair is too high" . . . "Oh, I thought it was too low" . . . "The eyes are too blue" . . . "Oh, I thought they weren't blue enough," and so on.

Neither Kay nor Jouett could make up their minds about the expression and she had to go to New York, and then developed a bad stiff neck at the last, so I couldn't possibly finish it although there is not much to do. I like the face and don't want to touch it, but must do some work on the hand and garden hat. Jouett offered to pay the $600, but I never like to accept the full amount until the painting is entirely finished so I said 1/2 would do so he sent me $300 and I will let them keep the portrait this summer while I am away. That may prove to be a mistake.

Lionberger Davis wrote that he is going to England, is moving to a new house and remodeling his museum so he wants to wait until fall to commission a "small portrait" of my mother-in-law.

Love,
Marcella

Center Sandwich, N.H.
August 1, 19477
Dear Tat,

Now that I am back in New Hampshire waiting for my house to be habitable, my mind has gone blank and pastoral. I wonder if I will ever be interested in world affairs again! All that is important to me now is to have the leak in the roof fixed, get the old wallpaper scraped off, the paint washed and the bathroom IN. Chester Weed's old carpenters are doing it all.

I have had a letter from Karl Shapiro telling me he was leaving my portrait of him (which I lent him for the summer) with Mother as they were packing to leave and he was worried something might happen to it. He had recommended that the poets' portraits be hung in the Fellows' room, but the Librarian would have to approve and he hadn't heard yet. He said that purchases other than books were rarely made, but he hoped one of the funds could be tapped for the pictures as he felt they would add enormously to the room and the Library's art works. They are expecting Cal Lowell as the next consultant on September 15th.

Everyone is so helpful to me here. Carl Beede, a descendant of one of the earliest settlers in Sandwich, had a little Franklin Stove sent to me from his house in Hartford, as he said he was so pleased that an artist had come to live here in summers. There was only a coal stove in the house as the open fireplace had been bricked over.

Love,

Marcella

The contractor who repaired the house, Chester Weed, paid his fine carpenters a dollar an hour, and they worked the entire month of August. He broke out in a sweat, horrified, when I said I would take out a mortgage to pay him. He told me I could pay him when and how I pleased, with no interest at all. He seemed perfectly satisfied with this arrangement, for I never saw him again. Some months I paid him fifty dollars, some months twenty-five perhaps, some months nothing at all, but he got it all eventually.

Center Sandwich, N.H.
September, 1947
Dear Tat,

How about naming my house for the book which paid for it? Would you suggest A Quiet Neighborhood, the title of the book, or just Quite Quiet, or Anne's Folly? I considered calling it Two Bells because all I found that could be salvaged from the fourteen truckloads of trash carried from the house were two sleigh bells on a broken leather thong. They could make a doorbell—since I have neither a sleigh nor a cow.

I am discovering other things that people born in Sandwich seem to want to discard. I found a fine old family bed in a neighbor's attic. It is solid maple with hand-turned bedposts, and a bargain at $50. So I thought. However, there was a difference of opinion from the old carpenter working in my house when he saw it come in. He asked: "What ya pay for that bed?" When I told him $50, he gasped incredulously. "We used to throw 'em on the dump!" he exclaimed.

My little Cape Cod house is very old and only 30 × 19 feet. An architect, who summers here, has advised me how I can get in three small bedrooms, cupboards and a bathroom, as well as the living room, by removing a partition. He insisted on making blueprints for me (his portrait will be painted at some point) but when his plans were put up for the old carpenters to follow they viewed them with undisguised suspicion and refused to look at them. They KNOW how to build houses. Learned from their "pappies."

Mr. Gotchall, who is a silversmith, let me have some Japanese iris bulbs and some white delphinium from his garden, and has taken us around to see the views, even to the other end of Squam Lake to the estate of a Boston millionaire named Webster [of Stone and Webster] whose hobby is hummingbirds—dozens of them feeding from stations which supply them with honey and water. Quite a sight. I saw some white clematis, a vine I love, which I wanted, and asked Mr. Gotchall if I could have. "No," he replied, "we've got your garden all filled up." A wonderful character. I expressed a desire to paint him but he said there would be no money in it.

Johnny digs patiently and futilely for worms to go fishing. I called up a neighbor and asked hopefully: "Mrs. Daigneau, do you have worms?"

In late August Karl Shapiro wrote me that the picture project for the Fellows room seemed a fine idea to the Librarian, but there was no mention of the money needed to purchase them. "That, I may add," wrote Karl, "is quite like the hieratic language of government. We are still in the dark." And the dark is the way it all remained.

Love,
Marcella

Mary Winslow Chapman, Mrs. Winslow's daughter, wrote me a note on September 18, 1947:

> The QUIET NEIGHBORHOOD advance copies just arrived. We live in a world of Anne G. W. All the previous books and all the English editions of them, and now this, plus a lot of correspondence about the next one, which is already in Knopf's hands. Name unknown. Secretive Tat is not giving out anything.

In October, 1947, *A Quiet Neighborhood,* by Anne Goodwin Winslow, was published by Knopf. The New York *Times* reviewer, Orville Prescott, felt that this second full-length novel should delight Mrs. Winslow's admirers and win her more. "Like most of her stories it is laid in the south some fifty years ago and is a study of the inner life of its principal characters. It isn't so much what we do or what happens to us which matters, Mrs. Winslow seems to say, as what we are and what we think. Experience is only significant when it is digested, when its meaning has been absorbed and when it has contributed to intellectual and spiritual growth." The reviewer remarked that no one was likely to claim major importance for this book but that it was good to know that wise and artful novels were still being written and noticed. "Secretive Tat" had her say in a Memphis newspaper about the condensed version of *A Quiet Neighborhood* that appeared in the *Ladies' Home Journal:* "The editors seem to have tried to remove every passage in which I had tried to do a little thinking, or the reading of which might have required some thinking on the part of the reader. . . . The author is going into utter seclusion until it is all over. Now, all that remains is for someone to distill it into a capsule so that it can be swallowed." Her comment in a letter to me was, "My story is even more cut up than the proofs. Hopeless—and the illustrations, hideous. But the money has its place. I am glad I abandoned the planet when I did."

P Street, N.W.
Washington, D.C.
October 13, 1947
Dear Tat,

I am glad I read A QUIET NEIGHBORHOOD when down with a cold. Only at such a time would I have had leisure enough to get into the mood of "serenity and peace of mind of a bygone day." A sort of untouched-by-today beauty. I know there is no one today writing as you do—so I know why the Knopfs feel the way they do about not wanting to change you. Your contemporaries will get so much more out of it than the group under 40. How many of those would understand the idealistic love of Mrs. Fairleigh, or why sex didn't rise and smite Maury on the approach of Amy? The whole setting for me was laid in your living room, though I could see Amy packing in my bedroom and Nellie making the candy in that marble-floored kitchen. As in every one of your books, the atmosphere that has enveloped my married life is overpowering in your written words. I hope it will be your greatest success.

Three cheers for Orville Prescott! That was such a review that the Book of the Month must be hiding their heads in shame for having been the ones who overlooked serenity. "There are not enough people who are excited about Anne Goodwin Winslow." I am! I saw Terence Rattigan's *The Winslow Boy* (your period, 1910) with the original English cast— dignified, well-bred people, or acting as though they were.

I told you Jim Simonds sold his house next door and the people are in it. I called on my new neighbor and she is delightful. Intelligent, old enough to be a grandmother but smart, young looking, very chic, natural and friendly. The house is in exquisite taste, beautiful paintings. She asked which side I lived on and then exclaimed: "Then you paint!" Marjorie Clay had told her to get in touch with me. She later told me she wanted to take lessons, so I will introduce her to Andrea Zerega who has a class. Of course he will soon feel she is his special property, but no matter, he is just the one she needs. Her name is Mrs. Christian Herter. Her husband has been a Congressman from Massachusetts for six years. [1] I am sure she will be a great addition to my life.

Love,
Marcella

1. Christian Herter (1895–1966) later became governor of Massachusetts and served as secretary of state under Eisenhower, in 1959–1961. A week after the Herters moved next door to me, *Time* magazine ran a long article about the "52 year old, 6 ft. 5 in. handsome gentleman politician who cuts a fine patrician figure on Boston's Beacon Hill" heading up a congressional committee on foreign aid.

October 18, 1947
Dear Tat,

Come and cheer us up! We all have colds and the house is as dark as pitch. The weather is lovely now but I have gone into autumn doldrums after the freedom from want and everything else that the country life provides. I need Mrs. Glassford's iron pills to face another winter. Also, I have just received the tax bill for my N.H. house before I am even in it! $75. I ought to be very happy because Etta is back and as wonderful as ever and the children are wonderful but, at this time of year, the world is going to the dogs. I will feel differently tomorrow as I have a lot to be thankful for. I am thankful to Malvina Hoffman who brought Mestrovic to tea after we saw his exhibit at the National Gallery, and I also was included in the dinner Anne Archbold had for him—only me,

Malvina, Mestrovic and the Secretary of the Navy [James Forrestal, who served from 1944 to 1947]. I can understand why Malvina likes Mestrovic so much. He was the second sculptor she studied with after Rodin, and an influence on her work. She made a life-size statue of him.

Love,
Marcella

November 3, 1947

Dear Tat,

So many impressions of New York! First and foremost was my joy at meeting Louise Dodd, your good friend. She was like a breath of fresh air in the murky, overdone, decayed atmosphere of New York. The Fishers and the Tates, of course, are all decaying rapidly. I won't say rotten, though I might apply it to some remarks set off by Caroline and Allen about their "friends." More of this when I see you. They are in a dither because you didn't invite Nancy and baby to come by when she was in Memphis. I couldn't take up the cudgels because I knew nothing about it. Isn't it hard being nice to people and not treading on toes? The Tates' toes are easily tread on these days it seems because so many of their friends are being more successful. Red Warren has three plays going— movie, radio and stage of ALL THE KING'S MEN—and the Lowells, of course, are all the rage at the moment in literary circles, which probably doesn't help. I hope they saw the Orville Prescott review of your book. Allen mumbled something about seeing a review but no comment. Caroline has been delving into Catholic philosophy and says she will become a Catholic if she has time!

I took several pictures to *Harper's Bazaar* and *Town and Country* and both art editors were more interested that I hadn't painted Lowell than that I had painted Shapiro, Welty and Biddle. Now I shall have to ask him to sit having told them I would paint him!

Betty [Fisher] has gone suburban after Guatemala and the Foreign Service dream. Keeping up as ever—cutting down the gold damask for draperies and having wainscoting put around the dining room walls, which was never meant to be there, with the tables FULL of Guatemalan dolls and bric-a-brac. Dear Betty, with chin up, and kind as usual, is not too thrilled to find herself out of Georgetown.

I went alone to see *The Heiress* with Wendy Hiller, Basil Rathbone and Craig Kelly. Adapted from Henry James' WASHINGTON SQUARE and superbly done. I loved it.

Portraits Inc. were very nice to me indeed, and even suggested that if I had a large interesting portrait there by next April, Homer Saint-Gaudens [the director of the Carnegie Institute] might invite it to the Pittsburgh International next fall, as he was rather influenced by what they suggested! You see how it works.

I went in to say hello to Alfred Knopf as I was passing by. It seems that is not what one does—you know—the usual appointments weeks ahead. He managed to say hello, but the "publishing game is way off." In fact, he looked glum, but I hope that was just New York and not me. Faces in New York say, No Trespassing, On Private Property. One nice exception was an engaging young Patrick O'Higgins, a new art editor at *Town and Country*. He wants to see my portrait of Katherine Anne Porter when he comes to Washington.

Mother Barry wants me to paint an overmantel in the Reception Room at Stone Ridge, Mary's school. Surprisingly, instead of a religious subject, she likes the idea of my making a copy of the painting by Savage of the George Washington family (which is in the National Gallery), since it represents Family. I asked if I could do it in fresco directly on the wall so it wouldn't seem to be such a direct copy. Barry was given $1000 for a statue in the garden but said she much preferred the mural for that sum.

It looks like another batch of kittens is imminent. A 5-year-old grandson of the Herters called over the fence to ask if they had come yet and, when they did, would I mind if he could "come over and join them."

Love,
Marcella

November 6, 1947
Dear Tat,

I have probably lost a good opportunity to have a New York gallery. After Mrs. Dodd and Mrs. Albrecht showed some of my pictures to the Ferargil Gallery on E. 57th Street, I had a letter from the President, Frederic Price, saying that he liked my paintings and believed a N.Y. show would further my career. He said the gallery was not endowed and they could not pay extra expenses, which did not put me off as much as his admonition that I line up an exciting selling exhibition, that New York was very tough and I should have light, bright, airy and cheerful pictures—landscapes etc. because their public wanted to be pleased and enjoy looking at the pictures they bought. A later letter repeated that "New York and, let us say America, is tough on artists. It's got to be colorful and alluring—red, white and blue, with, if possible, a theme song that runs through the exhibition." Well, I haven't done that many landscapes and I certainly have nothing in the least red, white and blue, but I understood well enough to realize that he would be expecting pretty subjects and my work would be too gutsy. How could I pay all the expenses and get all the work framed and shipped by next spring? I wrote him of my reservations and we decided to drop the matter for the time being. In the meantime he said he would be glad to see any "masterpiece" that I might bring in for them possibly to show in the De Beers Collection (the famous ads in publications). So—back to my portraits which, if they have white in them, seldom have red and blue as well. Still, landscapes have their points. Imagine the utter peace of not worrying about people objecting to their portraits, finding always something wrong with the mouth! Speaking of which, the Shouse portrait has been waiting for the final touches. We are still waiting for the last sitting—she for a miraculous different face, and I for the remaining $300.

Love,
Marcella

I felt I needed to do more work on the hands and the hat of Mrs. Shouse, although I considered the head and the rest of the portrait finished. Her husband, however, wanted "more sparkle in Kay's eyes," and I would have added an extra sparkle or two had I been able to get her to sit again. That never happened, so I completed the painting without her, framed it, and left it at her door. A few years later an artist, on a house tour, told me that he had seen one of my best portraits. It was resting on the floor of a bedroom in the Shouse house. At least it was not in the cupboard.

November 13, 1947
Dear Tat,

Mary's ham has arrived. It is my Christmas present, isn't it? There is no way a Virginia ham can compete with a Tennessee ham, and everyone who tastes one realizes that is so. She is so generous to share her bounty with us. The sending is so fraught with difficulties that I appreciate it all the more. I will cook it after you come and perhaps we could share it with Lionberger Davis. He is determined to meet you and is arriving in Washington for that purpose on the B & O at 11:20 Saturday, December 13th, and wants to see us on Saturday or Sunday. Do please come up in plenty of time to be here then.

I am painting Mrs. Meade Fletcher now—evening dress, family jewels and brocades. She had all sorts of gorgeous things to choose from. The Ferargil Gallery would like her coloring and her looks. She is almost too pretty to paint. Hard to get a likeness as she looks like those pretty girls in cigarette ads, features so even.

On a pretty day I decided to try some landscaping and, while I was painting Anne Archbold's garden, she and her luncheon guests came out for their coffee and got put into the picture! Mrs. A immediately bought it and then expressed her delight at the sun on a beech tree which sounded like a commission—but it turned out not to be. I think she prefers *not* to do the expected. She said it was her favorite view—late afternoon shadows falling across a grassy slope and highlighting the breasts of the two stone peacocks—brilliant reds and yellows of leaves through the trees in the distance. But no whites and blues!

I had Cal Lowell over for dinner last week which, in spite of being a Lowell, and because of being a poet, he dived into like any starving artist. More talk of the Tates which you will enjoy hearing about when you come and we get into the literary gossip.

Enclosed are two clippings from the *Post:* one of Molly Thayer's rating of you as a "prodigy" for A QUIET NEIGHBORHOOD; the other about me publicizing the Stone Ridge Bazaar! Clever Mother Barry got me to pose with six children of alumnae, with my portraits on exhibition.

Love,

Marcella

Years later, when I showed the photograph to Mother Barry just before she retired, she could remember the names of every one of the children, even the men the girls married.

November 24, 1947
Dear Tat,

It is 11 P.M. but I must get off a letter, which many things have interrupted, mainly the suicide of my last model, Augusta Fletcher. She killed herself yesterday evening before she was to come to my studio for a sitting today. Now, if Mrs. Shouse had done it, I might have felt responsible (the easy way out you know) but Augusta was loving the picture and all seemed rosy. I won't take the blame, but it was quite a shock as I saw her frequently last week. She had phoned me the day before to ask to put off the sitting because she thought I did not like to work on a Saturday, but I told her that made no difference and I wanted to get on with the portrait. I was preparing to go to the studio and saw the headline on the front page: "Socialite Dies of Pistol Shot After Party," and this was how it was described: After being at a cocktail party near their Georgetown home, Mr. and Mrs. Fletcher returned to their house with dinner guests (the prominent L. Corrin Strongs), and Augusta and Mr. Strong went up to the library. Augusta asked Strong to turn his head and count ten. She then fired a bullet into her temple. The news account said she had been chic, charming and gay at the Auchinloss party and no one could give a reason for her act. I thought right away of the difficulty I had getting a likeness. I had not been able to "get" her and it was frustrating to me. It would be nice if I had been able to finish it for her husband, but it was to be a surprise to him and so he knew nothing about it.

How did you answer your fan letter from the guy who wanted to have a role in the "movie" of A QUIET NEIGHBORHOOD? Don't you want the letter back for his marvelous line: "As you might have guessed, I am a writer by talent and determination, and have plenty of both?" Too bad his signature shows him to be unbalanced. I had a letter once from a nut with that identical handwriting.

The Institute of Contemporary Arts was founded by Robert Richman, a teacher, editor, and poet. Starting on a shoestring, he was permitted after a few years to have the institute's events at the Corcoran Gallery. He and his wife, Maida, were called the world's greatest experts on the care and feeding of artists. Their guest room, which overlooked Dumbarton Oaks, was seldom without one. Richman would say the writers, musicians, painters, and sculptors were all well mannered and fit into their family life: "Aldous Huxley is the best baby-sitter, Herbert Read a keen dishwasher, and Nogushi his own breakfast-getter." Occasionally I was asked to have these artists to my house, not far from theirs, after the various events.

In the fifties the lecture series cost only ten dollars annually for the likes of Sir Kenneth Clark on painting, Martha Graham on modern dance,

Elizabeth Bowen on the novel, Naum Gabo on sculpture, Bernard Leach and Hamada on pottery, James Johnson Sweeney on abstraction, John Cage on expressionist music, Eric Bentley on modern theater, and Lewis Mumford on architecture. The series also included memorial lectures—for instance, by Allen Tate. A membership, at five dollars a year, entitled one to films, concerts, and exhibitions as well as poetry readings.

December 6, 1947
Dear Tat,

The pecans came yesterday. Just in time to have a dessert for Allen who arrives to give a reading tomorrow at the Corcoran. We all agreed they are extra good. Tomorrow I am having dinner with Robert Richman. They live across from Dumbarton Oaks and usually entertain the poets.

I will wear my new coat and the dress I had made over from the discarded velvet of Betty [Fisher]'s posing dress and the blouse from the dress I got in Paris in the 30's. Très chic! Pink velvet petals on chiffon. I wore it one night to dinner at Mrs. Scriven's on Bancroft Place. Remember that nice lady whose English-sounding voice you didn't like on the telephone? She has the kind of house which is supposed to bowl you over with its luxury items but only makes you wonder why anyone would buy such enormous objects. Suits of mail etc. The kind of things the Finnegans would have bought if they had had a bigger house and had gone to a few more auctions.

Mrs. S has Mrs. Woodrow Wilson's cook, I was told, sotto voce, and no one said why, as Mrs. W is still living, so it must be because the cook doesn't know how to cook. Mrs. Wilson undoubtedly hired her for her lemon meringue pies for we had one that quite made up for the undone meat, forgotten potatoes and over-salted vegetables.

Caroline [Gordon]'s portrait was in a Corcoran exhibit and a review said it rose above the usual style in portraits. I hear that she entered the Catholic church two weeks ago. I wonder how that will affect things.

Having left photographs of my portraits of poets at *Harper's Bazaar,* I got a note from the Fiction Editor saying that there was no chance of reproducing them in color, and the art department decided the black and whites did not stand up as a feature. Sorry but thanks etc.

Love,
Marcella

December 15, 1947

Dear Tat,

Your decision not to come for Christmas is quite a blow! The children each took it as something they wouldn't believe. "What! Grantat not coming for Christmas! She can't DO that." I realize how everything has been just waiting—the kittens haven't been given away until you could see them cavorting; the ham not cooked for Lionberger so it could be saved for a party for you; Mother's plum pudding neatly tucked in the icebox; even an old fashioned coffee grinder waiting to help out—but I refuse to think you won't be able to make it. I need your cheerfulness. I have no active worries about health, or even life, to say nothing of safety, but the weight of grief makes me wonder what the future holds with so little hope. I wonder how anyone takes more, the way you are doing. But some nice things are happening. Fredrica just bought a painting and Anne Archbold had me for drinks to meet Witter Bynner.[1] A society poet? He has all the pat, charming phrases. He is pleasant and there were two musicians who played and improvised on her two pianos. I felt very gay for the first time in ages.

Allen's visit was at a bad time for me. Rather a strain melding him, the Cairnses, the Biddles, the Richmans, Alexis Léger and Lowell at my dinner. After Allen's reading (he reads so beautifully, of course, those unintelligible words), all of us, but the Biddles, went to the house of Caresse Crosby and indulged in heavy slander heaped on all writers' heads. I'm awfully tired of it, but fascinated of course.

I like Cal. He is like a big awkward bushy dog who wags his tail, but never in tune with anyone else. I feel that he is sincere but groping. Anyway, *Time* says no other poet has taken his place this past year.

Lionberger Davis was a complete and total flop. I practically had nightmares after he left I was so depressed. You can gather how I felt listening to those verses of his. He talked of how no one is buying paintings and of how broke he is—though he admitted he is in the top income taxable class. He never even LOOKED at your painting or any other, though I had decided NOT to sell you at any price, you may be glad to know. Sorry for this gloomy letter. I start the mural at Stone Ridge tomorrow which I am looking forward to.

Love,
Marcella

1. Witter Bynner (1881–1968) was a translator and a literary editor for publishing companies. He served as president of the Poetry Society of America from 1920 to 1928.

December 20, 1947
Dear Tat,

I am feeling so much better since I started work on the mural. Why do these weights lift like a mist and then descend again? Doing the fresco technique up on a ladder is hard work but relaxing. I just love it and it is going to be beautiful. The colors are all blocked in. I am painting with casein tempera using small brushstrokes which give the appearance of true fresco.

The enclosed letter from the Corcoran Gallery tells me that a Mr. Lovejoy came to the area show and "carried off" my "lovely watercolor" *From My Georgetown Window*. Enclosed was a $100 check. I came down from $125 or Mr. L would have brought a different painting. There is no rise in art prices, unfortunately, but I am pleased to sell from an exhibit to a perfect stranger. The picture was done looking down P Street where the children were playing in the snow. I'm sure Mr. Lovejoy lives up to his name and likes gay things.

Elizabeth Wilcox [an interior decorator] is decorating the Fort Myer Officers' Club and wants a picture of mine for over the mantel. The budget allows for only $100, but every little bit helps. (The rug cost $1000.)

Does the *Atlantic Monthly* always ask for a list of names of people who might buy the edition in which you have a poem? Well, I will buy the January number for "Thus to Revisit." Thanks for letting me know.

Just in time for Mary's birthday today I got a lovely letter from Mother Barry which eases my mind. I quote:

> Please do not think of taking Mary away from Stone Ridge for financial reasons—she is exactly the kind of child we want, and I am already planning something that will make it possible for you to leave her here with us until she is ready for college. And her excellent work last year makes me hope that she will eventually win a college scholarship. She has it in her to do so, and I am going to see that she is carefully guided towards one.

Then more about the new wing and my helping her with color problems. She is a super Mother Superior, that's for sure.

Love,
Marcella

December 31, 1947
Dear Tat,

I am, as usual, not letting the New Year in. It always gets in nicely without me. I am catching up on my mail before life picks me up and deposits me on the merry-go-round of 1948. Enclosed telegram from Alfred Knopf, who was disappointed to find you had not come yet.

December has required additional services from Charles (because of more furnace ashes), one being portrait sitting. He has such fine features, added to that benign expression, that I asked if he would let me paint him. I wanted to get his hands in (with those extra-long fingers), so have made a three-quarters life-size painting. It is one of my very best. He sat as long as I was able to work, nodding off occasionally. To keep him awake, I asked him about his life. I didn't question him about his "white grandmother," when he came to that part, but did a bit of wondering since he comes from Virginia. Nothing said about the color of his grandfather, but the tar brush had to come in somewhere. I think that even Miss Nichols would concede that he is a fine old gentleman. I enjoy him tremendously and have begun to quote his wise and priceless remarks which I think should be recorded. Here are some good ones: I asked him to shovel snow from the front steps last week, which brought on his dismay at the condition of my coal shovel. I had to tell him that the reason the end was so "curly" was because, in my ardor to get the coal in the furnace, I often missed the door completely, spilling coal all over the floor and hitting the furnace instead. Old Charles, in his 70's, looked at me, so many years younger, and ruminated, "Yas'm, you so strong, somepin' hadda give." Another time I was reaching for a dish on the top shelf which he could not get without a ladder. He made up for his short stature by assuring me that I could reach up farther than he could, but he could stoop just as low!

I picture him seated on an old tree stump, with a Delta background landscape. I have made a lot of his hands on his knees, and the differing browns of flesh and earth. His expression is just right. One can see that I care about him.

Today an editorial in the *Washington Post* declared that Washington was the most expensive city in the country, the chief reason being the outlandish cost of housing—that people affected were the ones who had forgone dollar butter and 79-cent bacon.

Love,

Marcella

As the year ended, Mrs. Winslow wrote that there were a thousand things she wanted to ask me but it would mean more wielding of my pen than she had a claim to; that it seemed a miracle that I had time for letters at all, adding,

> How do you manage it—not only to live your life but to capture it as it flies? Some day you may be glad to have these records—some day when you want to do the autobiography of an artist who was so much else besides.

January 3, 1948

Dear Tat,

A long "Happy New Year" newsy letter from Katherine Anne who is staying long enough in one place to have a printed address on her stationery—8706 Sunset Plaza Place, Hollywood. Wait! I knew that info. had to be wrong. Rereading the letter I notice she is stopping with friends until she can "pull herself together and decide what to do"! Remember Mr. Knopf's remark, when we told him Katherine Anne had gone to Hollywood, that no writer was ever known to have gotten out of Hollywood except Faulkner? She sends thanks to you saying it is fine to be read, but to be reread is what any writer really longs for. Most of the letter was taken up with her comments about Caroline's conversion to Catholicism—such as: "In the last few years I have known such a scrabble of damaged souls who simply resort to the church as almost an act of despair—they cannot stick—they backslide like the old fashioned Methodists they are at the core" etc. Several other quotes: "You are right about Witter Bynner; he is an old fashioned society poet who waters down Chinese philosophy for the kind of people who like to be soothed with nice thoughts without having to think for themselves, and he floats around rich people who float around him, and he is as empty and not half as pretty as a grasshopper shell." She suggests we get a copy of the December *Harper's* magazine (not the *Bazaar*) to read her piece on Gertrude Stein. No doubt vitriolic, as she loves to be. Says she still wears the gray dress she posed in, and is glad she didn't die in my house when she took all those sleeping pills. She is still shuddering about that.

Awaiting your coming. Let us know as I want to have Charles hang up all the frames now on the floor in your room. They do seem to accumulate. Charles made an amusing remark the other day: I felt I needed some boards under my mattress (the doctor suggested them for my back). I found them so expensive and realized I had many packing boards in my basement, so I asked Charles to find the best boards and put them in my bed. Later, he told me he had done so, but added: "Couldn't find but jest one. If you is plannin' on havin' company, they gotta git along best way they kin."

Love,
Marcella

Robert Lowell had offered to take me to see Ezra Pound at St. Elizabeth's Hospital, a mental institution, provided I could get permission from the Pounds and Dr. Overholser, the superintendent. Pound's visitors' hours had been extended to two hours in 1948 from fifteen minutes during the first year. He seemed to have regained his balance and enjoyed having company from near and far. Later he was granted privileges that permitted hordes of young disciples to flock to him, drinking in his every word. Conversation was his chief recreation.

I wrote for permission and got a cordial letter from Dorothy Pound, who spent every afternoon with Ezra. She said her husband raised no objection to my doing a color sketch of him, especially if I needed only two or three sittings. She said she was there nearly every afternoon "unless the wintry weather catches me by the heels." Although it was necessary for me to get written permission to visit, Mrs. Pound suggested that I not mention that I wanted to make a sketch, since that would entangle me in red tape, perhaps for months. She asked if I would consider the "somewhat conspiratorial method" of carrying my supplies in a small shopping bag. I would and did.

It was a very cold, snowy day in February when Robert Lowell and I drove to the hospital in what was to me an unfamiliar section of town. Lowell came often, so climbing the long flight of steps and waiting to be let in the locked door at the top was no surprise to him, but I was trembling, not knowing what to expect. Ezra put me at ease immediately, giving me a big bear hug. He was bigger and better looking than I had expected. I noticed at once his beard, which was divided into three parts. We sat by a window in an area he seemed to have claimed for himself, and to the tune of a noisy radiator, we tried to make ourselves heard. Some of the din was just the passage of strange figures talking to themselves—one, I remember, wandering around in his underwear. There must have been a special chair for Pound, for he found it necessary to rest his neck. Leaning back on it was the way I drew him—one hand upraised as he talked, in a characteristic gesture. Since conversation goes over my head when I am concentrating on my work, I can never repeat the fascinating things intelligent men, such as Lowell and Pound, say to each other at such a time. I came away with visual sensations: snow out the window, the bareness of the room, and the apparent pleasure Pound was getting from the visit. I had a keen desire to get a faithful rendering of this controversial man. The drawing was finished, but I asked if I could return for a color sketch, and that was agreed. The next time Lowell and I could get together for the trip was in May. I was not able to use the same pose, however, because Ezra and his wife were sitting outside under the trees on an unseasonably warm day. I painted a new version of just his head and shoulders, with casein tempera on board, a 10 × 12 size, which I was able to finish on another warm day in June.

I made a number of visits after these, since the Pounds enjoyed company and I was sometimes asked to take out poets who wanted to meet the famous—or at that time, infamous—man. When I wrote for permission to bring the English poets David Gascoyne and Kathleen Raine in 1951, I received one of his cryptic letters:

S LIZ   21 Nv

O.K. bring 'em along.
Will leave their names at the desk
preferable one at a time / BUT, no abs
/ prohibition
of their gangin up on grampaw.

In one of my letters to him I enclosed a photograph of my portrait of Robert Frost, asking if he recognized who it was. I got back an answer immediately:

Yes, my dear Marcella,

I recognize the portrait, a low down pusillanimous son of a bitch, my opinion of whom has sunk with increasing velocity during the

past 5 years. A mindconditioned ape, and sycophant to popular opinion. The mental and moral cowardice of a lot of puffed native writers
is more than a nice gal like you can imagine, taking only the surface.
Details viva voce, cant use typing ribbon on same. portrait excellent
I shd/ say. Why not RAISE the standard of american writing instead
of blubbering about submediocrity.

Pound had been helpful in reviewing Frost's first book, *A Boy's Will,*
when they were both in England, and Frost was helpful in getting Pound
released from St. Elizabeth's, but there was little love lost between them.
When I was painting Frost in 1952, he told me that when Pound objected
to the line "Home is the place where when you want to go there they have
to take you in" in his poem "The Death of the Hired Man," he decided that
he had had enough of Ezra's influence.

During the fifties at some point, Ezra asked if I could house his daughter, Mary de Rachewiltz, if she came to Washington. That was a complication I could not take on even if I had had the room. I can't recall if she
ever came, but I vividly recall the occasion when Dorothy Pound was invited to one of Harriet Winslow's musicals. She spotted the Supreme Court
justice Felix Frankfurter in the august throng and asked me to introduce
her so she could ask him to get Ezra *out.* Poor Justice Frankfurter made a
hasty retreat when I approached him with the request, and nothing more
developed in that direction.

My solo show of forty-four paintings was arranged by the Whyte and
Bader Gallery and held at the United Nations Club from March 10 through
March 29, 1948. Besides twenty-three portraits, including eight of the
poets, I showed the designs I had made for murals in a Pittsburgh library,
done for the Public Works of Art Project (a New Deal effort to help artists)
in 1933 and 1934, just before I married. I also showed some compositions,
one being a Washington scene with figures, lent by Mrs. Eugene Meyer,
who had bought it from a show she sponsored in 1935 (also to help artists
sell their work, with the cooperation of retail stores and women's clubs).
The Noel Macys lent the oil of their house, which I had done out of grati-
tude for the use of their studio.

Mrs. Winslow, visiting at the time, was as interested in all this excitement as she was in the negotiations that went on over the sale of my portrait
of Charles. It had been selected from a Pittsburgh area show to be included
in a group being considered by the Latrobe High School, in Pennsylvania,
for their permanent collection.

I received a phone call from the school offering me a price for the painting that was only half the amount put on it. I felt I could not accept this offer for the portrait's first showing, although I regretted turning down any sum from the young students who had voted it their favorite for the art collection. While I was feeling somewhat guilty for my lack of beneficence, the school called again and said that they had gone over the books and could raise the amount a bit; they added that the kids raised money for their purchases for the collection by selling hot dogs. Their get-up-and-go succeeded where money had failed. Charles did not leave Latrobe until 1985, when the portrait was selected to represent me in an exhibition celebrating the seventy-fifth anniversary of the Associated Artists of Pittsburgh, at the Carnegie Mellon University.

Charles always treasured the letter he received from the student council in Latrobe: "Our eleven hundred students [they were all white] selected Comès' painting, not only as the very best of the ninety-five that were brought to Latrobe, but as their first choice of paintings that they especially wanted to remain in Latrobe. Miss Comès has shown through her painting the very pleasant characteristics that you possess. Your picture says that you are a delightful old gentleman!"

April 26, 1948
Dear Tat,

To accent the misery of your leave-taking, the weather has put on a raw cold spell which I hope is not insulting you too. Etta and I are holding down the damp, dark fort.

Even being up in your ivory tower, 3rd floor back, you DID make an impression. Mary found words for it, returning from the airport: "We are going to miss Grantat. Every time she comes I learn something more. She is brilliant. And she laughs in all the right places in the Pip books!" I wanted to get that all down before I forgot it. Certainly, on my tombstone, instead of In Memoriam there should be No Memory Mum.

The Christian Herters and I had dinner at Chauncey Stillman's last night.[1] Mr. Herter, who insists that I call him Chris, sat next to me and said he thought I was going to follow up taking him to my show with doing a portrait of him, and added: "A commission!"—the only hitch being a time for him to sit. This evening the Herters had a huge cocktail party in their garden, guests who all looked like Congress from my window. None of the ladies dressy—mostly in suits, and Mrs. Herter (now Mac by her wish) stood out tall and regal among them. I was impressed with Chris and said he should run for President, but it seems he cannot as he was not born in this country. His parents were professional painters living in Europe at the time.

I will start a portrait of Carley Dawson soon.[2] Cal Lowell has proposed to her, she says. He is now divorced from Jean Stafford. She also says my small portraits are certainly worth $350, but she can't pay more than $300. She is the daughter of Mary Chess (cosmetics) and has beautiful clothes to choose from. Very attractive and does some writing herself.

I was delighted to have my small portrait of Denis Devlin accepted for the Phillips spring exhibit. Mother told me she was near Duncan when he was commenting favorably on it to someone. Forty-three Washington and Baltimore artists in it. The only portrait in the show.

Love,
Marcella

1. Chauncey Devereux Stillman (1908–1989), a New York investor and philanthropist, was an alumnus of Harvard and of the Columbia School of Architecture. In World War II, he was a squadron air combat intelligence officer. In the sixties he was commodore of the New York Yacht Club and founded the Wethersfield Institute, a Manhattan group that sponsored religious seminars. In March, 1947, when this elegant New Yorker heard from Miss Rose Standish Nichols that Anne Winslow was visiting in Washington, he simply presented himself at the door, taking the most direct, if somewhat unorthodox, way to make her acquaintance. His friendship and his admiration of Anne Winslow's writing continued as long as he lived.

2. After two failed marriages in England, Carley Dawson came to Washington, buying a Georgetown house. She met Robert Lowell at a dinner in honor of Alexis Léger and was briefly engaged to him.

May 13, 1948
Dear Tat,

I have gone along with Marceil's idea that I paint the current crop of debutantes. Not only will her daughter be introduced to society, but she feels this will be a lucrative venture for me, since the proud parents will hardly be able to resist portraits of their daughters at such an alluring age. So far all the "debs" have agreed to sit—at least their mothers have agreed—and I start this project with every ounce of strength I've saved up by not painting lately—unless one can call Ezra Pound my

Pound of energy. I worked on him yesterday, outdoors, with yells and whoops accompanying my every stroke, although not coming from him—or me.

Nikolaki writes to me today: "I urge you to work less and spend more time to know people." I spent some time to know people at the Herters' cocktail party a few days ago; music at Harriet Winslow's house; concert at Marceil's, she at one piano, Russell at the other; and feel full of knowledge, at least as much as I need at the moment.

What I need, more than knowledge, is strength to continue to paint portraits. I have discovered that Betty Vincent has told everyone that she doesn't like the first painting I did of her (she likes the second). [She] tells me that she thinks I should put it away. She says I should show the portrait I made of Margaret Cox to people who want portraits; but Margaret Cox thinks I should put hers away. However, all agree that they like my portrait of Katherine Biddle—which *she* thinks should be put completely out of sight.

So I am going to have a special morgue exhibition of "Put Aways" served with tea. I expect it to be a big success with people admiring other people. If in between this I can achieve a reputation, then everyone will like themselves and be proud to own the pictures—but I may be dead by then. Mrs. Biddle wrote from St. Croix that she was sorry to miss my exhibit and enclosed a check for $350 for her portrait! No doubt Léger's influence.

Love,
Marcella

May 20, 1948
Dear Tat,

After a visit from Lionberger Davis saying I had MADE his day, I got a very flowery letter. Not only a "God be with you," but how good to find a "person here and there who really loves beauty and is not afraid to have enthusiasm." However, he didn't express a desire to own the work I showed him with that same enthusiasm. But in his usual literary style he thanked me for taking in a "pilgrim on his way to the promised land."

Having heard of an excellent model, I decided recently to ask a group of artists to join me in a life class in the beautiful studio at the Macys'. We meet once a week and all has gone well until yesterday. The model is inventive in her poses and has a beautiful figure, so we were all pleased with her and feeling very disappointed when she didn't show up on time. She finally arrived, breathless, when we had almost given her up. Without a word, she took one of her graceful poses but couldn't hold it, and suddenly announced that she had just run over a man in her car. The man was a Negro and other Negroes set upon her, one with a knife, to whom she gave her watch to be let free. She had posted a $2500 bond and her victim was taken to a hospital. After her next pose she phoned the hospital to find that the man had died! If the story hits the newspapers it will no doubt read: "Nude model posing for Mrs. Hugo Black, Lady Jellicoe, Bill Walton, Marcella Comès, and George Hamilton in the Noel Macy house in Georgetown is wanted for manslaughter." (Hamilton gives weekly talks at the Phillips Gallery.)

Mrs. Shouse called to cancel a sitting. Says she will call me when she can come—which is beginning to seem doubtful. Mother has gone off to Pittsburgh for a wedding—looking very smart. She can look young and pretty when she goes gallivanting.

Love,
Marcella

One of my most pleasant experiences was painting the portrait of the poet Juan Ramón Jiménez (1881–1958), who left Spain during their civil war and won the Nobel Prize for literature in 1956. He was then living in Puerto Rico, after teaching at the University of Maryland. He is famous in Spanish literature for his *Tales of a Donkey*. Platero y Yo is as well known in Spain as Peter Rabbit is to readers of English. Jiménez' Vassar-educated wife, Zenobia, who took such good care of this sensitive recluse, trying to draw him into some communication with the outer world, was the one to decide that I could paint his portrait. Jiménez left his fine collection of books, pictures, and pottery to the beautiful new library at the University of Puerto Rico and never returned to Spain.

May 27, 1948
Dear Tat,

Carley Dawson said I MUST get Jiménez to sit for me while he is in this country. He lives near the University of Maryland where he teaches. I got in touch with his wife, who is half American, and she invited me to go to see them, and, if the great man would agree to sit to me, I

238 / BRUSHES WITH THE LITERARY

would have to arrange to paint him there. This I have accomplished, for two reasons. First, because he knew I had painted Pound, and, secondly, when I asked him why he had agreed to let me paint his portrait (after it was finished) he pointed to my fingernails and, in a Spanish that I could get the drift of, let me know it was because I didn't wear nail polish! We communicated in sign language, after I discovered that my Italian can't pass for Spanish, as I had hoped. I was told (in English) that J had fled Spain because of Franco. We worked in one of the only rooms that did not have his papers covering the entire floor. The papers were in neat piles so he could find what he wanted, WHEN he wanted them, I presume. Considering the language difficulty, we got along amazingly well and even laughed at what we must have each hoped were good jokes. He has a strikingly handsome head, is thin and aesthetic— just the way a poet should look. I am very pleased with the little painting. It should add a great deal to my collection.

I have enjoyed working on the George Washington family mural at Stone Ridge. When the mural was almost complete, Mother Barry asked if she could made a few strokes. She got up on the ladder and found out what is was like to wield a brush. It delighted her.

Mary loves the school. Last night she told me she was giving herself an exercise in spirituality by going over virtues she lacks. She started with: "Do I lack humility?" "No," said I. "Patience?" "No." "Long-suffering?" "No." "Charity?" "No." "Well, then," she said with a sigh, "I will just put Miscellaneous."

Love,
Marcella

June 1, 1948
Dear Tat,

I know the clipping I sent you of Eleanor Roosevelt's daily column, "My Day," was a disappointment, but it was the best I could do when you asked for some signs of life.[1] Now I really don't know where to begin.

Would you like hearing about a prominent historian, Francesco Aquilera, at the Library of Congress, coming to see my portrait of Juan Ramón Jiménez, "the greatest Spanish poet since Cervantes," to ask about acquiring it for the Hispanic Room?[2] Or about the quart of Mr.

Neam's last, and best, olive oil which fell and broke all over the newly painted kitchen and garden pillows? (It was mopped up into every corner and cranny by the industrious children, who called themselves cleaning up the "vinegar.") Both are fascinating. But more follows: Are you interested in the low trick my expected tenants pulled by backing out of their promise to take my house this summer after I had told a General and a Colonel's wife that it was rented? They were also the last people to call about my "ad," still running at a small fortune. You may, however, prefer hearing that Lionberger Davis bought two paintings that netted me $400, and that I have finished one of my debutante portraits which the mother is crazy about; or that I have just started a commission of a precocious 12-year-old [Jennifer Lee] who won't sit still unless I talk about Laurence Olivier and the state of the theater.

You may also want to know why my neighbor's son shot the black cat, or why the neighbor's sister, marrying next week at age 34, took to bed with "sexual frustration" (according to the same neighbor, who says the fiancé has rallied, the marriage must go on). And shall I tell you about the Biddle garden party where the intellectuals rubbed elbows with the "haut (and I mean 'haut') monde" and were sometimes indistinguishable? Even Melvyn Douglas and Helen Gahagan were hardly noticed. Or about my lunch today at the Little Tea House, as the guest of Mrs. Jiménez, with Katherine Biddle and Mrs. Aurelio Valls, when we pulled acquaintances to pieces with polite murmurings? Or maybe, knowing you, you would prefer to hear the gossip about a friend's divorced daughter who has no heart, no sexual frustration and no popularity, but knows the most interesting people and writes rather good poetry.

I'm sure you *don't* want to hear about a choice dinner I attended at the C——s' with fourteen people. Half the guests were French and the other half send their children to Jackson School and just love it. What I carried away from there was the story of Johnny (who had only that day convinced me that studying music with Miss Armstrong was a waste of money during the baseball season) writing out a musical composition for the daughter of one of the couples present, and telling her, at school, with a flourish, to go home and play it. The mother was distracted trying to work it out for her daughter, who had lovingly copied it complete with "By John Winslow." (Johnny said it was just a little thing he made up.) David Osborne [expert on the Far East], who was here for dinner tonight, says I should not go into detail on any of the above points, as the effect would be spoiled. I told him I was grappling with getting it all down. It looks as though I can't even worry about the effect because it is now near midnight and tomorrow I go to New York.

Love,
Marcella

P.S. The paintings Lionberger bought were *Dumbarton Oaks* at $250 and my self-portrait drawing for $150. He thought he got such a bargain on *D. Oaks* that he upped the price on the drawing! Mrs. Valls called today and asked to bring the Spanish Ambassadress on Friday but I won't be here. She paints too.

1. "My Day" was a newspaper column Eleanor Roosevelt had been writing since 1937 describing events in her busy life.
2. Francesco Aquilera was a specialist in Hispanic culture.

Anne Winslow's reply to this letter was that it would be easier for her to think that Johnny could write a symphony than that the C——s could have a choice dinner party.

June 14, 1948
Dear Tat,

I have before me several blissful days of nothing to do but pack for New Hampshire. That used to be such a chore but now I am relieved to have no scheduled debutante to look at from 10:30 to 1. You have no idea how tired that makes me! I have two "debs" finished and four on the way to be. Also, my precocious, ferocious Jennifer Lee is approved and paid for. She found out all I knew about Olivier and the state of the theatre, which wasn't much.

A honeymoon couple has taken my house for the summer. A charming Captain in the Navy named Hunnicutt, who says his wife will love the piano. She was an art major from Philadelphia, but, since he says he doesn't know if she will be able to keep the butcher bill paid, he could only pay $150 a month. He seemed so nice I figured some things are better than money.

The back of the house next door is being torn down with great flourishes. Charles is painting the back door and Mary is quietly reading a book. She got the English and History prize in the Middle School. Her teacher said she wrote such good compositions and never had to be told anything twice so maybe she will be a BRAIN. Johnny plays baseball madly every day. He surprises me. When I returned from New York I found a faded rose in a Pyrex dish on the "mepple" table with a note: "To my dearest mum, Johnny." Thrilling, because I thought he would never miss me.

I have not tried to paint Robert Lowell. I have been so busy and cannot bring myself to ask him, anyway, when he dislikes the idea of sitting. He never got over the pain of sitting to a Miss Stackpole when he was sixteen.

Love,
Marcella

In a letter in May, Mrs. Winslow wrote, "I wish I could be there to pose Robert Lowell. I can't bear for you not to get the innocent wild good dog look."

Center Sandwich, N.H.
July 1, 1948
Dear Tat,

Our own house at last! To think that I own as much land as the eye can see from my window! That gives me a sense of power lacking in me all these years. We arrived after a stop at Sears, Roebuck in Concord, getting numerous things that could only be shoved into the car for a 50-mile stretch, and no longer. We were really well packed in. Charles, helping me pack the car, suggested that a small bus would be what I needed. Looking at the entire pavement in front of my house strewn with boxes, bags, pillows, lamps, toaster, suitcases, games, paint boxes, dishpans, food, lunch basket etc., I had to agree. However, I asked if most people going on trips didn't have always as much as that. "Not 'ceptin they's gypsies," said Charles with finality.

So the gypsies arrived in New Hampshire with many prayers to St. Christopher answered, since there would have been no way to get to the jack had we had a flat tire.

When we left Washington my nice tenant, Mrs. Hunnicutt, was waiting on the threshold (literally there was no room for Mrs. H on the threshold—or anywhere) to take possession. She seemed to love the house, the piano and the pictures and showed such a liking for your portrait that I left you in the hall, so she can look at you when she reads your books.

We got a late start and ran into a terrific thunderstorm after going through the worst traffic in record-breaking heat, so I stopped at a hotel in Elizabeth, N.J. The Irish porter was so helpful, rescuing us from a cloudburst and seeing that we got some dinner after closing hours, that Johnny announced that he wished everyone was Irish. We got up at 6 a.m. to get through N.Y. before the traffic rush, but there is no such thing as no traffic around N.Y. We made it through the Holland Tunnel (I must confess, though not to the children, that the closed-in feeling with the traffic rushing through there just terrifies me) and onto the wonderful Merritt Parkway, the road through wooded areas and no trucks allowed.

I got so sleepy around 2 p.m. that we stopped on an abandoned road; I pulled out a comforter and pillow and had a good rest under a tree. I drove 10 1/2 hours so we had another stopover. It is usually easy to make the trip up in two days, as the mileage is less than 600 miles, but, because of the load, I didn't like to drive fast.

When we arrived in Sandwich, and I got the key to my house from my neighbor, Bob Mudgett, we stood breathless, the three of us, excited to be entering our very own house. I turned the lock. Nothing happened. I turned again. Nothing! Locked out of our own house with our own key! I yelled across the field ignominiously to Mudgett and he yelled back that it was only the dampness, our door was stuck! So we all three gave a mighty heave and entered our house in what might be called the bum's rush. Once in, however, the house relented and became extremely hospitable. We are very happy. Mary keeps saying, "Aren't we lucky!" We are, indeed, especially to have it all paid for—by you.

Love,
Marcella

Center Sandwich, N.H.
July 7, 1948

I enclose a picture of Mr. Mudgett and his house in the field beyond mine. He can't be over 40 and has been raised here. He supplies me with all the local color as well as stories of the past. It is hard to believe that his father butchered "beef critters" and peddled them from house to house. The other night when he brought me milk from his cow and some cider (sour as anything), he stayed to chat. His grandfather, who was a champion mower and woodsman, was also a seventh son of a seventh son and was born with a caul over his face which, as you know, allowed him to make predictions. All his predictions came true. Now the old ways are gone. Mudgett gets done in an hour what his father got done in a day. His wife, Thelma, works, and he eats store cake which he says is sawdust and hot air. There is a flavor in New Hampshire, expressions and accents, which is delightful. The New Englanders set about doing things in a quiet but very capable way, never hurried or intense—and so honest and PROUD of their work. This is the true New England that I am discovering—and I love it.

A letter from Cal Lowell written in late August tells me Robert Frost's address: c/o Theodore Morrison, Breadloaf Summer School, Middlebury, Vermont. He says he hasn't heard much from Allen who has been going to one conference after another all over the country. He repeats that he DOES hate to sit, as it makes him feel self-conscious. He expects to be back in Yaddo about September 20th, and said he had summered in Maine and Massachusetts which was a wonderful change after the heat and wet of Washington.

Love,
Marcella

Miss Rose Standish Nichols' four-story, Bullfinch-designed house was situated in the most proper of proper locations in Boston, facing Mount Vernon Street, on Beacon Hill, just off Louisburg Square. It was in this house that she held meetings of the Beacon Hill Reading Club, which she had founded, and entertained Harvard students at weekly teas, to keep up with her interest in international affairs. When she died in 1960, she left the house as a museum and headquarters for the Boston Council for International Visitors.

In her later years, when I knew her, she made yearly trips to the Cosmopolitan Club, in New York, and to the Sulgrave Club, in Washington, always starting with a tea at the clubs, to which were invited old and new acquaintances. Her guests soon learned to settle down to long monologues, mostly on current affairs, by the hostess, who expected invitations in return. In 1948, I got the full treatment, and when, at the luncheon in my house, she saw the portrait of Gretchen Green, she expressed a desire to be painted in her own surroundings. I was able to do her portrait in her Boston house during the summer of 1948.

55 Mount Vernon Street
Beacon Hill, Boston, Mass.
August 27, 1948
Dear Tat,

Are you reading about the blistering heat wave up here in New England—100 degrees and high humidity? In this house of Rose Standish Nichols I seem to have gone underground—from the world, as well as from the heat. She wrote me in May inviting me to visit her and said she would be delighted to pose at her fireside and even added: "You can have a free hand to improve upon my appearance." So that is what I am attempting to do.

There is a slight touch of GREAT EXPECTATIONS about us here. I am Estella, grown, back on a visit. (However, Miss Nichols is quite different from Miss Havisham.) The house, which sits at the very top of Mt. Vernon Street and almost directly in back of the State House and within spitting distance of the Athenaeum, is one of three or four houses designed by Bullfinch. It is filled with so many antique treasures that you can't get around to seeing all of them—and also, if you pick one up (provided the door isn't too stuck to get at it), you get so black with the years of dust that you think twice before you try again. I tried going through some of her wonderful books yesterday and came up looking like Pussy out of the coal bin. It isn't that Miss Nichols enjoys the dust—she laments it—but finds too many other things more interesting to attend to. She has an old Irish woman and a Negro who come every day part time. I think they just look in to see if she is up and around because I have yet to find out what they do. Mrs. Donahue gets breakfast and makes the bed, 'tis true, and she must take care of the "swill" because Miss N and I can never find anywhere to put our leftover melons which we eat all the time.

You will, I'm sure, never forget our luncheon in Washington when Miss Nichols ate the last of the Tennessee ham and quantities of butter and bread, but no salad. Well, that is what she does when we order at the Parker House where she takes me every evening for our only real meal of the day. The food there is the way the Peabody Hotel in Memphis was when at its lowest ebb. The Parker House is not air-conditioned, you can't hear yourself think and it is frightfully expensive, but it *is* the old Parker House. Miss Nichols says she doesn't have to pay because she has a charge account. We always are seated at the same table and are shown a menu. Her finger goes down all the selections of meals until we get to the least expensive and she gives me a choice of two of these and I try to like whatever it is. She eats meat, a vegetable or potato occasionally, but mostly bread heaped with much butter, and she drinks pots and pots of coffee. For tea, after our sitting, we have a slice of melon and then some ice cream and then the cup of tea. The afternoon I arrived she met me at the door, closed it quickly, and said: "Now we will have our melon," which we proceeded to do (grimy as I was after my drive in the heat), the melon accompanied with melted ice cream and a discussion of Russia and Alger Hiss.

The large room on the first floor has a big table and high-back chairs which Miss N carved herself, and a desk and lots of books, some of them on landscape gardening which she wrote, as that was her profession; also Japanese prints, beautiful old tables and vases and sewing boxes. She has dozens of old sewing boxes from many countries as she embroiders everything—even the canopy over her high-posted bed. (She told me how bare the Thomas Watsons' house in New York was—no chair beside a window where one could sit and embroider.)

Miss Nichols herself is in keeping with her house. She wears ancient-looking voile dresses with real lace collars and choker pearls and English-matron hats, but most of these things come from Bergdorf-Goodman or Paris. I have grown very fond of her. Besides being a museum piece she is kind, generous, and most broad-minded. She just does not get around to straightening up things—everything she has is so interesting to her. She has been in the act of straightening up her room ever since I came, but it gets worse and worse instead of better. I have seen her—while talking of military affairs in Japan, or about Mrs. Lowell or Mrs. Cabot, or the Queen of Greece—go through one pile of old letters, clippings, string, embroidery skeins, and all she does is move them to another place.

Being mesmerized by the Alger Hiss hearings on the radio, she also mesmerized me watching her attempts to clear out her drawers while she was tuned in.[1] She placed a wastebasket at her feet and took out a tangled mass of beads that she wears in clusters around her neck usually, and while following accounts of the papers in the pumpkin, and whose old typewriter it was, and Whittaker Chambers's accusations, they got untangled and I waited to see them dropped into the wastebasket. She would pause, consider, but not the beads, just whether Hiss was guilty or not, and then they would go into a different drawer. She threw away only one envelope while I watched. Every drawer in my bedroom has string, embroidery, and letters postmarked as long ago as 1883. I know it was an effort for her, but she managed to clear out one half of one drawer for my things and placed four coat hangers at my disposal. I can count from my bed, where I am writing, three chests of drawers, two desks, three tables and a dressing table. There are also seven chairs and a settee, a window seat, a bookcase, a sewing table full of thread and yarn, and a stool, as well as an open fireplace. This room, like the dining room and kitchen, are seldom used anymore. I can hardly believe that it is possible to live in a four-story house where only three windows are ever opened—one in my bedroom, one in Miss N's bedroom (come to think of it, I am not sure she does open hers) and one in the living room where we have set up our painting space.

For the portrait, which takes place in the most comfortable spot, Miss Nichols is seated by the big fireplace wearing a long white lace dress, the usual tortoise-shell comb in her hair, and a crimson velvet jacket. Her whole figure is shown—but less than life size. The chair is covered with rose brocade and the walls are a lovely apricot color, so the atmosphere is warm and inviting. She particularly wanted a bust, made by her uncle, Augustus Saint-Gaudens, especially for her, to be shown on the mantelpiece. She has quantities of mementos of him. It seems they were very close and corresponded a great deal. She has even kept, and produced for my interest, drawings Chauncey Stillman sent her as a child of eight or ten. His mother was a friend but Chauncey seldom sees her now, I believe. One of his letters, naturally a recent one, tells her he had met the two Winslow ladies (you and me) who are "both remarkably charming and interesting." That must be why I got the invitation! Except, unlike the other septuagenarians, who seemed to care nothing about my portrait of Gretchen Green, she wanted to be painted the same way I had painted Gretchen—seated in her familiar surroundings.

If you ever come here to visit, since you got an invitation, you must bring some salt, a flashlight, and a few wastebaskets. Miss Nichols's room has the only wastebasket. She never uses salt so there is none, except a tiny bit in a little Canton China dish which I discovered when

I needed some desperately while eating a tomato I had bought for my lunch. I have given up even the thought of pepper.

There are about two small lamps with 40-watt bulbs on each floor, which are all on the opposite end of whatever room you are going into and, since there is a lot of furniture in every room, you feel victorious when you make it without breaking the old Staffordshire or Sandwich glass, or tripping over the Queen Anne chair or John Hancock dressing table (a table that belonged to him).

Miss Nichols has a sister [Mrs. Shurcliffe], a famous bellringer who lives next door, but there seems to be no communication. The only person I have seen is a young Anglo-Frenchman. (She habitually has groups from Harvard for tea in order to ply them with questions on subjects dear to her heart.) She likes this ardent Catholic because he seems to have answers. I heard her on the phone. It went like this: "Can you come to tea tomorrow? I have a Catholic staying with me and we want to discuss whether any wars are just wars." Then, when he came and was immediately set down to work on his melon, she started right in on the holy wars.

I think the painting is turning out well, and her appearance is being improved, as she suggested (or, shall I say, hoped for?), since there is nowhere to go in the opposite direction. I have one of her feet peeping out from below her long lace dress. The most interesting thing in the portrait is the feeling of length in those legs and her aristocratic look.

Love,
Marcella

1. Alger Hiss served in the State Department from 1936 to 1947. In 1948, he was accused by Whittaker Chambers, a senior editor of *Time,* of having acted as a Soviet spy. After one hung jury, he was retried, convicted of perjury, and sentenced to five years in prison.

Mrs. Winslow's response to my Boston adventure was gratifying. I sent her photographs of Miss Nichols, not only in the pose by the fireplace but also posing in front of the Winslow house in Marshfield, Massachusetts, where she insisted I go to see the old family homestead. For that photo I wrote, "Then we have Miss Nichols in her everyday costume, vintage 1915, the hat, vintage 1925." She would have liked to take me to her usual stopping-off place on the way to the Parker House, the Athenaeum, but told me that since I was not a member, I was not permitted to enter its portals. Since she customarily left off five or six books that she had borrowed, and came forth with five or six new ones, I thought she could have wangled me in, perhaps as a prospective member. But that is not done in Boston, it seems.

I conformed to everything expected of me the week I spent with Miss Nichols, except that I was unable to get the kitchen windows open in the torrid weather. In commenting on my letter, Mrs. Winslow wrote:

It has been too wonderful, both to read and to read aloud and to discuss afterward, and keep discussing. "This is literature," Mary said when she got to the kitchen windows. My favorite bit was the salt, the flashlight and the wastebasket. I know Miss Nichols is impressive because of the way I remember her. I would, as they say, know her in Africa. And, from me, that means a good deal, for my habit is to forget the human face completely. And when I think how I enjoyed that letter and how I would have NOT enjoyed the experience, I know again how superior art is to life.

I have Rose Nichols' reaction to her portrait in a letter she wrote me after I returned to Sandwich: "The picture you painted here I think will stand out in any exhibition as a work of art. It would appeal to other painters, I think, because the drawing and the values are so good. I shall be much interested to hear what the critics say about it in your exhibition." She thanked me for letting her call me by my first name and said she associated it with one of Mrs. Humphry Ward's heroines who had fired her imagination in her youth and who had dwelt in a settlement house but was courted by an aristocrat who eventually married her. Miss N forgot whether she was happy ever after.

Center Sandwich, N.H.
September 3, 1948
Dear Tat,

When I saw the half-hearted string on my birthday package with the cranberry glass, my heart sank. Miraculously, the bowls came through OK and I love them. Will I ever dare use them since they were meant for finger bowls? I could place them on the crocheted mats that you say the Misses Eveleth made and gave to you when you were married—as they must be of the same vintage. Such exquisite work!

How soon we are all going to fit into the past, the way the Misses Eveleth have! [1] Sad that they never married—their heirlooms come to those who have, you and me, who aren't born Winslows or Eveleths. Of course your books and my paintings may be a living reminder of us, but they may not be around any longer than the mats at that—if anything lasts after the atomic bomb.

A letter from Mac Herter that she won't be back in D.C. until after the elections. Chris is doing some work for Foster Dulles [secretary of state] and campaigning for his own election for governor of Massachusetts. I know she would rather work in the garden than "do" politics, but she will go along with whatever happens.

We just saw a doe with her two fawns at the end of our pasture. They gamboled around for a while while we stood transfixed!

A letter from Francesco Aquilera about the Jiménez portrait. He writes that, as much as the Hispanic Foundation admires the picture, the Library cannot justify the purchase now. Nothing to do with art and poetry, simply budgets and taxpayers. I had met Aquilera at the Biddle garden party and he couldn't believe that Jiménez had allowed me to paint him. He told me that J had always seemed adamant about having even a photograph made. I offered to give them a photograph of the portrait, but they said "everything or nothing."

Love,
Marcella

1. The Misses Eveleth were General Eveleth Winslow's aunts by his mother, Kate Porter Sanford Eveleth, of Alexandria, Virginia.

P Street, N.W.
Washington, D.C.
September 25, 1948
Dear Tat,

We hated to leave our little house (still unnamed) and I do dread the two days driving back through New York (so uninteresting) but, once back, interesting things began to happen. Before I even had time to feel low about the dirty house and all the electric lights and gadgets that needed to be fixed, I found myself running out to get a bottle of bourbon to entertain the nice poetess Léonie Adams.[1] She is the new consultant in poetry at the Library. Cal Lowell had called and asked to bring her to see me the day after I returned and, as he was leaving to go to Yaddo, and I had not seen him since the dinner party with Chauncey (or was it Cairns and Joseph Lalley [editorial writer for the Washington *Post*], I

wanted very much to have them. It was still warm and we had a delightful chat in the garden. I asked Cal if he didn't think I had been noble
not to insist on his sitting when he hated to do it so much. He said
yes, and hadn't he been noble to offer to sit when he felt that way etc.
He looks more handsome as he matures. Did you read in the last *Time*
magazine that old Santayana enjoys reading Lowell's poetry? When Miss
Nichols and I discussed Santayana's cold analysis of his mother in his
book PERSONS AND PLACES, she said quietly, reflectively, but with finality, "Well, Santayana is *not* a gentleman."

Léonie Adams (she is a first cousin to James Truslow, you probably
know) is very nice and gentle and small, with no side or manner, or
looks, but rather compelling none the less. Cal said, "I hear you are getting a screen from Mrs. Boit," and, since that offer had been made only
that very morning on the phone, I was startled to realize news could
travel so fast. It was true. Cal had just been to call on Harriet and she
had told him.

Love,
Marcella

1. Léonie Adams (1899–1988), educated at Barnard College, won many prizes
for her poetry, including the Bollingen Prize in 1955. She was a Fellow in American Letters at the Library of Congress from 1949 to 1955. From 1959 to 1961 she
was secretary of the National Institute of Arts and Letters.

September 28, 1948
Dear Tat,

I am leaning against your goose down pillows right now and thinking
about Jo and Hattie plucking the geese. I remember the day you suggested I make for the back yard where the plucking was going on, but
not to tell Jo I wanted to paint them or Jo would put his shoes on. I
have done several versions of that wonderful subject, Jo hanging on to
the webbed feet, sitting on those two bricks, and Hattie in the broken-
down green chair stuffing the pillows. I have had time to be thrilled
with my best birthday present every day, or night rather, and to get
plenty of sleep on them. I feel so full of energy and am not sure but that
I got a touch of the Vigoro I was giving the flowers. Did you think
about sending the pillows when I wrote you of my first days back, when
I said I had finished two of the debutante portraits, and had been to the

milliner, shoemaker, electrician, grocer, dressmaker, dry cleaner, radio repair shop AND the PX? For whatever reason, a hearty thanks. Homemade pillows!

The house on my east side has been remodeled, the old kitchen removed, two bathrooms added with a new little porch on the back; a far cry from its former self with its rented rooms. I often saw the front-room-first-floor boarder (a taxi driver) hang his coat on an old light fixture, as he never pulled the shades. Georgetown is really looking up. The house sold for $17,000, or that was the asking price. If I owned this house, which is now the only one in the block that has not been remodeled, and did a little fixing up, and painting, I could no doubt rent it furnished for $300 and take the children to Europe and live on the income! Of course Europe would have to quiet down a bit. I think my place has possibilities. When you said you were sure this might be my last year in "this queer, dear, comfortable place," did you think it might be sold under me? The rent was just raised to $88 a month, and for only a one-year lease, so you may be right.

Love,
Marcella

October 19, 1948
Dear Tat,

I know you would enjoy meeting Léon Masson, the French artist who was sent to me by Mary's school. He came to the great land of plenty to make a fortune with his work and went directly to the nuns at Stone Ridge. The nuns had no answer to how this could be done, but thought I would. I do. However, not in the way he expected.

When he came, he produced his portfolio of drawings unaware that I do that sort of thing myself. He told me about his six children and his dire need for a show. I knew that would be impossible on short notice, so I had the idea of sending him around Georgetown to draw houses. He has illustrated limited editions of literary classics and has had many shows in Paris. I figured I could get him a show at the Peabody Room in the Georgetown Library, since I knew Americans would buy anything that concerns their interests—houses, children whatever. It worked like a charm. I am his headquarters. He brings the finished results to me and has already sold to owners on the spot, since he sets up his easel on the street and the owners of the houses can't miss him. Leon was surprised that I suggested he draw that adorable, typically old Georgetown house of Rose Greely on O St., because, to him, a frame house would certainly mean low class in France. He could not realize how we cherish such houses and long to buy them but he follows my suggestions. The very scent of a new commission sets him off like a bloodhound, looking to neither right nor left. He is not a prepossessing person, but quite nice in a homey way and certainly clever. His show is scheduled for late November in the Peabody Room.

Love,
Marcella

Léon Masson's exhibit of drawings of Georgetown houses was so successful that he sought to engage me as his agent, to sell his Christmas cards, after he returned to France. He felt he had barely grazed the land of plenty; it all seemed so easy.

November 1, 1948
Dear Tat,

I have been invited, with three other artists, to have a showing in the Peabody Room at the Georgetown Library—two painters, Alice Acheson and I, and two sculptors, Alice Decker and Maxime Elias. We all live in Georgetown and that is what the Peabody Room is all about, having been given by a Mr. Peabody to house Georgetown memorabilia. The curator and I are doing all the preparations as Mrs. Acheson is too social and Alice Decker is too vague. It will take place next week.

While I was admiring the glorious mass of red chrysanthemums in my garden, I looked over the fence and saw a worried-looking gardener of the Herters' watching Mac overseeing a full transplanting of autumn flowers. On my other side, Mrs. Van Kaathoven, of old Washington, who has supplanted the former boarding house, has been busily getting settled, with chauffeurs drawing up to deposit rubber plants etc. sent from Sumner Welles, I was told.[1] She calls me often to chat—but, so far, I have not set eyes on her. She has the reputation of having been a great belle. Her friends can't understand her leaving Massachusetts Ave. for the "slums" of Georgetown. They must be particularly surprised that she rented a house that is pink with green steps. Perhaps for that reason the rent was reduced from $300 to $250.

I enclose Lady Vernon's letter with the good news that her daughter, with husband, Tim Marten, is coming to Washington while he is with the British Embassy. I know I will like them, since Randolph did—and they can tell us what they know about him.

Love,
Marcella

1. Sumner Welles (1892–1961) was assistant secretary and undersecretary of state from 1933 to 1943.

November 8, 1948
Dear Tat,

I am writing just after the opening of our show. You would have been gratified to see the number of people who turned out for it. If it weren't for Alice Acheson's name on the invitations I would think that a great art revival was taking place! As it is, Oh! human frailty, too many people saw the *Post,* or know the sources that say Dean Acheson might be the next Secretary of State now that Truman is in. Be that as it may, we were deluged with very high "sassiety," but mostly Georgetown, which was to be expected. Columnist Mary Van Rensselaer Thayer was there, taking in Mrs. Cornelius Whitney's news and Mrs. Whitney bought a piece of sculpture and said she would like me to paint her garden and to come to tea next week to talk about it. Fredrica bought my still life *Constituent Elements* for $200, throwing in two of her Duncan Phyfe chairs as well, and Alice Acheson sold two landscapes to Mrs. Morris Cafritz for $300.

Elias is just an artist with a capital *A*. He revels in being liberal and, on the day of the hanging, never offered to drive a nail. He lifted a finger only on his sculpture. We did everything ourselves. The curator's husband paid for the notices we sent (the trustees of the room wouldn't give a cent as it might set a precedent). I bought the poster paper, extra stamps, fresh flowers and wire, but you know me—I like everything to be a crashing success. I am most gratified with the results. I have 13 paintings and was pleased that my portrait of Miss Guest received so many favorable comments, especially so from Dean Acheson. The James Restons were there, Marquis Childs and hundreds of others, which surprised Mrs. Acheson as she had asked for only 50 invitations, not expecting many people to come to a library, she had said. (Her butler hung her pictures.)

The Fellows are arriving on the weekend of the 20th. I have two tickets for the T. S. Eliot reading on Edgar Allan Poe. Going to a dinner at the Richmans' for him. Maida Richman says wistfully, "I am having twenty-five guests and have only service for five. Also, with T. S. Eliot, one HAS to sit down at tables." Léonie Adams is helping and I will take some food to help out too.

Love,
Marcella

Gwen Cafritz had offered to buy the two Acheson paintings if Mrs. Acheson went to her house and told her where to hang them. The three-hundred-dollar sale suggests that that is what happened.

November 22, 1948
Dear Tat,

Such a busy weekend! The dinner for T. S. Eliot was at the Richmans'. I took my contribution (potato casserole) and sat at the big table between Red Warren and Allen. Eliot is perfection. I could hero-worship him! He is every bit as good on repartee, wit and the perfect word in the proper place as Allen. To hear him and Allen and Red converse was worth the whole evening. Along with this, Eliot is so gracious and charming— and simple. He nodded understandingly when Mrs. Robert Woods Bliss blew in late, excusing herself with "I have just been doing the Byzantine." All the poets were in evidence. The magic of being with T. S. Eliot brings them all flocking. Allen says Eliot does NOT care about linen napkins and sitting at a table, but the Richmans keep saying he does, so we sat.

The following evening I had dinner at the Biddles' with the Merrells and Mrs. Frank West and we sat in the 3rd row to hear Eliot read an excellent paper on Edgar Allan Poe. Allen, by the way, is writing a book on Poe, after Eliot had turned down the offer.

The next day Allen asked to come over with Cal Lowell, Alexis Léger and Léonie Adams. Afterwards they insisted that I go to dinner with them at the Cosmos Club, where we joined Auden and Richman.[1] Then we went to the Cafritz Auditorium to hear Auden read.

Auden did not impress me personally but he is terribly bright—rather like a young Charles Laughton—the same unctuous voice and smug conceit. I can imagine him being quite obnoxious in an English public school. I may be quite wrong about him. He was fascinating to listen to. Lowell was fencing with him in his adept and awkward manner. Lowell likes him.

I called on my new neighbor, Mrs. Van Kaathoven. She is a faded beauty. Also, her furniture is faded. All of it gold and French. I like her. She has a light touch. In a heavy way. Or vice versa, if you know what I mean.

Love,
Marcella

1. Wystan Hugh Auden (1907–1973), educated at Oxford, came to the United States with Christopher Isherwood in January, 1939, and became a citizen of the United States in 1946. He returned to England later, however, and was elected professor of poetry at Oxford in 1956.

November 23, 1948
Dear Tat,

We not only opened Léon's show—great success—but sold almost everything. There were 40 drawings. The three done at Mrs. Archbold's house were the only ones not sold. This Standard Oil heiress, whose house has been appraised as being the most valuable in Washington, came to the opening but, as I told you, she never does what people expect her to do. I had taken Léon to meet her and he had made three attractive interiors which she had seemed to like a lot, but nothing will induce her to buy them at $25 each.

I have a very nice roomer for a few weeks. I am now finding out what the unattached male does—which is never staying put. He is only here long enough to change and go out again, usually in tails, tux or Navy dress. You can bet that he gets plenty of invitations. No trouble, always remembers the lights and doesn't get in the way. He and Léon have run into each other but I pretended that I didn't know, so each can wonder about the other. Léon had asked about finding a room in Georgetown, but of course I didn't want him and did not tell him I rented to someone else! They each know where the key is on the rubber band, so it's sort of funny.

Mrs. Cornelius Vanderbilt Whitney asked me to come by and talk about doing a sketch of her garden. I had to wait almost an hour while the owner of the house, Mrs. Paul Bartlett, went over everything from soup to nuts and was so difficult, according to Mrs. Whitney, that Mrs. W was exhausted and then said she might never even want to remember the garden or the house she was renting, and offered me only $100! She said they had poured $5000 into the house and still the furnace won't work and the cook can't bake in the oven. They own a Renoir, a Bellows, a Grant Wood and a portrait by Boutet de Monvel. I'm not sure yet if they will own a Comès!

I took a few paintings to the Stone Ridge Bazaar and offered to paint a portrait of "your child, house, or yourself" for a dollar chance. In doing so, I am helping the school in the only way I know how.

Love,
Marcella

Thanksgiving
November 25, 1948
Dear Tat,

I have had a delightful day of rest. Etta cooked the dinner, Mother bought the turkey and I had the family over at 2 o'clock. Now at eight p.m. I think that I will never be hungry again. I think, in spite of taxes, hell, high water, and the stock market, I have much to be thankful for. You, for instance. And your interest in my letters and my life. It must sound funny at a distance of over 900 miles—the key on the rubber band, the poets on the wing, the pictures up and down and, always, something going on, or in, or up (poets, turkey, and pictures.)

There was one afternoon that the two men in my present life shared the top floor when everyone else was out. They still had never been introduced and they still must have wondered who the other guy was. Léon was pasting and stamping invitations to his show in the studio room and Mr. H was doing whatever the popular man-about-town does the short time he spends in his own room. You ask what he looks like. Nice-looking, dresses very well, and always has a proper rejoinder. He is well brought up, leaves before we get up in the morning and returns after we go to bed so I don't mind him at all. In fact, it is rather intriguing to get a glimpse of him and his $12 every Thursday. That helps to pay for Etta.

Blanche Knopf phoned today to ask if you were here and said she would call later. Also, a friend of Mary's who goes to Mt. Vernon School, says that their English teacher (a male, you will be pleased) told his class that Anne Goodwin Winslow was considered by the critics to be the most versatile woman writer in AMERICA! He must read Barzun and Prescott, but he could not have got the word "versatile" from either of them. They have used so many better words.

Yes, I got the Danish edition of A QUIET NEIGHBORHOOD. Thank you. I can understand "Stille Krog" but that is all. It is impressive. I was sorry that the only time Allen was here recently he didn't notice it.

Love,
Marcella

Barbizon Plaza Hotel
New York
December 16, 1948
Dear Tat,

Rev. Mother Barry keeps having ideas of things I can do for the School. She would like a Madonna to be painted like the one in their Rome headquarters they call *Mater Amirabilis* that seems to have special significance for the French order. For this purpose, she has brought me to New York and Philadelphia to look at other *Mater* shrines in three Sacred Heart convents, so I stayed on to partake of the art scene, and bring a portrait to Portraits Inc. I am depressed with that setup. So many stuffy, sweet, painted renditions of overdressed people! Not my dish of tea. However, I have been encouraged by the Art Directors of *Life* magazine. They are interested in my idea of having them print portraits of the poets I have painted along with poems by same. They asked to keep my album and will send it back after they decide. The Assistant Manager always has to have the last say.

I was lucky to get a seat for Maxwell Anderson's play *Anne of the Thousand Days* with Rex Harrison. Many standing and a very electric audience.

Love,
Marcella

P Street, N.W.
Washington, D.C.
December 29, 1948
Dear Tat,

I hope you will be able to come soon. Miss Nichols has counted on seeing you. I am having a luncheon for her—her usual expectations after her Sulgrave Club tea. Christmas was good but we missed you. At a swank party I attended my feather got singed in one of the candles, which was sad as Betty [Fisher] had given it to me—a real Bird of Paradise which had belonged to her mother—and I had waited so long to have a black velvet hat made to put it on too! Mrs. Alice Roosevelt Longworth recognized me with a "You paint"!

Alex Böker had a party with the usual run of aristocrats and journalists; and my nice roomer has long since departed for more elegant surroundings, alas!

Mary has bemoaned your absence and so often wishes you could help her on musical questions. There are so many ways you are helpful, not least of which is your cheerful presence and being the nearest thing to Randolph on this earth. I think our winter has been interesting, though I realize I am still very emotionally unstrung.

Love,
Marcella

Denis Devlin wrote from London, "It was such a pleasant surprise to learn about your exhibition of paintings. . . . I did appreciate most highly the honor of having my picture on the book of words [the catalog]. . . . It all gave me a powerful whiff of nostalgia for Washington. I hear from one who has returned from those blessed groves that Dupont Circle has been ruined: I burn with indignation. I do look back on those parties in your Georgetown garden at the relaxed end of days in summer."

January 5, 1949
Dear Tat,

Excellent, excellent that you are coming. It has seemed such a long time since we have seen you. Imagine, another year, so close to another summer that seems to have ended so short a time back! The summer sustains me. Etta is another blessing. She improves all the time. Her luncheon today for Miss Nichols was a gem. It was going well when suddenly Miss Nichols rose and said Mrs. Robert Woods Bliss had summoned her to pay a visit at 2:30 and her secretary had given her the "go" sign. Everyone rushed to get her there on time so she could be "worked in" before Mrs. Bliss's next engagement. Miss Nichols looked wonderful in a navy blue dress and a jacket covered with braid. She had on an amethyst necklace, and wore a velvet purse with silver top attached to her belt with a chain. With this, she had on a black velour hat well festooned with crimson and black ribbon in front and a long blue cape with a chain clasp.

I wish you could have been here to enjoy Miss Nichols' story about Marie MacNeil and the Princess who sought Miss Nichols' advice on whether to take Marie's discarded husband, THE MacNeil, as her fifth husband. Marie takes a dim view of the idea and there are also complications about which one would then be THE MacNeil of MacNeil. Marie says the Princess (an American), whom she has known since childhood, has always wanted to do everything she, Marie, has always done, but this time it is going a bit far.

By the time I get my *Mater* for the convent finished I should be able to paint a few other things besides portraits. However, I can't quite see getting that far ahead.

Try to get the recent *New Yorker* that has Eudora [Welty]'s letter to the editors about Edmund Wilson's review of Faulkner's INTRUDER IN THE DUST. She takes up the cudgels for Mississippi which she writes had been "pushed down" 3 times in 2 weeks—that it's that combination of "intelligent despite," the "intelligent" referring to the books or their characters and the "despite" referring to their living in Mississippi. She is so clever the way she pulls apart, in one of the most amusing put-downs, Wilson's comment on Faulkner's weakness having its origin in the "antiquated community he inhabits" etc. You will love it—being a Southerner. The children are so thrilled you are coming.

Love,
Marcella

A letter from Miss Nichols told of her visit to Mrs. Robert Woods Bliss:

> Mrs. Bliss kept me waiting five or ten minutes so I was certainly on time and left promptly. We carried on a rather stilted conversation about international affairs. Fragile brownish white orchids, strangely resembling her, were sparsely placed here and there to decorate her salon. However she was very pleasant and seemed rather glad to see me in spite of my insignificance.

It was while Mrs. Winslow was staying with me that her fifth book, *The Springs,* was published by Knopf. On February 8, 1949, Orville Prescott's review in the New York *Times* again sang her praises: "The same virtues which have been cited before must be cited once again"; "There isn't anyone now writing at all like her"; "Other novelists write with greater power and a great many others with more sound and fury. But few write with greater delicacy of perception or with greater subtlety of craftsmanship"; "Already she has a discriminating following but the time is certain to come when her rare distinction will be more generally appreciated."

The Springs was Anne Winslow's only book to make the best-seller list. I learned much later—since she never mentioned her sources—that the story she told of a young girl's struggle for an understanding of life and love was her own. One of the young men who had stayed at the summer hotel built across the field from her home by the springs found her irresistibly appealing, and it was he who had become her husband.

April 10, 1949
Dear Tat,

I will soon have to think about showing my house for summer tenants, but the tea will get finished first, then the Madonna installed. I will have to supervise the painting of the room and do a few more things on the picture. Rev. Mother Barry thinks I have really caught the spirit of the original. A man who works at the National Gallery, named Stapko, is giving me lessons in how to manage the gold leaf. Very tricky. I have learned a lot on the Madonna, and we are both smiling, she sweetly and I because Mother Barry told me mine was the only copy of the *Mater* that looks as though she is smiling *at* you—the way the original does!

Cal Lowell has had a breakdown. Harriet Winslow had a letter from Robert Lowell's mother saying that they hoped Cal would be better in a few months. She felt the Tates could have done something sooner to help "Bobby." Mrs. Ezra Pound had also called Harriet, very concerned about Cal, wanting to know more about his breakdown. She said Ezra felt that Cal should come to St. Elizabeth's Hospital where Ezra could help him. Poor Cal—with so many people pulling at him!

I wrote the Tates asking about Robert Lowell's illness and Allen answered with the following letter on April 20, 1949.

Dear Marcella

We are delighted to get your letter but sad that its occasion was Cal's illness. The rumors will fly, and there's no way at present to stop them; but the truth will in the long run prevail, as it always does in these matters. I will not attempt to describe what happened here, or at Bloomington, where his psychotic violence was even more severe than it had been with us the day before. His mother and Merrill Moore arrived by plane from Boston the next day, and took him to Baldpate, which I understand is a private hospital. He was having messianic delusions, and in the five harrowing days here it was almost impossible to communicate with him. Merrill Moore writes that there is every chance for his recovery, that there may even be a very tangible physical basis for his trouble. We can only pray that this is so.

What his future will be depends upon many things beyond his powers of recovery. His mother, that misguided lady, feels (according to recent reports) that this is another instance of Cal's folly, like marrying Jean, becoming a Catholic, and writing poetry. (The Pulitzer Prize took the curse off poetry for a while, but doubtless it is now back on again.) In this view, if he had just done, at the outset, what she wanted him to do, and settled comfortably into Boston, he would have stayed out of trouble. She doesn't see—and one must not expect very many people to see very much—that her son carries his conflicts and crises as the price of his great distinction. As I see Cal, over the past twelve years, and no one I think knows him better, three things held him together: the Church, his marriage, and his poetry. He gave up the church; he gave up Jean; and some months ago he virtually gave up poetry. (He had been pushed forward too rapidly as a poet, and he had attempted a work beyond his present powers; he couldn't finish it. It is significant that he left the unfinished ms. with a casual acquaintance at Yaddo.) The result of these several repudiations was that he cut himself off from the obligations and routines that even well-balanced persons need to keep themselves going. The result was collapse. His going back into the Church at the end of February was only a temporary rationalization of his delusions. By the time he had come here, at the end of March, he had rejected the Church again, and had become his own religion.

He is a complicated boy, and I will not try to describe the nature of his conflict; it has been there from the beginning. I think the sensible thing to say about him is that more than most persons he needs external disciplines and loyalties to keep himself in order; when these, such as they were, failed him, or he failed them, he broke down. Our own relation to Cal has been one of great affection on both sides, but for us it has been especially difficult; he substituted us for his parents. It is a responsibility that no outsider can discharge properly.

We had a fine vacation in Memphis, and greatly enjoyed Mary; but we sorely missed Miss Annie. We shall hope to see her in June, when we go down again to take Nancy and the children to Kenyon for the summer. We are buying a house in Princeton but we shall not be able to occupy it until the end of August. You must come to see us there. Caroline joins me in love to you.

Affectionately yours,
Allen

Love,
Marcella

May 1, 1949
Dear Tat,

In preparation for the showing of debutante portraits, all finished since you left, I am having a "Hang the Debutante" party tomorrow, with a picnic supper afterwards as a reward: the Egidio Ortonas, the Tim Martens and Chauncey Stillman representing Italy, England and New York.[1] It was Chauncey's idea to have a preview. It was my idea to put them to work! Can you imagine Chauncey up on a ladder, driving in a nail? I am providing salad and pecan pie. Chauncey is bringing chicken and bottles of "an adequate little white wine." If it is nice we will eat in the garden.

Sorry you have not had an adequate little letter from me but you know my days. Yesterday was one of those: I was finishing the portrait of Eleanor Morgan when Eleanor Bishop was ushered in and waited her turn for finishing touches. I could just keep on saying, "Smile, Eleanor." After these two sessions I had to get a watercolor framed for a 4 o'clock deadline for the National Museum's watercolor show, and, while waiting for the frame, went to the *Star* and *Post* newspapers asking for publicity for the debutante tea in my studio tomorrow. Then I went to a late dinner at the Merrells with an assortment of State Department men, two of whom, TOO nice, were "au courant" with the latest book, joke, etc.—but no farther than Waugh's THE LOVED ONE or Helen Hokinson's cartoons. I finished the portrait of Marian Merrell which she wanted to use on her book jacket and which she liked, so I had told her to take it home to be pulled to pieces.[2] However, her daughter Julie phoned to say she liked it too.

Marceil, who of course instigated the Debutante Portrait Sittings, is not having much of a hand in it, but she wants to. She phoned me with questions: "What dress will you wear?" "Oh, a brown silk." "BROWN? WHY? Have you arranged the publicity? Get on the phone tomorrow, first thing in the morning, and tell them you want a big headline like Madame Rybar got for the showing of HER portrait. Have you invited all the members of the Music Club?" "No, I'm afraid not." "WHY?" Etc. Lida Mayo called to ask if she could bring Mrs. Justice [Hugo] Black to the studio tea.

Freida Leigh also called, over a week ago, to ask you to lunch with two of your admirers, one being Mrs. Woodrow Wilson. She is rounding up people for the studio tea.

Love,
Marcella

1. Egidio Ortona (1910–) came to be regarded as the dean of the Italian Foreign Service when he became the ambassador to the United States in the late 1960s. An alumnus of the London School of Economics as well as the University of Turin, he epitomized the urbanity of the skilled diplomat. In the twenty-three years he spent in the United States, he and his wife, Giulia, made a lasting impression in the music and artistic circles in Washington. I met them in the forties, when Egidio was helping to implement the Marshall Plan for Italy; they lived next to the Macy house—my studio—in Georgetown. On trips to Rome, Giulia would bring me the Italian paintbrushes I could find nowhere else that she knew I loved. Avice (Mrs. Tim) Marten, Lady Vernon's daughter, had known Randolph in England.

2. Marian Merrell used the pen name Clinch Calkins for her novels but wrote under the nom de plume of Majolica Wattles for a series "Forays into Nonsense" she did for the New Yorker. She was also a playwright and lyric poet.

May 11, 1949
Dear Tat,

A week after all the excitement, a tea to show the debutante portraits. It went well. I have had an unusually smug feeling—very much the way we accuse you of feeling over your best publicity and reviews. It won't last long. You see it was mostly because of the setting—the beautiful Macy house, going up to the fourth-floor studio, seeing everything along the way. An opportunity one seldom gets in anyone's house! Also, a write-up and photograph of the Hoover girl's portrait in the morning *Post,* a list of prominent mothers who poured tea, and an impressive guest list: Mrs. Dean Acheson, Countess Jellicoe, Mrs. C. V. Whitney, Mrs. Francis Biddle, the Assistant Director of the National Gallery, representatives of the British, Italian and Spanish Embassies, and hundreds more. I don't intend to repeat this lucrative project, but for a one-time thing it has paid off. I have gotten a commission over the telephone from a picture in the paper; get checks in every morning's mail as regular as clockwork; refused to paint a portrait from a photograph of a distinguished, aristocratic old Virginian, according to his wife, who isn't one; and have been besieged with invitations, requests, regrets, and thank-yous. Famous for a day and for all the wrong reasons.

I came home from the studio after the party to find Johnny laid out on the sofa. He had fractured his arm the hour of the tea and was patiently waiting for my return. He is fine, but has his arm in a cast. It is a small fracture but I have spent many of my recent hours at Walter Reed Hospital. He said it happened, in his own words, "jumping over six boys." All is well now.

The day after the showing one of the mothers called quite furious because her daughter's name wasn't mentioned in the newspaper—"the only deb not mentioned." She had been rankled at the tea, also, coming to me and asking, "What is the portrait of that girl doing in such a prominent place when she is not a debutante? Everyone is talking about it." Someone had discovered it, but she got the picture back in a dark corner—immediately.

The party for hanging the debutantes' portraits the night before the tea was delightful. We had to eat in the studio as we had one of the worst rains in years. It just poured, beating against the big window. Everyone settled down to the chicken, sliced beef, salad and delicious adequate vintage—as though eating on the backs of pictures in an unstaffed studio was what they had always longed to do. In fact, Signora Ortona suggested to her husband (First Secretary at the Italian Embassy) that they let their servants go and give a spaghetti dinner just like it. It is a marvelous place to entertain—the whole top floor of that big house. Isabel made coffee for us and left it in the kitchen so we had that with the pecan pie. I wish the Macys had been there to enjoy it with us and watch us enjoy it too.

Most of the pictures got hung. Chauncey got right down on the floor with a picture, hooks and wire, intending to get them in the proper places. I pointed out where to put the hook, how to measure the wire, how to twist it and then, how to hang it. He carried food and trays up and down those four flights of stairs and was no doubt worn out completely by 11 p.m.! Avice said it was the most fun they had had in ages. Few diplomats have such studios, or if they do, such ways to use them.

You didn't let me know nearly enough about Alfred and Blanche [Knopf]'s visit—what they said, what they did, how they reacted. Did you do the talking? Did you have tea on the marble table and have Fine Chick come and join you? I can't see Mr. Knopf in a pink or green shirt seated there. Of course I can't see Mrs. Knopf anywhere as I have never met her. I feel sure your place would have a bit more of the "genuwine" than Louis Bromfield's place would—where they visited first.

Lionberger Davis was in town again. I showed him around the studio and he liked the little color painting of Ezra Pound and my mural sketch better than anything. He offered me $100 for the mural sketch and then, out of the blue, "I'll give you $150 for Roscoe Pound!" Of course I'm not putting a price on the old gray head—Ezra, or Roscoe—but I let him have the mural sketch. That is another little drop in the bucket.

Love,
Marcella

In 1989, a painting by Pontormo owned by the late Chauncey Stillman broke a record for the sale of an old master. The Getty Museum bought it at auction for $35.2 million. Other paintings on Stillman's fifteen-hundred-acre farm estate in Amenia, New York—including works by Degas, Lautrec, and Cassatt—will remain in the Stillman collection at Wethersfield, which will be transformed into a museum and the headquarters for a charitable foundation, I understand. Chauncey learned how to hang debutantes, but I doubt that anyone trained him to hang impressionists, much less Pontormos. On a visit in 1986, I saw one of my paintings hanging over the mantel in his guest room, *Magnolias in a Glass Bowl,* which was the only painting sold from my exhibit in 1948, when no one was buying paintings. I was happy to get the asking price of two hundred dollars for it.

May 15, 1949

Dear Tat,

I have had another one of my suprising adventures with someone who buys art and knows nothing about it. Mrs. Cornelius Vanderbilt Whitney came to the Macy house looking for me but I was not in my studio, so the houseman would not let her in. She was muffed and huffed. I phoned her and suggested I bring her garden picture over in my frame, which had been shown at my tea. "What?" she asked. "Doesn't the frame come with it, all ready to hang, when I pay $100 for it?" Also, "Weren't you going to put me and my little son in it?" It was my turn to huff and puff, but I tried to explain that commissioned pictures don't come already framed and figures don't get in automatically and she should see it with her little dog in it. Finally she said, "I'm so disappointed. I'm not sure if I want to see it with no frame. I don't have time to get a frame—and you never put us in it. Now, if it were $30 or $40, but $100!" I calmed her a bit by saying Mrs. Archbold gave me $250 for an identical-size painting of her garden. So, she let me take it to her, and even liked it with the little dog, and she said she would go to that framer "whose named started with a V" on Connecticut Avenue.

People like telling me who their favorite deb portraits are, but *your* friends liked Ezra Pound and Juan Ramón Jiménez the best. (Imagine them as debutantes? They were also put in dark corners.)

I wish you had been with me at a tea yesterday to hear a Helen Hokinson type (appropriate build and hat) whom I overheard proudly saying, in answer to an "I'm afraid I didn't get your name," "Just remember the first governor of Massachusetts and THAT will be *me*."

My house is going to be painted, front and rear, including vestibule, porch and front steps. It is costing $200 and I am paying $100, with a two-year lease and an option to buy. In two years the owner will be 82—but she may be another Grandma Moses! There will be only one coat of paint, but that will freshen it up a lot and give me every bit as much spit and polish as Mrs. Van K. As a matter of fact, the pink on her house is becoming a very dusty rose. Mrs. Van Kaathoven's garden looks very much like her Marie Antoinette interior—the birdbath in the very center, surrounded by six pink rose bushes. She amuses herself by saying that all she needs to make it cozy is her tombstone in Arlington. I am wondering if my gravel yard and four antique ice-cream chairs show up my character to my right and left neighbors. On my right, yesterday, I saw Mrs. Robert Woods Bliss gesticulating wildly to Mac Herter in her garden, changing all her planting with one sweep of the arm. Dumbarton Oaks gives her that authority no doubt. The $100 for my share of painting my house is an advance (and what Chris Herter calls his "gamble") on paints and canvas for the small portrait which is being put aside for another try when he has the opportunity to sit.

Love,
Marcella

I could not buy my house on P Street as long as the owner lived, so it was not until six years later that I was able to call it mine.

Before I was lucky enough to have the use of the proper studio at the Macy house, I started a small portrait of Christian Herter. In spite of his willingness—notwithstanding an arthritic condition—to climb three flights of stairs to the room I was using for my work, and in spite of my anxiety to produce something special, we were both disappointed with the result. Upon receiving a hundred dollars from him, with a charming note saying that it was to be considered an advance on our next effort, I wrote that, until then I would put the money into another form of paint that would be more pleasing for them to see from their windows. Unfortunately, the opportunity never arose for a second sitting, since he became governor of Massachusetts and then secretary of state.

On May 17, 1949, President Truman decorated Major General Lucius Clay with the military's highest peacetime decoration, the Distinguished Service Medal, in a ceremony in the Rose Garden at the White House. Afterward, Clay went to Capitol Hill to address both houses of Congress, and then to New York, where he was given the traditional ticker-tape parade through lower Manhattan.

May 18, 1949
Dear Tat,

There was a reception in honor of Lucius Clay at the White House which was most impressive. General and Mrs. [Philip] Fleming took me in their official car. Nice day in the Rose Garden. Marjorie [Clay] looking beautiful. I had a good view of the whole proceeding, of Truman and Lucius too. There were about 150 people. As American Commander and Military Governor in Germany for four years, and hero of the Berlin Airlift, Lucius was given an elaborate homecoming, 17-gun salute etc. He deserved it all. One of the most brilliant engineers in the Corps, Randolph always said.

I had a letter from the *New York Times Book Review* asking if I could let them have glossies of my paintings of you and Robert Penn Warren, adding: "At the moment, Pound seems out of the picture." They said everyone there liked my portrait of Eudora Welty.

Mary Van R. Thayer put me in her column as renting out paintings—with my phone number, but so far no callers. The idea is too new but is being done at some museums.

Love,

Marcella

Léonie Adams served a grueling year as consultant in poetry at the Library of Congress during 1948–1949. That was the year the Fellows awarded the Bollingen Prize in Poetry to Ezra Pound, provoking widespread controversy. Another of Adams' tasks was overseeing the preparation of the library's first series of recordings in which poets read from their works—an album of five records representing twenty-one American poets. The album was issued in January, 1949.

The award of the Bollingen Prize to Pound brought uninvited celebrity to the library. On February 20, 1949, the day after the award was announced, the New York *Times* ran a headline typical of the press's reaction: "Pound, in Mental Clinic, Wins Prize for Poetry Penned in Treason Cell." Indignant articles and editorials followed. Robert Frost called the award an "unendurable outrage." Pound, he said, was "possibly crazy but more likely criminal." Congress called for an investigation.

What came about, however, was not an investigation but a resolution, on August 19, bidding the library to abstain from giving prizes or making awards. After the Bollingen Prize was banned there and the subsidy returned to the donor, the Bollingen Foundation granted the Yale University Library funds to continue making the awards. On this chapter in the history of the Library of Congress, see William McGuire, *Poetry's Catbird Seat: The Consultantship in Poetry . . . at the Library of Congress, 1937–1987* (Washington, D.C., 1988), esp. 108, 114–15, 121, 124.

Center Sandwich, N.H.
June, 1949
Dear Tat,

Back to New Hampshire, refreshed and rested!

Léonie Adams let me paint her at her desk in the poetry office at the

Library of Congress before I left Washington a week ago. I used casein tempera which dries quickly. She was terribly upset about Ezra Pound the last day I was there—or rather the attacks in the *Saturday Review* by Robert Hillyer, who was gunning for all the "new deal" poets, it seemed, because of the prize Ezra got for the *Cantos* given by the Bollingen Foundation. Léonie said the *Saturday Review* Editors were backing Hillyer even if they got run out of business!

Love,
Marcella

Center Sandwich, N.H.
August 15, 1949
Dear Tat,

The days are beginning to get just a touch of fall. We were so glad to get back here after our trip to Maine, though it was an experience for the children just to see how a few others live. Harriet Winslow's summer place in Castine was the high point, and shall I say Betty [Fisher]'s was the low? Betty couldn't have been sweeter, or more hospitable, but the way she lives is incredible. Though the kitchen was of a primitiveness which defies description, there was never any letting up of the butter plates, or little plates under little plates, and fresh linen napkins and silver butter knives, which no one ever has at summer camps! However, the boys are so engaging and helpful, and must be used to remnants of former splendor by now.

Harriet's house is a big rambling white frame with an attached and converted barn, which she had painted aluminum to the town's horror. She and Mary have separate summer places, Mary's being in Canada.

Harriet says they saw Bobby (Cal) [Lowell] and his new wife and thought her very nice. I believe that must be Elizabeth Hardwick whom he met at Yaddo.

Lady [Merrie] Vernon is finally getting to the States. She will be visiting her daughter, Avice, and wants to see us both. She says she hopes to get to Memphis at the time of the publication of your new book. Will you be preparing the Lady Vernon Room?

A reproduction of my portrait of Eudora will be used with her publicity for GOLDEN APPLES, I understand. Look for it in the *New York Times*.

I forgot to tell you I completed the Madonna for Stone Ridge, spending a day putting on the gold leaf and helping Gid Legg get it installed. Although his bill was $675, leaving me the balance of only $325 for my own work, I had to agree that it was very special. Not only the prie-dieus and the fine wood, but the frame and a contraption that permits draperies to enfold the painting. I had to buy the draperies and dye them blue as well. The experience has been rewarding and Mary, after all, is getting almost a full scholarship. (I find that portraits done for teeth straightening are also very helpful—dentist-wise.) At Pearson [brother of Harriet] Winslow's cocktail party I met the sister of the donor, a Mrs. Ravenel—New Orleans and Charleston—who told me the Benoit family has not seen the completed shrine. I hope they like it so I can continue to smile about it.

Love,
Marcella

After Harriet suffered a stroke, she offered the house to Robert Lowell for summers, and she willed it to him after her death.

Léonie Adams wrote me a letter on September 28, 1949, while I was still in New Hampshire:

Dear Marcella,

I was very pleased to have your note—how pleasant it sounds up there! It has been awfully hot and damp here, almost unbearable and the *Saturday Review*'s campaign is having all sorts of effects. It has now been brought up in the House, and we are waiting to see what comes of that.

I was glad to hear the last news of the [portrait] sketch and shall certainly bring Bill to see it in the fall. Before writing you I waited for a reply from Frost, who was difficult to track down. He is at Homer Noble Farm, Ripton, Vermont; and in writing to him about the records the other day, I tried to prepare him for hearing from you about a sketch. I hope he will consent to have it done.

Cheering news did come of Cal—Merrill Moore wrote me that his illness had been much exaggerated by well-meaning friends, and that the various forms of treatment had put him in remarkably good shape. He too wrote briefly but cheerfully, and said he was back in circulation, or soon would be.

Just now Bill is in Connecticut and I am trying to get out from under the load of official worries and do a little writing. Fate seems against me. I shall have at least to stay within reach in case the congressional committee does decide to "investigate" us. It all seems fantastic, to have been fomented chiefly by a literary quarrel between the modernists and the oldsters.

Thanks again for your note—and best wishes for peace and coolness for you and the children.

Affectionately,
Léonie

The last novel Anne Winslow wrote, *It Was like This,* was published by Knopf in October, 1949. Although she said it was her favorite book, Orville Prescott felt her characters did not seem to be speaking in their own voices but in Mrs. Winslow's. He remarked that, although the book had "numerous shining phrases," there was little plot, and he ventured that since only seven months had passed since her last book, it might be that she was writing too quickly.

After Prescott's halfhearted review came out with a very unflattering photograph that Alfred Knopf had taken of her, she wrote to me, "I am glad you felt the way I did about Orville's review and Alfred's picture—as if they were connected by an evil spell of some kind. And so the old woman was turned into a frog—only she looks more like a camel, and to think he came six hundred miles to do this to me!" Whatever reason Mrs. Winslow had for forsaking the novel, she continued to write poems that were published monthly in the 1950s. They appeared in *Harper's,* the *Atlantic Monthly,* and the *New Yorker.*

P Street, N.W.
Washington, D.C.
October 7, 1949
Dear Tat,

Having two books come out in one year is almost TOO much! It seemed to me that I had just finished reading THE SPRINGS when along comes IT WAS LIKE THIS. I picked that book up the night before we left N.H. and became so engrossed I forcibly made myself stop reading or I knew I would never get off the next day. I had been so much in the mood of the story that several times I had the illusion of being IN it! Since returning to D.C., the leisure to take up the story again has come fitfully. Etta won't be back until next week and the children had to get ready for school, and there has been the usual refurbishing and overhauling of clothes and house.

Two bits of news: Robert Lowell has married Elizabeth Hardwick (the girl that Allen [Tate] fell for, remember?) and Charles is back, looking better than ever.[1] I think he is meant to be perennial. He has made his wisest comment yet, concerning the beautiful Italian table that Fredrica inherited and gave me in exchange for the painting I had always refused to let her buy—the still life Randolph liked so much, the semi-abstract one. I asked Charles to be aware of the table's age, the single piece of walnut, a refectory table which might have spent many years in an ancient Italian monastery and needed loving care to keep the rich patina. Charles gazed at it a long time and finally said: "Yas'm, it so old, must be when they said, Let's start makin' tables."

Léonie Adams writes that she is back in New York; that she saw Allen and Caroline in Princeton at an unofficial meeting of the Fellows. A and C love their new little house and there is a fine growth of mushrooms in the region to delight Caroline. She wants me to be sure to look up Elizabeth Bishop and hopes Robert Frost will let himself be sketched. I hope Frost will still remember me if I can make it to Vermont one day.

Betty and John Carter Vincent are enjoying being at the American Legation in Switzerland. She writes that she sees reviews of your books over there and is keeping them to paste in her copies—"such complimentary appreciations of your special kind of writing."

Love,
Marcella

1. Elizabeth Hardwick (1916–), a writer and a book critic for the *Partisan Review* in the 1940s, met Robert Lowell at Yaddo and married him in 1949. She founded the *New York Review of Books* in February, 1963, at the time of a labor strike against New York's newspapers. Lowell and Hardwick divorced in September, 1972.

Thanksgiving
November 24, 1949
Dear Tat,

Etta gave us a delicious dinner, but it was buffet style. The children all ate on my new Italian table in Johnny's room as he is still recovering from bronchitis. Lady Vernon took two helpings of turkey and sweet potatoes and liked the pumpkin pie which she had never eaten before. Poor Avice [Marten] had the flu, but Mother and Eleanor made up the family. Merrie Vernon is devastated that they couldn't get to Memphis as she has to return to England sooner than she expected.

November 15th was a busy day for me. The opening of my exhibit at Chequire House in Alexandria, Virginia, was very well attended. Lida Mayo, who runs the gallery, was surprised at how many people came from Washington. I must say the setting for pictures is so much better than the UN Club where Whyte had put on my last show. Because I was invited to a swank party at the Greek Embassy, which was in honor of a Greek dress designer from Paris named Desses (as well as for the Venizelos), that evening, I had bought a new dress that I saw advertised in the morning paper. I enclose a clipping of the Ceil Chapman copy of somebody famous—the original had appeared on the last cover of *Vogue*—and because I felt so stylish in that and my aigrette (which came by way of Betty's mother replacing the singed bird-of-paradise on my velvet hat), I longed to meet Mr. Desses who would know who were the famous designers and their styles. Fortunately, Mr. Salvago, a Greek diplomat whom I had met recently, saw me, searched around in the crush, and brought Desses to meet me. Wondering if the famous man would spot a copy, I courageously asked if he recognized the designer of my dress. With a quick look of interest, he answered promptly, and diplomatically: "The top looks like ME, the bottom, Fath!" It was all worth my hasty trip to town that morning.

I would like to think that the young Shah of Iran reads his publicity. At the end of a long article in the morning's *Post* which says that his Imperial Majesty, Mohammed Riza Shah Pahlavi, would be spending a night at a Guest House in Georgetown, as guests of President and Mrs. Truman, there is a final paragraph stating that the young Georgetown artist Marcella Comès, known in private life as Mrs. Randolph Winslow, would be having an exhibit of paintings in Alexandria!

Aside from all this going on, I have had a luncheon for Susan Ertz, the writer, born in England of American parents. The combination of Ertz, Katherine Biddle and Elizabeth Bishop was a happy one. They got along famously considering that not one of them seemed to have read anything the other two had written. Since [they] had come promptly, meeting each other on the way in, I couldn't explain any of them, so it was fun to see their efforts to recall just "who was she and what in God's name had she done"! Miss Ertz knew nothing of the Ezra Pound controversy, but had lots to say about Elizabeth Bowen and Elizabeth Taylor. She and K. Biddle compared notes on having gotten in to see Emily Dickinson's house in Amherst which, apparently, is quite a feat. Harper

(Miss Ertz' publisher) had asked her to write something on Emily D. but after she met Millicent Todd Bingham, she felt Mrs. B was covering the field thoroughly. Remember Mrs. Bingham, whom you did not like?

Speaking of writers, my portrait of Red Warren was borrowed for the showing of a movie made from his book. *All the King's Men* opened at the Playhouse a few days ago and my portrait of him was displayed prominently in the lobby for opening night. It was suspended from the ceiling in the center of a number of his books. I had lunch with Zenobia Jiménez just afterwards and I asked her to ask Juan Ramón if he wouldn't like to be suspended somewhere. And about Anne G. Winslow—couldn't she write a movie and get suspended?

Nikolaki came by one day. He looks even more like Mussolini in his old age and still goes on about good and evil. I haven't seen much of Marceil and Russell. Marceil says they are "burning the flame at both ends." Have you seen the piece Katherine Anne wrote on Willa Cather in the *New York Times Book Review?* Allen phoned briefly one morning. Apparently the poets are on shaky ground just now.

I took Augusta Fletcher off her stretcher and threw her in the wastebasket. Her husband, Meade, remarried in June. The stretcher is going to support Mrs. Henry Fowler, who, I hope, will have a happier fate than poor Augusta.

Love,
Marcella

Mrs. Winslow's answer to this letter was, "Such an exciting life! I see you madly clinging to the swift coat tails of time. I wish I could see Nikolaki's reaction to Venizelos. How much I had to hear about that idol in the past!"

Anne Winslow submitted to having a photograph made, which Blanche Knopf "expressed herself delighted with." Mrs. Winslow was never delighted with a photograph of herself of any kind, however, saying that it had been filtered out beyond recognition.

Mrs. Winslow sent me a note from Johnny to Cousin Harriet that Harriet had shared with her. Johnny had typed the Christmas thank-you on the typewriter Harriet had given him: "I dont know how to thank you for the MOST wonderful present I ever got in all my life. I dont know if I will get a good chance to use it with my mother liking it so much and my grandmother a writer. Mabey she will even write a new book on it."

ART SUFFICES, 1950—1959

Practice an art for love and the happiness of your life
you will find it outlasts almost everything but breath!

—Katherine Anne Porter

P Street, N.W.
Washington, D.C.
January 5, 1950
Dear Tat,

You will soon be here and preparations are already under way—your presents stacked up. Nikolaki has left you what shakes like Greek brandy. (For me, an article entitled "Modern Arms and Free Men," by Vannevar Bush. I am memorizing the title as I will never get beyond it. Meant subtly and indirectly for you.)

Three paid-up portraits just before Christmas have occasioned the refurbishing of your room, and the whole third floor. Some of the clutter is either thrown away or, alas! more often put into a different drawer or behind something, à la Miss Nichols.

Alex Böker has bought nine copies of your last book, IT WAS LIKE THIS, and presented them to friends for Christmas. Mrs. Nicholas Longworth was the recipient of one. Alex said she would like so much to see you again and wondered if you would remember her! Let's do the unexpected and not know who she is if she drops by.

Since you like, or I should say "prefer," males, you will be glad to know that I had three callers of that sex on New Year's Day. All new to you and one of them brand-new to me. A young man named Deeble, grandson of Chester Harding, who wants to write an historical novel about the *Kearsarge* and *Alabama* battle in the Civil War.[1] Now should be the time to tell you the remark Mary made to Midgie, relayed to me by Russell—Midgie said she wished you could pass on her new boyfriend and Mary agreed saying, "Yes, Grantat's boy crazy. Always has been and still is."

I am sorry that your friend Canon Douglas will be thanked for sending nuts. He will be wondering how you can make Pecan Pie out of Oregon pears. Surely I wrote "pears" and you can blame my handwriting and not my confused mind! I kept them in the icebox but they were getting too ripe so we feasted on them. We all thank you and send regrets.

Love,
Marcella

1. Chester Harding was one of the best-known of the early portrait painters in this country. A grandson, also named Chester Harding, was a classmate of Eveleth Winslow's at West Point.

Mrs. Winslow was not always happy to see visitors at Goodwinslow these years. On January 25, she wrote, "Several Boston products of real distinction have been here, and it was one of the better occasions. They were headed to stay longer, but I simply can't have people around the way I used to in the old days. I get tired of them. If they are charming, they make me long for Randolph, and if they are obnoxious, they still make me long for him."

January 20, 1950
Dear Tat,

Mary says, "The winter isn't the same without Grantat!" We can hardly call what we are having winter. Yesterday was 73° and I had my lunch outdoors. How about you? Don't tell me your life is becoming complicated in that quiet spot. The two young men from the effete East looking for atmosphere sound promising. I wish I were there to see them see it—though not to lend it.

I lent my atmosphere to the poets and, now that is all over with, you can come. I invited Katherine Anne to stay in her old room when I found you were not coming, and her answer was typical KAP: "Deluged under paper; When the novel is finished; Redecorating the large house; Five floors, four families; All that's needed is time and money etc." You were undoubtedly right in your prediction that she would never write anything more for these very reasons—People, Paper, Time, Money. She couldn't pull loose from New York for two days.

My cocktail party for the poets was such a success that Robert Penn Warren said I must have them every year. They presented me with a big box of flowers, which Robert Lowell had selected himself and brought as far as the door. He had to leave for a train to Iowa where he will teach. I was quite touched. Caroline was here, as well as the Percy Woods and Allen, of course, much more subdued. There was no one outside the D.C. poet group invited except Huntington Cairns and Léger (who was away), and the Robert Richmans. Afterwards, we all went to the Biddles' for dinner and acted out Charades. Katherine [Biddle] was really wonderful in that game. Lots of fun. The first group, composed of the two Biddles, Red Warren, Louise Bogan, Willard Thorp, Mark Merrell and myself acted out HUNTINGTON CAIRNS. It was guessed immediately. Probably because the second group had also chosen that name which they put on in a different manner. The second group was the Tates, Léonie Adams, Elizabeth Bishop, the Cairnses, Karl Shapiro and Marian Merrell.

Love,
Marcella

January 30, 1950
Dear Tat,

I had the most amazing experience yesterday, or maybe I should say, macabre—a trip to Baltimore with a character whom I met at a party for the Prince and Princess of Hesse: a woman completely fictional and not of flesh and blood, who took me to an American BRIDESHEAD REVISITED, where we had tea. The owner of the manse was also unreal—in fact, he was Sherlock Holmes, and his Scottish friend was more Dr. Watson than the Conan Doyle one. The house was full of priceless art treasures. The family is one of the oldest in Baltimore, and the lord and master (Sherlock), a "Brideshead" Catholic, is related to many of the titled families in Europe. I understand he managed to have a beautiful wife who is now in an insane asylum and he is reportedly pining away, although he told me he had gained 50 pounds within the last few years.

After the fantastic tea (which I will have to act out for you), he left to buy sheep, and put on a long flowing cape which went well with his 6′2″ frame and long Thoroughbred horse face. I hope I can do justice to the whole thing when I see you but what I haven't conveyed is the feeling that everything was all wrong from beginning to end—like a very vivid nightmare wherein you know you don't belong but can't run away. Maybe just my astral working overtime.

How nice it was to come home and find a cute note from Mary telling me that there was to be a dramatization of Katherine Anne Porter's stories "Pale Horse, Pale Rider" and "Flowering Judas" on the radio and that she had done the dishes. Reality at last!

Love,

Marcella

Mrs. Winslow came for her usual three-month visit, leaving in late April to get her garden started.

May 1, 1950

Dear Tat,

I hated to leave you at the airport but I do get gloomy at parting, so it ends up as a strain for even your powers of conversation.

My portrait of Howard Mitchell is so good at this point that I am afraid to breathe.[1] I had two sittings last week. Mary says he looks just like Rochester. She is into JANE EYRE now. I will be painting Clagett Wednesday. When I phoned and asked to speak to Mr. Contee Bowie Clagett, he answered: "This is HENRY Contee Bowie Clagett." All the ancestors have to be accounted for!

Love,

Marcella

1. Howard Mitchell (1911–1989), a cellist, was the director of the National Symphony, in Washington. He was named director at the age of thirty-seven, in 1947, becoming one of the youngest conductors of a national symphony.

May 7, 1950

Dear Tat,

Are you surprised that the portrait of Henry Contee Bowie Clagett, by Marcella Comès, will be shown in Weston, the family seat of generations of Clagetts, during the Maryland house tour? Yes indeed. As quick as that. We had two sittings of 3 1/2 hours each, with only one rest and presto! The 9th-generation Clagett is captured permanently for the 10th—and on up (or down?)—for, I feel sure, that in his bright red hunting coat he will outshine all the ancestors, and descendants too, for some time to come. He did ask me how soon the colors would mellow. I obliged him by carving in paint the initials of his hunt on his gold buttons for all Upper Marlboro and horse-conscious Virginians to identify his outfit. I practically "stuck on" a miniature riding whip pin when it came to his cravat but, outside of those few touches to please him, it was all Comès and, I must say (and he did say), the portrait was a speaking likeness—as "they" say. I like Hal. He will go far as an ancestor I am sure.

Katherine Anne writes from Beaulieu that she got my Christmas card in France at Mardi Gras. Appropriate, since it was my self-portrait with the mask. She said the carnival was fun.

Love,
Marcella

May 8, 1950
Dear Tat,

I have had two interesting days since you left and shall class them as Dowager Day and Literary Ladies Day. D Day started out with a sitting on Howard Mitchell (I get him started on music and off he goes; since he is Director of the D.C. symphony, I asked him to sit), a drink with the Macys around noon, and then a meeting of the Arts and Letters at Mrs. Cornelius Whitney's, where we planned the Scholarship Benefit and saw the work of some of the young scholarship students who explained their paintings (most engaging) and then tea at Mrs. Herter's where the Dowagers started in earnest. There must have been at least ten, including Mrs. Dean Acheson, Mrs. Robert Woods Bliss and Harriet and Mary Winslow. Mrs. Bliss described an Indian fakir's gestures in subduing a python to such effect (with her skinny hands and neck) that I felt hypnotized myself. Needless to say, Mac Herter was out showing her garden at that point—a mass of white azaleas and dogwood—so beautiful. Then I went to a long-dress dinner at Mrs. Corcoran Thom's house. Only dowagers again. No men, alas! They all could have been my mother, or even my grandmother, and I never heard so much gossip. Mrs. Mesta and the Marquess of Milford Haven came in for most of it. Perle Mesta is "The Hostess with the Mostess"—as she is referred to in D.C.

Literary Ladies Day revolved around a lecture given by John Mason

Brown. I had been given a box for this occasion, so I invited my most literary friends, Marian Merrell, Lida Mayo and Agnes Hale, all of whom had books, or various publications to their credit, to join me. Although we enjoyed Brown's comments on the theatre, we were probably most impressed by the poem that Congressman Hale, husband of one literary lady, Agnes, told us was to be published the following week in the *New Yorker*.[1] It was his farewell to Congress:

> Adieu, sweet dome, Ye roofless halls, adieu,
> Where I have swinked and sweat the summer through,
> Pondering the work of Messrs. Taft and Hartley
> Which we did not undo, not even partly;
> Probing the problem of the nation's health
> And various plans for squandering its wealth;
> Intent on coping with inflation's ills,
> And with deflation's monitory chills;
> Trying to chart an economic course,
> Steered now by Keyserling and now by Nourse. Etc.

Love,
Marcella

1. Robert Hale was the Republican congressman from Maine.

May 29, 1950
Dear Tat,

I have been made art chairman for the National Arts and Letters Scholarship Benefit so am in a whirlpool of publicity. My studio (the Macy house), pictured in the *Post,* is called the "glamour studio of the lot." Bill Walton [a painter friend of the John Kennedys] posed with me, which made it more glamorous. Andrea Zerega is shown in his studio with the usual egg hanging from the ceiling—à la Piero della Francesca. I am really keen about the idea of helping young artists and was able to tell my interviewer, Mrs. Carl Spaatz, about it on the radio. For the first time, Johnny is impressed with mum, on account of radio! The government offers so little in the way of support or commissions to artists that an exhibition and sale of the invited ones, which will raise money for scholarships for young artists, can only be a help. In some cases the professional artists are donating, but most will receive a percentage from sales, so everyone will benefit. Don't expect to hear from me until the whole thing is over.

Caroline Gordon is more like her old self—much more serene. She is all wrapped up in her conversion to Catholicism, which she says saved the day for both her and Allen. Allen indirectly.

Love,
Marcella

June 16, 1950
Dear Tat,

Benefit over. Portraits finished. Besides Howard Mitchell and Clagett, I painted Tim Marten and Elizabeth Bishop.[1] The latter came to P St. instead of the Macy studio, with one floor less steps. It was my last chance to work on Bishop as she leaves this year and Conrad Aiken takes over the poetry job at the Library. I have enjoyed knowing her. She is quiet but takes everything in. One feels that her poetry is her life. It took a while to convince her to leave her job long enough to pose for me. No doubt Léonie Adams had led her to believe it was the thing the Poetry Office expected. All of it going back to Allen and his passion for portraits! That is southern, isn't it?

The portrait of Elizabeth is the size and technique of Denis Devlin's which has been so well liked. I have her in a brown jacket and white blouse with her hand under her chin—a natural-looking pose. The paint quality makes it one of my best.

The President of the Arts and Letters phoned me yesterday to ask if I would run the whole benefit program next year—I was so businesslike! Imagine me in a new role! Of course I refused, but I agreed to do the art show again, as I frankly enjoyed working with the artists and will hope to make it something big and very good. The art show was very well received, considering it was shown at the Shoreham Hotel. We made over $1000 in one afternoon on sales since the calibre of the art work was excellent.

I had a garden party to show Howard Mitchell's portrait on a beautiful day. A Fish House punch and lots of men, oh me, oh my! Sounds thrilling, doesn't it? There is a photograph of Mitchell in the recent *New Yorker,* but it is too glamourized. He is very good looking though.

The British diplomat Peter Stephens (the first man in Washington to invite me to something before I invited him) had an interesting dinner party—the new Counselor at the British Embassy named Bernard Burrows, and our young Louisiana Congressman Hale Boggs, and their wives.[2] You would have liked them. I did.

Love,
Marcella

1. Elizabeth Bishop (1911–1979), a 1934 Vassar graduate who had won a Guggenheim, a Pulitzer, and many other awards, took over from Léonie Adams the chair of poetry at the Library of Congress in the fall of 1949, and she gave the customary readings. Although she felt that she had made no discoveries of poetic talent and that poets needed to read their poems more effectively, she also thought there had been an increase in interest in poetry in the United States after the Second World War. She remained cautious in her assessment, however, since no poet could earn a living by poetry, magazines paid very small sums for it, and various awards were just drops in the bucket. Her disturbing visits to Ezra Pound inspired a poem that started,

> This is the house of Bedlam.
> This is the man
> that lies in the house of Bedlam.
> This is the time
> of the tragic man
> that lies in the house of Bedlam.

2. Sir Bernard Burrows (1910–), educated at Eton and Oxford, was a specialist in Arab affairs and one of the few British diplomats who knew Arabic. He represented the authority of the British government for all the protectorates of the Persian Gulf—the oil sheikdoms of Kuwait, Bahrain, and Qatar, and the seven Trucial States. In 1957, during the crisis in Oman, the New York *Times* wrote that the judgment of "this cool man in a hot spot" could have important consequences, especially since the British press was leveling accusations that arms and money from the Untied States were making the revolt in Oman possible. In January, 1950, Burrows was named counselor of embassy in Washington.

Center Sandwich, N.H.
June 23, 1950
Dear Tat,

It is so restful to be in New Hampshire. I am sitting happily in the sun on my old mustard-colored bench under the beech tree, looking over my still unmowed fields and the blue mountains beyond. The shadows haven't yet come over the lawn from the large elms. The grass is cut and the mailbox out to welcome us—still with no name on it except Winslow. That will have to do. The place was cleaned and beds made by my neighbor, so we are able to relax after our extra-long trip up. We went 150 miles out of our way to stay in Aurora, N.Y., in the inn Tom Carruth and his wife are managing for Wells College. Tom wanted to stay in the Army after the war but couldn't get a commission (he still calls himself Major). So he and Camilla (unfortunately from the poor branch of the Morgan family) have had to take all sorts of jobs. They seem to love it there and have taken the inn out of the red. They have an attractive suite and, as usual, Tom's stories are pages from the *New Yorker*. Even if he had time to write them, it is better to hear with your own ears his description of the undertaker who took a room but let his small son sleep in "the box" in his hearse, or of the jealous wife who got out her pistols one night in the corridor.

The prize story of all is their five months with the writer Rachel Carruthers in Danbury, as her couple. After a hair-raising account of their duties, which included butlering, chauffeuring, gardening, cooking, cleaning and even doing the laundry, Tom casually remarked: "We were only two pages ahead of her in the Social Register." Although there was continual entertaining, with sometimes 12 for dinner—which Camilla would cook and Tom would serve (6 1/2 miles, he figured, he walked passing things)—they got very meager tips and, very often, the guests would be old friends of the Morgan family. One financial wizard, who had given a $2 tip on her first visit, after hearing who they were, came to the kitchen after her second visit and said: "You poor, brave, young things!" and gave Camilla a lottery ticket for a religious benefit.

Love,
Marcella

The Korean War was scary. An old-time Bostonian who summered in New Hampshire told me her family had made plans to meet in New Hampshire if the cities got hit with an atomic bomb dropped by the Russians. I thought I would as soon be in the cities and get it over with. I could not bear the thought of rationing and hoarding again. I also decided I had better make improvements on my place in New Hampshire while materials could still be had. I needed a studio in the barn where the cow stalls had been, more light, and a floor laid so we could use the extra room for activities.

Mary, her cousin Sara, and Johnny required space for their playacting. They went in heavily for Edgar Allan Poe. Insisting that an adult audience was essential to the success of their first effort (a macabre story about a mummy, called "The Curse"), I inveigled the three little Munoz ladies— who loved children even enough to look forward to participating—to sit in their car just outside the open barn door so that it could supply its headlight on the eerie scene. There were no screens or electricity in the barn at that time, and the mosquitoes arrived in swarms for the performance. Although badly bitten, the three children were encouraged enough to plan and carry through their versions of "The Masque of the Red Death," "The Tell-Tale Heart" and "The Cask of Amontillado," complete with bodies bricked up and hearts pounding offstage. They named themselves the Bornactors, since that sounded like the Barnstormers, the summer theater group in nearby Tamworth. One day, inspired by a play by Noel Coward, the Bornactors were improvising loud and vivid town gossip, when a neighbor on the four-party line came by to tell them their receiver was off the hook.

The Munoz ladies were Cubans who had run the first girls' summer camp in the States, which their mother had started on Squam Lake. They summered in Sandwich after retiring.

It astonished us that these tiny old ladies could drive. When we saw a car coming with no one in it, we were sure that Inez or Adele was inside driving and we gave it the right of way.

P Street, N.W.
Washington, D.C.
September 20, 1950
Dear Tat,

Back to P Street.

Last evening Lon [Brainard] Cheney came over and told me Fanny [Cheney] had gone to Japan until June, I presume on Library business, and he has just completed a novel. He had been to a writers' conference with the Tates and put them on the train for Minnesota. Allen is taking the place of Red Warren teaching at the University.

Do you have any intention of reading Caroline's book, THE STRANGE CHILDREN? If so, let me know what you think of it. Orville Prescott's review was excellent. He says it is first-rate, beautifully written and distinguished. Of course all the characters would be recognizable. Lon made a retreat with Caroline and seems to be on the brink of Catholicism. All he lacks is faith, he says!

The children are back in school, so the worst is over. I don't like the city or my old house, but I will get used to it. When Etta comes back next week I will begin to like it again.

Avice and Tim Marten will be leaving the U.S. soon. They were staying in Millbrook, N.Y., near Chauncey [Stillman]'s place at Amenia, this summer and Avice, in spite of coming from one of the "stately homes" in England, was much impressed with his estate. Two butlers to serve breakfast—little houses in the woods and ponies for the children—more magnificent than anything she has seen in a long time. Chauncey has quit his job here and expects to live the life of a gentleman farmer, she says.

A scathing editorial in the *New York Times* about Mrs. Mesta going to Luxembourg as our Ambassador—such as: "Are our embassies to be treated merely as playthings for palace favorites whose renown is registered only in Broadway musical comedies?" Eleanor gets all the repercussions at the Embassy.

Love,
Marcella

December 13, 1950
Dear Tat,

Last weekend I spent with the L. M. C. Smiths in Philadelphia. The occasion was the opening of a modern British show. They had invited me for dinner—fashionable and staid Philadelphians had cocktails right in the museum, with dinner served under the pictures!

Eleanor [Smith]'s amazing old father, Mr. Houston, aged 83, sat next to me. We took him home after the viewing and went through his huge house in Chestnut Hill, where he decided one day to remove the top two floors. It is the type of house which is fast disappearing—comfortable, overstuffed, occasionally something possibly picked up in Europe. Eleanor told me all the numerous "undistinguished" family portraits were painted by imported European artists—when Thomas Eakins was available in his own town![1] Eakins's portraits would not have been appreciated at that time, I'm sure.

Love,
Marcella

1. Thomas Eakins (1844–1916) was a professor at the Pennsylvania Academy of Fine Arts and is one of the most famous of American painters, especially for his revealing portraits.

January 19, 1951
Dear Tat,

Do please make up your mind to come up. I am craving oysters, mushrooms, beer, artichokes, shrimp and all the other things I never get if you are not here. I am saving Mother's plum pudding too. You needn't worry about war talk. You would never know there is a war going on. Few are interested in Korea, it seems.

The Bernard Burrowses are back at the British Embassy after their trip south. They said that meeting you and seeing your house was the high point of the trip. You must have lived up to what the English expect southern women to be. Gone with the wind?

Howard Mitchell brought his portrait back, which I had lent him, without explanation. It is such a good portrait and a likeness as well, but of course he isn't smiling. He is still directing the National Symphony. I am going tonight to hear the guest conductor, Leonard Bernstein, who is the young genius who wows them in Boston.

Chauncey looks fine after a vacation in Jamaica. At the dinner I gave for the Burrowses he surprised (but delighted) me for a gesture so unusual for that sybarite by picking up the blue Staffordshire dessert dish at his place, and turning it over to see its markings. Nothing was said, but I was consumed with curiosity.

The children have gone square dancing. Mary and I have noticed that Johnny has invested 59 cents in a bottle of Wildroot Creme Oil.

Love,
Marcella

February 10, 1951
Dear Tat,

If you wonder why I haven't written for a week or so, it is because of "Season in Swing." The newspaper column under Society Notes I enclose explains it all. I get mentioned only once but you can see I am swinging. The reporter describes the guests of the "SPECIAL" little buffet supper, given by the First Secretary of the Italian Embassy and Signora Bounous (who writes as Alba de Cespedes) as being "suitably intellectual," since the hostess and her guest of honor, Count Piovene, are well-known writers. It seems that Count Piovene is here to write his impression of Americans and to give a talk on Italian Literature at Georgetown University. I seemed to be the only American at the party (the nice Ortonas had suggested me for some reason), so what impression did the Count get when he got me? Quite a lot! I can hear you saying to Mary—and you would both agree if you had seen me towering over some of the smaller men.

Signora Bounous (Alba de Cespedes) is almost too glamorous to be so talented, but she tells me her first book was translated into 24—are there that many?—languages, and the next, soon to come out, is under Knopf's auspices. She says Blanche [Knopf] doesn't like the translation. I was invited for 8:30 but we did not eat until 10 and were having our demitasse at midnight. We were hungry enough to eat the three meat dishes, the lobster and six desserts. Now it is up to you to come up so that I can invite the Bounouses to my house for one meat, one dessert and to meet one writer.

You may meet the Piovenes as they are driving south. The Countess does all the driving. They left New York on the afternoon of a blizzard at 5 p.m. and drove until 3 a.m. to Washington, so I must say they have guts—or she does.

Love,
Marcella

February 12, 1951
Dear Tat,

Gertrude C. Whittall has given $100,000 to the Library of Congress to be used to encourage poetry, buy manuscripts, have readings and so on. She has furnished the old room the poets used, and refers to it as the Poet's Corner, which makes them writhe. Allen Tate is resigning this year as the oldest member of the Fellows, to make room for newer members. He looks years older. I don't know if that is due to getting religion, and the strain of same, or just cracking up after all these years. John Crowe Ransom said charming things about you and your books at a buffet supper which the Biddles gave. Nancy and Percy Wood seemed the bright spots—Nancy with her hair pulled straight back, most be-

Henry Contee Bowie Clagett, painted in 1950
Courtesy Henry Contee Bowie Clagett

Howard Mitchell, painted in 1950

Bob Mudgett haying my field in Center Sandwich, 1950

Walter de la Mare and his son Colin, at their house in
Buckinghamshire, 1931.

Elizabeth Bishop, painted in 1950

Showing Mrs. Christian Herter the art work at the scholarship benefit at the Corcoran Gallery, 1952.

Courtesy Katharine Graham, the Washington Post

Sir Bernard Burrows, sketched in 1952

Robert Frost, painted in 1952

Cornelius Weygandt, painted in 1952
Courtesy Ann Weygandt

Jim Beede, sketched in 1953

With Mary, John, and Massa in New Hampshire, 1954

Alice Roosevelt Longworth at home, with portrait of Joanna Sturm, 1956

Father Martin Cyril D'Arcy in my studio, 1957

Father Martin Cyril D'Arcy, painted in 1957
Courtesy Georgetown University

Robert Lowell, painted in 1974

Chauncey Stillman at his place in Amenia, New York, in the 1980s

At home in Center Sandwich, 1979, painted by my son, John

Courtesy McDermott, Will and Emery

coming. Much talk about Allen's letter to Cardinal Spellman in the *New York Times* about the banned movie. They—the poets—are all fuming about "Spelly's" forthcoming novel. I must say I agree. From the way Red Warren talked, I felt he wanted to do another ALL THE KING'S MEN on him.

Nancy and Percy are going to Princeton until Percy gets settled in psychiatry somewhere and they asked me if I would come to Princeton before Easter to be godmother to Nancy. I will. Everyone was so quiet and orderly at the Biddles but, somehow, two of Katherine's bric-a-brac got knocked over and broken. Thornton Wilder broke a glass full of ivy and Richman broke a lamp base which looked sort of Ming—but ended Bing!

I met Duncan Emrich who told me of his article on Georgetown which he is writing for *Holiday*. I asked him over last night, as he wanted to discuss Georgetown artists. (I hope I get in!) I also asked the Robert Hales. Agnes told of writing her article on Portland, Maine, for *Holiday*. Between the two of us, we practically rewrote his article. Emrich is in charge of the folklore section at the Library of Congress and is long on folklore but short on Georgetown, where he has lived only one year.

Love,
Marcella

February 20, 1951
Dear Tat,

Having just got the FM attachment, which gets the good music station, I invited the Bounouses and the Robert Hales in to listen to Katherine Biddle read her poetry over that station. Alba de Cespedes (Signora Bounous) is editor of a paper in Rome for which she writes every week, and at the moment she is writing a play and another book. Blanche Knopf wants 100 pages cut out of the translation and Alba is thinking of giving it to Harcourt, Brace. Alba was unhappy in her role as a diplomat's daughter and said she ran away to marry at age 15. She knows diplomacy as her father was President of Cuba and Ambassador to this country for a while. Everyone was intelligent enough to know what everyone else was talking about and Blanche Knopf's ears should have burned. I start a portrait of Robert Hale this week. Agnes says she wants one of him.

Dinner with Chauncey Stillman, with some of his *own* Angus (raised on his farm) and Yorkshire pudding. C was in such good form that he carried a glass of water on his forehead all the way up the stairs. Somehow, it was not his sort of thing. He seems to prefer no contacts over Angus cattle and champagne, as he sent a note saying he wanted a chance to discuss your story "Seamiles," a discussion which will have to wait for a more informal occasion, or for a different type of dinner party.

I am going to Princeton over Palm Sunday to be godmother to all the Tates who are not already Catholic.

Red Warren's wife and Léonie Adams's husband are both falling apart in hospitals, and Johnny went to his first dance at Landon School. His only comment: "There were 33 girls and I danced with 25."

Love,
Marcella

March 14, 1951
Dear Tat,

Juan Ramón Jiménez left protestingly for Puerto Rico today—in fact, forcibly. He has had a nervous breakdown—as who hasn't?—and the doctors feel he would do better in a Spanish-speaking country. So poor Zenobia, who has made a career of indulging Juan Ramón's every whim, has burned her bridges temporarily to take him away. An English translation of some of his poems was just received at Whyte's Bookshop so I bought a copy, since I understood there had been nothing of his work in English before, and decided to pay him a visit in the hospital and have him autograph it. His illness (he is perfectly well physically) is all that concerns him now and our conversation ran like this:

> Marcella, this hospital is terrible. No good doctor. (He has Dr. Overholser, head of St. Elizabeth's.) They try to poison me on the food.

> Juan Ramón, I bought the last copy Whyte's had of your book.

> Can you get me a doctor of yours? They have only five copies probably.

Are these good translations, Juan Ramón?

Nothing matters but my situation. Look how thin my leg is. No good poems. Early.

Would you please autograph my copy, Juan Ramón?

I cannot hold a pen. Too weak. See how my hand trembles? (Reaching for his spectacles and taking the pen.)

If it is too much trouble . . . (But I hold the book and he writes clearly: *For Marcella,* in his hieroglyphic handwriting).

Love,
Marcella

April 6, 1951
Dear Tat,

I read your story in the *Ladies' Home Journal* and told Betty [Fisher] I couldn't see how you could get your people in such a predicament and find there was only one paragraph to get them out. She replied that was what you did best. I think she is right. Of course this town is in too much of a whirl to expect that anyone will get around to reading it—or anything except a horrible smutty book called WASHINGTON CONFIDENTIAL. Names, addresses and telephone numbers in that one are worse than Drew Pearson at HIS worst.

Betty was here to be with her Aunt Muffie and when I would ask her to a meal, she would look martyred and say she couldn't leave Muffie because two of Muff's friends were feeling low and she had to be on hand to get messages. All of which proves how noble she is, and makes me wish I were noble, and cared whether anyone who was a friend of an aunt of mine were low or high. I never know whether to be edified or irritated by all this. I'm sure if I were the low one I would be edified, though I am not altogether sure. There is something peaceful about being left to be low alone. When Betty would hold forth on the phone about an 84-year-old in Bethesda who was as spry as a chicken, and what she said and did, there was no doubt about my irritation, as I was usually in a mad rush to be spry myself in some place other than Bethesda.

To show what a small world: Miss Inez Munoz, who has been helping

Zenobia [Jiménez], and is an old friend of the Jiménezes', is one of the little Cuban ladies who have a house in Sandwich just a mile from mine. She is old—and would you like to know how spry?

Back to the Merry-Go-Round. I was invited to a symphony concert by the Ciechanowskis (pre-war Ambassador from Poland),[1] preceded by dinner in the lovely house of Mrs. Leland Harrison, whose husband used to be our Minister to Switzerland—the kind of dinner where the chef hovers over the artichoke entrée. Many Sully portraits throughout the house and TWO portraits of Fanny Kemble, the actress, who was an infatuation of her husband's great-grandfather in Philadelphia. The atmosphere was ultra-Republican, anti-Acheson, others considered outside the pale. [Leopold] Stokowski conducted the symphony. All of it enjoyable.

I received the *Virginia Quarterly* and perceive that you are in distinguished company. Without reading who the author was, any paragraph would indicate AGW. Now, I want to know *which Harper's* you will be in.

At an Arts and Letters meeting at Polly Guggenheim's house, we heard a talk on the UNESCO in Art by Sam Smith, who is the President of the American Federation of Arts, and I showed a painting that Mrs. Vogel liked at an exhibit afterwards.[2] She seems interested in having a portrait of her grandson.

I can't take on a description of my Princeton trip for Tate baptisms, which should have been in my last letter. I *did* go, and I did meet Maritain, who comes up to all expectations.[3] However, the Tates shouldn't mix baptisms and cocktail parties, but they do. When someone started calling Jacques Maritain "Jacquey," I thought it was time to go to bed. So I did. My one regret is that Allen induced me to lend him my hard-won autographed book of poems by Jiménez (which I took to read on the train), making promises to return it immediately, but it is presumed lost. If found, I hope the *For Marcella* in Jiménez' distinguished calligraphy will, some day, find its way back to me.

Your room is being thoroughly slept in, even if you are not here to do the sleeping. Fredrica [Fields] asked me to keep her 7-year-old Stephen for the weekend while she is away.[4] We call him Ferdinand, since he is "into" flowers. When I got him at school, he was holding 3 lilies in one hand and a bunch of violets in the other. After he got here, and found the proper vase and greenery for them, he has spent his time either digging, or planting, or growing roots in water, or just plain sniffing. All conversations revert to growing things, or naming bushes, or exclaiming over bushes already grown or named. He asks for ice cream and movies in the same breath, laughs incredulously at only one bathroom, and asks every minute, on the minute, when Johnny will come home—when he is not asking me to buy him topsoil, seeds and rakes. I will take him for a walk in Dumbarton Park to see the spring flowers. After that, you can send ME a lily.

Love,
Marcella

1. Jan Ciechanowski represented the Polish government in exile during World War II. The author of a book called *Defeat in Victory,* he felt keenly the defeat and loss of Poland's independence—Poland having been the first to fight against Hitler in a world conflict that brought victory to its allies. I made a start on a small portrait of him but unfortunately never completed it. I believe I was not satisfied with the likeness, to his disappointment and, of course, mine.

2. Polly Guggenheim, patron of the arts and a painter herself, was the wife of Robert Guggenheim, the financier. Townsend Vogel was about ten years old when his grandmother, Mrs. Martin Vogel, asked me to paint him.

3. Jacques Maritain, an influential and widely read Catholic philosopher and theologian, was a leading modern disciple and interpreter of Saint Thomas Aquinas. T. S. Eliot once called Maritain "the most conspicuous figure and probably the most powerful force in contemporary philosophy." At the fall of France, Maritain was lecturing in the United States and later served as a representative of the Free French movement of General Charles de Gaulle. He taught for a number of years at Columbia and Princeton and, while at Princeton, became a good friend of the Tates'. They asked him to be Allen's godfather when he became a Catholic.

4. Fredrica Fields, wife of Brigadier General Kenneth Fields, is a prize-winning stained-glass designer. We were both Engineer army wives, with a common interest in art, when our husbands were stationed in Vicksburg, Mississippi, in 1939–1941. Fredrica posed often for me.

May 17, 1951
Dear Tat,

I elected to take over again the National Arts and Letters Benefit Art Show (to raise scholarships for young artists) as I wanted to be sure that my good work of last year would not go down the drain. Apparently it hasn't. We are making such strides that the Corcoran is interested in taking the show on next year. All the best artists are taking part and next week Mrs. Carl Spaatz, wife of Air Corps General Spaatz, will interview me again, this time on TV.

I am toying with the idea of converting my coal furnace to oil. I called on my 83-year-old landlady, who lives around the corner, to ask if I could get a long lease. She is a dear—a nice old devout Catholic who has most of her interests in heaven. It would be too easy to take advantage of her—so, as Mother asked, "Which advantage are you taking?" I'll have to think about all the possibilities with the real-estate agent.

The Vogel and Hale portraits still hang fire. Agnes and Robert [Hale] have to be reconciled to the fact that (1) Robert is not really good-looking to start with. (2) He is Old, Father William. And (3) It is really a good likeness. I knew when Agnes brought her favorite photograph of Robert to the studio to show me how she expected him to look, that there was no way she could be pleased. Every bit of character had been neatly removed by the retouching. As for Vogel, she is not parting with the $350 without a struggle.

I am soon to meet Alec Waugh, brother of Evelyn, at the Burrowses', Maritain again at the Richmans' and, perhaps, but unlikely, Elizabeth Bowen at the Frankfurters'.[1] Eudora Welty wrote me a glowing letter about Bowen whom she has been visiting, saying it has been the nicest thing that has happened to her in years. She is hoping we will meet when Bowen comes to Washington to stay with the Frankfurters, working on a mission having to do with the Royal Commission on Capital Punishment—nothing to do with books. Eudora writes that she wishes Bowen could see me and my house and paintings—that the minute I saw her I'd want to paint her, and she hopes I will. Eudora is having a holiday in England—which she says is ill deserved but heavenly.

Love,
Marcella

1. Elizabeth Bowen, an Anglo-Irish writer, said that from the time she was twenty, when she wrote her first short story, she thought of nothing but writing. Some critics compared her to Henry James, Katherine Mansfield, and Virginia

Woolf. She lectured often in the United States in the 1950s, appearing regularly on college campuses.

After Lillie Vogel asked me to paint her grandson, Townsend, I learned that she was one of the Lewisohns of New York, a family always busy founding or financing settlements or stadiums or homes for wayward girls and the like. Mrs. Vogel said she really cared more for pretty clothes than her sisters did who built New York's School of the Living Theatre and tried to persuade their father to give all his money away. "My dear," she would say, "they went downtown and never came up." She, herself, preferred an upper-class swirl of activities, such as meeting Winston Churchill, dancing with the Prince of Wales, or knowing the "beautiful people" like Gertrude Lawrence and Lady Diana Duff Cooper. After her husband died and she came to live in Washington, she made her house a headquarters for the entertainment of servicemen, and for receptions of mind-blowing proportions for all sorts of causes. An invitation to dinner could mean two hundred seated, sometimes with an ambassador next to a hairdresser. She liked them all.

May 30, 1951
Dear Tat,

Here is a full account of the portraits that you seem interested in. The Vogel boy gave me the most trouble and, after I had finally finished it, his grandmother gave me more. I left it at the IFA Gallery with other portraits as she couldn't make up her mind how she liked it. Then, every week she would call to ask if the portrait were still there (as she needed to send people to tell her if she should like it). Finally, I told her to take it home. All was quiet for a few weeks, so a few days before I left for the summer, I wrote a note suggesting that she send the $350 to my N.H. address. The mention of money galvanized her into action. Every day I would get a message to please call Mrs. Vogel.

When I pulled myself together to do so, I found out that the boy wasn't "animated enough" and would I do another, or what should she do? I told her to return the painting and I would decide, since I was pleased with the one I had done. So she sent me a check for $150 with hopes that I would do another.

I finished the Hale portrait at some point but, knowing of the resistance I would run into, decided to have a photographer come to the studio to take a photograph of Robert in his pose. I felt nothing more could be done to improve the likeness and I wanted her to be convinced as well. The unretouched photograph was such an improvement over the one Agnes had shown me (that had been so worked over) that I showed her the photograph with my portrait when she came to get the painting.

However, she soon returned the portrait to me. Her only comment being that Robert didn't look pleasant enough. As Agnes was leaving the studio, having deposited the painting, she paused briefly and asked casually for the name and telephone number of the photographer. So now I own one Congressman—or the best likeness of one.

Love,
Marcella

P.S. The Clagett portrait is to have the stickpin more carefully painted, the red coat made "richer," and the face "redder."

Center Sandwich, N.H.
June 25, 1951
Dear Tat,

My activity in the arts was varied and active before I left D.C. We cleared $2500 for scholarships at the Benefit Exhibit, which won support from professional artists. The show was run, not like a formal exhibit, but more like an art market. I had been so frantic, running the whole thing, that only an emergency could reach me by phone. So, when it was over and I returned home exhausted and Etta told me N.Y. had called and I was expected to call the operator, I felt I would have to forgo a relaxing moment to get this mysterious message. After many delays, I got through—to discover that Betty [Fisher], calling from Larchmont, wanted me to buy 2 dozen water lilies for Mrs. Holton (head of Holton School) by the following day! Such are the things that make me realize that some people are still leading normal, uneventful lives.

Johnny asked if Betty's son Peter could visit us for a month this summer so Betty and I cross-lettered about my stop to pick up Peter on the way to New Hampshire. After a few calls and a telegram whose message read: "Going to Tommy's commencement. House all yours night of 15th. Do you want dinner prepared?" I accepted with alacrity, so felt reasonably secure of a stopping place overnight. I bent every sinew, and all of Charles's sinews and Etta's sinews to get me packed and away by 9:30 on the 15th, so we could make it for dinner prepared.

It was therefore somewhat surprising, on driving up to their door, to see Betty, Evan, Tommy, Burnett, Mona, Peter, and two of Tommy's friends all safely returned from the commencement and filling adequately the "house all yours." I tried hard to look happy to see them but it was difficult, and continued to be so when we ate a horribly expensive dinner in Larchmont's least swanky restaurant and slept in an old ladies' inn, which was the only one we could afford in that gold mine in Westchester County. Also, the weather had turned cold and I found I had left my only wrap hanging in my cupboard—on P Street! However, we did enjoy breakfast the next morning with the attractive children in the "house all theirs." Sara said afterwards that, looking at the three portraits I had done of members of the family, hanging in the living room, I examined them in all lights and then declared: "What feeling!"

Love,
Marcella

In answer to this letter, Anne Winslow wrote: "Some day some of us have GOT to write a story called THE HOUSE IS YOURS. . . . Everybody could write one."

On the way to New Hampshire we acquired Massa. Mary had been begging for a dog for a long time, but I had told her that I could not take that on. Nevertheless, I said that if one came our way, I would consider it a sign of God's will that she and I were the chosen ones—I to buy it and she to take care of it. Mary continued to read dog books and even entered a contest in which the second prize was a dog. (She was worried about winning the first prize instead and having to take a trip to Alaska.)

Whether God's will or not, it was a sign by a gas station that brought us Massa. A sign on the border of New Hampshire and Massachusetts read, Stop! LAST GAS IN MASS. Massachusetts gas is cheaper. My economical streak stopped me dead. Four children—Mary, Johnny, Peter, and Sara—and I got out to stretch our legs and saw in this rural spot a litter of adorable, furry puppies. Without hesitation, I told Mary to select her dog. I had no time to inquire about the breed or pedigree, or even the price. His papers were "lost," so he came for twenty dollars. He was named, of course, Massa—southern for Master, and Yankee for Massachusetts. He was such a success that the children invented a Massa language, and as befitted a true member of the family, he wrote our Christmas messages, which drew replies from our friends' dogs, and even a few cats.

Center Sandwich, N.H.
August 15, 1951
Dear Tat,

If you wonder what I have been doing with my letter-writing time, it has been spent composing, destroying, and recomposing epistles to my real estate agent and my landlady attempting—so far, unsuccessfully, to change their minds about raising my rent 20% this August. I had not signed next year's lease before I left Washington because I had been to see my landlady and she had said: "Dearie, don't worry, I'll never raise your rent." Unfortunately, that was not in writing. I won't sign until I can brave them in their dens however.

Massa keeps us in trim. John was asked by our new friends, the Walter Sharps from Nashville, to keep their Doberman pinscher for a day. He liked us so much he returned (on his own) to be underfoot while my luncheon for Rose Nichols was going on. Miss Nichols and TWO of her young men were motoring through, so what could I do but invite them along with Dorothy and Phil Fleming—realizing that Rose N would be in seventh heaven sitting next to a General who was also an Ambassador, or about to be one. Besides, Miss N's aura has not worn off Dorothy as yet, so they were pleased to accept.

I was put on my mettle for the meal as I was also initiating the new floor in the barn, which is now our dining room; but I knew I had a success when Miss Nichols asked for a second helping of my homemade peach ice cream. She was appropriately decked out to be escorted by a budding author who had just resigned (don't be suspicious) from the State Department and is now writing a novel. They all thought my house was too cute for words.

The Sharps drove up from Nashville with 5 dogs—2 collies—and their 8-year-old daughter. Walter is working for his Ph.D. at Harvard summer school so he can teach History of Art at Vanderbilt University.

Walter is charming in the way that Southern men are when they are intelligent—or even when they aren't. They provide what was, as yet, missing in my life up here. He studied with John Crowe Ransom and helped Strickland start the Nashville Symphony.

I found a house for the Howards too this summer. John is now with the Ford Foundation and they insist I should stop over with them in Scarsdale on my drive back and forth from Washington. He has just returned from a flying trip around the world, unbelievably having . . . tea with Nehru in India, visiting Pakistan and seeing Eisenhower in Paris. He traveled with Chester Davis, Hutchins, Cowles and Paul Hoffman. He is definitely the one to talk to you about the "sitch."

Love,
Marcella

P Street, N.W.
Washington, D.C.
November 8, 1951
Dear Tat,

I am full of Music, Greeks, Wine and Art. I was asked to make a drawing for the cover of a catalogue of a concert Gina Bachauer gave with Dimitri Mitropoulos and the New York Philharmonic, to benefit the children of Greece. An Athenian head with laurel leaf seemed the appropriate design. I was told that visiting Greeks, of some importance, could not find their tickets to this event. Too late, they discovered that their four-year-old had sent them to a favorite aunt—in an envelope with an indecipherable address! Wouldn't that be a good clue for a mystery story?

Portraits don't fare well in exhibits these days. The Director of the Corcoran told me the composition I made of you, Randolph and Mary seated at the marble table got in the coming show, but a portrait he especially liked—of 12-year-old Charlie Saltzman—was not chosen by the jury. There seems little use sending portraits these days. It always surprised me that Duncan Phillips chose my portrait of Denis Devlin for one of his shows. Portraits are rare in Phillips exhibits.

Love,
Marcella

December 11, 1951

Dear Tat,

We are looking forward to having Christmas with you. I am especially happy to get away as I watch hostesses steamed up over the usual efforts to catch the elusive male for parties. I am thinking of Marceil, mostly, who is now a hound in full cry, with a daughter about to be launched in society. She talks so much about the college graduates of the male gender that I finally asked if she felt being a college graduate meant THE ELUSIVE MALE was automatically moral, attractive and eligible. "Oh, it's the brain deal!" she said emphatically.

I will bring down as many groceries as I can manage. I remember that last year we ate you out of ham and turkeys. Ham and turkey sounds almost as good as having Bessie to help out—although Bessies are never as reliable as hams, are they?

The last ham I had here was cooked for some British poets who are booked as being the best three of the current crop in England—David Gascoyne, Kathleen Raine and a guy named Graham, who is a Scot. They seem about the same as the American poets—less money (if possible) but with the same neuroses. All except Graham, the Scot, who is an extrovert of the deepest dye. Please remind me to tell you, when I come down, about how I got trapped into taking them to see Ezra Pound two days in succession. Also, how I had to extricate Graham from what he called "the stiff British Embassy dinner" because he had to be what he was and couldn't go to another of those affairs where his dinner partner asked him so many questions but answered them all herself, and went on to more before he could get in a word. I heard Elizabeth Bowen give a talk. She was superb. Never used a note and talked in those amazing, involved, but fascinating sentences. Kimon Friar (does that name ring any bells for you?) is going to read his translations of modern Greek poets this week. That probably means another trip to St. Elizabeth's, if he is as anxious to meet Ezra Pound as the others were.

Aside from the poets and Hale and Vogel, and a new portrait commission of a vivid brunette with a Siamese cat, my life has been flowing as usual.

I will have a beautiful surprise for you in my dining room. I have become increasingly disenchanted with my old DR table and chairs. Just about the time the table refused to pull out, the chairs refused to do anything else but; and yet I knew I could not afford new ones. Then, when I mentioned to Dorothy [Mrs. Philip] Fleming that I wished I had some Queen Anne chairs to go with the refectory table Fredrica gave me in exchange for a painting, she told me she had just inherited sixteen such chairs from her mother's house (sitting in her garage) and would love for me to use any I needed! So I can now seat eight people, and there is still room for Etta to get around BOTH sides. The table is only 2 feet wide—one big solid plank of gorgeous walnut.

> Love,
> Marcella

We enjoyed Christmas in Memphis vastly and also our visit to the Walter Sharps' home, Cheekwood, in Nashville, on our return to Washington.

Cheekwood
Harpeth Hills
Nashville, Tenn.
January 3, 1952
Dear Tat,

I am lying in luxury at 9:30 a.m. in a very grand room in Cheekwood (a room with a 12-foot mahogany door with a brass key 6 inches long), recovering from the cold I picked up the last day of my visit with you at Goodwinslow.[1] The children have been taken by Walter Sharp to see the Hermitage.

The day is misty but not freezing. The house, however, is. I shouldn't call it a house though; 20th-century mansion would describe it better. When Huldah invited us to stop over on our way back to Washington (since it is directly on our way from Memphis) she had not prepared me for all this. The "park" I was lost in (carefully following directions) turned out to be their grounds which led us to a mansion of vast proportions. Huldah welcomed us at the door, where I rather expected a footman in livery. Since dogs are Huldah's true passion she greeted Massa with the greatest enthusiasm and directed Johnny to the second floor via the elevator. We all met again at dinner. In all the elegance her five dogs wander about and Massa was allowed the privilege of the dining room along with us and the distinguished guests. Huldah placed Johnny at her right, which I thought was a nice gesture as the editor of the Nashville *Tennessean* was one of the company. I never saw Mary so composed, and even conversing (sitting next to a Nashville man who lives in New Hampshire), which may have been due to the whole glass of sherry she had before dinner.

When Massa got tired following the houseman who served, he lay down under the table at our feet and seemed just as much at home as he was in his first humble abode. Have you ever given thought to his rise in the world? The steps upward seem carefully planned. From the filling station where we found him to the small frame house in N.H., the middling brick on P Street, the large stucco in Memphis, and now, the immense stone in Nashville. I don't see how he can go any higher.

But no place can equal Goodwinslow. We loved every minute of our time with you. The atmosphere you create, the food, the fun, the comfort—at least the side nearest the fire until it gets too hot—and, most of all, being understood and appreciated. Among the many things we appreciated were the books by every chair (some covered by dust, but well-read dust), the ever-present magnolia leaves in oversized containers, and the huge fireplace harboring logs as big as tree trunks— brought in by strong men but mainly struggled with by genteel ladies manipulating a four-foot iron poker. After all, who can visit a place where one can have the newborn calf named for one—just for being there? I like the name Ching picked: Aunt Marcella. It is a nice name if no one can think of an udder. Ooh!

Love,
Marcella

1. Cheekwood, with its botanical gardens, was given to the city of Nashville by the Sharps, and it has been functioning as a museum since 1959. When Mary, John, and I returned to Washington and were invited to dinner at my mother's house, Mary remarked that, in comparison with Cheekwood, Grandmummy's delicious but simple meal and small house seemed on our first night back like Bob Cratchit's.

P Street, N.W.
Washington, D.C.
January 12, 1952
Dear Tat,

It is always so nice to get cheerful missing-you letters before settling with a thud back into the mournful routine. I got around to unpacking and thought you would like to know that Etta is one Negro who doesn't have the race question on her mind. I showed her the lovely photograph of Mary Chilton [Mrs. Winslow's eight-year-old granddaughter] seated between Schoolboy and Studebaker, both as black as Mary is white, and she studied it with interest. Without flicking an eyelash when I told her that girl was my niece, she asked: "The one in the middle?" That is my private name for the picture, no matter what you call it.

Etta is now all mine. Considering my state of dependency I can't say I'm sorry in spite of the extra $10. Now she seems quite happy and even the beaus seem to have quieted down, to say nothing of funerals.

Betty [Fisher] sent Peter to cheer up Muffie, who finally lost her good friend. Peter comes out in the afternoon to walk Massa, then waits to see Johnny before he has to return to play Russian Bank with Muffs. Betty still finds time to write—whatever it is she writes.

Love,
Marcella

January 23, 1952
Dear Tat,

A letter from Chauncey Stillman that the news of your continued writing fills him with anticipation. "It's as if you reported that the sturgeons were bulging with caviar this season." I quote him:

> How did you like Caroline Gordon's STRANGE CHILDREN? Although I've hardly seen the Tates for years and have lost touch with mutual friends except you, the goings-on in the book were so intensely Caroline and Allen, so reminiscent of the single weekend I spent with them at Monteagle in 1937, that I felt Caroline's physical presence piercingly, mystically and ashamedly, as if I were watching them through a keyhole. That's how Baring said Sarah Bernhardt made him feel.
>
> Please give Mrs. Winslow my respectful, fearful, but warmly affectionate regards. I wish I still lived around the corner in Georgetown as I long to see you all.

Love,
Marcella

Chauncey Stillman wrote me some time after Mrs. Winslow died, "Anne Winslow was one of the few really *civilized* people it has ever been my privilege to know."

John Carter Vincent (1900–1972) was one of the most important China experts, both in rank and influence, in the State Department, yet his career was cut short when, fifty-two years old, he was declared a security risk and John Foster Dulles dismissed him. His friends and the media rallied to his defense. Vincent found the charges against him absurd, but he never seemed to hunger for vindication.

January, 1952

Dear Tat,

Can you believe that John Carter Vincent has been dismissed from the Foreign Service with only a small pension? Marquis Childs' column says he is being punished for his judgment in connection with the failure of our China policy. He and Betty are living in Cambridge and I don't see how they can live on so little after all their years in the service. What a blow to them and their children!

I had a small and very interesting group for a luncheon for Betty Vincent. The hearing about John Carter's loyalty is being held now and is certainly an example of hysteria on the part of Foster Dulles and the State Department. After all, John Carter has served his country devotedly for 27 years and all he has done is to advise and record honestly what he saw and what he believes about China today. There seem to be frightened men who are offering him up to propitiate Senators McCarthy and McCarran. Betty is certainly very amusing talking about it, but how ghastly for them both!

For the luncheon I invited Gretchen Green (who ran a tea room on a barge at Windsor Castle last summer—having the little boy who played "The Mudlark" open doors etc., proceeds going to charity, of course), Elena Macy, Mrs. Marquis Childs, Katherine Biddle and Marian Merrell, whose new book will come out soon.

I had a lot of fun the other day helping Elena Macy hang Noel's and her ancestors. We hung a dowager with long white gloves, an old Quaker lady in a white lace cap and grandparents galore. Some of the later portraits were by Chris Herter's mother and father who were successful painters.

Mary took an aptitude test and came out in the art-literature-music category. I went with her this morning to hear talks on same by career people in same who encourage studying same. It all seems a little . . . same. Did you see our house in the last number of *Holiday?* Our bay window serves as a foreground to the Herter steps in an article on Georgetown. One way to make it.

Love,

Marcella

March 7, 1952

Dear Tat,

Léonie Adams was here with the poets the other day and I drove them out to see Ezra. That is always a bit exhausting as he never wants one to go until the bell rings. His hair is long again, so he looks better than he did when one of the inmates cut it all off. He is deep in his Chinese translations.

Léonie has become a Catholic like everybody else. Did I ever tell you of Lon Cheney's reaction and surprise to realize that I am a "born Catholic"? "Do you really go to church every Sunday?" is the question I am most often asked. Really, one would think the converts would like a few catacombs, where they could all meet subterraneanly. They seem amazed to find someone else thought of it before they did. Katherine Anne can't bear to have Caroline Tate become what she felt was hers by rights, though she started as a Methodist, I believe.[1]

I heard Dylan Thomas read with Auden the other night.[2] Did you ever know how electrifying his reading can be? Dylan Thomas', I mean. His voice is unforgettable. The Robert Richmans asked me to dinner to meet him, but I couldn't go until 10 p.m. and the group had already broken up. I never felt such congealed air as I walked in. The Richmans don't dare to show favoritism by hanging paintings, since they entertain so many different artists, so they end up with just two pieces of pottery on the mantel. I asked Dylan to pose for me and he agreed. That is something I must approach with caution from everything I have heard about him.

Léonie said the meetings without Allen Tate, for his first absence, didn't have the usual zip. KAP was supposed to have come, in fact everyone at the Library of Congress felt she meant to come this time. However, had they asked me (she was going to stay with me), I would have said: "Just be on the end of one of her departures and you would never be surprised at no arrivals."

Love,

Marcella

1. Although Katherine Anne Porter was a Methodist when she married her first husband, John Koontz, she was baptized a Catholic on April 5, 1910, in Houston. See Joan Givner, *Katherine Anne Porter* (New York, 1982), 100.

2. The Welsh poet Dylan Thomas (1914–1953) gave readings that were always well attended—six in Washington in the 1950s. Huntington Cairns said Thomas could read the headlines of the New York *Times* and make them sound like poetry. His magnificent voice could be heard throughout the first-floor rooms of the Phillips Gallery. I found him surprisingly quiet at the luncheon the Phillipses held for him before one talk I went to. I had heard stories about his life in the "Rabelaisian Third Avenue" period in New York. He died of alcoholism; there was never an opportunity for a portrait sitting, alas.

March 29, 1952
Dear Tat,

I am in the throes of putting on the big show at the Corcoran. I must say the Art Fair has taken on important proportions being in the Corcoran, and I feel all the hard work I have put into this show in the last three years has been justified. We have graduated into the big league. The scholarships will be presented at a Preview and a Gala Concert in the Atrium. Six Directors of Museums are sponsors: Finley of the National Gallery, Duncan Phillips of the Phillips, Adelyn Breeskin of the Baltimore, Leslie Cheek of Richmond, Williams of the Corcoran, and Wenley of the Freer, as well as the Librarian of Congress, Luther Evans, Howard Mitchell, conductor of the Symphony, and Mrs. Whittall. It all takes place on April 30th. The portrait of Charlie Saltzman was the one of my three paintings selected for the Washington Society of Artists Show. Isabel Bishop, the Juror, whom I met at a dinner, told me she had taken two of mine but had to choose because she found she could have only one of each artist. She chose the portrait as she said there are so few good ones these days. The I.F.A. have three of mine in their window so, maybe, when I am too old to hold a brush I may suddenly become the rage!

Love,
Marcella

April 12, 1952
Dear Tat,

Happy Easter! The children are excited and dyeing Easter eggs. Lent is over. On Good Friday we decided to spend some time in church and

I admonished Johnny to get some uplifting reading to take with him. When I asked what he had selected, he produced a very large fat book entitled THE STORY OF PHILOSOPHY.

Love,
Marcella

May 18, 1952

Dear Tat,

I am coming out of my exhaustive art chairmanship for N.S.A.L. and am now running the art competitions for scholarships. Next year I have declined all jobs of responsibility and will rest on my laurels.

Dolly Clagett [wife of Henry Contee Bowie Claggett] is posing for me now and I "finished" Townsend Vogel (the second version) last Saturday. So far, his grandmother has not seen it but I trust I will never have to look at either of them again. I would like to leave the picture wrapped up in a blanket on her doorstep.

Last night I had a call from a man who asked how much I would charge to paint his portrait. I went into the usual about size, medium, pose etc. He kept referring to what he wished to wear, which I finally learned was a G-string! That is what he wanted to be painted in, so we didn't get much further as how much further is there left to go?

I had a good chat with Robert Frost at the Biddles' one evening. He seems to be expecting me to turn up in Middlebury this summer. A letter from Caroline in Minneapolis where Allen has been in the English Department since last fall. She writes that living out there is exciting for a convert as the French Catholic influence is still quite strong—"the churches themselves are so modern and handsome." I'm not sure if she knows that one of my father's finest churches, St. Luke's, is in St. Paul. She is teaching a seminar in fiction at St. Catherine's, a girls' college, enjoying it enormously.

A letter from Duncan Phillips invites me to be in a summer show at his gallery. They select one out of three of each artist invited.

Love,
Marcella

May 28, 1952

Dear Tat,

I am sitting at home on a cold cloudy Sunday waiting for people (couples, I asked for) to answer the "ad" for my house this summer. Two nibbles—both for girls who want to pay $100 instead of $160. But every year I think no one will take it. This year, being election year, is not good, I hear. One sees many For Rent signs on the larger, more expensive houses. Mr. Conant's beautiful house has been up for sale all winter. He left it to Princeton but no one wants to pay Princeton the $80,000 that is being asked for it.[1] This is the first year my wisteria has bloomed. It is so beautiful, trained across my upper balcony. The Herters' wisteria still hasn't bloomed. Chris is going to run for Governor of Massachusetts. If Eisenhower comes in he will no doubt get it.

Since Simon and Schuster is using my portrait of Marian Merrell on the jacket of her new book, CALENDAR OF LOVE, why can't you maneuver Knopf into using my portrait of you on your next jacket? You see I want to become known as a painter of writers and *fascinating people*. By the way, having been picked to be the "Fascinating Lady of the Week" by the *Washington Times Herald,* I get a "treasure chest" in leather with my name in gold on the cover, with the compliments of P. Lorillard, maker of Old Gold cigarettes. Naturally, I have switched from Pall Malls and Camels, Lucky Strikes and long black cigars to Old Golds—or would, if I smoked. I pass them around at my literary salons, saying, "A treat instead of a treatment." Can't you write a poem about authors in a cloud of smoke?

Love,

Marcella

1. Recently the same house was listed in real-estate references as worth more than a million dollars—making it the most expensive house in Georgetown.

While Anne Winslow was visiting me in 1948, we were invited by Robert Lowell, who had the chair of poetry at the Library of Congress that year, to a private reading by Robert Frost (1874–1963), the most popular and widely read poet in the history of American letters. The purpose was to record his poems for the library. When I was introduced to Frost after the reading, I asked if he would let me paint him, recklessly promising that I would require only two sittings. He agreed, and that summer Lowell sent me Frost's address in Vermont. I was not able to get to Vermont until 1952, however. In July of that year, I thought if I was ever to paint him, I had better do so soon. He might forget or not be around too many more years, so I wrote to him from New Hampshire.

July 22, 1952
Dear Mr. Frost:

I'm afraid you were hoping that I would forget about your agreement to let me make a sketch of you this summer. Alas! It means too much to me so I write with the hope that you will remember your generous offer to give me two sittings.

The heat has been bad for this part of the country, so I have waited, hoping for a cooler spell as I do not want you to be uncomfortable for me. If you still feel disposed to let me come, I would appreciate knowing what would be the best time for you. After I hear, I will write to the Waybury Inn for a room and dispose of my two children. I promise I won't put them down the cistern, as I know you are fond of children, and I happen to be fond of mine.

Yours,
Marcella Comès (Winslow)

Mrs. Theodore Morrison, Frost's secretary, answered on August 5, suggesting that I start the sittings on August 13. The date had to be put off until August 19 and 20, though, since Frost was to be interviewed for a television documentary in a series to be called "Wise Old Men."

At the first day's sitting, I got the pose and placement and sketched in the features with fast-drying acrylic paint. I was nervous about the time constraint but knew I could not go halfway if I was to finish the next day. I would have to see him in one burst of energy to get it right. Although I had my camera with me, it did not occur to me to photograph the pose or even to take a picture of him. I did not believe in using such props, and I disliked portraits from photographs. Frost was jolly and talkative, telling me that the production crew for the interview was "wiring the mountain." I tried to listen to everything he said and, at the same time, concentrate on what I was doing. I attempted to think of topics that would set him to reminiscing—which he enjoyed doing, since he was so expert at it—and not to lose the likeness emerging. I seemed to be someone else, hearing what I was saying, but hardly knowing what it was—the whole thing turned over to my astral. I was too excited to sleep that night, but next day I did manage to pull it off after some bad moments.

I still have part of a letter that I sent to Frost a month after the portrait sittings:

August 24, 1952
Dear Mr. Frost,

I hope by now your ordeal by television is over and that you can agree, with me, that it was not as bad as you may have expected. It makes me sad to think of the words of wisdom that went untelevised while I was going through MY "ordeal."

It was only an ordeal in the sense that the outcome seemed dubious until the last two precious hours that were granted to me, like a reprieve, from that wonderful Mrs. Morrison—not to mention the extreme kindness and understanding from you both in agreeing to give them to me. I felt like a driver of a car, desperate to reach a destination, who had pressed too hard on the accelerator, that last day with you, to have been able to slow down enough to get any reaction. Now that I see the picture at a full stop, I feel that I have done one of my best portraits.

Did I really hear you say—or just imagine it—that you liked the painting better than any that had been done of you? Somehow, the photographs in your books don't seem to do you justice—the eyes lost in shadow, and they are so important . . .

Frost had said it and did mean it. When he stopped to see me and the portrait the following year, he wrote in my guest book, "Robert Frost, who would be willing to be remembered the way Marcella Winslow made him look."

Center Sandwich, N.H.
Labor Day, 1952
Dear Tat,

After I returned from painting Robert Frost in Ripton, Vermont, I stayed under his spell for a week. I was sorry too much had piled up for me to write to you then because I would have liked to have gotten it all down. If you remember Frost's voice reading his poetry the day we heard him recording, perhaps you can imagine what it was like to listen to it for one whole day (not counting the hour and a half of the first day when I started his portrait), rambling on about his views, his philosophy—quoting various poets—telling me about knowing Ezra Pound in England—not caring for much of the modern poetry—he thinks Robert Lowell has something—getting a bit fidgety about the television interview which was to come off the day after I left—and reminiscing about

326 / BRUSHES WITH THE LITERARY

many things in his life. We got along just fine and when lunch time had come, which was the hour I had promised to be finished, and I had not gotten him yet, he was distressed for me and said if he didn't have to give a lecture at the writers' conference, which was taking place at Breadloaf College nearby, he would sit longer. I was too heartsick with disappointment to even know what I was eating for lunch. But a reprieve was granted. His secretary, Mrs. Theodore Morrison, whose husband teaches at Harvard, and who lives in one of Frost's farmhouses and keeps house—giving him his meals and generally taking care of him (although Frost lives in his own cottage farther up the hill)—said he COULD come back after half an hour as his talk was not scheduled until the next day.

I quickly changed mediums, from tempera to oil and in two and a half hours "got" him—so that he said when I let him look at it: "I like that better than any picture that has been made of me, and I wouldn't say that if I didn't mean it." He called Mrs. Morrison in and she had no criticism so I left to drive back across the most beautiful countryside feeling as though I had been granted wings.

The picture is only 10" x 12". Frost has on a light blue dust jacket, which matches his eyes, and a white shirt. His hair is very white and the background is a gray lavender. He said he would like to "snitch" the painting but I told him I could come back next year and do one for him. He said, "I might be gone!" He looks very well but told me he had had a cancerous growth removed from his cheek last year.[1]

When Frost's old friend Cornelius Weygandt came in to see the portrait after I returned to Sandwich, he told me I had caught F in a mellow mood and was surprised that the bitterness of his often tragic life was not more evident.[2] However, I never saw that in Frost's face. I think the last four years *have* made him mellow. He has been on the cover of two magazines, proclaimed the greatest poet of the day, and certainly has a peaceful, secure life now. Weygandt, on the other hand, says the publishers don't want HIS work now because they say it is too old-fashioned. "But," he boomed, "I can still hold them in my classes and talk louder than anyone else. They (the University of Pennsylvania) kept me on ten years after the retirement age!" This Pennsylvania Dutchman has been coming to Center Sandwich for 35 summers and just retired in his 80th year. He was one of the first to recognize Frost's talent and has often entertained him and his whole family here in his early Colonial house (still with the Indian shutters) which he bought from one of the old families in this New England village so long ago. He has written dozens of books about both Pennsylvania and New Hampshire. He brought Yeats and a number of the Irish poets to this country, probably for his English classes. The patchwork quilts I bought in Georgetown were from his Pennsylvania Dutch collection which he sold for $15,000 recently. He is the most decided personality I have met in some time and one of the most interesting.

Weygandt agreed also to let me paint him, life-size three-quarter view, so I have both portraits in my studio, two of my best. It has been a good summer. I wish I had this exact place in Washington, including sound of cowbells and hayloft studio.

Love,
Marcella

1. When Frost died in September, 1963, the Washington *Post* used a reproduction of the portrait in color on the front page, in one of the first uses of color in the newspaper.

2. Cornelius Weygandt (1871–1957) wrote a number of books, many concerned with folklore. He was one of the first to make the new Irish drama known to Americans. After he died, I let his wife have his portrait. She wrote, "It is so exactly like him—the hands crossed on his cane, his necktie askew and the familiar old brown hat. He is relaxed and content, just as I like to remember him."

October 5, 1952
Dear Tat,

You may be hearing from a new magazine called the *Washington Spectator*. I got an unsigned letter, a typical Ezra Pound, which went as follows:

> anonymous information/
> Washington Spectator / 17 Dupont Circle / Wash / 6
> sacked its edtr/ yester a.m.
> can MARCELLA do the kind of drawings they want , dont
> take current issue as model / as that is what got the
> ed/ fired.
> better drop in and hv/word with pubr/ Bill Gales

also / society column needed / and very little makes at
least that much for rent.
case for quick action

       (a) because the void will Fill
       (b) cause the mag/ has got to
make its hit before end of De.

So I acted quickly, as he cautioned, and have been asked to make a
drawing of a Georgetown professor [Dr. James Tansill] who has just
written a book on Political Science. I am promised a steady income once
the magazine gets going. If it doesn't fold up by Christmas, it may have
a chance. The "pubr" wants a sort of Washington *New Yorker*.

Love,
Marcella

Gales's magazine survived only three issues.

October 23, 1952
Dear Tat,

Betty [Fisher] has been in town helping Muffie move to New York.
Dear Betty . . . she does manage to disarrange things for me. The day
she called and asked to come over at 1 o'clock couldn't have been a worse
day for me. I was painting and also expecting the "pubr," Gales, to pick
up my drawing for his magazine, having the Clagetts for dinner and
seeing Mary dressed and off to her first dance. I told Betty all these
things, but she said she wanted to see me THAT afternoon. So I agreed,
if she would come at 5 (which was between everybody), but she over-
lapped with the magazine people so got introduced as a writer. (She says
she has been doing some writing.) Seeing Ezra, Allen, Denis, Caroline,
Mark, Juan Ramón, Robert Penn, Léonie, Frost and Katherine Anne all
over the place, the Galeses thought they better take her name and address. That may be an opportunity for her. Only, I fear that Betty's luck
would be to have something accepted for the number that folded.

I am going to cultivate fewer new friends so, later, I will have fewer
old ones—says the cynic. No—I don't mean to be hard on Betty. It is
just that she goes on being more the way she always has been. She is
darn well going to get martyred on this Muffie move, and the more
luncheons she has to give up, the more hair on her shirt—the more
coals of fire on Muffie's head. Only Muffie never gets burned.

Johnny, now 14, is growing so fast. He grows while my back is turned. He has shot out of all his clothes and is getting straight A's now, determined to get scholarships.

Love,
Marcella

A woman who called herself Lady Montague phoned me in May to ask for the address of Anne Winslow, saying she greatly admired Mrs. Winslow's writing and wanted to look her up when she went south. I was not forthcoming, but she persisted with many phone calls, saying she was a writer herself. She also let it be understood that she was working to elect General Eisenhower. When she would not take no for an answer, I finally allowed her to take me to lunch in Georgetown.

November 10, 1952
Dear Tat,

Lady Montague turned out to be a fraud! I almost fell into her trap this August. On a leisurely summer day I had a frantic phone call from her in a Hanover, N.H., hospital asking if I could send her $100 to pay her hospital bill. She said her nephew who had her power of attorney had just died, and everyone she knew in Washington who could come to her rescue was off on vacation. She had yet to get her affairs in order but the hospital was obdurate about her bill . . . her nephew's death a deadly blow . . . such a wonderful man . . . the Superintendent of the hospital so mean . . . frightens everybody . . . her chest was in such bad shape . . . and she would return my $100 very soon. A letter followed the phone call thanking me for the money which I never sent—the reason being that I had consulted my good friends here, both Generals (Tompkins and Moses), who asked how well I knew this woman. When I admitted how brief was our acquaintance, they advised me against sending any money, since I never have any to spare anyway.

Love,
Marcella

This American woman, who had certainly never married Lord Montague, gained some notoriety a few weeks after she worked on me in New Hampshire, when it came out that she was keeping the contributions she had solicited for Eisenhower's election. Most of her victims were professional people, professors and the like, from whom she could hardly have expected to gain much financially. But they were especially likely to take her at her

word, being rather trusting, and at times naïve. I myself believed her stories (she obviously had an educated background) but balked at handing over
a hundred dollars even to a lady in distress. My naïveté did not go that far.

John spent Christmas with his grandmother in Memphis. A letter from
Mrs. Winslow said she felt John had liked being there in his "quiet Ran-
dolphian way . . . being as near perfect as you (or even I) could want him
to be."

January 25, 1953
Dear Tat,

How did they get you to introduce Elizabeth Bowen and pose for a
picture with her? Was it Knopf? Her subject sounded interesting.
Thanks for rare clipping.

I received the enclosed letter just after Christmas from Cornelius
Weygandt, and the other one from Ralph Hodgson who has views similar to yours. Weygandt had told me Hodgson was one of the foremost
living English poets and that he was living in a little town in Ohio
avoiding attention, and he thought I should paint him. In fact, he offered to give me a letter of introduction which I promptly sent off, as I
was intrigued with one of the columnist William Lyon Phelps's "Daily
Talks About Books and Authors" on Hodgson. Phelps wrote that it was
impossible to obtain much information about H's life because he was a
recluse by nature and had successfully avoided both biographers and
interviewers. He explained that Hodgson had published very little, but
that every poem he ever published was so remarkable that one always
wanted more. Then I remembered that when we were living in London
the Rothensteins, Sir William [head of the Royal College of Art from
1920 to 1935] and his sons, John and Bill, had talked a lot about this
mystery man who was a great English poet [and had said that] no one
ever knew where he was, which was the way he liked it to be. Naturally
I wanted very much to track down this elusive man and paint his portrait for my usual reasons—that poets should be recorded from life.

Love,
Marcella

Ralph Hodgson (1871–1962), a Yorkshireman who loved good talk, bred
fine dogs, and lived in London before the First World War, made his living
as an editor and publisher of broadsides. In 1959, *Time* magazine ran a
page on Hodgson, who had just won a gold medal in London for *The
Skylark and Other Poems*: "It was the second major book published by Poet

Hodgson, 87, in a long life of deeper privacy than most poets ever dream of. Strangest part of his story: for 19 years Poet Hodgson has lived in the U.S. in a shabby farmhouse on the side of a hill near Minerva, Ohio (pop. 3,800)." T. S. Eliot, when asked where Minerva was, replied, "Minerva isn't on the map, though it is rumored that a bus from somewhere will take you to it once a day." Eliot also wrote,

> How delightful to meet Mr. Hodgson!
> (Everyone wants to know him)—
> With his musical sound
> And his Baskerville Hound . . .

Weygandt's letter was written on Christmas Day:

6635 Wissahickon Avenue
Philadelphia 19
XII–25–1952
Dear Mrs. Winslow

This genial Christmas weather makes me wonder are you planning a foray to Owl Acres, Minerva, Ohio to paint Ralph Hodgson? If you are maybe you could use the letter of introduction I send along. I doubt if you need it, but one never knows.

I was wrong in thinking you made Robert Frost less hard than he is. I have seen two photographs of him this winter that show him softened.

Cornelius Weygandt

To Ralph Hodgson:

This letter is to introduce Mrs. Randolph Winslow of Washington, D.C. who wishes to paint your portrait. This past summer she painted Robert Frost, up near Middlebury, Vermont, and me in Sandwich, N.H. Both portraits are masterly in catching likeness and personality, in composition, in all detail.

Cornelius Weygandt

The gracious but disappointing reply came:

Owlacres, Box 56, Rt. 1
Minerva, Ohio
September 18, 1953
Dear Mrs. Winslow:

I hardly know how to word the only reply to your courteous request I find possible; a line from a young English poet's letter I received a week before your own helps me: "I cannot even momentarily close my eyes to this knowledge of mankind's tragic destiny." I have been in that funereal condition of mind and spirit, almost hourly, since what they call the Atomic Age opened.

The dear old world we all loved, whatever its shortcomings, for me has already gone, and like many others still living, I have gone with it.

I do hope this explanation will free me from the charge of churliness: I could never have made it in the old days. So I can only thank you for the handsome compliment you pay me, and herewith return the enclosures, all of which had great interest for me.

Sincerely yours,
Ralph Hodgson

February 26, 1953
Dear Tat,

You may have as many children as you like. Why not? If it will help on your income tax, I will hand them over on a silver platter. Why don't you come up and discuss it with me in the usual furtive way we reserve for tax talk? I have a sneaking suspicion that you don't intend to come, and I can't even wish you to freeze as a result. If you were here, you would be cozy and warm and I would feed you and fatten you, which you could stand a little of.

Alex Böker was in town and came by to ask for a photograph of you. He somehow looks more German—something about the way his hair is plastered down—said he was rushed, although he does make time for Mrs. Longworth, of course. He likes his job under Adenauer but still likes us all and the U.S.A.

Johnny has applied to both Andover and Exeter. So far Andover has been way ahead on seeming to want to give him a scholarship, or else the Director of Admissions is livelier. Mary has applied to six colleges and I am relieved as we near the March 1st deadline. I don't want to look at another catalogue!

You should be here for some of the good programs the Institute of Contemporary Arts is putting on at the Corcoran. Kenneth Clark will be speaking on Henry Moore, March 16th (with slides);[1] Allen reading his poems on the 24th and, HOPEFULLY, KAP on April 1st—if you stay that long. The newly formed Women's Committee is the latest thing at the Corcoran. I have been asked to be one of the 20 members, along with one other artist, Alice Acheson. I am not sure what our roles will be, but I know that museums need all the help they can get.

I sold my painting in the Corcoran Area Show to a guy from Georgia who bought up all the prize winners; and the three Clagett portraits are paying for improvements in the house and applications for Mary's college. Yes, she graduates from Stone Ridge in June. We have been to see Goucher and Swarthmore (whose Dean of Women has read all your books), and I noticed in the college *News* at Sweet Briar, when we went there, that Katherine Anne was going to speak (wrote they, confidently) on the novel. I hope the next number will be able to contain the news that she HAD spoken.

Rose Nichols replied to my Christmas card, expressing surprise that Chauncey Stillman had entered the Catholic Church—"He and his family have always been such good Episcopalians that I can't understand why he felt any need to change."

Love,
Marcella

1. Kenneth Clark (1903–1983) was director of the National Gallery in London from 1934 to 1945. He served as chairman of the Arts Council of Great Britain from 1953 to 1960. Created the baron of Saltwood in 1969, he developed the art-history series "Civilisation" for BBC-TV.

March 5, 1953
Dear Tat,
I want to send you a few suggestions gleaned from Katherine Anne. I left her in Mother's hands as she was getting a train out today after staying with me for two days.

She said many nice things about your work and style and about how well you write. She may use "To My Geese" on her radio program. Mary said she saw her saying it aloud to herself.

I told her you were about to have a book of short stories published, and I thought some of them were new. She exclaimed: "Don't let her have them come out in book form until all have been published." She suggested you send three of them (or any other three) to Miss Cyrilly Abels on *Mademoiselle* and said she would speak to Cyrilly about you. They pay well and have published some of the best writers. Any that you have not had luck selling she suggested sending to her and she would give them to her agent who would try to get them placed. She approved highly of getting things published in the best-paying magazines like the *Ladies' Home Journal, McCall's,* the *Saturday Evening Post* etc.

The *New Yorker* pays well and she could not understand your not getting anything in that. Says she feels it is more "open" since [Harold] Ross the Editor died, so a better chance for others outside the charmed circle. They write her twice a year religiously to send them something, but she never has.

She was on her way back to New York after two speaking engagements at Washington and Lee and Sweet Briar (which she liked very much) and I induced her to take a breather. She badly needs to as she gets herself into a state of exhaustion and goes frequently into paroxysms of coughing in which she can't get her breath. It is dreadful and I feel so sorry for her.

She looks older, but one can see the early beauty still in her face and trim figure. I was glad she still liked the old portrait from 1944 and that she sat nicely for a redo of the undone eyes. She wants to give me a commission to paint a smaller one. I would like to go to New York and paint it if the children are away in school. However, an interesting experience may take place when she returns. Before her last book, THE DAYS BEFORE, came out, she had much correspondence with Ezra Pound, who asked her to come to see him so he could correct some things she had written about him. She wanted to go, so I took her out (always having to get permission beforehand), and they got along so well that she wants to spend more time with him—*Notes on EP by KAP!* Since I had introduced her to Robert Richman and paved the way for a paid reading from the Contemporary Arts at the Corcoran April 1st, she will come for about a week then and we will "DO" Pound. Maybe I will take my sketch pad and "do KAP 'doing' Pound."

KA's address is 117 E. 17th St. Her agent is James Oliver Brown.

After we left Pound, Katherine Anne stopped in a Georgetown store and had an elaborate cheese tray sent to him. For me she bought a bottle of cherry brandy with a music box on the bottom that plays a Christmas carol. You wind it up and then you know when someone decides to have a drink when you are not looking.

Love,
Marcella

Katherine Anne and I were both glad at last to call her portrait finished, with her eyes successfully looking somewhere.

March 10, 1953
Dear Tat,

The great news of John's scholarship at Andover brought this kind note from Landon's Headmaster: "We are all so happy John has his scholarship at Andover. He is in one of the country's best schools, and in John Kemper is under one of the finest headmasters. I predict a most brilliant career for him there, and also for his usefulness in later life."

Katherine Anne writes that she really wants your poems for her thirteen programs for radio. The dates and hours are not set yet. She also hopes to see your unsold short stories. She says she had a note from Ezra saying he loved the "house cheese" and round crackers which he ate as soon as they arrived. She felt she had a refreshing visit and wants me to visit her in New York and repay me in kind. "You could do a little picture and I could give a little party." She likes to think of the portrait finished after so long, "the eyes really looking somewhere now, after all these years."

Mary has decided to go to Newton College of the Sacred Heart (in Newton, a suburb of Boston). They offered her such a good scholarship she couldn't refuse. It will be nice to have her in New England. Especially with Johnny in Andover. I can pick them both up on my way to New Hampshire at various times if our schedules can be worked out.

Since I was asked to be a sponsor for funding the new building of the Workshop Center of the Arts, I have participated in their exhibits (enclosed photo with my contributed painting: *Boys and Boats*) and an exhibit of the faculty wins a lot of praise for the newcomers, Kenneth Noland and Morris Louis.[1] You have always said you could understand pictorial compositions if they were explained in flower-arranging terms, so I don't think you would appreciate the abstractions these two go in for—dribbling and pouring paint on canvas. Would that be equal to upsetting your vase of flowers?

Love,
Marcella

1. Ken Noland and Morris Louis were among the first Washington artists to use canvases that were stained and unsized. Their method was to pour color in large areas on unprimed canvas.

March, 1953
Dear Tat,

I loved your goose poem in *Harper's*. I typed it out for Katherine Anne's radio program, along with the poem "Thus to Revisit" that
she asked for. Any corrections?

> *To My Geese*
> [*Harper's*, February, 1953]
>
> I wonder why you always wait
> For me to come and let you through the gate
> Before you waddle on your way
>
> To do today what you did yesterday—
> To crop the field that has no field beyond,
> To flout around the same round pond,
> Drying the pillows that you floated on?
>
> You were outfitted for the far-off things—
> Feathered for winters at the pole, for springs
> Whose freshets overflow
> Fields I shall never know—
>
> Why do you stay in this dull place with me?
> Go rise on your incomparable wings
> From meadows I shall never see
> To wider skies;
>
> Go launch your squadrons on the foam
> Of rivers far from home—
> Be emblems of some high emprise,
> Screaming in triumph, saving Rome!
>
>
> *Thus to Revisit*
> [*Atlantic Monthly*, January, 1948]
>
> Deep in the ground the dead
> should be, in lead fast bound,
> their names in marble overhead;
> but you went free;
> you were given to the wind instead,
> and to the sea.

The spells by which a ghost is laid
I know; the amulets made
to wear between the midnight and the dawn
I have them on
What charm avails
for ghosts that go
not when cocks crow
nor come in witches' tales?

Under a mound, under a stone
they bide, who wait for the
last day;
but your way is the way
of wings that ride,
of sails that come
on every tide, home.

> Love,
> Marcella

April 8, 1953
Dear Tat,

Katherine Anne has come and gone in the usual breathless flurry. Instead of the visit we had planned—going out to St. Elizabeth's to "do" Ezra Pound, as he had wanted her to do—she wired that she could come only for her reading at the Corcoran. How foolish to make plans for any sort of future; with KAP a future is always nebulous. She said she was so tired that she would have to go to a hotel so she could get back early to New York to start her radio broadcasts of poetry readings. I was disappointed but not surprised. She read for two hours and mesmerized her audience at the Corcoran. She looked beautiful in a gray organdy dress with a voluminous skirt. The talk was truly electric and I had not expected it to be.

You may not be as interested in KAP as she herself is, but everyone was thrilled. When we told her how entranced everyone was, she agreed that she had that spark that gets across at all her readings. Certainly the talk I heard Elizabeth Bowen give did not have the same spark. Mary and her cousin Alison attended and loved every minute, even the poetry translations at the end. There was a party for her at a house on Sheridan Circle after the reading, with champagne and Justice Douglas, at which Katherine Anne was so up on the clouds, after the sensational performance, that she spilled champagne on the gorgeous dress. She says it is ruined.

The following day Katherine Anne had promised to come to lunch. She wanted to autograph the three books she had sent airmail just before she came "so that Mary and Johnny could have them 30 years from now" and then I had said I would take her to her train.

She called at 10:45 to say she was pulling herself together to get here in time for the 1 o'clock train to New York. At 12:30 I phoned the Willard Hotel, since she had not come, and they said that she was still registered but did not answer the phone which rather alarmed me. I asked them to investigate. Just as they called to say she had checked out at 12:20, she arrived. She had given the taxi driver the wrong address and, of course, was out of breath and not hungry—until I said "crab-meat casserole," upon which she stayed and had two helpings. Then, suddenly, she remembered that she had told Mary McGrory that the only time she could give her an interview was at the railroad station at 12:45. She had become so interested in telling the young girls (who were hanging on every word) how she had written her story "That Tree" that we almost missed the 2 p.m. to New York—especially since she had neglected to tell me her bags were still at the Willard. For her overnight trip she had brought a very large hand trunk which, I presume, was necessary for the gray organdy, now ruined.

As I rested exhausted upon my return, I had a phone call from Mary McGrory, frustrated and exhausted as well. I gave her a vivid description of why KAP had not turned up for the promised interview.

Katherine Anne had left mumbling about a return trip for a "pleasure visit," which she invariably says, and never makes, for all the reasons given above.

Love,
Marcella

Mary McGrory, now a columnist for the Washington *Post,* wrote in her *Evening Star* column of April 12, 1953, "Katherine Anne [Porter] charmed the audience right out of their seats at her reading and was hurrying back to New York to make tape recordings for a radio broadcast of American poetry [the one in which she used Anne Winslow's poem]. Although of an age to be a grandmother, Miss Porter somehow still commands the aura of the southern belle. Her snow-white hair frames her delicate features and an elegant dress brought out her beautiful deep-set gray eyes. Her throaty, drawling conversation is sprinkled still with the 'La, me's of her Texas and Louisiana girlhood. She says it's more profitable giving readings [than writing], and, of course, more fun."

April 12, 1953
Dear Tat,

This seems to be the month everyone turns up in Washington even though the cherry blossoms have come and gone.

Someone had told me that Alex Böker was coming over with Adenauer and had added that Alex was the No. 3 man in Germany now. As he has always had a "thing" about you, I thought he might phone to inquire about your whereabouts but never expected that he would ask to pay his respects in your absence. Good old Alex was dashing into Georgetown to see the journalist Joe Alsop, so he figured he could dash by P Street at the same time and do his inquiring in person.

After the No. 3 information, all my young fry, including Mary, Alison, and Alison's friend, rallied round to catch a glimpse. The friend, who is interested in politics, had worked herself into a frenzy of excitement over Washington—particularly since she and Alison had been received by [Vice-President Richard] Nixon, a friend of her father, who is a lawyer in Pasadena. Even hearing that Adenauer himself was coming would not have surprised her. Alex did not disappoint them.

He arrived so very tall, such VERY long striped pants, Homburg and cane—looking every inch the diplomat if not No. 2 himself. He looks well and is as attractive as ever. Though he pooh-poohed the No. 3 idea, he was obviously pleased to know the rumor had gotten around. After a proper ten minutes, in which he talked mostly of you, he arose with his German camera and asked to take a picture in the garden—recalling the evening we had listened to Denis Devlin and some of his colleagues singing Irish ballads on numerous Scotch and sodas.

Upon leaving he turned, paused, and, impressive in his sartorial splendor, announced: "The Third Man!" All we needed was the zither music as he strode down the brick pavement toward Alice Long-worth—or someone equally equal.

The Arts and Letters Scholarship Benefit took place last week, at the Corcoran Gallery, ending today. I invited Sir Kenneth Clark to come to the opening so he could be impressed with the work being done here. I had met him at a dinner and he had asked me about the art climate in D.C. I suggested he come to see some of it. Just before coming he sent me a card on which he had written: "I am assuming that you do *not* expect me to make a speech, simply to be present, shake hands and make benevolent noises." He called me and left a ticket at the National Gallery desk to be sure I would not miss his last talk on "The Nude in Art Today." His audience has been faithful for six weeks on Sundays. Besides myself, others who have been anxious to further our knowledge of nudes in art have been the usual Bacon-Bliss-Beale-Longworth contingent, and even the Duncan Phillipses who hardly need to be informed who is in art and who isn't.

When I put the question to Clark on what he thought was the best art America had to offer, he answered without hesitation: "The *New Yorker* covers!"

Love,
Marcella

April 15, 1953
Dear Tat,

Chauncey Stillman is coming to Washington next week and, to be sure he gets the guests he wants for a dinner at the Metropolitan Club, cards are sent beforehand so his friends can check whether he should phone Friday or Saturday; and in my case, whether my address should be studio or home. Such efficiency! It is nice to see so many old friends in such a short time—Allen, Katherine Anne, Alex and, now, Chauncey—"but better if you have a maid"—quoting THE DWELLING PLACE.

Speaking of which: Charles whispered to Lena, who whispered to me, that Etta had lost her job. Fired! You know she left me to work for Freddy. I did a very good job of looking surprised when Charles said to me confidentially, "That woman jes wanted to show you she had more money than you." They have all loved the intrigue, if it can be called such, and, according to Lena, Etta is supposed to be receiving her just reward . . . "She never should have left a nice lady like Miz Winslow, even if she don't have no money." I hope to have a little more after I start a commission tomorrow of the wife of a real-estate operator.

Robert Frost was in town and came to see me with his daughter, Mrs. Ballantine, to show her my portrait of him. She found something wrong with the mouth, which is what Sargent said should be the definition of a portrait—invariably, the mouth! However, few seem to agree with her—as yet, anyway.

We went to a reception at the National Catholic Welfare Council recently and I talked with Senator Kennedy, Vice-President Nixon—and Senator Green [of Vermont], whom you met at Harriet Winslow's party, and liked so much. No doubt they were all courting the "Catholic vote."

When does your story come out in *Perspectives*—the [issue] Jacques Barzun edits?[1] I would have missed your poem "To My Geese" in *Harper's* if I had not been told. It was hard to believe Allen didn't understand the reference when I DID! Does anyone know about this magazine except the intellectuals who write for it?

Love,

Marcella

1. Jacques Barzun (1907–), critic, scholar, and university administrator, when asked to be guest editor for an early number of the magazine *Perspectives,* selected a story by Anne Winslow for it. He was one of the distinguished advisers to this publication, funded by the Ford Foundation, whose purpose was to advance all countries' understanding of the art, letters, and thought of the United States. It was published four times a year but survived for only three years.

April, 1953
Dear Tat,

The semi-abstract painting which I did under the influence of Karl Knath (after attending his group at the Phillips) got into the Society of Washington Artists show at the National Collection of Fine Arts. You knew they were *Bottles on a Blue Cloth* (its title) so almost liked it, remember? I have offered to paint a portrait of the winner of chances at the Benefit Art Fair at American University to help their Art School

survive. Being on the committee, I will try to do my share when the
FUN DAYS take place next month. I admire the artists who teach there:
Sarah Baker, Bob Gates and Bill Calfee. This is the Art School I told
Kenneth Clark has the greatest influence in Washington today.

Aside from all this art activity, I have not neglected my literary
friends—certainly not Allen Tate, who brought Natasha Litvin out to
see me one afternoon.[1] She was giving a concert and he has been on her
trail for a while I gather. He is quite frank about how much he likes her
and I am always sticking up for Caroline and trying to get them back
together where they belong. When I put my feelings in writing, he
wrote back that the trouble between him and the wonderful woman he
is married to is that she has never been able to say she loves him, re-
gardless of what he does. Had she been able to say it, he thinks things
might have been different between them. At fifty-four he knows his own
mind and is capable of complete commitment, he says, but he deeply
desires it in return. He ought to realize that there has never been anyone
in Caroline's life except Allen, whether she says what he wants to hear
or not.

As for Ezra Pound—after a recent request to bring Howard Comfort
out to see him (Howard being into Greek translations),[2] he sent me one
of those cryptic letters:

> STUFF an' NONsense, Cara Marcella. Don't wait till you have a
> visiting fireman, come when you have the time, alzo, Young
> MacNaughton has made a start translating Zielinski's "La Si-
> bylle," but there ought to be some decent friends for him in
> Washington, vot's the town come to if it can't make use of an
> unattached almost educated young male?
>
> Love,
> Marcella

1 Natasha Litvin was a concert pianist and the wife of Stephen Spender.

2. Howard Comfort and I had met in Rome, where he had a Prix de Rome for
classical studies at the American Academy. Later he taught Latin at Haverford
College and came to Washington occasionally. He told me that he originally met
up with Ezra Pound through a mutual interest in Catullus. When during one
of his visits to St. Elizabeth's to see Pound, the poet said that he had once set

Carmen 61 (Collis o Heliconii) to music, Comfort challenged him to recite some of the lines. Pound at once launched into the whole 235 lines, at least some of which he composed extempore. Comfort said it was a good show, particularly because of the baritone voice Pound adopted in declaiming, in contrast to the squeaky treble he used in conversation. When I checked this information with Howard in 1989, he corrected my spelling of *Heliconii,* and added that it was the first time he had ever had the pleasure of being in a footnote.

Center Sandwich, N.H.
July 12, 1953
Dear Tat,

The weather is dry and quite ideal for an overnight climb with Huldah Sharp who is very 4-H. She is continually planning outdoor picnics and steak fries and outings which I like once I get going, but never before. She will bring her four dogs and we will bring our one, Massa. He is equal to four, personality-wise. Johnny will miss the climb, being off in Andover, catching up on math for next year.

Mrs. Corcoran Thom wants me to meet an Andover cousin who teaches English there. That makes three cousins of people I know who teach at Andover. I will track them all down, one by one, and let Johnny "finish" them after I "start" them. Hers is a bird watcher. Goes to bed at dusk so he can get up at 5 a.m. When Mary was there recently she came back with her head reeling from meeting an up-and-coming intelligentsia who talked of Strindberg, Paul Klee and whoever is the latest thing in poetry.

Love,
Marcella

Center Sandwich, N.H.
August 15, 1953
Dear Tat,

There are some colorful characters here in New Hampshire including one I have been able to catch for a portrait sitting. An old-timer named Jim Beede (from one of the earliest families to settle in this area generations ago) has finally agreed to let me make a drawing of him. He has been completely suspicious of my motives in wishing to do this, as he doesn't realize how fascinated I am with his general appearance—the oversized mustache, the craggy face showing the . . . character built up over his more than seventy years, and the stalwart figure. He is never seen without a hat and a bow tie and the watch chain across his chest that connects the watches he collects, and I have displayed them all. I am so pleased with the result. I told him I would give him a large photograph of the drawing. "No," he said, "I HAVE a large photograph of myself in my Mason's outfit, and I never saw a picture of anyone with a hat on." The Historical Society is drooling over it but I doubt that I will ever be able to give it up. I just title it *Yankee*.

Love,
Marcella

P Street, N.W.
Washington, D.C.
November, 1953
Dear Tat,

I think I will have to run down and tell you everything about my life. Not as exciting as it used to be with all the literary lights going on and off (mostly in my house) but always so full—also like the poets. I haven't had time to be lonely as I expected to be without the children. I am doing more of the things I have always wanted to do. Aside from painting, there's the theatre, music, lectures, and seeing more of the people that I enjoy most.

I went to a party at the Red Warrens' recently. He and his new wife (Eleanor Clark) have a 4-month-old baby. They seem very happy. I see Bill and Helen Costello often. She is a talented painter and Bill is one of the radio commentators and political writers. I think the newsmen are the most clear-headed thinkers one runs up against now. I was appalled to find even Betty [Fisher] eating up McCarthyism! You would enjoy talking—or listening—to Bill. He liked your poem in the November *Harper's*.

The play I have enjoyed most was *The Prescott Proposals* with Katherine Cornell—a story about the UN by Lindsay and Crouse. It will go to Broadway next. Then we get Judith Anderson in *The Summer House*. We have three live theatres here now so have a chance to see most everything. I was sorry to miss Deborah Kerr in *Tea and Sympathy* earlier this season.

Katherine Anne is teaching in a university in the Netherlands. She writes that from her upper window she sees landscapes as Brueghel did. She hopes something nice will get her back to Washington.

Love,
Marcella

December 12, 1953
Dear Tat,

I wish we could get caught up. Or are we caught up enough? I asked Charles if he was ready for Christmas and he answered: "I stays ready." He has waxed all the floors which gets me ready for something, and makes Massa slip all over the place. Having Massa all to myself is hard on me as he always needs to go see a tree, which means I have to be on the other end of the leash. The children miss him more than anything else, or anyone else, including me.

I enjoyed my Thanksgiving in New England and stopped with Betty [Fisher] overnight on the way up, which would take several pages to describe adequately. Somehow, seeing the same red velvet hangings and oversized Victorian lamps and relics and remnants of former splendor in that, to use Betty's word, "nasty" suburban little house gets me down. My bed was spotlessly done up in magnificent linen with blanket covers turned down. All in the best tradition—even if the only light was across the room and the drawers stuck and the cobwebs had settled on the toiletries. There is the usual cat smell and dinner materializing from nowhere (the freezer) and an endless array of beautiful china and glassware passing under our noses. The relationship between father and sons can be envied very much. Betty has produced some fine sons who have inherited the good manners and sense of noblesse oblige that come with a background such as theirs.

I had Thanksgiving dinner at Mary's college [Newton] which used to be the Schrafft estate and she put me up in her room, as all her roommates were away for the holidays. I felt like Goldilocks getting to choose my bed among five in the huge room. It used to be the guests' quarters when the Schraffts lived there. I was about to close my eyes in much-needed sleep when Mary remarked: "Mr. Schrafft hanged himself from that chandelier." Few colleges can claim a chandelier, much less a possibly haunted room!

Love,
Marcella

December 27, 1953
Dear Tat,

I am sitting across from your grandson, resplendent in tuxedo, looking too gorgeous for anything. He has grown so much and his shoulders have become too wide for his suits. In 20 minutes he goes to a formal dance. His dances have come so close together he could almost own his rented tux. He insists on a maroon cummerbund (sash to you) and bow tie to match. He is quite unchanged inwardly, but I now have to look up to him—outwardly. He loves the book on mobiles that I gave him for Christmas and has spent hours in his room making these great contraptions. He has admired so much the Calder mobile his art teacher, Pat Morgan, has in his house in Andover. He is delighted with his room, painted blue with a white ceiling and venetian blinds. (Freddy gave me six pairs.) I was crushed, however, when his eye lit on the four model planes so lovingly made only a few years ago which I had placed conspicuously on his mantelpiece; he picked them up and threw each one in the waste basket, declaring in a disgusted voice, as he did so, "How immature!" We are both so delighted to hear that Andover gave him a $900 scholarship award for 1954–1955.

The Talbotts (renting the Herter house) have been away over the holidays and I have been accepting packages for them which come in a steady stream.[1] Epicurean delights in large quantities—all needing refrigeration, or special handling, or This Side Up, or *Don't* Freeze, or *Please* Freeze, Special Delivery Airmail etc. Consequently when I saw the largest poinsettia plant ever waiting to have the door opened for it, I calmly announced that I was accepting all packages for the Talbotts, as Mrs. T had requested me to do. It has reposed on our piano in all its glory ever since December 23. When a large box of long-stemmed American Beauty roses came for them on Christmas Day I left a note in their door (I was told the Navy chauffeur picked up the mail), addressed to the Honorable Harold Talbott, marked IMPORTANT. Can't you imagine the consternation in Navy circles over the hush-hush secret official matter which should be rushed to the Secretary of Air? A dozen roses breathing their last!

Love,
Marcella

1. Harold Talbott (1888–1957) was secretary of the air force in 1955. He was a Republican prominent in the presidential campaigns of Wilkie, Dewey, and Eisenhower. His wife, Peggy Thayer Talbott, a Philadelphia belle, won acclaim as best-dressed woman and the like.

January 21, 1954
Dear Tat,

Before I get another warning postal from you on the passing of time with no letter from me, let me hasten to tell you that all is more than well at this end. By this, I mean that my good luck is working overtime in the person of a young Virginian named John Prince, who is paying me $100 a month for the privilege of occupying Jay's bed and cooking Cordon Bleu meals in my kitchen! He came by way of the Tates and is looking for a job that will pay him more than his teaching of English at the University of Missouri. He studied with both Caroline and Allen and, like Cal Lowell, has visited them at various times. However, he is not the creative litterateur I have come to know, often painfully, in the past. He makes his bed and helps wash the dishes and walks Massa occasionally, and also fixes the furnace whenever he sees me going down to the nether regions. He even returns packages for me at the stores. A true Southern gentleman! Let's hope I will not overwork him. Last week he returned from his home in Norfolk bringing copper pots, meat cleavers, French measures, wire whisks and other gadgets he felt I needed in the kitchen. That is because he has recently taken a course in cooking at the Cordon Bleu in Paris. We have eliminated most cans and eat heavenly French food flavored with Southern.

After a week of partaking of the latest Parisian recipes, I was delighted when he offered to cook a lunch I was having for Mrs. Harold Talbott (renting the house next door), but I was confronted with how it could be gracefully managed—a young man living with me? Who would serve it? I decided to just feature him. I would whet their appetites beforehand—this great cook from Paris who had come my way, who would not only cook but serve our meal!

The ladies loved it. He had drinks with us and then served the luncheon of scallops soaked in tarragon vinegar; Potatoes Anna (thin layers baked in butter with a touch of mustard until crispy); salad; and a flaming banana dessert with a curaçao sauce. None of the guests left until 3:30, and all of them with recipes in hand.

I have just used Miss Nichols as an excuse for a cocktail party. She loves to be the center of attention, questioning all guests at great length, but encouraging only short replies. So here I am in full swing after all I have said about leading a changed and quiet life.

Love,
Marcella

John Prince later turned successfully to catering and real estate.

February 17, 1954
Dear Tat,

People are getting wind of a new man in town and John Prince has had to get an engagement book. He invited Mrs. Gertrude Whittall to a Cordon Bleu luncheon here. She is one of the people John had a letter to, from someone hopeful of finding him a job. Although she hardly seems the one to ask for Library of Congress employment, she did us both a favor by putting us on her list of recipients for concerts (her money makes possible) in the Coolidge Auditorium at the Library of Congress. She is somewhat deaf but delightful. Gay AND spry!

Social Notes

The Corcoran Gallery had a private opening of an exhibition of paintings by Mrs. Dean Acheson. You would think elite Washington had gone Democratic judging by the large number of people for whom I poured tea! The non-elite Washington has always been Democratic but some tea drinkers may have been Republicans in disguise.

John Prince gave a reading of work by Eudora Welty to the Arts and Letters group. If Eudora only knew how he is spreading her fame! He had once called on her at her home in Jackson, just to let her know how much he liked her work.

I was invited to the Biddle party after Karl Shapiro's reading at the Library of Congress. He is the new Consultant in Poetry, so it was given in his honor.

My portrait of Cornelius Weygandt got in a Corcoran show and another of my paintings was accepted in a Carnegie Institute exhibit in Pittsburgh.

It seems that General Battley suggested me to paint a portrait of him, which he is to get as a "surprise gift" (!) since he is retiring as the President of the National Paint and Varnish Co. A big commission. A letter from Wm. Burden, President of the Museum of Modern Art in N.Y., expressing interest in my making a painting of his house in New York. Says Mrs. C. V. Whitney told him I did an excellent one of her house in Georgetown. The one with the little dog in it which she apparently learned to like.

Love,
Marcella

May 1, 1954
Dear Tat,

I have completed the portrait of General Joseph Battley. Joe would speak of the subject of the portrait (himself) in the third person. He kept saying: "He is not looking at me. His eyes don't follow me around the room." I finally made a small change and he was content. When Joe left, his eyes watched him go down the stairs. I have yet to warm up and loosen the mouth, however. My problems are not over. Joe is only worried now about showing the portrait in the most important window in Washington.

I must finish all my work in one month. If I succeed in doing so I will be in a fine state of mind, and richer too.

I enclose the obituary of one Mr. Draper who I am painting from a photograph, of necessity since the poor man has been ill for some time. Mrs. Draper liked the portrait of you so much that she wondered if I could paint her husband like that—instead of "modern"—and took me to the hospital so I could see what he looked like! J. Prince kindly offered to be helpful by sitting for the flesh tones and the gray suit, since I was so desperate working from the photograph. We had one sitting and were starting for the studio yesterday when the news came about Mr. Draper's demise. John said: "I feel so queer."

Sad news. Robert Lowell is back in a mental hospital as the result of his mother's death, I've been told. He never should have been permitted to go alone to Europe. . . . Mrs. Lowell died before he saw her and it must have been a shock to Cal and a complicated procedure for him to arrange things without help. Cousin Harriet told me he had been getting along so well and was planning to have a family and live in the house he had bought in Duxbury, Massachusetts.

Caroline Tate returned from Europe to be with Nancy who had a nervous breakdown. What price genius—or children of same!

Love,

Marcella

Ian Hamilton's *Robert Lowell: A Biography* (New York, 1982) tells how the Duxbury house became superfluous for Lowell after Harriet Winslow left him her summer place in Castine, Maine. One of my letters to Hamilton expresses my feeling on Lowell's death: "Cal's life was almost more than I could bear, and how he could write through it all was amazing. The end of his 60 years seemed somehow appropriate. At least I felt it was better for him. I had no idea that the poor man had had so many manic attacks and such an unhappy childhood."

Center Sandwich, N.H.

June 10, 1954

Dear Tat,

I got off to N.H. with the usual rounds and scurrying. Without the children (they always helped pack the car), I was glad of John Prince's help. He will keep my house this summer. I directed Jan Karski, too, when he came by, assuring him of my superior packing experience when he asked if he could use his own initiative.[1] Finally, he said to JP, who was absorbed in how there could be room for all the art supplies, food, luggage, and Massa yet to come: "I was like you at first, joyous, carefree, full of ideas—now I simply say, Where does it go?"

I got paid up for all my commissioned portraits before I left, and feel so rich. Battley's portrait will get presented to his company in July—as a "surprise" to him. He wants 33 color prints of it! The young Clays loved their 5-year-old; the board members of the settlement house passed on their retiring director approvingly, and the English couple didn't even want to part with their portrait long enough to have it photographed. I hadn't counted on the money for the poor dead Mr. Draper, as I had my greatest struggle with that one—he being missing etc.—but, at the last, he seemed to take on a little life, as I breathed out so much of my own. Mrs. D, in widow's weeds, asked only to have a "little more expression." So, I took another hour, the last day of packing, to express him and, lo and behold, she paid me for it!

I had a glimpse of Johnny at Andover. He looks great, and was nominated for president of his class next year. I drive down to get him next week.[2]

P.S. The National Paint and Varnish Co. was so pleased with the Battley portrait that they INCREASED my price to $1200!

Love,
Marcella

1. Jan Karski, a Polish diplomat captured by the Russians and also by the Germans for his underground activities in World War II, was the first to report to Eden and Roosevelt on the Nazi concentration camps. He teaches political science at Georgetown University.

2. My letter to Mrs. Winslow in July was written on a playbill for a performance of *Arsenic and Old Lace,* to benefit the Sandwich PTA. Next to John Winslow's name is printed, "Sound Effects," after which I penciled in, "4 bells and 1 squeak."

P Street, N.W.
Washington, D.C.
November 9, 1954
Dear Tat,

On my mantel is a painting I know you would like. A landscape. I worked on it today from 10:30 to 4 o'clock. It is a painting of a manor house and grounds, fall foliage and outhouses, rolling hills and grazing horses. It is to be a Christmas present for the Lord of the Manor—a prominent lawyer in D.C., John Laylin. I must say it is cold on the windy knoll where I am working. One day I had on two hats, two pairs of gloves, four sweaters and galoshes over heavy shoes and socks and was very glad to be invited into the manor house for hot coffee and a nip to keep me going. The last two days have been warm enough to paint without gloves. I am glad, as I don't see how I could paint the lacy treetops and fences in the distance with clumsy gloves on. I take Massa, of course, and he roams about, but not too far, as he stands over me, barking at curious cows and livestock. One cow was so entranced with my shiny blue car, which I drive into the pasture, that she licked it all over and finished by rubbing her horns on its horns—or something similar.

Peg Woolen, who had introduced me to Jan Karski—a fellow Pole—was here for her yearly jaunt, and we gave a dinner party to celebrate Jan's becoming an American citizen. Our Americanization dinner consisted of an American menu, presents, and American flags for decoration. My favorite item in the menu was Asparagus Vespucci, but we also had, as a start: Oysters Rockefeller, then Beef Eisenhower with Rice Lincoln, Boston lettuce with White Russian Dressing, and Siberian Salt Sticks. We finished off with Pulaski Pieway. I must make that pie for you at Christmas—rum, eggs, whipped cream and shaved chocolate on top.

My landlady died in August. No doubt after the estate is settled this house will be put up for sale and I am not sure what I should do. I would like to own it if they don't ask too big a price. I have got to live somewhere!

Love,
Marcella

January 12, 1955
Dear Tat,

It is now calm after the holidays. The children back in school.

The Laylins loved the landscape, which is always so much easier to love than portraits. Apparently, the lord and master had not seen me freezing up on the knoll, as it was a complete surprise—different than the Battley kind.

Although Mary was locked into the Library of Congress for a week doing research on Chaucer, she found time to go with me to hear Lowell give a reading of his poems. She said he was worth giving up Chaucer for. Also, we enjoyed meeting his wife, Elizabeth Hardwick, at the

Biddle party after the reading. Cal told me he hoped I would ask him to sit for me . . . that he wasn't ready before—he has left Washington alas! Elizabeth Hardwick is lovely looking and very nice indeed. Cal is certainly OK now.

The children and I had a nice visit with Cousin Harriet there. She loved hearing about our delving into John Ancrum Winslow's horsehair trunk on our last visit to you and launched off on her own Winslow-niana, which Johnny told me later he hadn't listened to, as he had had enough of THAT! Harriet is an authority on the family. I am getting pictures off to shows, seeing Katherine Cornell in a play next week, and plan to go again to see the marvelous *Romeo and Juliet* movie with Giulia Ortona. I predict even you would like it, if you would consent to attend a movie.

Love,
Marcella

The horsehair trunk under discussion contains all the surviving material on the Winslow family, and the original log on the battle between the *Kearsarge* and the *Alabama*.

March 16, 1955
Dear Tat,

Members of the Corcoran Women's Committee are asked to entertain for artistic events on occasion, so I had a dinner for the prizewinners of the Corcoran biennial—all three youngish New Yorkers who paint very large and very bold. The two boldest painters liked my earlier work—at least the painting of Randolph and me over the sofa, and the big still life of your DR table, *Southern Sunday*. The first prize winner, John Hultberg, seemed especially complimentary.

The three were so relieved that the dinner was informal as they were uncomfortable in their rented tuxedos. I could see the strain depart from their faces. John Prince gave us a superb meal of veal scaloppini covered with creamed spinach, tomatoes and cheese, salad and Peach Melba. The Director [and] Assistant Director of the Corcoran and the Art Critic of the *Washington Post* came, and relaxed as well.

Larry Rivers, the third-prize winner (a seven-foot canvas), phoned, waking me at 2 a.m., long after the event at the Corcoran, to say he liked Washington, asking when would be a good time to come back—"the fourth of July?"[1] Also, he liked me and my guests and what material was my dress made of, and that Peach Melba was almost *too* good. Even at 2 a.m. that was pleasant to hear! Rivers found the excitement of the award ceremony too much (his first), so he said he had left the museum to find a bar. The nearest was blocks away and, when he returned, the museum was closed! I figured he had gone back to the bar and found a telephone to call when he felt mellow enough to do so.

Obregon, the Colombian artist, had a sellout show at the Pan American Union. The prices were so low that I bought a lovely small oil for $25. He sold two paintings to the Museum of Modern Art and one to the Phillips Gallery.

I heard Glenway Wescott give a talk. He read several of KAP's letters. Amusing, lively and informative. Afterwards he told me he reads everything you write and thinks you write beautifully.

Love,
Marcella

1. Larry Rivers (1925–) is a New York artist who believes in the coexistence of nonrepresentational art and realism. Born Yizroch Loiza Grossberg, in the Bronx, he has a humorous memory of bad art: a tapestry at home that was a "cross between a Fragonard and a Minsky " (Sam Hunter, *Larry Rivers* [New York, 1989]).

April 5, 1955
Dear Tat,

My house has been authorized to be sold! I am given the first chance to bid on it, although the heirs of the owner (all out West) asked their lawyer to put it on a general listing. I am worried since people will offer impossible prices just to be in Georgetown. My agent told me he had appraised it at $25,000, but the lawyer's appraisal may be lower, as they won't say what it was. However, I was able, through a friend, to get one of the best R. E. Investment Loan men to look at the house and he suggested that I offer $21,000. I did so, with a (good old General Battley) $1000 deposit, and will wait to see what happens. I am going on a "bird-in-the-hand" theory. If they agree, I could get a loan at 4% and hope to get it paid for—some day. My R.E. agent tells me that small houses with one bath and two bedrooms are going for $23,000 BELOW the canal—very undesirable (but still Georgetown). Unfortunately, real estate is booming after a slump of a year ago. I could have bought the big house on the corner for $18,000 at that time.

Love,

Marcella

May 7, 1955

Dear Tat,

My offer for the house was refused! Being desperate and sunk in gloom (I can't visualize myself in the boondocks, in a tiny house with no garden and certainly no atmosphere), I got the address of the lawyer who lives in Iowa, representing the heirs, and wrote to him describing my situation; the only home my children remember, the old kitchen fixtures and claw bathtub; the coal furnace; telling him how much would have to be done to make it salable etc.; then I offered him $23,000. If I let them throw it on the open market, my nervous system will suffer, having to show it! I must admit I have made the garden lovely and the high ceilings keep the house cool, and there is lots of wall space for pictures, and enough bedrooms, so I realize I DO want to make P Street my permanent address. Mary calls that letter my widow act. I really can't rustle up $25,000!

The reason $1200 is not too high a price to pay for a portrait like Battley's is because, after loving it madly, he writes me a letter with the following suggestions: "I feel the watch should be shifted and the cuff and sleeve moved down to cover more of the wrist. As it is now, a couple of the fingers since the last change do not look quite natural to me, so when we look at that together we can consider that also." Togetherness again!

When Johnny was home for Easter I painted his portrait. He had never shown much interest in my painting but has been taking a course with Pat Morgan in Andover, which has such an excellent little museum [the Addison]. I was amazed when, upon arriving home, he immediately noticed my new painting over the mantel, so I asked if he would pose to show off the big *A* he was sporting on his jacket, which he had won in a track meet. His answer delighted me: "I will, if you promise you won't try to worry about a likeness." We went to the studio as soon as he unpacked, and he fell into the most ideal pose immediately. Having no canvas on a stretcher, I just tacked one on a board and soon had the thing almost finished, life size, 3/4 figure. One more sitting got him—looking his relaxed sixteen years.

I love it.

Love,
Marcella

In May, *Harper's* published one of my favorite poems by Anne Winslow, "Sing, O Goddess, the Wrath":

There was no printing press in Homer's day;
What a man felt he simply had to say.
He simply said:
He was listened to, not read;
And in the case of an important thing,
Singing was better still—if he could sing.
War was the thing that Homer sang about—
And love, which are important still no doubt.

We have renewed the battles in the plain;
The skies are lit, the rivers red again,
And Helen back again upon the wall;
Her olive drab is different from the stuff
The songs are made of; and Achilles too—

Achilles seems no longer mad enough,
Or long enough, to do.

Center Sandwich, N.H.
June 23, 1955
Dear Tat,

Good news! I had a letter from my real-estate agent enclosing one from the estate lawyer that all heirs had agreed to my offer of $23,000 for the house. However, he wrote: "Marcella C. Winslow cannot count on this sale until all parties sign the contract." But it's in the bag, I feel sure. Strange. I had been so confident that I had put it off my mind. I made all the arrangements before I left in case I got the house. What a relief!

Johnny is liking his job working for Chauncey [Stillman] at his summer place in Amenia, N.Y. He has his own room and bath at the head gardener's house on the grounds. J drives a tractor and helps out wherever needed. Returns in August. Mary is working here at the N.H. Industries, selling crafts.

The night before I left Washington I went to a lovely dinner at the Talbotts'. It was outdoors—lanterns, airforce band and all. I sat near Kay Shouse, and she seemed embarrassed. She thanked me "for not mentioning" her portrait. (She never came for a last sitting.) As you know, I delivered it to her house after finishing it without her, in MY frame, and that was the end of it. . . .

Did you read Peter Taylor's story in the *New Yorker* called "A Sentimental Journey"?[1] It is about a trip he and his roommate from Kenyon (Robert Lowell, whose name is not mentioned) take to New York and Boston. I think it is so good I am keeping it for you if you did not see it.

Love,
Marcella

1. Peter Taylor (1917–), born in Trenton, Tennessee, is often referred to as the dean of the American short story. He is the author of several plays, two novels, and seven collections of short stories. He taught English at the University of Virginia from 1967 to 1983. For the novel *Summons to Memphis,* he became the first American to win the Ritz Hemingway Prize.

P Street, N.W.
Washington, D.C.
October 26, 1955
Dear Tat,

I had a visit with Robert Frost at a reception in the Library of Congress after his reading two days ago. He is still going strong. They borrowed my portrait of him for the exhibit illustrating his work for more than half a century, which opened at the same time. A photograph was taken of Frost with my painting, but alas! not with me. Another portrait of him has been painted by Gardner Cox [1906–1988], a very good portrait painter who lives in Boston, so I don't know if he can still say he likes mine the best, but maybe he says that to both of us! I think I will go on liking mine the best. He has received the Pulitzer Prize four times for his books and been awarded honorary degrees by Harvard, Columbia, Dartmouth and Yale, as well as all sorts of other honors. His readings are so popular and are always PACKED.

John Prince was married to that nice Catherine Graves and their rehearsal dinner was held in my house. I will certainly miss him. More reason for me to be grateful for your handsome offer of a gas furnace when the time comes, which should be soon. I will have to get back to stoking in the meantime.

Love,
Marcella

December 20, 1955
Dear Tat,

Thank you thank you for my very best Christmas present—the gas furnace. It went in today with the temperature down to 15. The old coal furnace is out with the old year. (Though not old Charles. He *stays.*) Anyway, I have no more coal and have been burning Coca-Cola boxes, and willow-tree branches and anything burnable I could put my hands on. I can't believe just turning a thermostat will adjust the heat, and I keep going down cellar to see if the furnace is still working.

I am trying my hand and brain at teaching art. I met the wife of the Attorney General (Herbert Brownell), a charming Texan named Doris, at a luncheon at Peggy Talbott's and she asked if I would give her lessons. She and Mrs. Herbert Hoover, Jr., have been talking about studying but would like that idea to be kept secret from their husbands—in case they turn out to be flops! I thought it might be an interesting new challenge, so have just given them their third lesson. Both of these attractive women act like little girls about the whole thing. Today I had them mixing colors—very messy—(since I told them they would be just ordinary students to me) until Mrs. Hoover said: "I just HAVE to get my hands clean as I must go directly to a luncheon being given in my honor." I make them wash their brushes before they leave to get them in good habits and, so far, they seem to be enjoying themselves tremendously. I find that after three lessons it is easy to use first names. However, I find it easier to call Doris Doris, than to call Peggy Peggy.

Katherine Anne is in Southbury, Conn., in a house she has taken for two years. She says she is surrounded by birds and squirrels in a kind of glass house on the side of a hill. As usual, she says she hopes to get a little writing done.

Love,
Marcella

January 7, 1956
Dear Tat,

A telephone call I had today so amazed me that I asked Etta if she could vouch for the fact that it had happened. I will write it down exactly as I remember it. A girl with a definite Brooklyn accent said she was calling from the Credit Bureau to ask if I could tell her something about my next-door neighbor, Allen Dulles, who had sublet the house of Christian Herter while he is in Boston being the Governor of Massachusetts. The conversation:

Mrs. Winslow?

Yes.

This is the Credit "Beerow." Do you know Allen Macy DULLS who has moved next door to you?

I know that Mr. DullESS has moved in. (Correcting the name.)

Would you please give us some information about him? I must tell you we have been asked not to contact Mr. DULLS personally.

I will do what I can.

Can you tell us where Allen Macy DULLS works?

Mr. DullESS is the head of the Central Intelligence Agency.

How old a man is he, do you know?

I should say in the late fifties, or early sixties. (I made a rough guess, having seen Mr. Dulles only once, tipping the garbage man under my window just before Christmas. He could have been Santa Claus himself with the right suit.)

Is he married?

Yes.

Children?

Three, I believe. I heard that one was wounded in Korea.

Then we don't have to worry about him. Can you tell us what Mr. DULLS' job is at Central Intelligence? What exactly does he "dew" there?

Do? He is HEAD of it. Director, you know. (I didn't know how else to put it, so added that his brother was John Foster Dulles.) She didn't seem to know that was the Secretary of State, but tried to reassure me by adding:

I don't know why we aren't supposed to get in touch with Mr. DULLS himself. He probably wants to belong to a club or something.

I was recovering from that remark when she briskly brought the conversation to a close by cheerily asking: "Well, then you think Allen Macy DULLS is OK?"

The Credit Bureau voice, though unwilling to accept my pronunciation of the Dulles name, was quite willing to accept my judgment of the man who headed the most powerful agency in the United States. I muttered something like how sad it would be for our country if he wasn't OK, but instead of worrying about our country, I was thinking how amusing it was for me to be passing on whether my distinguished neighbor could belong to a club.

The picture of the contrast between the elegant Herter house, a model of the best Georgetown has to offer—shown in all the yearly house and garden tours, beautifully landscaped with the two large magnolia trees (which drop their leaves on my side and shade my flower garden), the fancy fishpool which Mrs. Herter liked to move often, the fragrant potted plants which arrive in large terra-cotta pots already blooming—and my bay-windowed house, 18 feet wide, with a "back yard" (where old Charles and I toil away with one trowel and a few bulbs) was striking to say the least.

Our fence joins, but I could see over it and did enjoy the parties and dinners held by candlelight (with guitar music) from my back windows; while, from their side, they could get whiffs of my barbecue (if they cared to smell) and sounds of my coal deliveries (if they cared to hear), as well as the sight of the peeling paint on my back porch (if they cared to look).

Of course none of this ever bothered the Herters when in residence. Chris asked me to paint his portrait and Mac was always sending over flowers and pretending she really wanted to know why I was spraying my woolens out back come warm weather—"*Maw*cella, what ARE you doing? I must try that. What a good idea!"

I loved having the Harold Talbotts sublet, too, before the Dulleses moved in. All the fascinating boxes and presents I received for them over the holidays when Mr. Talbott was the Secretary of Air and they flew to Greenland to cheer up the Air Force. Particularly one huge poinsettia plant which I enjoyed all one Christmas; and the corsages that the flower stores sent which Mrs. Talbott said to keep when she was not home to receive them—one from Prince Obolensky which I wore at Easter with his card in my pocket.

I thought what a wonderful idea for a *New Yorker* story. Would you like to write it up? As a preamble to the story you could mention that the White House called me to ask if I would send someone next door to deliver a message asking Dulles to phone the White House, as their phones were not yet connected. I sent myself. I thought of telling that to the Credit Bureau girl, but decided she might not have heard of the White House.

Perhaps you could contrast the splendor of the neighboring house with my "celebrity" room on the third floor back where poor but talented artists get a clear view out of their window of what life might be like if a best seller gets written or a masterpiece painted. If Katherine Anne could just get that famous novel finished! Who knows? Getting on the best-seller list with your fifth novel, THE SPRINGS, qualifies you certainly for a permanent place in the "celebrity" room but I'm sure you will always prefer your own DWELLING PLACE.

Love,
Marcella

When Katherine Anne's famous best seller, *Ship of Fools,* came out in 1961, she was able to rent her own expensive house in Washington. All the book-stores were overwhelmed with orders, and the most popular one in George-town, the Savile, asked to have something of hers in their window. She decided to let them show the original manuscript, asking if my portrait of her could be displayed along with it. After some weeks, Katherine Anne had me request the return of the borrowed items. When the portrait was delivered, I assumed that the manuscript was on the way to her and thought I had better alert her. But she answered the phone in a chaotic state of nerves and exhaustion, or perhaps a hangover, declaring that she was in bed and had no intention of answering the door, or even the tele-phone, and would not be disturbed for anything, or anybody. The book-store assured me that the delivery had been made, and it showed no concern in the least. The concern was mine; I felt responsible that the manuscript of one of the longest-awaited novels in memory might be picked up as trash. Because I knew there was no one in Katherine Anne's house to accept the package and there was no vestibule or cranny where it might be left, I decided to go to the rescue. And rescue it was. The bulky pages were in a large paper bag forlornly lying on the doorstep. Feeling extremely guilty, I walked off with the precious bundle, wondering what it would be like to write a best seller.

January 20, 1956
Dear Tat,

So glad you have decided to write up the Dulles story. Will you try the *New Yorker?* If you have not yet sent it in, I caution you not to use an address. Jan Karski, who knows the Far East and foreign entangle-ments (having been in the Polish underground and written the Book-of-the-Month selection STORY OF A SECRET STATE), tells me . . . that in other countries no one would ever know where the head of their secret organization lived; his movements would be heavily watched and guards would be everywhere. He kept tapping on the table whenever we said anything "important," to break the contact. He said every word spoken in my house would automatically go down on some tape—not that anyone would look at it, but when I became suspect (after the piece in the *New Yorker*) THEY could go back and check up on me. Pleasant thought.

I haven't been able to spot a security guard yet, but recently I saw a young man standing on the Dulles steps and, when I tried to engage him in conversation, he wouldn't answer me. That was when I was trying to move cars so I could get my last ton of coal in the proper window. I think I was the last person in Georgetown to have a coal furnace. I am cooking with gas now since the house is all mine.

Love,

Marcella

Anne Goodwin Winslow did send her version of the Dulles story to the *New Yorker*, but it was turned down. I was not surprised, after my briefing by Karski, and decided I should feel relieved.

January 30, 1956
Dear Tat,

The process of face-lifting has been going on these days with the house—shelves where the dumbwaiter used to be and paint jobs. I got rid of the gas burner and opened up the fireplace and we are getting to look more like Georgetown—*indoors anyway.*

The track coach at Princeton has written to say that Princeton is a great college and John should go there. The coaches are all on his trail since he broke the record set in 1951 for the hurdle race against Harvard freshmen. No doubt one can say he is "way out front" in track, particularly broad jump and hurdles. He is still debating between Harvard and Princeton, having been accepted by both.

Mary has the lead in her college's new play, *You Can't Take It with You.* I haven't told the children about the house improvements. The garbage disposal is the best of all. Everything just goes down the sink!

I have completed a portrait of 90-year-old General "Billy" Harts, as you always called him. It is hard to believe he was your husband's best friend at West Point where they both graduated in 1889. He still wears colorful cravats so I have painted him in one—crimson with a stickpin—beige vest and gray suit. It goes well with his very pink complexion and manicured white mustache—every hair in place. I have enjoyed hearing the stories of his brilliant past. He doesn't forget anything—being military aide to Woodrow Wilson, Commander of American forces in Paris after World War I, and the Engineer in charge of the beautification of Washington which interested me the most. Still with erect posture, he deserves all the accolades you always bestowed on him.

Love,
Marcella

April 9, 1956
Dear Tat,

Mary went back to college yesterday wearing a large white straw hat. I see in the paper this morning that a snowstorm paralyzed New England. Newton had no power as heavy winds had knocked out the system—and probably Mary's hat as well.

I, myself, was nearly knocked out three weeks ago when I drove to New York to meet Johnny and go with him to Princeton where he had an interview with the track coach (J is still trying to decide between Princeton and Harvard). Sara was with me, fortunately, when we got caught in a very unseasonable snowstorm and had to abandon the car on the highway, or I would have had no one to keep me company during this traumatic event, or to laugh about it later. I had brought Massa along too, so when we three had been rescued by a state trooper and deposited in Baltimore, I found a nice Mrs. Skunkle who "loved dogs" and agreed to keep him so Sara and I could take the last train to New York where friends were expecting us and surprised we had made it.

The blizzard kept up until late the next day, but J and I eventually made it to Princeton. When we got back to where we had left the car, it had been broken into and the battery was dead so we had to be rescued again by the same trooper. It was wonderful to return to what J calls our Dream House. It seems a dream after all the improvements.

John spent the holiday working on a history paper. (He is in Dudley Fitts's honor class now.) His subject was the battle of the *Kearsarge* and the *Alabama* as he feels he has an inner track, having access to the original log in the old trunk of Captain Winslow you have in Memphis. I wonder if Fitts will believe that! Mary is Literary Editor of her college magazine in which she will have a story and a poem. I like its title: "Inscape," from Gerard Manley Hopkins, a word which he used to express an inner beauty of form and pattern, she says. Do you have the same interpretation? I know he is one of your favorite poets.

Doris Brownell says she has never had as much fun as she has had painting with Peg Hoover and "Teacher." They work so differently, but I do not let them DAUB—and I must say I am proud of their progress. They are now ready to inform their husbands of the lessons!

Love,
Marcella

May 3, 1956

Dear Tat,

Now comes the subrenting time. I decided to get Central Intelligence to work for me since they should be concerned about who moves next door to its director. I went over to see Mrs. Dulles and told her I wanted to be sure the "right" people came in next to them. She said that was quite right and phoned Allen Macy "Dulls" immediately. I had a call from his office and a man came out. So far, however, they have produced no one. They said they would not interfere with my private business but would appreciate my letting them know who took the house. We have decided to get Jan Karski out in the garden, using his best Slavik accent, sometime when the "Dulls" are sitting out in theirs. Then we will see what happens.

Next Monday I take my two pupils, Doris Brownell and Peggy Hoover, on their first step into outdoor painting. They graduate from shells and boxes to roofs and treetops. The Princes have offered us their roof garden with a gourmet lunch thrown in. I will take some Pouilly Fuissé and John will have soft-shell crabs. We will have only one more lesson and I told them there had better not be anyone official interfering. Last week the President of Brazil was the interferer. I can't go on putting up with that! They went so far as to have a private showing of their work at the Brownells'. Only cabinet wives invited (very exclusive as each has to first catch a cabinet member): Mrs. Sherman Adams, Mrs. Arthur Radford, Mrs. Dulles, and I don't know who else.

I have finished the portrait of Alice Longworth's granddaughter, Joanna Sturm, age 9.[1] Her mother, Paulina, likes it a lot. When I went to Paulina's house, expecting a "best dress" sort of thing for the pose, I found that the child was dressed in dungarees and had on basketball shoes. No move was made to suggest anything else so I realized that was acceptable and perhaps preferable. When I commented on the attractive color scheme of the outfit with a red, white and blue target which I saw there, Paulina was pleased with such an unconventional setting for a portrait, so the result is a landscape and a child with bow and arrows seated on the grass in front of the target. Quite effective.

Love,
Marcella

1. Alice Roosevelt Longworth, the daughter of Theodore Roosevelt, acquired the status of a monument in the capital, and her caustic wit was widely admired and repeated.

June 17, 1956
Dear Tat,

Harriet Winslow, who is able to write now after her stroke, wrote me that the Robert Lowells are expecting. They have returned to Boston to live and, what's more interesting, the OLD part of Boston. "Robert is fussy about the old silver and where the furniture should be placed." If that isn't heredity getting revenge! He seems willing to take on the Lowell mantle since his mother's death.

I have almost completed my house improvements. The last thing added makes an elegant statement—a huge burnished gold pier glass which misses the ceiling by 1/2 an inch. Given to me by Mrs. Fleming whose grandfather had it sent from France. Since giving up the family house in Iowa, she has kept it in storage for sentimental reasons and because the ceilings are not high enough for any of her family to use it. She has been paying large storage bills but insisted on paying for its installation. When it was delivered, a man rang my bell to ask if he could use the crate for a chicken coop! It came in a huge van and required five men to install it. What a difference it makes in my hallway! The house looked beautiful for the party on May 24th to show my portrait of Joanna Sturm. One hundred people were invited and we spilled into the garden.

Old Charles answered the door in a white coat, looking like an old family retainer. Joanna's portrait was over the mantel, the young Lucius Clay III on her left side, Howard Mitchell's portrait on the right.

Mrs. Longworth came with Paulina and Joanna, seeing the painting for the first time. She stood entranced, paying no attention to anyone (was this for effect?) and fairly shouted: "I love it. I just love it!" She seemed enchanted with the pose, especially the basketball shoes which Joanna insisted on wearing with her dungarees for the painting. Mrs. L seems to like the idea of Joanna as a tomboy.

Many of the older viewers expressed their delight with the portrait but were sure, with such an outfit (as they carefully explained to me), the painting could never hang in a formal drawing room! Joanna played Hide-and-Seek with Massa who was welcoming one and all.

Love,
Marcella

Center Sandwich, N.H.
July 23, 1956
Dear Tat,

John sprained his ankle two days before commencement so he graduated from Andover with crutches. Afterwards he went to aquatic school so he could be a lifeguard here this summer. Mary is taking care of children with a family on the Cape. Massa and I are here doing the usual.

I let four young Lieutenants have my house this summer. They made all sorts of promises and were highly recommended, so I will take my chances. One of them was excited about all my new cooking gadgets as he aims to do the cooking.

I am definitely planning to come to visit you in September after John and I drive to Princeton. I will go on to Washington, leaving the car and Massa, and take a plane. I will check up on tenants. I hope the house will still be standing.

Have you read that Congress voted to boost the monthly benefits of widows of veterans who died on active duty? That should help John's college tuition. He will have to furnish his room at Princeton. I am trying to be philosophical about his turning down Harvard after he originally accepted. I think New England Winslows belong where their roots are, but I am not being vocal about his decision. It is too late now, anyway. I hope he won't regret it.

Love,
Marcella

P Street, N.W.
Washington, D.C.
October 9, 1956
Dear Tat,

Johnny is settled in Princeton.

Massa *loved* being at the Tates' house, as Caroline asked me to stay with her on my way down to Washington. He and Caroline have empathy. She is much more tolerant of beasts than of people. People continue to be human and erring and this Caroline can't take, especially she can't take it from Allen. She was her usual very generous self, insisting that Johnny borrow a rare vase for his room, as well as an Etruscan one that Allen had given her (she much preferred a horse and chariot that he had given Nancy, which Nancy has no place for, and has not thought yet of giving to her mother), and also a portion of a foot, which Caroline herself had dug up in Greece—or somewhere where they dig. Caroline said it probably had been planted. It looked old to me. In fact, it all looked too fine for a freshman room at college—even though the freshman IS Johnny. The trouble is that J has such good taste that he wanted the things badly and I couldn't restrain either one of them.

Johnny has a "suite"—a room with deeply recessed windows and a fireplace, with a small room off that which has a desk and bed. He had painted all Peter [Fisher]'s cast-off furniture black and had splurged on a sort of room divider. He has taken the dividing seriously. The sofa is divided from the fireplace and, as you come in the door, you are also divided from the room. Peter had given him his old sofa which had large holes in both arms, as though rats had gnawed through and were still in there. All in all, it is a lovely room with, what's more, ivy trailing up the window.

Allen sent me a card from India saying he was leaving for Rome after giving 11 lectures in 14 days. He simply couldn't eat the food, he said. "Ever try betel nuts? Wonderful time . . . Rome two weeks; Paris 10 days; London 7; then home."

Love,
Marcella

Caroline, never aware of her excessive generosity, was "dazzled by the munificence" of a gift of paints and brushes that I sent her on my return to Washington. She wrote, "For heaven's sake, do not give that vase another thought. I would not care if Johnny stepped on it and smashed it and as for Allen, he flies about the world at such a rate that he doesn't recognize the existence of any of our possessions, and would never miss it. Please don't bring me any more house presents. I must now get to work on my novel whose working title is 'How to Read a Novel, Damn It.' How much nicer it would be if I could attack the Prophet Elijah!"

October 26, 1956
Dear Tat,

October has been beautiful. I have been glad to get back in my house after two weeks with Mother and the enjoyable visit with you. The Lieutenants left my house in good condition and even had me to luncheon before they left. Nick, my favorite, said the kitchen in their new house is terrible after cooking for the first time in mine.

Mary is frantically busy directing a play, rehearsing in one, writing editorials as well as the inevitable test papers. She says vitamin pills are all that are holding her up—like baling wire does in the South. Katherine Anne, who spent several days in town last week and had all her dinners here, was, she said, pleased with the story Mary had written, and said she would gladly recommend her for a job in publishing houses or the like. The Princes and I drove with her to Gettysburg for the next lap of her tour. She looks fine and is taking care of herself. She says the *Atlantic Monthly* pays her $500 a month on the strength of getting their hands on her novel which she says is almost finished. She gave a beautiful reading at the Library of Congress. Eudora [Welty] will also give a reading there soon.

My portrait of Cornelius Weygandt got first prize in the Sandwich Art Fair and I got the horse picture that I painted in your pasture in the Laurel [Maryland] Race Track show—which netted me a pass to the races!

Love,
Marcella

December 5, 1956
Dear Tat,

Ward Dorrance and I have been attending a group of three lectures on "Modern Trends in Thought" given by Father Martin D'Arcy, the English philosopher, at the home of Mrs. William Corcoran Eustis.[1] I used to hear D'Arcy talk at the Farm Street Church in London the winter

I lived there. He is famous for his oratory as well as his writing. Sorry you weren't here as I am sure you would have enjoyed his subjects. The first lecture was on man's search for something outside himself: the Eastern religions, mysticism etc. The second one was on Existentialism, and the last on Christianity. It was a sort of Dumbarton Oaks atmosphere—retired John Walker, former Director of the National Gallery, introducing and commenting, a smattering of diplomats and the old standbys Katherine Biddle and Alice Longworth. Yesterday the Archduke Ferdinand of Austria was there, a Russian Prince Toumanoff (Catholic), Mrs. Eugene Meyer and many others. I saw old Mrs. Boit who hasn't been around for so long, looking so frail and tiny; Mrs. Corcoran Thom, not understanding much but unwilling to miss any of it; Ambassador Jan Ciechenowski and wife; Mrs. Dunlap, all done up for an evening out and, at the end, asking a question which was really not wanting to know but wanting to tell. There is a large cleavage between political Washington, as it is now, and the old Washington cave dwellers.

Political was the Brownell wedding—the marriage of one of their daughters. Some of the politicians seemed rather out of place in the elegance of Anderson House where members must be descended from Officers in the American Revolution but it was impressive. The receiving line waited hours to shake hands. When it was my turn to greet the Attorney General, who was first in line, after seeing him kiss and shake hands and pat backs of everyone in front of me, I had to think fast to get him to greet me like an old friend, so, when I took his hand, I announced, "I'm Teacher!" (which is what Doris calls me and I thought he would know) but, not getting the drift at all, he exclaimed, with a loud guffaw: "You look too young to be a teacher!" His wife, Doris, had not told him I gave her art lessons!

Love,

Marcella

1. Ward Dorrance is a novelist and professor of English literature and was a friend of the Tates'. He has taught at the University of Missouri and at Georgetown University. Father Martin Cyril D'Arcy (1888–1976) was educated at Oxford University and entered the Society of Jesus in 1906. He was master of Campion Hall and lecturer in philosophy at Oxford from 1932 to 1945. From his church on Farm Street he guided the conversion of many distinguished English writers, among

them Evelyn Waugh (who depicted him as Father Rothschild in *Vile Bodies*) and Edith Sitwell. In a book of Avedon's photographic portraits, Truman Capote commented, "Impossibly erudite D'Arcy . . . lecturing the already enlightened . . . converting to the Faith many of the Century's cleverest minds."

December, 1956
Dear Tat,

Your Christmas gifts this year will be geared to the limp budget. The dollar is now worth 50 cents and I do wonder how long the prices will continue to go up. The stock market is far removed from reality. Money is REAL money when it comes through painting. I don't recognize it on paper, going up and down, as it does on the financial reports.

The Herters are expected back. Everyone seems to think he will be the next Secretary of State. They are coming early in January. Allen has also been here, staying with the Biddles. When he came for lunch he said he wants to go back to Caroline but dreads living with her. He is a lost soul without Caroline and I don't know what the solution is. He isn't writing—no doubt will go back to Minneapolis. He looks so old and thin, but still has the wit and sparkle. One is still fascinated when he is in good form.

I haven't heard from Katherine Anne since she was here giving a reading at the Library of Congress. She looked fine.

Since Juan Ramón Jiménez won the Nobel Prize for literature I am more than ever grieved that Allen never returned the book of poems I had so much difficulty getting Jiménez to inscribe to me before he left Washington.

Miss Nichols suggested that I read Jean Stafford's article in the *Atlantic*. She said it sold out so she couldn't get a copy, but shouldn't have dreamed that Mrs. Robert Lowell would set the house afire with such acute criticism.

Love,
Marcella

New Years Day, 1957
Dear Tat,

Festivities are on the wane. Dust has settled over everything. Decorations look pitiful—holly dropping on piano, red berries all around.

The children deep in biology and playwriting respectively—preparing for exams when they go back to college.

We are still eating Chauncey's 22-lb. turkey but looking forward with tremendous anticipation to Mary's Tennessee ham. I had all the family for Christmas dinner after which we went to the new Arena Stage theater which was moved down by the river to a converted brewery. The play was *Tartuffe*—excellent cast. That whole section, between Georgetown and Constitution Ave., is being developed.

Could you come for a visit in late January after Nixon's inauguration? Not that I am having any part in that, but Jay will be home on a break after his exams. The Herters will be back like old times.

I started two portraits last week. One is of Carley Dawson who, I understand, declined to marry not only Robert Lowell but also Alexis Léger. She is beautiful and writes books. She has been definite about what she wants in the small portrait: her cat on her lap, a favorite chair, tulips in a vase on a table beside her with the right book whose color complements her outfit which, of course, is most becoming.

The other portrait is of a young girl of nine whose mother is Russian and wants her darling to pose in her "tutu." I try to discourage the mother from coming to the sittings as she makes the child put on her sweater over her costume for fear she will catch cold. She says: "There now, isn't she sweet when she puts her head that way?" or, "Perhaps we should wait until spring when there will be more color in her cheeks." That goes along with wanting the lowest price.

Love,
Marcella

On January 29, 1957, my letter to Anne Winslow enclosed a letter I had from Caroline Gordon and included my comments on it: "Enclosing Caroline's last letter. The 'savage attack' she refers to was a few words on the subject of Allen, such as 'Do you love him? I haven't heard you say a good word about him' etc. This goes back to my visit with her in October which she never objected to at the time. Allen may have caused a new rage to make her lash out. She is off the beam. I didn't answer as everyone says she will forget it in a short time."

Vigil of the Epiphany, 1957
Dear Marcella
    Thanks for returning the article. I need to use part of it in a book I am writing or you could have kept it indefinitely.

I think that you and I had better come to an understanding—if only for the sake of our friends in Washington who are embarrassed and inconvenienced by this rift between us. I feel sure that I will regain my old affection for you in time, but at present I do not feel as kindly towards you as I did before you attacked me so savagely. I know well that this is wrong and I am striving to overcome my resentment of the harsh things you said. At present my resentment shows itself in a reluctance to accept hospitality from you. I am sorry to be so weak, but what little store of charity I have has been almost exhausted lately, and your attack couldn't have been at a worse time. I am certain, however, that you would not have said the things you said if you had understood the situation and that certainly enables me to hope that we can be friends again. But I think it is better to tell you frankly how I feel rather than to express my resentment in acts of veiled hostility.

The last paragraph spoke of family doings like any ordinary letter, saying that Allen was "a little better physically and much better spiritually" and that she could have him off her mind. She ended with, "Best wishes for a good year for you all."

I was not aware that we had had a rift—but I never saw her again. I did, however, get a letter from her later the same year, advising me about a college for Mary and telling me where the key to her house was if I came to Princeton.

April 2, 1957
Dear Tat,

The date for my exhibition at the Corcoran is set for October 8th. Bill Williams, the Director, wants to make a selection next month and has agreed to keep the work over the summer, and said if I have recent paintings which I would like to show, I can send them from New Hampshire in late August. He leaves that decision to me.

I have been too busy to write, getting two pictures off to the Carnegie Museum's Pittsburgh artists show, two to the Baltimore Museum and five to a four-artist show at the D.C. Teachers College, besides getting my garden in shape, taking on the presidency of the Professional Artists Guild, giving final lessons to Hoover and Brownell, whose husbands are retiring, and arranging portrait sittings.

The most interesting sitter last month was Father D'Arcy, the English Jesuit philosopher who has been staying at Georgetown University while he lectures and gives readings. Robert Richman asked if I would have some people in to meet him after his talk at the Contemporary Arts series. I was so taken with his aesthetic looks that I asked if he had ever been painted by an American. He replied that there were a bust of him and a pastel in American museums, but there was no painting in oil by an American. I recalled a phrase in *Life* magazine about the Very Reverend Martin Cyril D'Arcy, S.J., mentor of young British artists in the 30's, being a "photographer's delight—so emaciated and mysterious looking," and asked if he would let me be the American to paint him.

He took out a little engagement book and after studying it awhile, put it back in his pocket. When I asked why he had done that, getting my hopes up, he said there would be no time for sittings except at 4 o'clock on Sunday. I heard myself saying: "I will pick you up at 4 at the front entrance of Georgetown." Which I did, and got such a good start that, halfway through, I interrupted his fascinating stories of the Bloomsbury group of writers, to ask for one more sitting. Again the little book came out and Father D'Arcy asked: "How about 4 o'clock next Tuesday?" It is one of the best paintings I have ever done and he agrees, even asking for photographs of it.

I saw Betty Fisher OFF Friday afternoon, after seeing her ON. ON her bags, unexpected, seated in my vestibule waiting for a welcome from me. She stayed a few days and, in spite of what I was led to believe, which was no money, and no job, she was going along as usual: taxis, flowers, avocados, Swiss chocolate etc. I managed to keep her from taking me out for a meal. I can't imagine what her family is living on. The pearls and piano etc. were long given, lent, or lost, weren't they? I did produce Mary's Tennessee ham for her delight and will do so again when Eudora comes to Washington to give a reading—if there is any left!

Love,
Marcella

April 7, 1957
Dear Tat,

This has really been a busy time for me. I started two large portraits this week which I must finish this month, and had Eudora for two days which was pure pleasure, as I like her so much, and have been making out Johnny's scholarship form which is worse than an income tax.

The best news is that Mary has a job in Switzerland. This is my luck working overtime. As you know, she graduates from college on June 3rd, but had no idea what she would do this summer. I hated the idea of her having again to take care of someone's unruly kids and wanted to get in touch with the woman who was hiring Mary's friend for a summer-school job in Europe. However, the woman had left Philadelphia and no one knew where she had gone. Can you believe that she turned up buying the twin house on my right that had been vacant for four months? Naturally, I lost no time greeting my new neighbor, and she hired Mary after an interview! Mary will be responsible for dramatics for 9 weeks and Johnny will again be the swimming teacher and lifeguard at Squam Lake this summer.

Carley Dawson asked me to paint her mother—known as Mary Chess, the famous beautician—but she turned out to be impossible to do. She has a very white, creamy face, with pale green shadows and white hair. The general effect was like a ghost of beauty creams.

I do hope I get paid for some of these portraits—the attractive girl in her ballet outfit and Admiral Hillenkoetter in his Navy uniform.[1] His will go to the CIA bldg. as he was its first Director, who also set up the Agency. There have been only three Directors. He, Beedle Smith and Allen Dulles. The Admiral should be good for Uncle Sam's money, and is turning out well.

Love,
Marcella

1. Admiral Roscoe Henry Hillenkoetter (1897–1983) graduated from the United States Naval Academy in 1919. After serving as chief intelligence officer for Admiral Nimitz, he was appointed first director of the CIA by President Truman in 1947.

April 10, 1957
Dear Tat,

Sad! My beautiful willow tree has been uprooted and is now sprawled over four gardens like an immense giant.

There was a terrific wind night before last and the crash sounded like doom. The tree had been weakened by having its roots cut on the Herter side at the time they had put up a new fence in late March. Mac Herter says she will get me a new tree—whatever I want. What do you think would be suitable for a Georgetown garden? Luckily, Johnny was home for spring semester as it is always better to have someone to exclaim with; and he had come just after the last excitement.

I had let a young Radcliffe girl (daughter of a friend of a friend) have my front bedroom for two nights and found she had sneaked in her boyfriend! A nice little girl from Kentucky. My friend told me the girl's mother wanted to be sure her daughter would be in a safe place in the big city and would I accept the girl as a favor, also accept a payment of $5.00 a night. I was so displeased to have had the girl use me this way that when the time came for her to leave, I left her a note with a bill for $20 for "Room as occupied."

What with paintings going to various exhibits; a party showing the Howard Mitchell portrait (which won a prize); getting a commission to paint Mary Chess; having two Fulbright painters to dinner (a Nicaraguan and a Chinese); being a judge at an art exhibit; painting Admiral Hillenkoetter; and not yet accomplishing my Income Tax; all I needed was a letter from Betty [Fisher] asking me to send her black shoes which she said she had left here last week. It seems hard to believe that they walked off and out of the house on their own since they are nowhere to be found. Unlike Massa, they have not come back. I lost Massa one day at the museum on the Mall where I was taking a painting. Our routine, which we both understood, was that he could wander about while I did my business but that he was to return to the car as soon as he heard the horn. That had always worked perfectly, but this time he was nowhere to be seen. I drove around for an hour vainly searching. When it got dark and started to rain, I gave up and alerted the park police. Then I sat at home worrying. After five hours of misery I heard his familiar bark in the vestibule. I don't know which of us was happier. He was so proud of himself. The museum doorman told me later that a furry yellow dog had come to the door, stood on his hind legs and looked in, and when I, and the car, were not around, he started in the direction from which we had come—in the rush-hour traffic, the dark and the rain. What a dog!

Love,
Marcella

Center Sandwich, N.H.
June 17, 1957
Dear Tat,

Happy Birthday! May you be that "last leaf" you are always talking about. You have made it to 82, so you are really the last leaf in the Goodwin family tree. I am sending you some N.H. pottery which is the specialty around here—my neighbors have their own kiln.

Sara came up with me to be at Mary's graduation and John will be here soon. This is his year to be on all the "lists." The boys get passed over while freshmen and start being tracked down by "debs" as soon as they have shown enough stamina to finish a year of college.

Eleanor [my sister] phoned that John was smart to leave D.C. early so he could get through Baltimore before the mid-June traffic. That is the worst part of the trip. He will have clear sailing on the new N.J. Turnpike and then the new Mass. Turnpike. How I remember the awful trips through towns before those were built!

I stayed over a few days in Newton after graduation while Mary got her literary magazine printed. We took time to see both Cal Lowell and Miss Nichols: a delightful lunch with Cal as host and a not so delightful visit with Miss N. She must be about 87 now and was in bed recovering from a fall, propped up on pillows with a transparent veil covering her head and falling into her eyes. She is so deaf now that there is no way one can get in a word, which was always difficult even in the best of times, and she goes right on allowing no interruptions. It was almost impossible even getting her to hear that we were leaving, which we had started to tell her the minute we were fastened down by her first sentence. It took 1/2 hour.

After luncheon with Lowell, he took us to his four-story house in the heart of old Boston, on Marlborough St., to see his new baby, Harriet, and Elizabeth [his wife]. With a nurse and a maid he seems to have all the comforts so many poets never know. He is a most devoted father. He also mentioned that he now appreciated Robert Frost's poetry more than he used to. As Harriet said, he seems to fit willingly into the role he struggled so long to escape while his parents were living.

I am driving Mary to New York next Sunday for her ship to Europe and her big adventure.

Love,
Marcella

P.S. Betty [Fisher] found her "lost" black shoes carefully put away in—of all places—her shoe bag! It had never occurred to her to look there.

I plan to come to Memphis after I get Mary off to Marquette Graduate School this September after she returns from Europe. What to do with Massa is always my problem. The trouble leaving him with willing friends is that they might treat him like a dog.

For my show in 1957 at the Corcoran Gallery, Eudora Welty, true to her promise, sent her portrait in the box she had someone make. She asked if Anne Winslow had arrived, and sent her best wishes, saying she hoped to meet her someday "in other ways than portraits bowing to each other."

P Street, N.W.
Washington, D.C.
October, 1957
Dear Tat,

My Corcoran show went off well. There was a large crowd at the opening, good reviews in both papers, and it was well hung on the first floor. I got together my recent work; the semi-abstract still lifes (I sold two), some landscapes and six portraits. The Corcoran had selected four of the literati: Eudora Welty, Robert Frost, Denis Devlin, and Martin D'Arcy. No doubt they are the best of the small ones. A collector, Mrs. Edward Bruce, wanted to buy D'Arcy but I feel he has to be saved for the proper setting. Mrs. Longworth came to admire Joanna's portrait (lent for the occasion) and I showed the life size of Johnny. The Brownells sent a huge bunch of flowers. I missed your being there.

Love,
Marcella

In December, 1957, our dog, Massa, sent out the usual Winslow news and Christmas greetings. The first response was from my Nicaraguan artist friend Armando Morales, whom I had met in Washington at his exhibition in the Pan American Union before he achieved fame internationally and went to Paris to live. We always enjoyed his letters.

Managua, Nicaragua
Dear Marcella:

Was a very nice letter that which you sent me along with the one "writen" by Massa. This last, believe me, made me laugh for a while.

I suppose it is the most delicate, and fondnessful (and vanguardist too) way of participate the family strategy and moving plans for the near future.

My congratulations and best desires for your trip to Italy. Oh, that is a true dream! a fairy fancy becoming real facts!

I am so glad to hear that you are working in a new way . . . I don't want to say that I didn't like your former style but I know that every change means new life, and I know that the passional enthusiam and the furious love to each inch of work (furious and new, but serene too!) is the only spark capable of starting, you know, that "something" inside us, that formless and dim shade lying quietely in deepest depth of our soul of our artists' soul full of the best Kiruna steel springs ready to jump, full of tension and stress!!! I mean changes often symtomatize progress.

And that exhibition in the Corcoran? That is fine news for me.

And tell me about Mary, what is she writing? Does she keep in the career of writer? (or writress?) Say hello to John. And give to Massa, in my name, two or three pieces of good paper for he enjoys tearing, hopping, runing, going and coming.

And about my work: I am working hard and have finished eleven paintings and have the sketches for eight more with such titles: Birds Fight (in Spanish: Pajaromaquia), Signals, Two Nighty Figures Singing, Birds and Poisoned Fruits and Sardines, Night Fruit, Dead Guerrillero II, Fading Out Woman, Dissolving Man, Man-Horse with Insomnio.

Best regards and warm greetings to Mary, John and you, and Massa of course. Drop some few words if you have some free minutes, Yours,

Armando

Katherine Anne Porter, who usually answered "Massadog"'s Christmas letters, wrote from Southbury, Connecticut, on December 20, 1957:

Dearest Marcella:

Good news often travels very fast and comes in from several directions, so I had heard about your show—from John Prince—and about the proposed Italian journey from your mother, *our* darling Honora, let me say, because I love to feel I have a little share in her. And as these two I take to be authorities on the subject of you, I just said Hosanna on each occasion and felt nicely cheered up. Now comes

Massadog's letter really spilling the beans, and I already have my own dream of being in Italy next year too, at least for a little while, and wouldn't it be fun for us to see each other there? I saw Rome for the first time Christmas week 1954, saw all the sights one can see in five days, being hauled around by a tireless sightseer—I would have preferred to sit in restaurants with friends and let the sights go by under their own powers—throwing a lira in the Trevi fountain. Denis gave me a cocktail party and it was astounding the number of Princes and Princesses and Literary Lights turned out on a day's notice! We went to midnight Mass Christmas Eve at Ara Coeli, and to the Children's Fair in the Piazza Navone—in fact, did you ever hear of anything more touristy? Then I took the Blue Train for Paris for New Year and so back to that awful miserable dark cold smoky dull beastly town of Liege where I blew up with exhaustion soon after, resigned, and came home—sailing from Cannes in—of all ships!—the *Andrea Doria,* as it happens I have a very beautiful photograph of her—or him? Wasn't Andrea Doria a sixteenth century pirate admiral, so to speak?

Well, next time in Italy I shall stay long enough to shake down a little, and live there, as I did in Paris. Sooner or later one sees everything without even trying, and that is what I like.

My play—that is, an arrangement made for the theatre by some one else of a short novel of mine, will close alas, this Sunday evening the 22nd December after a run of just twenty-one performances. Nobody liked it but the audiences, small but enthusiastic and faithful—the critics just simply cut its throat and let it fall. I saw it twice and loved it, and the young actors were superb. Never mind, they all got good notices, and I got good notices, too, but the poor woman who "arranged" it caught Hellfire from every side. Now somebody else, this time an actor and successful playwright, are talking about making a regular play out of "Noon Wine." We'll see. I send you one of the little advertisements that were in all the papers day after day. It was fun while it lasted!

I'd love you to stop by here on your way to N.H. and make a little portrait of me. I remember those very well, and Allen and Nancy and Robert Frost especially, but you do these so well you could very well have the field to yourself.

Love,
Katherine Anne

Eudora Welty wrote me a note at Christmas telling me that it was fun to have news of my Corcoran show—that she would have liked to have seen it, for she still thought my painting of her one of my best pieces of work. She remarked that there was something inspired about the day it was painted, in the way it telescoped so much into an hour or two.

On June 28, 1958, Katherine Anne sent me about sixty pages of her still-unfinished novel, *Ship of Fools*, with a letter:

Roxbury Road, Southbury Connecticut
28 June 1958
Marcella my dear:

There is some kind of obstructive pixy at work on our plans for you to paint my portrait. I didn't make myself clear enough when I wrote Honora, but I am in the last throes of this book—enclosed find a chunk of it just now published—and have got to pack up my household and leave on the 31st of July. So I can't see you here, or anybody else either—I have got a little gadget on my telephone so it doesn't ring though I can call outside if I need . . . I don't read my mail but once a week, and I don't answer any but urgent letters. I am in such a state of high voltage I upchuck violently without being in the least nauseated—just my midriff contracts and that's that! So I have to keep very quiet and stay on the rails. This isn't time for flying apart!

BUT—in September I'll be in Charlottesville, Virginia, from about the first, I think. And there we won't be too far away from each other, and I have week-ends and I hope you have too, and oh how happy I should be to have one of those lovely small portrait heads you do so beautifully; of course, I'm not getting any younger or prettier, and by the time you get to my face I maybe shan't be able to bear to look at it! But let's worry about that *then*—

Meantime, have a good summer. All the news about your children is so interesting and exciting, especially Mary. . . . Must stop and get to work. I'll see you DV in September, angel.

Meanwhile goodby with my same old affection

Katherine Anne

The pages I am sending you were chosen by the editors out of about sixty pages of manuscript I sent them, and [I] told them they could pick out anything they liked that made a sequence of some kind, and this is what they did . . . I can't imagine what bonehead made the mistake about the title in the little box at the head, nor why they couldn't get my publisher's name straight, but that is what happens one way or another, always! You'd think I'd get used to it, but I never have.

KAP

In November, 1958, Rose Nichols let it be known to all Robert Lowell's acquaintances that his book *Life Studies* was "horrid and outrageous." When Miss Nichols died, in 1960, she left her house to the Boston Council for International Visitors. The New York *Times* reported, "It is the only house on Beacon Hill open to visitors. World travelers can glimpse a bygone era of gracious Boston living."

In 1958, toward the end of the summer, I flew to Memphis for a visit with Anne Winslow before leaving for a year in Europe with my sister Alice and meeting up with Mary after she had had another summer in Switzerland. I could not know that I would never see my mother-in-law again. It was on that visit that she told me she had saved my letters and that they would come to me. Eventually, when the big box was delivered, it took its place with many other relics of my past in a P Street cupboard, the contents of which never saw the light of day and were almost forgotten.

When I returned from Europe, in August, 1959, Johnny met the ship and drove me to Center Sandwich to finish out the summer. I planned to go on to Memphis and have a visit with Anne Winslow. I knew she would want to hear about my fruitful months in Rome—and especially about my early-summer stay in Siena with the fascinating Vivante family, whose guests were likely to enjoy poetry readings of an evening. I wanted to show her my color sketches of Roman street scenes and Siena landscapes, and tell her about the whole Italian experience—which she always said she preferred hearing about to observing on her own. In a letter welcoming me back, she wrote,

> It gave me quite a shock to get that nautical looking letter from dear little homey Sandwich. And how glad I am to have it! You seem almost near enough to talk to. It seems to me such a nice arrangement for you to be in the country for a while to sort of get back in step. It is always complicated going back to town—even when one has not been so far away. I love to think of Massa and his joy at seeing you again. Think of what a success his life has been—when it might have been so many other things! That is one of the successful things you have accomplished.

Your last letter sounds like a story book, and your picture looks more like an untrammeled boy than the mother of two grown children. I am keeping your letters of course. They will make good reading in the future. This brings you a tremendous welcome home.

Love to both of you.

We had left Massa with our dog-loving neighbors, the Mudgetts, the summer before, and we grieved to hear how he did not leave our driveway for months, waiting for our return. He never quite forgave us for leaving him.

I became concerned that no letters followed from Mrs. Winslow, and I learned from Mary that her mother did not feel up to writing or seeing visitors. My letters were aimed at cheering her up. I knew she would find my description of my fall commission to paint Lionberger Davis amusing.

Center Sandwich, N.H.
September 21, 1959
Dear Tat,

I decided to go to Princeton and paint Lionberger Davis. You must remember the millionaire who fell in love with your portrait and wanted to buy you? Well, even though he is now quite old, and way past his prime, I think, or should say *I know,* that the reason he wanted me to paint him is that he needs someone to listen to his stories. He had many opportunities while I worked. Then in the evenings, when he did not have guests (never more than four), we sat side by side in front of the cold fireplace—it burns wood and only gets that treatment for 4 guests—while he got out old photographs, old copies of the sheet he put out which he called the *St. Louisan,* and museum catalogues. With the latter he would go down the line saying, "I gave that, I gave that, I gave that—gee, I don't remember that one I gave—my! I gave a lot that year." The photographs were often fascinating as I got life histories of all the people. I always listened the first time but then he told me the same thing at dinner, and immediately after dinner—while his mind was on the same track. I learned to steer him off which was easy, as anything at all brought on a new story. I also learned to set up my easel in the living room and study my painting, with the noise of talking in my ear, but no need for me to emit even an "izzatso," since he was so engrossed in what he had done, or written, or said. We were both content.

Besides the small portrait, which went too quickly, he asked me to paint a still life. He had more fun getting out the objects to arrange than I did. He hardly looked at the result because he was already arranging objects for another still life and told me if I were broke in the spring I could return and do some more. Perhaps he will begin buying now with the idea of what goes well with what. He bought $30,000 worth of art last year and made so much money that he is in the 80% income bracket. As hard as he tried, he couldn't sell anything at a loss last year that equaled more than $900—to take off his tax.

His Hungarian couple are used to his ways. Barta wants so much to cook tasty dishes but she told me: "Mr. Davis say he no eat, he no want a cake but I make good-a-cake"—so I gave an order for a layer cake, telling Mr. D that I CRAVED a cake. The last day of my stay she asked me if I liked liver since, up to then, we had had stuffed pepper and shepherd's pie as the main courses, so I asked, "What about chicken? Surely Mr. Davis likes chicken?" Barta wrung her hands. "We have chicken only on Sunday," she bemoaned. So we had liver and bacon. She told me she buys fruit for herself with her own money. He goes over all bills and never buys fresh flowers. The house is filled with vases of artificial tulips, lilies of the valley, delphinium and lilies, all mixed up.

At my last dinner Barta's Hungarian soul rigged up a vase of imitation white tulips, with electric lights in each tulip, for the dining room table. Mr. D said, "Look at that girl—she's a whiz—thinks of all those clever things." Of course he always turns off all the living room lights when we go into the dining room.

I came away with $350 and am promised $100 for the finished still life to be paid in January. Do you think that will come under CHARITY for his 1960 income tax?

Love,
Marcella

Center Sandwich, N.H.
September 28, 1959
Dear Tat,

When you next look over your canceled checks for 1959 don't be surprised if you see one for $10 dated 1955. I found it in an envelope tucked away in a drawer, long forgotten but not unappreciated. I hope you deducted it! I am always finding money in old pockets stashed away at some earlier time and have come to expect it. It isn't that I have a disregard for money, I just can't let money rule my life, as Lionberger does!

I wish you could join us for Thanksgiving in D.C. Mother is already planning to have all the family for dinner and I am hoping to get tickets for an English play, *Five Finger Exercise,* directed by Gielgud and starring Jessica Tandy. Sounds wonderful. The review says it is one of those complex things where *no one faces reality.* I love other people not facing reality and wonder if I do, or don't. I think I don't.

Katherine Anne has taken a house for two years just around the corner from me on Q St.; and has a $15,000 Ford grant and will finish the novel. John Prince says it is REALLY almost finished and KAP has taken a vow of Chastity—since she is way up in her 60's anyway. Her 50th birthday at my house in 1944 was really her 54th, she now admits.[1] Maybe Social Security is reminding her.

I just saw a tremendous bull moose, with huge antlers, walking across our back pasture. He slowly ambled over the field as I rushed to every available window not to miss any of him. I was worried that he might be hit by a car when he got to the road, but I have been told that it is the car and its driver one has to be worried about. Apparently, it is the mating season and the moose are more in evidence. He isn't the only one mating. All the hornets that get in the barn at this time of year are in mad revelry and mad pursuit. When two buzzing balls land suddenly with a thud at my feet, I try to imagine what it is like to leap with joy on a hornet.

I hope you will soon feel like having visitors, as I want to come see you.

Love,

Marcella

1. In my copy of the 1940 edition of *Flowering Judas,* on page 1, in the biographical note, I find a comment Katherine Anne inked in on a visit to me in June, 1965. Where the second paragraph read, "Born in Texas in 1894," she had crossed out the 4 and put a zero. In "Miss Porter had little formal education," she had crossed out the last three words and written along the margin, "Rome, Basel, Madrid and Washington, D.C. . . . . I had a good sound classical humane education in private schools. I never set foot in a University until I went there to teach. KAP"

P Street, N.W.
Washington, D.C.
October, 1959
Dear Tat,

Back in Georgetown.

Mary says you are still under the weather and I do wish I could do, or write, something to cheer you up. Perhaps some news on Katherine Anne. I have had several days with her in the house she is renting on Q street, a block away. It is lovely and she wants to buy it and live here always—but she always starts out that way. She bought my Siena fruit picture and has a frame for the small portrait she wants me to do if we both get time. She says her novel is FINISHED, which is hard to believe. She expects to make a fortune on it—movie rights and so on. She had me to lunch which she always cooks herself. She starts with 6 lbs. of beef for a wonderful soup to which she adds potatoes and lobster; then after that she made a shrimp dish in scalloped shells and homemade rolls. She can bake 6 kinds of bread. In fact, *Life* magazine came to photograph her for an article on celebrities' hobbies to which she invited me to come along (with my portrait of her) and watch her hobby— baking bread. She loves this sort of thing and wants her friends in on it. *Life* is bringing children to watch (photographing little children watching the star "vamp" of the age). She is living on a Ford Foundation grant of $25,000 for two years—or something of the sort. She bought a huge round slab of marble in Vermont for her dining room table top which cost $28 and which she paid $149 to have sent. She told me she had suggested my portrait of her go to the library in Texas "at a big price, a Texas price." She is not as beautiful now, being 69, but still fascinating.

The evening Mrs. Christian Herter entertained Mrs. Nikita Khrushchev for dinner we were alerted beforehand, as our houses adjoin. We had time to invite Katherine Anne [Porter] to join us for a peek from our bay window. It was exciting to watch all the security and to see Mac Herter greet Mrs. Khrushchev with a kiss no less—on her way up their spiral staircase. The security had taken pains to see that there was no one hiding below our cellar steps, but they never seemed to worry a bit that a well-directed shot from our window could precipitate a world crisis.

Much discussion on politics now which may bore you. Jan Karski has bets that the Democrats will deadlock on candidates and that Adlai Stevenson will be nominated, run against Nixon and beat him. Nelson Rockefeller is getting much talked about. Nixon is so nauseatingly ambitious—eating five helpings of cranberries in Wisconsin right after the cranberry cancer report.

I am longing for a letter from you to say you are better. When do you think you will feel up to visitors?

Love,
Marcella

On November 17, 1959, my last letter to Anne Winslow crossed with her last letter to me.

Mine was telling of my consternation at changes in Georgetown after a year's absence—from sleepy small town to city chic: Neams Market supplying the French embassy; newcomers, lured by a Georgetown address, struggling to park near their expensive houses; restaurants replacing antique shops; and even an inn to accommodate tourists. Mrs. Winslow would have been unhappy to know that the huge elm tree down P Street, and the old Catholic home beside it, had made room for a new street and a dozen new houses. But I am sure she would have wanted to hear the latest news about Cousin Harriet and Allen Tate. I wrote,

> Harriet looks just the same. She still has three nurses around the clock since her stroke, and so does her brother, Carlyle, but they won't have them together although they live in the same house. When I am as old I intend to stay in one place and paint and have people make appointments to see me as Miss Harriet does.
>
> I have seen Allen, who was here with his new wife, Isabella Gardner, who writes poetry. Allen said, "I've done something awful, but couldn't live without a woman. I can't live with Caroline so had to make it legal." He says he will use my portrait of Denis Devlin on the book he is compiling of Denis' poetry.

The handwriting of Mrs. Winslow's letter was shaky and wandered over the page:

> Dear Marcella,
> I have written this on many sheets of paper already. I am planning to send this one before it goes any farther than to tell you that I still love you and am planning to do something about it one of these days.

Perhaps be more the person I used to be. I didn't care too much for
HER, but compared to my present running mate . . . few words, but
much love,

Faraway,

Tat

Anne Winslow died a week after her letter to me. The following unpub-
lished, undated poem entitled "Lady Leaving" can be found in papers of
Anne Goodwin Winslow given to the Mississippi Valley Collection of the
Memphis State University Library. The poem expresses not only the lighthearted manner in which she depicts leaving this earth but the manner in
which she chose to live on it:

> Dear Earth, goodbye;
> It was lovely being here
> Your sunshine and your good air,
> And that blue sky!
> To say nothing of the food—
> My dear, your food
> Is just too marvelously good!
> And all those thousand little things you do—
> Like putting flowers everywhere
> And all those candles that you light at night,
> I loved those too.
>
> I just can't tell you how I hate to go
> And not to know
> When I'll be coming back this way
> Not soon, I fear;
> But I must manage it some day—
> Let's say in spring;
> So till then, goodbye my dear,
> And don't change anything.

I understand why Anne Winslow saved the letters I wrote to her in the
1940s and 1950s. I am sure she wanted me to have the pleasure of reliving
the most momentous two decades of my own life.

INDEX